HISTORY OF WEST AFRICA

History of West Africa

The Revolutionary Years—1815 to Independence

J. B. WEBSTER
AND
A. A. BOAHEN

WITH A CONTRIBUTION BY
H. O. IDOWU

PRAEGER PUBLISHERS

New York · Washington

BOOKS THAT MATTER

Published in the United States of America in 1970
by Praeger Publishers, Inc.
111 Fourth Avenue, New York, N.Y. 10003

Originally published in Great Britain by Longmans Green & Co. Ltd., as
The Revolutionary Years: West Africa Since 1800

Library of Congress Catalog Card Number: 79–88616

Maps by Maureen Verity
Illustrations by Peter Verity

Printed in the United States of America

Contents

Part five
Return to independence

List of maps

Publisher's Note

In the present state of African historical research, it is inevitable that much of the most up-to-date knowledge and interpretation is as yet unpublished or, where published, is in the form of learned monographs. For this reason, the authors of this book, from universities closely in touch with current knowledge and thought in African history, are particularly well qualified to present a text containing new information and analysis.

J. B. Webster is head of the Department of History at Makerere University College, University of East Africa. He has done research on the African church movements in Nigeria. He has also taught history at the high school level and is the founder-editor of *Tarikh,* a journal of African history for secondary schools. Professor Webster has been responsible for the writing of most of this book, which was planned jointly by Professor Boahen and himself.

A. A. Boahen is head of the Department of History at the University of Ghana. His research interests have ranged over the history of Saharan trade and are now concentrated primarily on the history of the Asante Confederacy and its external relations both within Ghana and with the outside world. Long concerned with the presentation of African history in schools, he is the Ghanaian member of the *Tarikh* editorial board, and he has delivered radio talks designed for schools. He has written the chapters dealing specifically with Ghana, as well as the chapter on changing trade patterns. In addition, he has helped Professor Webster with the over-all preparation of the book.

H. O. Idowu, an expert on French-speaking West Africa, contributed the chapter on French assimilation policy.

J. B. Webster wishes to express his thanks for the generous assistance he has received from scholars such as A. E. Afigbo, for his expert comments on Chapters 12, 13, and 17, and J. F. A. Ajayi, for his valuable assistance with the book's over-all organization and specifically on Chapter 7. He also wishes to express his indebtedness to D. M. Last, of Ahmadu Bello University, for his generous permission to use his thesis *Sokoto in the Nineteenth Century with Special Reference to the Vizierate* and for his comments on the first three chapters of this book. Special thanks are also due to Abeodu Jones, of the State Department, Monrovia, for permission to use her thesis *The Struggle for Political and Cultural Unification in Liberia in 1847–1930* and for comments on Chapter 10. Professor Webster also wishes to express gratitude to Professor Boahen for criticism of the entire manuscript and to acknowledge the pleasure he derived from the exchanges of ideas that the co-authorship of this book engendered. Each author, however, is ultimately responsible for the final form and content of his own contribution.

Acknowledgements

The publishers are grateful to the following for permission to reproduce photographs:

Héléne Adant for p. 170; I. Bandy for p. 27; British Museum for p. 184; Camera Press for p. 299 (middle), (a), (b), (c), (f) and (g) opposite p. 321; Clarendon Press for p. 307; Commander H. C. Maclean for p. 213; Commonwealth Office for p. 144; Culver Pictures, New York, for p. 206; Edinburgh University Gazette for p. 223; Eliot Elisofan for p. 48 and the opening to Part Two (right); William Fagg for left-hand figure opposite p. 91 and the opening to Part Three; John Hillelson for the opening to Part Five; Historical Picture Service, Chicago, for p. 143; *Illustrated London News* for p. 279; Keystone, Paris, for p. 274; Akinola Lashekan for p. 327; Linden Museum, Stuttgart, for p. 181; Mansell Collection for pp. 13, 31, 81, 133 and 212; Ministry of Information, Lagos, for (d) opposite p. 321; Museum of Primitive Art, New York, for right-hand figure opposite p. 193; National Portrait Gallery for p. 86 (top left and bottom left); New York Public Library for the opening, Part One; Nigeria High Commission, London, for (h) opposite p. 321; *Nigeria Magazine* for figure opposite p. 3, and for pp. 146 and 182; Paul Popper Ltd. for p. 324; Radio Times Hulton Picture Library for pp. 64, 231, 299 (foot) and 132; University Museum, Philadelphia, for the right-hand figure opposite p. 91 and p. 183; U.S.I.S. for p. 86 (bottom right) and E. G. Waterlot: Les Bas-Reliefs des Batiments Royaux d'Abomey (published by University of Paris in 1926) for pp. 99, 109, 114 and 119.

You will often come across the phrase 'contemporary print' in the captions to some of the illustrations. This term is used to signify that the picture was drawn for publication in a magazine of the period. It should be noted, however, that an artist's aim was to create an atmosphere of drama; thus, many prints were exaggerated in order to stimulate the reader's imagination, regardless of whether the facts were accurately presented!

Part **one**

States of the western Sudan in the nineteenth century

A nineteenth-century drawing of a nomadic Fulani village

A Hausa trumpeter

1 The jihad of Uthman dan Fodio and establishment of the Sokoto caliphate

At the opening of the nineteenth century the western Muslim world around the Mediterranean and in the Middle East found itself on the defensive in relation to the growing power of Christian Europe. Throughout the Muslim world scholars were concerned that Muslim communities which had once led the world in the arts, sciences, government and military prowess were now in decline. In the western Sudan Islam had established itself strongly in earlier centuries under the empires of Songhai and Bornu. By 1800 Muslims formed only small minority groups in non-Muslim states. Scholars of the western Sudan attributed this decay to the abandonment of the moral standards, simple living habits and purity of faith of their ancestors. During the nineteenth century a number of reforming movements aimed at restoring the Muslim world to its former greatness by a renewed devotion of Muslims to the the highest ideals of their religion. The most important of these movements were the Wahhabiyya of Arabia in the eighteenth century, Sanusiyya of Cyrenaica, Mahdiyya of the eastern Sudan and the three jihads of the western Sudan led by Uthman dan Fodio, Hamad Bari and al-Hajj Umar.

The western Sudan at the beginning of the nineteenth century

At the beginning of the nineteenth century Bornu remained the most Muslim of the states of the western Sudan, under its Mai (king) of the thousand-year-old Sefawa dynasty. The Hausa states, of which Gobir and Katsina were the most powerful, were ruled by Pagans, or Muslims in name only who mixed Paganism and Islam to satisfy all sections of their populations. South and west of the great bend of the Niger the Bambara people of Macina and Segu and the powerful Mossi federation were under Pagan dynasties. In the Senegal area three Muslim states – Futa Toro, Futa Bondu, and Futa Jalon – had been born out of Islamic revolutions in the eighteenth century.

3

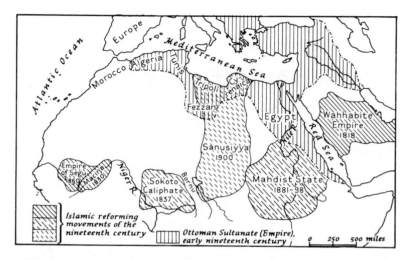

1 The western Muslim world in the nineteenth century

The success of the Muslim revolutions in the Futa kingdoms was an inspiration to the Fulani all over the Sudan, who looked upon the Futas as their homeland. The largest number of Fulani, many of whom were nomads, lived among the Hausa and Bambara. They were often Pagan or at best Muslim in name only. Although the Hausa and Bambara farmers valued the manure of the Fulani cattle as fertilizer for their crops, arguments arose, especially in the dry season, when both farmers and herders wanted water from the small pools.

A number of the Fulani had settled in the cities, so that there was not a Hausa state without its town-dwelling Fulani, who had married Hausa wives and spoke the Hausa language. Some were wealthy traders, while others, because of their literacy, education and knowledge of the outside world, held high positions as teachers, judges, scribes and advisers to the Hausa aristocracy, and in the courts of the Sultans or Sarkuna.

Devout Muslims valued education, and young children began their education in the local Koranic school. Upon completion a young man who showed aptitude moved about the country seeking more qualified teachers. In time he might begin to gather pupils of his own while at the same time continuing to study under more learned men. Agades, located on the caravan and pilgrimage route to the north, was a famous educational centre where mallams (scholars) from North Africa, Bornu and Hausaland gathered to discuss law, philosophy and the affairs of the Muslim world. Occasionally Sudanese mallams moved on to the educational centres of North Africa and the Middle East. The majority of Sudanese scholars were either Fulani, Tuareg, Kanuri

4

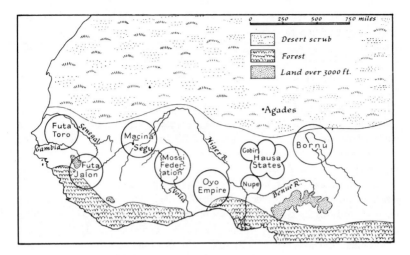

2 *Major kingdoms of the Sudan in 1800*

or Shuwa Arab but a number of other peoples such as the Hausa were also becoming mallams.

There were two types of scholars. Some settled in the cities of the western Sudan and enjoyed high positions of trust, wealth and power in the courts; they married into the aristocracy, and lived in luxury close to the throne, so that they saw clearly the difficulties of the rulers in attempting to govern mixed Muslim and Pagan populations. Other scholars preferred to wander alone, or with the Fulani or Tuareg nomads, preaching or teaching as they moved from place to place; they had no connections with the governing classes and, being closer to the people, they were critical of the abuses of Hausa rule which affected them, and frequently became spokesmen for the people.

The grievances of the Muslim community, both Hausa and Fulani, against the aristocracy were religious, political and economic. Muslims objected to conscription into Pagan armies to fight brother Muslims; they hated the practice of selling Muslims into slavery; they despised the Sultans for their sacrifices and belief in spirits, for the luxury and sinfulness of court life as well as for the servility demanded from commoners. They complained about the judgements in the courts, and bribery and corruption in appointments to office. Most important of all, the merchants disliked the heavy market taxes, while nomads hated the tax on cattle.

The scholars pointed out that all these things were illegal by Koranic law. They preached reform, and attracted not only devout Muslims and those who were Muslims only in name, but also Pagans ready to support reform even if they did not like the Muslim religion. What the reformers needed was a powerful scholar, who could lead the common people and thus force the aristocracy to listen to their complaints.

Victory for the jihadists in Gobir

The most famous of the wandering scholars, and the one whose influence eventually spread throughout the western Sudan, was a Fulani from Gobir named Uthman dan Fodio. Uthman and his brother Abdullah received the normal education of Muslim youths, studying under various teachers and finally ending up at Agades under the famous Jibril b. Umar, an accurate, demanding and devout scholar. Eventually Jibril was forced to leave Agades after announcing an unsuccessful jihad among the Tuareg. Dan Fodio returned to Hausaland at twenty years of age, to begin teaching and preaching in Kebbi, Zamfara and Gobir. The fame of his knowledge and piety surrounded him with student-disciples, who in time returned to their homes to teach and preach in Hausaland and beyond. Dan Fodio continued to write to his former students, so as to improve their knowledge and keep their faith strong.

Uthman dan Fodio settled at Degel in the 1790's and from there his fame continued to spread and attract students and scholars. He demanded complete acceptance of the spiritual and moral values of Islam, and condemned corrupt and unjust government which, against the teachings of the Koran, oppressed the poor and the weak. He attacked those mallams who supported oppressive governments and sultans, and it is reported that over a thousand scholars gathered at one time to hear him speak. However, dan Fodio always preferred conversion and reform to violence and bloodshed in achieving Muslim aims.

3 Gobir at the beginning of the nineteenth century

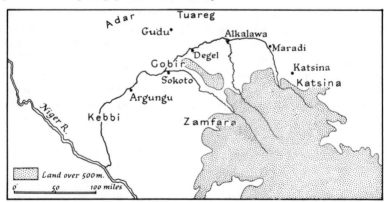

Dan Fodio's prestige further increased when he successfully negotiated an agreement with Sultan Bawa of Gobir which granted Muslims freedom of religion and guaranteed respect for the turban, which was the local symbol of Islam. Taxation was lessened and Muslim prisoners released from jail. Gobir was very powerful under Sultan Bawa, who wisely decided that he could relax his rule to allow greater freedom for his subjects.

However, the Pagan aristocracy disapproved of such tolerance, and would have preferred a policy of reducing rather than encouraging Muslim activity. After Bawa's death they persuaded Sultan Nafata, 1796-1802, reluctantly to issue a proclamation which withdrew the privileges. In addition, Nafata ordered all converts to return to Paganism. Many Muslims, of whom the most outspoken was Abdullah, wished to oppose Nafata's proclamation by violence, but dan Fodio advised restraint.

On Nafata's death his son Yunfa became Sultan, and, since Yunfa had probably sat as a pupil of dan Fodio's at Degel and dan Fodio had supported his claim to the throne against his rivals, there was hope that Yunfa would negotiate with him. Yunfa, however, found the anti-Muslim faction strong in his court, and many opposed him because he was believed to be friendly towards the Muslims. Some of his rivals for the throne were ready to act against what they felt was the destructive behaviour of the Muslim community. Moreover, Gobir was not in as strong a position as in the days of Bawa, for Zamfara was in revolt, Kebbi was not paying tribute, the Tuareg were raiding the northern frontier and Katsina was moving into Zamfara from the east. The pressure from outside the state, and from his own court, decided Sultan Yunfa to strengthen Gobir's internal unity which was now threatened by the Muslims.

In an effort to prevent the development of a separate Muslim group in his kingdom he attempted the assassination of dan Fodio in Alkalawa, the capital of Gobir. Tension increased further when the followers of dan Fodio forcibly freed some Muslims, disciples of the Hausa scholar, Abd al-Salam, who were being taken as captives to Alkalawa. Gobir was seriously divided and civil war could not be avoided. It was not merely Muslim Fulani against Pagan Hausa; some Muslims, Fulani and Hausa, were loyal to Yunfa while some Fulani and Hausa Pagans sympathized with dan Fodio.

Dan Fodio and his companions at Degel, including his father, his brother Abdullah, his son Muhammad Bello, Abd al-Salam and a number of scholars and disciples withdrew from Degel to Gudu on the western frontier of Gobir. This was the hijra (flight) in imitation of the Prophet Muhammad's hijra from Mecca to Medina. Supporters began to arrive in the following months both from Gobir and from all over the western Sudan. Most of Shehu Uthman's companions were Fulani, followed by Tuareg and Hausa. At Gudu. dan Fodio reluctantly accepted election as Amir al-Muminin

(Commander of the Faithful) and proclaimed a jihad (holy war) against the unbelievers just as the Prophet had done at Medina. Since dan Fodio was middle-aged, and not a warrior but a teacher and scholar, his two lieutenants Abdullah and Bello were given charge of military operations.

The first defeat of Yunfa's army sent against Gudu increased the flow of supporters to the cause of the jihadists. The jihad army in turn was defeated in its attempt to capture Alkalawa and turned south into Zamfara and Kebbi, where it was welcomed as bringing freedom from the oppression of Gobir.

The nomadic Fulani clans began to join the jihad, probably more for booty and the hope of political power than for reasons of religion. As the pressures of war increased their military leaders became more important than the scholars in the movement. Furthermore, the cruelty of the army, especially in seizing food in the dry season, created hunger among the peasant farmers. The Hausa scholars became uneasy as the political ambitions of the Fulani military leaders began to dominate their own religious motives. Some remained neutral while others fought for Yunfa. The peasantry grew hostile, seeing little advantage for them in the victory of either side.

Dan Fodio tried to assert the religious and social aims of the jihad, and thus to win popular support, by issuing two manifestos, *Wathiquat Ahl al-Sudan* and, later, *Kitab al-Farq*. In these he pointed out the duty of Muslims to resist Paganism and the evils of Pagan governments.

Then, in 1808, Sultan Yunfa was killed at the fall of Alkalawa, and serious resistance collapsed. The Gobir army and aristocracy withdrew to the north, while Kebbi forces reorganized in the country to the west around Argungu. The major parts of Gobir, Kebbi and Zamfara were occupied by the jihad army and were governed from the new capital of Sokoto, built by Bello in 1809.

The spread of the jihad

Even before the fall of Alkalawa made victory certain in Gobir, Muslims had gained control in a number of other Hausa states. Immediately after the hijra, Muslims from far away had travelled to dan Fodio to receive his blessing on their plans to start the jihad in their home states. The Shehu gave flags to those who were to represent him in the various states to show that they had his blessing and authority. By 1809 revolts in Zaria, Katsina and Kano had resulted in these flag bearers gaining control. The Hausa dynasties of Zaria and Katsina fled into exile and set up new states at Abuja and Maradi respectively.

In Bornu, the Fulani rebelled and sacked the capital in 1808. The Mai fled into exile, inviting al-Kanami, a scholar from the neighbouring kingdom of Kanem, to rally the scattered Bornu army. Al-Kanami won important victories, and made his position much stronger by carrying out a thorough reform of Islam, removing injustice in the law courts and bringing enthusiasm and efficiency into the government. By these methods he gained the support of those in Bornu who wanted religious and social reform, and left as a separate group the Fulani, who appeared as selfish adventurers looking for booty and personal power.

To the west in Macina, Hamad Bari, possibly a disciple of dan Fodio and a poor wandering mallam, was preaching religious piety and social reform among the Fulani and Bambara. He made the hijra and subsequently built Hamdullahi as his new capital after overcoming Pagan rule. For some time he was considered to be under the authority of Sokoto but finally was proclaimed Amir al-Muminin, and thus set up an independent Muslim state.

To the south of the Hausa states, near the Niger and Benue rivers, emirates were created among the Nupe and the peoples of Adamawa. In the capital of Nupe, a Fulani, Mallam Dendo, chief court advisor to the Etsu (king), had earlier received a flag from dan Fodio. In a dispute between two Nupe as to who should succeed to the throne, Dendo, as leader of the local Fulani, held the balance of power and supported first one candidate and then the other. Ultimately his son, Uthman Zaki, seized the throne, and the two rivals fled across the Niger to establish the small Nupe states of Shonga and Pategi.

Another Fulani educated in Bornu, Mallam Adama, visited Sokoto in 1806 and received a flag. He united the Fulani on the Benue and conquered a large area which before had been ruled by many petty chiefs. He founded Yola as the capital of the emirate of Adamawa in 1841.

Farther to the south and across the Niger lay the once powerful Oyo empire of the Yoruba, now suffering from instability and decay. In 1817 Afonja, the Kakanfo or commander of the Oyo army, revolted against his overlord, the Alafin, and set himself up as ruler of Ilorin. In order to keep his independence from Oyo he asked for help from the Fulani, and took Mallam Alimi into his service as advisor, a man whose son secretly possessed a jihad flag. Although Oyo was unable to bring Afonja back under its rule, he found himself more and more dominated by the Fulani. Aware of their aims, he tried to free himself from their grip, but he was assassinated instead. Alimi's son took the throne and brought Ilorin within the caliphate.

The Fulani-Ilorin army then sacked the Oyo capital, killing the Alafin and spreading the jihad south among the Yoruba, until their armies were halted in 1843 by Ibadan. The Yoruba were, however, thrown into a series of civil wars, as various Yoruba states tried in vain to re-establish the unity lost by the collapse of Oyo.

At the time of dan Fodio's death in 1817 the future frontiers of the caliphate

9

were roughly established. Almost everywhere the jihadists had been successful, for, with the exception of Bornu, the flag bearers had overthrown the old dynasties.

However, in the decade following the Shehu's death, the caliphate fought for its very existence. When Bello was elected Amir al-Muminin after his father, he faced an argument about the leadership, a strong Hausa rebellion, and external attacks first from Gobir and the Tuareg and later from the powerful army of Bornu. The quality of Bello's leadership between 1817 and 1827 decided the fate of the caliphate.

Prior to dan Fodio's death the emirates had been divided for administrative purposes, so that Abdullah, at Gwandu, was placed in charge of the west including Nupe and Ilorin, while Bello controlled the emirates to the east. It is not believed that this was meant to be a permanent division of authority, but, in the disagreement over policy between Abdullah and Bello, it became permanent. Abdullah disliked the development in the movement of the military leaders having more influence than the scholars; he claimed that the new leaders were turning away from the religious and social aims of the jihad by seeking power and rank for themselves and their relations, and by their interest in collecting booty, wives, fancy clothes and horses. He was particularly worried about the cruelty of the army to the Hausa peasants, and the fact that the Hausa scholars were no longer supporting the movement.

With the leaders in disagreement a rebellion broke out led by the Hausa scholar, Abd al-Salam, and this was followed by Pagan uprisings in Kebbi and Zamfara. Abd al-Salam said that the Hausa had been unfairly treated when the spoils and booty were given out and that the Fulani, including those not interested in Islam, were gaining all the benefits of the movement. Although Bello agreed with this, he also believed that internal revolts and external attacks must be overpowered before reform could be carried out; thus, while he wanted to negotiate with the Hausa rebels, he eventually was forced to declare Abd al-Salam an apostate (someone who has given up the faith).

The rebellion was particularly dangerous since the Gobir army from the north, in alliance with the Tuareg, were trying very hard to crush Sokoto. Although the Sultan of Agades, Muhammad al-Baqiri, had faithfully supported dan Fodio, both the rulers and the people of the Adar Tuareg were divided in their feelings. When in 1814 a jihad was proclaimed in Adar, and it failed, Muslim refugees poured into Sokoto, leaving the Tuareg ready to combine with Gobir to overthrow Bello. It was a tribute to Bello's leadership and military tactics that he succeeded both in defending the northern frontier and in crushing the Hausa rebellion.

These two dangers were hardly overcome when the Bornu army under al-Kanami invaded the caliphate from the east. The zeal of the Bornu

Fulani, Bornu's sympathy with the Hausa dynasties, and rumours that the Mai followed Pagan practices, had placed Bello in the embarrassing position of supporting violence against the oldest and most respected Muslim kingdom of the western Sudan. Al-Kanami's reforms removed the last excuse for war against Bornu. But, in the original attack, Bornu had lost some emirates on her western frontier to the Fulani, and al-Kanami now attempted a major counter-attack to reconquer the lost emirates. The army advanced to within seventy miles of Kano city, but was thrown back through the efforts of Emir Yakuba of Bauchi. The caliphate retained the Fulani emirates, and an uneasy though permanent peace was brought to the eastern frontier after 1827.

The attack which was inspired and led by Sultan Mayaki of Gobir ten years after Bello's death was the last serious crisis for the caliphate. After that there was little possibility that it would be overthrown, for, although external enemies remained, they were no longer able to organize large-scale revolts inside the caliphate. This was the result of the administrative work of Bello and his successors, who attacked the vital internal problem of the caliphate – securing the agreement and involvement of the Hausa people.

4 The Sokoto caliphate (mid-nineteenth century)

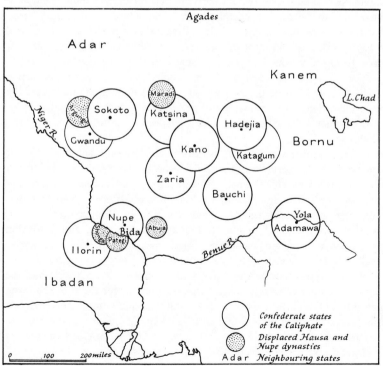

Organization of the caliphate

Bello made a determined effort to win the support of the Hausa people. His first task was to limit the power of the Fulani military chieftains and strengthen his own power, so as to reassert the intellectual, reforming and Islamic character of the movement. In order to achieve this he emphasized the importance of the scholar in the administration, regardless of whether he was Fulani or Hausa. His first move was to build ribats (walled towns or fortresses) on the frontiers for defence and to station the army away from the peasant settlements. He encouraged the nomadic Fulani to settle around the ribats, and both taught them agriculture and educated their children. This policy reduced the dislike between the Hausa peasants and Fulani nomads, removed army oppression of the peasants by keeping it away from the Hausa settlements, turned nomadic herdsmen into farmers and, through education, began their conversion to Islam.

In the peasant areas Bello gradually replaced the military chiefs in local administration by mallams, who were respected and supported by the people. Since stability of the caliphate depended in the long term upon Hausa support and acceptance he felt it unwise to drive the Hausa into rebellion by enforced conversion to Islam, and therefore relied on education to achieve this. According to normal Islamic practice Pagan Hausa peasants were allowed to pay special taxes, in return for protection against conversion to Islam by force. Even the famous Pagan Choka shrine in Kano was left untouched.

Since education was a key to efficient administration as well as conversion to Islam all emirs were urged to encourage it. Bello himself encouraged the better education of the mallams, and provided hospitality for scholars at his court, so that Sokoto became a widely respected centre of education and enlightenment.

Impartial justice was as vital as education if non-Muslims were to be convinced of the superiority of Islam. Bello checked the courts, and frequently overruled decisions which he believed were unfair. He also encouraged greater links between Fulani and Hausa, and himself married one of Yunfa's wives, entrusting her son with the command of a ribat on the northern frontier. Later caliphs continued to give Hausa positions of trust, and a Muslim Hausa, dan Halima, was encouraged to set up and administer a protective area on the frontier facing Gobir and Maradi.

Bello was also concerned with the relationships between Sokoto and the emirates. His policy here held the caliphate together, for the emirs had won their thrones with little assistance; as a result they ruled almost independently of Sokoto, which had no standing army large enough to compel the emirs to obey its will. Indeed the Sokoto army was so busy dealing with internal revolts and external aggression that it was already fully occupied.

A drawing of Kano in 1877

The Sokoto leaders never intended to create an empire, or tribute area ruled by force. Rather they wished to create a caliphate, a confederation of states held together by common aims and religious allegiance to the Amir al-Muminin. Sokoto's ultimate weapon was to declare a rebellious emir an apostate, which was a powerful weapon as long as the emirs were devout Muslims and was, in fact, very rarely employed.

The emirates might be considered self-governing but they were not independent, for the Amir al-Muminin had a number of important powers. While each emirate chose its emir, the Amir al-Muminin confirmed the appointment, and this gave him considerable power, especially in Zaria and Nupe where three dynastic lines competed for the throne, for the caliph as arbiter could see that his favourite was chosen. Sokoto also confirmed the appointment of the emir's chief ministers.

There was a great deal of correspondence from Sokoto to the emirs dealing with the Hausa administrations which the emirs had inherited and how to convert these to Islamic methods and policies. Regular tours of inspection by Sokoto officials were carried out to advise and oversee the practical application of policy. In addition, a conscious policy was pursued of linking the Sokoto aristocracy with the emirates by marriage.

The emirates sent two kinds of regular tribute to Sokoto. The first was of produce and manufactures, which included an annual tribute, and a percentage of the booty taken in war, as well as gifts at the great Muslim festivals, and from individuals on appointment to office. The second type of tribute consisted of military levies, usually made up of slaves.

An important link in promoting a feeling of Muslim brotherhood was the annual campaign when all the emirs joined their armies with that of Sokoto to extend the frontiers of Islam into Pagan territory. After 1880 the campaigns became less frequent, for religious enthusiasm had declined. There was anyway little desire for war, especially among the peasants and merchants who found trade more profitable, and, most important of all, there was no serious threat remaining to the caliphate. Rather than join the campaign the emirs preferred to increase their tributes of produce.

Emirs were not compelled to pay the tribute, nor was the amount of the payment laid down. Its size reflected the status of the giver, and if it was withheld this was a sign that the emir had withdrawn from the confederation. Many emirs, however, as their power and wealth grew, continued to increase the size and magnificence of their tributes to Sokoto; the fact that this was voluntary indicated the strength of the bonds of the confederacy which, though spiritual, were also remarkably practical.

Influence on Sudanese society

The success of the jihad and the establishment of the Sokoto caliphate had a profound influence on the nineteenth-century western Sudan. Dan Fodio's teaching and his successful jihad inspired the creation of large political units in place of numerous small competing units. Islam spread throughout the western Sudan and led to an increase in education and learning, which in turn led to expanded trade and prosperity.

The jihad united the Hausa states politically for the first time in their history, and, while they remained the core, the caliphate embraced a large number of non-Hausa, such as the people of Adamawa, the Nupe, Gwari and the Ilorin Yoruba. The caliphate was the largest political unit in nineteenth-century West Africa, made up as it was of fifteen major emirates spread over 180,000 square miles, which required four months to cross from east to west and two months from north to south. The boundaries of the caliphate and Bornu included rather more than the boundaries of present-day northern Nigeria.

Areas outside the caliphate were greatly affected by the jihad. It brought temporarily renewed vigour and a change of dynasty to Bornu, while it challenged Bornu's commercial supremacy in the central Sudan. It inspired the creation of the theocratic state of Macina, and influenced al-Hajj Umar who built up the Tokolor empire so that it was only slightly less extensive than

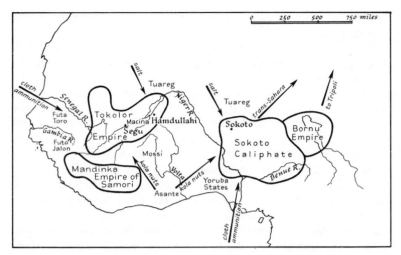

5 *Major political units of the western Sudan, mid and late nineteenth century*

the Sokoto caliphate. Indirectly it also influenced the career and policies of Samori Touré in his empire building among the Mandinka people.

Even more important than its political results was the jihad's stimulus to learning, education and the spread of Islam. The leaders were first and foremost scholars, and from their pens poured forth a stream of books (over two hundred known works from dan Fodio, Abdullah and Bello alone) which circulated throughout the Sudan, and were written to educate administrators about the kind of society they should aim at creating, and to explain Islamic law to the judges. Great libraries grew up at Sokoto and Segu; literacy became necessary for high office; Arabic developed as the official language of literature and correspondence; and Hausa spread in many areas as the lingua franca among peoples of different languages.

In 1800 Islam had been the private religion of a small minority in the Sudan; by 1850 it was the official religion of the majority. Islam undermined tribe and tribalistic loyalties, replacing them with loyalties to the brotherhoods; the Qadiriyya was the dominant brotherhood of the Sokoto caliphate while the Tijaniyya was favoured in the Tokolor empire, in the Futas and in Bornu.

Although conflict and violence continued around the edges of the larger units, internally there was a considerable degree of peace, order and good government which encouraged trade. Farmers could till their soil, herdsmen tend their cattle, artisans and merchants ply their trades. The caravan routes from Tripoli imported the luxuries of North Africa and exported the products of the Sudan; the northern Saharan salt trade, southern forest kola nut trade, and later the European trade through Nupe, flourished and brought prosperity and contentment.

Numerous criticisms have been made of the caliphate. It was said that a thorough reform of the Hausa administrations was not carried out, and that the evils of the old Hausa dynasties continued under the new Fulani aristocracy. Others said that Islam became mixed with Animism, that even learned scholars made charms and magic, and that the annual expeditions turned into slave raiding. Still others claimed that the unity of the caliphate was weak, and that the British found it falling apart, with the Hausa so oppressed that they welcomed the British as liberators. Finally the caliphate is blamed for the fall of old Oyo and civil strife among the Yoruba.

The leadership of the caliphate would have been the first to point out examples of misrule, lack of religious piety and devotion. Dan Fodio, before his death, expressed his doubts about the leadership when he said 'when I am gone, the whole country will go back to Paganism'. But successes outweighed failures. The criticisms of Islam in its involvement with traditional African religions could with equal truth be aimed against other world religions such as Christianity. The British criticized the caliphate administration only to turn around and employ it as the basis of indirect rule, becoming in a few years its loudest defenders. It can also be argued that the Yoruba caused most of their own confusion, for they failed to find unity even after 1843, when the caliphate ceased to be a vital force amongst them. In any case most will admit that the leadership was devout and sincere, fighting against enemies from without, and lack of interest and long lines of communication from within. Most would also agree that the caliphate leaders did a solid job of nation building through bringing the influence to Islam to one of the most culturally mixed areas of West Africa.

2 The Islamic revolutions in Macina and the Bambara states

The theocratic state of Macina

Uthman dan Fodio's teaching and the success of the Sokoto jihad were also important in the nineteenth-century history of Macina and the Bambara states of the western Sudan. Macina lies west of the great bend of the Niger in its inland delta where the river breaks up into numerous branches and passes through a dozen or so small swampy lakes. It is a fertile area, one of the best agricultural areas of the western Sudan though wasteland and desert lie close to its frontiers. At the beginning of the nineteenth century the people of Macina were non-Muslim Fulani and Bambara. The rulers were Fulani from the Dyalo clan, the most important king being the Ardo of Macina. The area paid tribute to the Bambara king of Segu. Within this non-Muslim world there were Muslim minorities of Fulani, Soninke, Songhai and Kenata Moors. Two cities were noted centres of Islamic learning, Jenne and Timbuctu. In the late eighteenth century a Kenata Moorish scholar, al-Muktar, had roused religious interest in the Muslim communities of Macina and under his influence the Qadiriyya Brotherhood had gained many adherents.

Al-Muktar prepared the way for the Islamic revolution in Macina which was led by Hamad Bari who studied under his own father and also under scholars in Jenne, perhaps under al-Muktar or one of his disciples and under Uthman dan Fodio at Degel. The teachings of dan Fodio were the formative influence in Hamad's life. The inspiration to change his own society in Macina arose from his participation in the early stages of the jihad in Gobir. Furthermore the scholars of Sokoto continued to influence both him and his followers in Macina. Hamad consulted dan Fodio on the timing of his jihad and because of the respect for Sokoto among his people, was able to settle disputes among the Macina scholars by reference to the Sokoto writings.

Upon leaving Sokoto, Hamad had settled in a small village under the authority of the Arma (ruler) of Jenne who later expelled him because of his popularity. He resettled at Sebera under the Ardo of Macina, teaching and

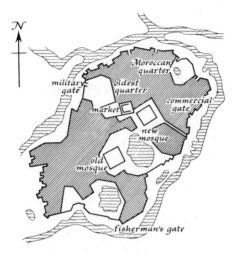

6 *Plan of the city of Jenne*

gathering disciples as dan Fodio had done at Degel. His fame as a scholar, reformer and devout Muslim spread until the Ardo, fearful of losing his own position and prestige appealed to his overlord, the Bambara king of Segu, for assistance in crushing him. Hamad performed his hijra to Hamdullahi, received dan Fodio's blessing and possibly his flag, proclaimed the jihad and was ultimately elected Amir al-Muminin by his followers.

Hamad defeated the Segu army and as a result the scholars of Jenne invited him to take over authority in that city, but the Arma was unwilling to step down and killed Hamad's representative. The jihadists then besieged and captured Jenne. Next, the Fulani Sangare clan revolted in Macina, overthrew the Ardo and like the people of Jenne invited Hamad to take over. Elsewhere Fulani chiefs, in order to hold their positions, declared for Islam. This was a political rather than religious move and Hamad spent a number of years in overthrowing them. In 1819 he established his capital at Hamdullahi.

Hamad conquered Timbuctu (1826-27) and established a Fulani garrison in the city not only to keep it loyal but also to defend it from Tuareg raids from the north. Although the people of Timbuctu were Songhai the scholar class was Kenata. After Hamad's death in 1844 Timbuctu, under al-Bakkai, proceeded to rebel against Fulani domination of the top administrative posts in its government. Hamad's son and successor, Hamad II, was therefore forced in 1846 to come to an agreement with al-Bakkai whereby Timbuctu would pay tribute to Macina but Songhai and Kenata would be favoured over Fulani in appointments. In addition the Fulani garrison was withdrawn from Timbuctu.

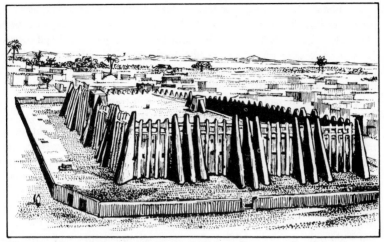

The great Mosque at Jenne before it was rebuilt in 1906

In the period of his rule Hamad Bari divided Macina into five emirates each under an emir and qadi. The state was governed by a Grand Council of forty scholars and a Privy Council of three, consisting of Hamad and two members of the Grand Council. In cases of friction between the Grand and Privy Councils, forty independent scholars sat as arbiters. Islamic law and rules of taxation were observed.

In religion, in law and in daily life Islam was thoroughly and permanently established. The Islamic code, regarding the number of wives and the prohibition of drinking and dancing, was rigidly enforced through the office of the Censor of Public Morals which operated a kind of inquisition which fell as hard upon the clerical class as it did upon non-Muslims and the common people. It was in part the rigorous clean-up of the vices of Timbuctu which led to the rebellion in that city. Because of its location on the edge of the desert, it attracted a large visiting population from the Sahara especially young men free from the watchful eye of their elders seeking the fun and sin which the city offered. Hamad's clean up of vice reduced the attraction of the city and its merchants' profits suffered from the decline in the number of visitors.

Macina was a theocratic state; theocratic because it was ruled by the laws of God as laid down in the Koran; a state because it possessed a high degree of centralization, a supreme governing body which legislated for the entire nation, the emirates here resembling provinces rather than the largely autonomous emirates of the Sokoto caliphate. But like Sokoto, unity was maintained more by the shared ideals and aims of the educated and thinking leadership rather than by the threat of a powerful army.

19

The jihad in Macina as in the Hausa states was at least partly a revolt of the people against the chiefly classes. Had the Pagan masses loyally supported their rulers the small Muslim communities could not have achieved success. It seems probable that many of the commoners or ordinary people felt oppressed under multiple taxes, arbitrary justice and corrupt officials. When the jihad commenced they therefore remained indifferent to the fate of their rulers and even though they may not have been attracted to Islam as a religion they could readily agree with the reformers' criticism of the present system and applaud their promises of reform. Some Animists even fought for the reformers because they believed they stood for a better life, honest government and fair and just courts administering laws which could not be altered at whim by the chiefly classes. In neither Macina nor the Hausa states was the new order imposed by an outside conquering army. The jihad was rather like a series of civil wars in each state where the Muslim minority won not so much the military battle as the battle for men's loyalty. It was the Arma and Ardo and the chiefly classes they represented which opposed the Muslims while it was the people who delivered both Jenne and Macina to Hamad.

We have seen how the jihad in Gobir almost degenerated into a Fulani struggle for domination. This was the result of a policy that 'the end justifies the means'. Thus, when the military situation was critical the Pagan Fulani nomads were welcomed into the Muslim armies and it began to appear that the ties of Fulani brotherhood were stronger than those of Muslim brotherhood. That the Hausa scholars grew cold and the Hausa masses grew distant was clearly indicated by the revolt of Abd al-Salam.

In Macina this process did not go as far. The military were not as powerful, and Hamad did not face as heavy a task as Bello in reasserting the influence of the scholars. This was partly because the non-Muslim nomads did not join the army to the extent they had in Gobir and partly because the split between Muslims and Pagans did not follow ethnic lines to the same extent as in Gobir. In Macina the struggle was mainly Pagan Fulani against Muslim Fulani but it also had its non-religious aspects in the inter-clan struggle for political dominance in which the Fulani Sangare were overthrowing the Fulani Dyalo with Hamad – of the Sangare – enjoying the support of minorities like the Kenata Moors. The tendency to favour one's own ethnic group appeared in the government of Timbuctu but this condition was corrected in the generous treatment of the Songhai and Kenata after the rebellion. Thus although the theocratic state was intolerant of Animism and immorality, on the whole it was tolerant of ethnic minorities. The resulting national unity was demonstrated in the resistance of Fulani, Kenata and Songhai to Umar, and support for Ba Lobbo's revolt.

Although the people resented the activities of the Censor of Public Morals, by and large Macina was remarkably stable. The succession passed smoothly from father to son, Hamad II (1844-52) and Hamad III (1852-62). Hamad III was killed by the Tokolor conqueror, al-Hajj Umar, but two years later a rebellion under Ba Lobbo uncle of Hamad III and supported by al-Bakkai and the Kenata of Jenne, killed Umar and threw back his Tokolor armies. After a long struggle al-Tijani, nephew of Umar, brought Macina again under Tokolor rule. Al-Tijani and his succeeding sons maintained the political system and strict morality laws of the Hamads, a tribute to the defeated Bari dynasty.

Al-Hajj Umar before the jihad

Between Macina and the Atlantic, in the Niger-Senegal area, were the Pagan Bambara states of Segu and Kaarta; the Tokolor Muslim states – Futa Jalon, Futa Bondu and Futa Toro – each ruled by an Almami; a number of coastal kingdoms, the Wolof state of Cayor being the most important; and a few European settlements on tiny islands off shore – the French at St. Louis and Gorée and the British at Bathurst. South of the Niger-Senegal were the Pagan Mandinka people with no political centralization but divided into numerous small independent town or village groups.

The man who revolutionized this area and was the dominant influence in its development was a Tokolor, al-Hajj Umar, born in Futa Toro in 1794. Umar left his homeland on the hajj in 1820 and did not return for almost twenty years. During his travels he witnessed two of the greatest Islamic reform movements of the nineteenth century; the Wahhabi struggle against the Turks in Arabia and Mohammed Ali of Egypt seeking to adapt the industrial techniques of Christian Europe to a Muslim country. Umar visited al-Kanami in Bornu, married into his family and was so impressed with this scholar-reformer that he wrote a poem in his praise. He also remained with Muhammad Bello in Sokoto for seven years, reading the Sokoto books and playing a part in the political life of the caliphate. Umar married two wives from Sokoto, one the daughter of Bello whose son became one of his military commanders, and another who bore him Ahmad, his successor. When he left Sokoto he was followed by many Hausa who later held prominent positions in his empire. On his way back to the Futa Jalon where he settled, he visited Hamad Bari in Macina.

Important as these experiences were, it was his belief in and deep attachment to the Tijaniyya Brotherhood which explains much of his later life. The Tijaniyya had been founded at Fez by Ahmad Tijani in the late eighteenth century. The brotherhood spread in Arabia and from Morocco to the Futas. It is probable that Umar had been initiated into the Tijaniyya before he left on the hajj but in Mecca he was appointed khalifa (head) of the order in the western Sudan by the supreme head of the brotherhood.

The Tijaniyya was a new and sensational way of salvation and combined with Umar's strong personality it spread in Bornu and Sokoto as a result of his visits. The ancient Qadiriyya emphasized that the fullest spiritual fulfilment came through study and intellectual activity. Since few men were born with great intellectual powers only a few – the elite – ever approached the ideal; because of this concept the Qadiriyya was favoured by the chiefly classes and because of its intellectual emphasis it did not spread widely among lower-class Muslims. The Tijaniyya rejected these ideas. It maintained that the faith was basically simple and easily understood by all men. Salvation came not through the intellect but through action, strict adherence to the moral code of Islam and zeal for the spread of the faith. There was no elite, all brothers of the Tijaniyya were equal as long as they obeyed the moral code and spread the faith. Although members of the brotherhood were equal the Tijaniyya fostered the idea that all those within the order were superior to those outside it. It was a Tijani's duty to show others the higher and better way to salvation. These beliefs appealed to the common men, the youths and the warrior classes to whom action was more attractive than tedious study.

Between 1839 and 1848, from his base in Futa Jalon, Umar made extensive preaching tours among the Mandinka and Tokolor, initiating members into the Tijaniyya. Most of his followers came from the Tokolor of the Futas but, as Samori Touré's career was later to indicate, Umar was having an impact upon the Mandinka as well. In 1846 on a preaching tour of Futa Toro, his homeland, Umar followed the example of dan Fodio and Hamad Bari by preaching an appealing message of social reform:

> You are like the unfaithful eating and drinking oppression and your chiefs violate God's law by oppressing the weak.

As Umar's popularity spread, his influence challenged the almamis of the Futa kingdoms for many Muslims left the Qadiriyya, which traditionally looked to the almamis for leadership, and joined the Tijaniyya. In 1848 the Almami expelled him from Futa Jalon. Umar performed his hijra to Dinguiray. Supporters flocked to him and by purchasing arms and ammunition in exchange for gold dust Dinguiray began to take on the appearance of a military camp.

Umar and the French

On his tour of Futa Toro in 1848 Umar had proposed collaboration with the French who for many years had been trading from posts on the coast of

Senegal. In return for a monopoly over firearms with which he could rule the interior and guarantee law and order, French merchants would be permitted to move freely in his empire. Umar returned to the interior and from 1852-54 his army overran the Bambara states of Bambuk and Kaarta. In a second tour of Futa Toro his military successes raised his prestige even further. Thousands responded to the call to join his army including a large number of literate and skilled artisans from St. Louis who helped him build his stone forts and man and repair his guns. The chiefly classes of the entire Senegal area feared for their positions and were alarmed at Umar's influence over their subjects and at his proposal to the French which he repeated on his tour in 1854. The French ignored Umar's proposals and when their merchants continued to sell arms to his potential enemies on the Senegal river he seized their traders and confiscated their goods.

The French maintained that their major aim was to open trade routes for the prosperity of the St. Louis merchants yet they failed twice to respond when Umar offered them what they wanted. As Catholics they mistrusted Umar and hesitated to support the spread of radical Islam. They felt much like the chiefly classes of the Futas; they too violated the laws of God; they too oppressed the weak and in St. Louis maintained a society where Christians ruled and Muslims served. The exodus from St. Louis was a warning. A powerful neighbour based on the equality of man would be no more acceptable to the French than to the Futa ruling groups. The common fear of Umar began to bring the French and the chiefly classes of the Futas into alliance.

In 1854, as Umar's popularity reached its peak, the Frenchman Faidherbe arrived as Governor of the French settlements along the coast. He was not anti-Muslim and he was attracted by the idea of co-operation with a powerful African state in the interests of commerce. However, he was determined that the Tokolor empire should not extend to the coast where Umar could dictate to the tiny French settlements. Rather he thought the French should expand into the Senegal area. Since Umar's popularity was frightening the chiefly classes, Faidherbe had an ideal opportunity to extend French rule by posing as the protector of the chiefs against radical Islam. It was thus that Faidherbe and Umar engaged in a partly diplomatic and partly military contest for control of the Senegal.

In 1855 Faidherbe, in a bold stroke, built Fort Medina on the edge of the Tokolor empire as a demonstration of how far French power should reach. East of Medina, Umar could create his empire and Faidherbe was ready to welcome Franco-Tokolor co-operation along the lines Umar had suggested. Umar and his advisors were divided as to whether to accept this division of the country. Some favoured destroying Medina, conquering the Futas and dictating to the French. Others, including Umar himself, were inclined to accept the Medina boundary. Umar saw little conflict between

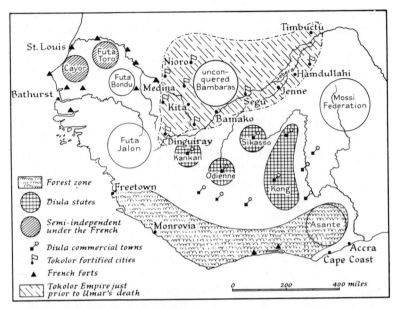

7 The far western Sudan in about 1863

French and Tokolor aims; the one wanted trade, the other empire. He failed to see that the French would soon want empire too, and the Senegal would be their base for the destruction of Tokolor authority. In a compromise Umar made a half-hearted attack on Medina in 1857 to satisfy his anti-French supporters, then turned east to enlarge his empire.

The battle of Medina temporarily determined the division of the country and while Umar turned to enlarge his empire in the east, Faidherbe began the French consolidation of Senegal. He built Dakar and a number of inland forts, recruited a battalion of Senegalese troops, played on the fears of the chiefly classes to secure a treaty of protection with Futa Toro, deposed the damel of Cayor, Lat-Dior Diop and replaced him with a 'friend' of the French.

Umar was killed in Macina in 1864; Faidherbe left Senegal in 1865. But even before Faidherbe's departure events began to turn against him and in favour of Umar in Senegal. Had Umar not lost his life in Macina he might have swept to the coast and overturned the work of Faidherbe who had alienated many by his methods. In the early sixties one disciple of Umar's became Almami of Futa Toro and worked secretly against the French; while another, Maba, a Tijani scholar declared the jihad around the Gambia river. Lat-Dior Diop, the deposed damel of Cayor, joined forces with Maba and by 1870 had regained his throne. In the same year in Europe, Bismarck's

24

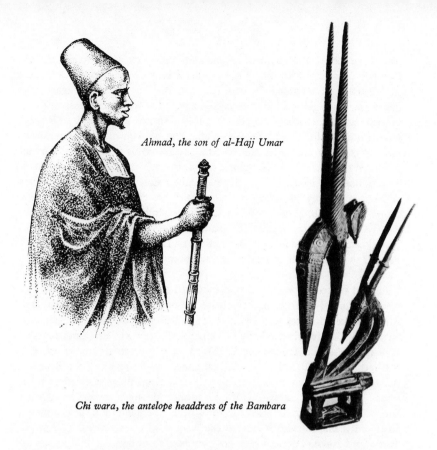

Ahmad, the son of al-Hajj Umar

Chi wara, the antelope headdress of the Bambara

Germany overran France and in a crushing defeat marched into Paris and dictated a humiliating peace treaty. The French were forced to cut back their activities in Senegal and ten years after the departure of Faidherbe had lost most of the advantages which he had gained for them. The Tokolors, however, could not take advantage of French weakness because of Umar's death and the empire's internal troubles which followed.

Ahmad and the Tokolor empire

As far back as 1854 Umar had invited Hamad III of Macina to join him in wiping out Animism in the western Sudan. Hamad refused. Following the half-hearted attack on Medina, Umar turned and marched against the Bambara of Segu whose Pagan king sought a defensive alliance with Macina. Hamad III agreed on condition that the Bambara king burn his images and declare for Islam. A series of letters passed between Umar and Hamad, like those between Bello and al-Kanami, in which Umar claimed that Hamad's alliance with Pagan Segu against a brother Muslim was apostasy, (the betrayal of religion). In short, he felt that to ally with Paganism *is* Paganism. Segu fell to Umar in 1861 largely due to his impressive use of firearms and an adequate supply of ammunition manufactured by his army blacksmiths behind the battle lines. The king of Segu fled to Hamdullahi secretly carrying the traditional religous images of his family which he had promised to destroy. The next year Umar entered Hamdullahi. Triumphantly he produced the images of the Bambara king before the assembled scholars of Macina thereby justifying the attack and his execution of Hamad as a traitor to the faith. Umar's forces swept on to Timbuctu and with its capture the Tokolor empire reached its greatest point. However, soon after this Umar lost his own life in a rebellion led by Ba Lobbo which resulted from the manner in which Qadiriyya members had been forced to adopt the Tijaniyya way.

Ahmad succeeded his father and inherited multiple problems. Umar had placed his sons, brothers and favourite slaves over the conquered emirates. Ahmad lacked the prestige of his father and the emirs gave him allegiance in name only. Macina revolted and two emirs (Ahmad's half-brothers) declared their independence. Large areas of Bambara right inside his empire had still not been conquered and there was real danger that a revolt of the Bambara under his control would be joined by attacks from these still independent areas. The Tokolor army divided its loyalty among members of Umar's family. Unlike Sokoto the army was foreign, recruited not from the conquered areas, but from outside. It treated the people with disdain and its excesses discredited Islam. The soldiers were exempted from taxation and possessing horses and guns were almost impossible to discipline.

By 1873 Ahmad had defeated his half-brothers. His cousin reconquered Macina but having gained this victory ruled virtually independent of Ahmad. To solve the problem of the army Ahmad began to disband it and rely more upon the subject people for support. Thus during the eighties Ahmad was cutting down his military forces for political and religious reasons inside the empire while he had greater need of them than ever to check renewed French penetration.

The French conquest

French interest in expansion into the interior was renewed with the appointment of J. S. Gallieni as political director of St. Louis in 1878. Work was begun on railway construction and on a road and telegraph to connect St. Louis with the French forts as far as Medina on the Senegal river. In 1881 Gallieni travelled to Segu to sign a commercial treaty with Ahmad. On this journey he sought to pursue an impossible double policy, on the one hand to pose as a friend of the Bambara, hinting at French support for a liberation revolt, on the other to pretend support for Ahmad and the Tokolor.

Tokolor policy was unchanged since the days of Umar. Guns for trade. In return for a French monopoly of the empire's trade they asked for four cannon and 1,000 rifles immediately plus 200 per year thereafter. The French were to agree not to build forts nor in any way infringe Tokolor sovereignty. In return they said, 'we shall open the roads for you everywhere; you may follow us and profit from our efforts'. The negotiators skilfully hinted that if France rejected their terms the British might be offered them. Gallieni accepted, but the French government in Paris, wanting more than just trade, rejected them. While Gallieni was signing a treaty which promised to respect Tokolor sovereignty, a French general was leading a military force to establish an armed fort inside Tokolor territory at Kita with instructions to act as liberator of the 'oppressed Bambara'. The Tokolor aptly summed up the diplomatic situation. 'We like the French but do not trust them, they on the other hand trust us, but do not like us.'

In the years between 1881 and 1885 the Tokolor empire lost its last chance of survival. While twice violating Tokolor territory by establishing Fort Kita in 1881 and Fort Bamako in 1883 the French blundered into a clash with Samori (see chapter 4), the Almami of the Mandinka empire to the south. Here was a chance for a powerful alliance, especially since trouble erupted behind the French in Senegal. Lat-Dior Diop waged a three-year war against the French in Cayor. At the same time a religious leader near Medina led a revolt against French forced labour and the commandeering of food supplies for railway construction. Samori proposed an alliance but Ahmad rejected it. By 1886 the revolts in Senegal had been crushed by the French and a treaty of friendship negotiated with Samori and Futa Jalon, thereby diplomatically isolating the Tokolor. A golden opportunity was thus lost and thereafter there was little chance of saving the empire.

In 1890 the French captured Segu and consistent with their pose as liberators placed a member of the old Bambara dynasty on the throne under the watchful eye of a Resident. Ahmad was in Nioro in Kaarta. The French captured Nioro and Ahmad fled to Macina. It was ironic that in Kaarta the French met their strongest resistance not from the Tokolor but from the Bambara whom they were supposed to be liberating. The following year they cast aside this pose in executing their newly-created Bambara king in Segu. In 1893 Jenne and all Macina fell to the French. Ahmad fled once again, this time to Sokoto, the homeland of his mother, where he died in 1898.

The French armies were now striking in two directions, south against Samori (see chapter 4) and east towards Lake Chad. One column captured

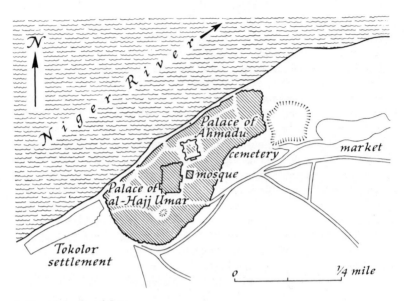

8 Plan of the city of Segu

Timbuctu in 1894. Another under Voulet and Chanoine left a trail of fire and blood behind them as they burnt villages and executed friends and foes alike. They placed a puppet on the Mossi throne and headed for Lake Chad. Their advance was slowed by water shortage, the vast quantity of booty they carried, and slaves. The French government sent a political officer to report on them and they so resented this action that they killed the political officer and declared their independence from France. However, their soldiers mutinied and killed both officers. It now appears that Voulet and Chanoine had gone mad with blood lust.

In 1900 three French forces, one from Macina, one from Algeria and one from Gabon converged upon Rabeh at Lake Chad (see chapter 3)..

Of all the outstanding Islamic reformers and reform movements of the nineteenth-century western Sudan, al-Hajj Umar, Ahmad and the Tokolor empire are the most difficult to assess. Some have called Umar a military adventurer using Islam merely as a cloak to hide his ambition for personal power and it is indeed true that the military aspect was of first importance. The jihad thus appears as Tokolor imperialism resulting in a Tokolor empire. Umar, unlike Muhammad Bello or Hamad Bari, led a foreign army conquering states where there were no civil uprisings against the Pagan rulers. Yet neither of his predecessors preached so consistently to the common people,

Ahmad's palace at Segu, late nineteenth century

expressing their grievances and appealing directly to them by emphasizing the equality of man. A further complicating factor was that Umar's preaching tours were mainly among the Mandinka and Tokolor while his empire was built over the Bambara states and Macina. The Tijaniyya was yet another complication. The Muslim minorities who elsewhere provoked the civil uprisings were, in the Niger-Senegal, divided in their attitude to Umar. Qadiriyya leadership and members were often Umar's strongest opponents. This division, Qadiriyya against Tijaniyya, hindered united action and plagued the empire until its collapse.

Much of the difference between Umar and his predecessors, between his empire and the Sokoto caliphate or theocratic state of Macina was the difference between the way of the Tijaniyya and Qadiriyya. The Tijaniyya stressed action in the cause of Islam. The quickest kind of action was war and sword-point conversion. Umar set the tone by turning Dinguiray into a military camp and precipitating the jihad. Dan Fodio, in contrast, sought conversion by persuasion and negotiation. Among the Qadiriyya the warrior was accorded least prestige, the scholar most. Dan Fodio retired from the distasteful business of war and politics to write and instruct the officials of the caliphate. The jihad in Gobir can thus be looked upon as an intellectual movement for dan Fodio, Abdullah and Bello were first and foremost idealists, poets, historians, writers and thinkers who produced many books in addition to their correspondence. They sought the ideal society and the just and upright ruler. War might be a necessary evil but peace was an essential requirement for the creative phase of moulding society towards the ideal. Education, not the sword, was the weapon in which they put their faith. Umar was neither as scholarly as the Sokoto leaders nor did his Tijaniyya way stress the intellectual. The military rather than the intellectual held the prestige and privileged position in the Tokolor empire. Nevertheless, Umar's methods were effective for, although his empire failed to survive, the Tijaniyya became the dominant brotherhood of the western Sudan as a result of his labours.

A further complication lies in Umar's relations with the French. This problem of an external power affected neither Sokoto nor Macina. Umar's curious 'softness' towards the French and his failure to make use of his popularity in the Futas to overthrow the chiefly classes and negotiate with the French from a position of strength raises a question not satisfactorily answered. While Umar has been accused of using Islam to arouse anti-European feelings the reverse appears to be the truth. Umar went to extreme lengths to meet French demands and this policy followed the general attitude of the Tijaniyya elsewhere. In Algeria and Tunisia, for example, it was a friend of French expansion and colonialism.

Ahmad followed his father in appeasing the French and refusing to exploit the unrest in Senegal. Various reasons have been put forward. He was a religious not a military leader. He had reduced the army and estranged the Tokolor by his policy of undermining their privileged position. He could not rely upon the subject peoples. In the early eighties Ahmad was the obvious leader of an anti-French coalition of African states but not only did he reject alliances but he estranged Samori and actually assisted French troops to suppress the Medina revolt. Since Samori was a Tijani, alliance with him ought to have come easily. But Samori's star had risen far above Ahmad's. Samori was not a Tokolor and not even from the scholar class, he possessed less intellectual sparkle than Ahmad. Samori might be typical of what a good Tijaniyya ought to be but while the idea of equality among men might be good in theory it appeared difficult for Ahmad to follow in practice.

3 Revival and decline in Bornu

Bornu lies between the western and eastern Sudan and has close connections via the Fezzan with North Africa. During the nineteenth century Bornu was continually affected by developments in these three areas. The most important of these was the profound influence of dan Fodio and the Sokoto caliphate which was probably as revolutionary in its effects upon Bornu as upon the Hausa states themselves. This was followed by the establishment of the Sanusiyya order in North Africa, whose spread into the Sudan and alliance with the military power of Wadai to the east created a challenge to Bornu's control around Lake Chad.

During the eighteenth century the Bornu empire, extending from Kano to Kanem, had been the undisputed master of the central Sudan. Neither the divided Hausa states to the west, nor Wadai, a vassal of Darfur, to the east, were in any position to challenge its supremacy. The empire consisted of Bornu proper, the petty chieftaincies to the south and west, the nomadic clans, the vassal states of Kanem, Zinder, and Bagirmi and the tributary states of Kano, Katsina and Zaria. Bornu proper, the heart of the empire and home of the Kanuri, was ruled directly by administrators responsible to the Mai. Areas other than the tributary states, which merely paid annual tributes, were governed indirectly through their own chiefs, under the supervision of a Kanuri resident.

Political organization

The Mai of Bornu was a semi-divine king surrounded by an elaborate court ritual. He could be approached only from a distance and gave audience hidden from view. This forced seclusion isolated the Mai from practical politics and encouraged him to turn to literary pursuits, excessive religious devotion, or the pleasures of his harem. Royal relatives were carefully controlled and were therefore powerless to challenge the Mai's position.

The Mai governed through a State Council of Twelve, made up of titled nobility and Kokenawa (administrators). The nobility held military titles which gave them responsibility for the defence and supervision of certain parts of the empire. They lived in the capital under the royal eye, and not in their areas of supervision where they might encourage rebellion.

Actual administration, tax collection, the raising of military levies, and supervision of local chiefs, was in the hands of the Kokenawa, either the Kambe (freeborn commoners) or Kachela (men of servile origin). Commanders of the army were titled nobles, but officers and lesser ranks were Kachela.

The high court of twelve judges presided over by the Mainin Kanendi (Chief Justice and second in rank to the Mai) sat in the capital. Judgements of local magistrates (Mallamai) could be appealed against to the high court.

The political organization gave unusual stability to Bornu, as was shown by the Sefawa dynasty, which ruled uninterruptedly for one thousand years. Succession disputes were few and, once in power, the Mai was unlikely to be challenged either by his relatives or the nobility. And, although it was the Kokenawa who in practice governed Bornu, since they could be promoted, transferred, demoted or executed on the orders of the Mai and State Council, they were powerless to rebel. The system was strengthened by the Kanuri idea of a centralized state and loyalty to the Mai.

Bornu's history was one of rise and decline but never fall. During peace and prosperity the Mai's seclusion would increase and a decline would begin;

9 Bornu and her neighbours before the jihad

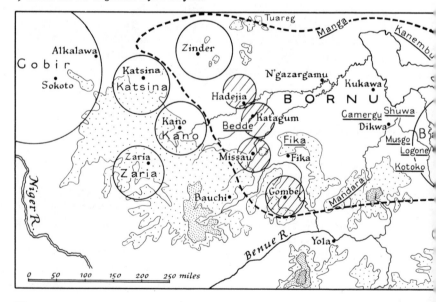

but under stress he could emerge and use his wide powers to restore the kingdom and prevent collapse.

The other Lake Chad kingdoms were also organized much like Bornu, with the Kolak of Wadai and Mbang of Bagirmi occupying a central position, similar to that of the Mai, in the political organizations.

The jihad in Bornu

The Sokoto jihad was a threat to Bornu's traditional policy of keeping the Hausa states divided. But when the Mai sent an army to the aid of Bornu's Hausa tributaries it was defeated, with the result that Kano, Katsina and Zaria fell to the Fulani. Then a number of leaders, among them Gwoni Muktar and Ibrahim Zaki, roused the Fulani of Bornu's western chieftaincies, and carved out the emirates of Hadejia, Katagum, Missau and Gombe for the caliphate. Muktar, having received a flag from dan Fodio, then swept into Bornu proper and sacked the capital in about 1808. The Mai fled to Kanem.

Taking advantage of Bornu's confusion Zinder declared its independence and Wadai, which was led by Kolak Sabun and had been independent of Darfur since the seventeen nineties, conquered Bagirmi and invaded Kanem.

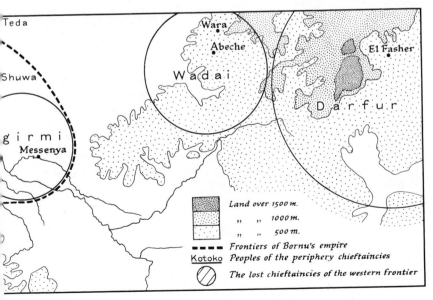

The Mai of Bornu holding court. From a drawing by the British traveller, Clapperton

No longer undisputed master of the central Sudan, Bornu was being crushed between two great expanding powers, the caliphate from the west and Wadai from the east.

But at this stage an important development took place. Mai Ahmad called upon al-Kanami, a scholar of Bornu who, supported by his own clan and the Shuwa nomads, was able to retake the capital and kill Muktar.

Al-Kanami, like dan Fodio, was really a Muslim scholar, who came from an influential family in Kanem. He had spent some time in the Fezzan because it was his mother's homeland and his father, who was also a scholar, had taught there. Al-Kanami had been on the hajj and had lived for long periods in Egypt and Arabia. He was married into royalty in Kanem and was friendly with the large Shuwa Arab scholar class in the Lake Chad region.

When Ahmad died he was succeeded by his son Dunama, who was driven from the capital in 1811 by another Fulani mallam and flag bearer, Ibrahim Zaki. Like his father, Mai Dunama turned to al-Kanami, and offered him half the revenues of the freed provinces if he would take control of the army. Al-Kanami accepted, and swept the Fulani from Bornu proper, forcing Zaki to retire to his emirate of Katagum.

34

Why the jihad failed

The Fulani nomads were concentrated in the western chieftaincies, and, after they swept into Bornu proper, both Muktar and Zaki found it impossible to keep their forces together, for the nomads returned to their homes after an early victory. Further, while in Hausaland the jihad was mainly a nomadic and scholar effort, in Bornu the Shuwa nomads fought against it and the scholars, mainly Shuwa, Kanembu and Kanuri, also remained loyal to the Mai; this left the movement without solid support or intelligent direction. The loyalty of the Shuwa was decisive for like the Fulani they were nomads, scholars and warriors. The failure of the jihad also showed the strength of the Kanuri political system. For while the Hausa peasants frequently seemed unconcerned about the outcome, the Kanuri remained loyal, and no rivals or discontented groups emerged to take advantage of the Mai's weakness. Lastly, Hausaland produced no leader of the military and administrative qualities of al-Kanami, whose reforms quickly removed possible causes of discontent.

Sokoto claimed that the jihad against Bornu was reasonable because the Mai allowed Pagan practices and persecuted Fulani Muslims while supporting Pagan Hausa dynasties. Al-Kanami claimed that, although there might be sin in Bornu as in all Muslim states, Bornu was not a Pagan state against which it was proper to launch a jihad. He accused the Fulani of seeking power and wealth under the pretence of furthering the cause of Islam.

Al-Kanami

Al-Kanami emerged as the hero of Bornu. By example and command he insisted that his followers should show the greatest respect for the Mai; the court continued to maintain its colourful ritual and the Mai to control the titled nobility. But effective authority lay with al-Kanami who, like a prime minister, was the power behind the throne and whose advice the sovereign was compelled to accept. His authority rested upon his position as chief justice and army commander. To increase his own influence he surrounded himself with Shuwa advisors and raised the Kambe and Kachela in the military and civil administration at the expense of the titled nobility. In addition he drew a large revenue from the provinces according to his agreement with Dunama and held the complete loyalty of his Kanembu soldiers who settled with him in Bornu. Al-Kanami took no title and was known as the Shehu until his death in 1837.

Following a similar policy to Bello in Sokoto, al-Kanami carried out reforms which called on the judges to enforce Islamic law, tightened control

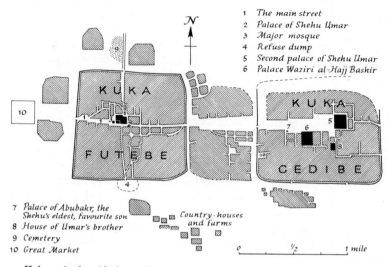

1 The main street
2 Palace of Shehu Umar
3 Major mosque
4 Refuse dump
5 Second palace of Shehu Umar
6 Palace Waziri al-Hajj Bashir

7 Palace of Abubakr, the
   Shehu's eldest, favourite son
8 House of Umar's brother
9 Cemetery
10 Great Market

Country-houses
and farms

0   ½   1 mile

10 Kukawa in the mid-nineteenth century

over the Kokenawa administrators and assisted education, so that by mid-century two to three thousand people were studying in the capital. In 1814 he built his own capital, Kukawa, which became the largest city of the kingdom. Bornu's dual capital – the ceremonial, inhabited by the Mai and titled nobility, and the administrative, dominated by the Shehu and Shuwa – symbolized the dual leadership and widening division in Bornu society.

Al-Kanami was only partially successful in his efforts to recreate the Bornu empire of the eighteenth century. He reconquered Zinder, Kanem and Bagirmi, but, following an unsuccessful invasion of the caliphate, he recognized Fulani sovereignty over the western chieftaincies in 1826 as the price of peace on Bornu's western frontier. Thereafter the caliphate and Bornu remained at peace but coldly hostile and suspicious of each other.

Thus in Bornu, as in Hausaland, the jihad transferred power from secular to religious leadership and from one ethnic group to another: from Sarkin to Emir, and Hausa to Fulani in Hausaland; from Mai to Shehu, and Kanuri to Shuwa Arab in Bornu. In Bornu the jihad created a dual headship which divided the society and progressively weakened the kingdom in facing the rising power of Wadai in mid-century.

The crisis of 1846

From the outset the Mai had resented the power of the Shehu. Twice Dunama

36

had conspired to throw out al-Kanami and twice the Shehu, showing great tact and diplomacy, had reinstated him. When Umar became Shehu in succession to his father in 1837, Dunama's brother Ibrahim was the reigning Mai. Umar reduced the Mai's revenues and exercised his power much more openly than his father had ever done. The personal hatred between Mai and Shehu reflected the Kanuri nobility's jealousy of the influence and power of the wealthy Shuwa and Kokenawa; it was this which led to civil war in 1846.

When a revolt occurred in Zinder, Mai Ibrahim took advantage of the army's preoccupation and opened secret negotiations with the ambitious Kolak of Wadai. Umar executed Mai Ibrahim, but the Kolak invaded Bornu and, supported by the Kanuri nobility, burnt Kukawa, drove Umar into exile, and installed a puppet Mai on the throne. However, the Kolak withdrew his army, on payment of 10,000 silver dollars, and possibly in return for Umar's recognition of Wadai's supremacy over Bagirmi and Kanem. The recently installed Mai, seventeen-year-old son of Ibrahim, and the last representative of the thousand-year-old Sefawa dynasty, was killed in battle and Umar mounted the throne.

Although Umar kept the title of Shehu, in every other way he took over the position of Mai, even to the elaborate court ritual which forced him into seclusion as it had the Sefawas before him. Power was entrusted to his Waziri (prime minister), al-Hajj Bashir, son of a Shuwa who had been advisor to al-Kanami. Bashir became the power behind Umar's throne just as the Shehus had been shadow rulers of the Mais, but his corruption and greediness kept alive the nobility's hatred of the dominating Shuwa and led to a second attempt to overthrow them.

In 1883, Abd al-Rahman, ambitious for the throne, and seeking the support of the nobility, led a revolt against his brother, Umar. Bashir was executed and Umar was forced to abdicate. But through the loyalty of the army Umar regained his throne and lived until he was very old and blind. He was succeeded in turn by three of his sons. Another Shuwa, Waziri Abd al-Karim, rose in favour and confirmed Shuwa dominance in Bornu in the last quarter of the nineteenth century. The division within the society resulting from the rivalry between Shuwa and Kanuri was a major cause of the decline of Bornu in the last half of the nineteenth century.

External factors in the decline of Bornu

In addition to internal divisions, Bornu faced serious external problems growing out of the rise of powerful neighbours to the east and west and their efforts to control the trans-Saharan trade. The burning of Kukawa in 1846 indicated the growing importance of Wadai just as the Fulani sack of Bornu's

Mounted lancers from the Bornu area. (a) *a Kanembu chief,* (b) *a Bagirmi lancer in quilted clothing,* (c) *a Kanuri lancer in chain mail*

capital forty years earlier had signalled the rise of the caliphate. Thus, while in the early nineteenth century Bornu lost its western vassals – Kano, Zaria, Katsina – as well as the frontier chieftaincies to the Fulani, in mid-century it lost its eastern vassals – Kanem and Bagirmi – to the Wadayans.

There was a close connection between the rise and decline of empires and their ability or inability to control and regulate trade. There was a further connection between trade and the brotherhoods, and thus the brotherhoods were vital in sustaining the political power of the empire they favoured. During the nineteenth century, therefore, trade and religion decided who should hold power in the Lake Chad area, with the major contenders for empire being Bornu and Wadai, while the minor states of Kanem and Bagirmi were little more than pawns in the power struggle.

During the eighteenth century Bornu had been the pivot of the two greatest trade routes of the central Sudan. The Saharan caravan route led from Bornu through the Teda country and Fezzan to Tripoli. Slaves were

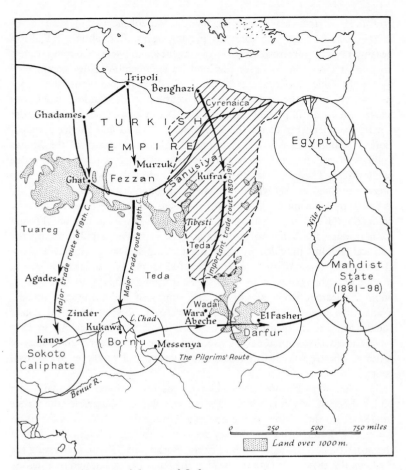

11 Saharan trade routes of the central Sudan

exchanged with the Tripolitanians for luxuries and firearms, and wheat was exchanged for salt with the Teda. The Mai customarily married a Teda wife to cultivate the friendship of the people who lived along the route and were responsible for the safety of the caravans.

Bornu also lay astride the pilgrim route between Kano and Darfur. Along this route Darfur copper was imported for Nupe, and Lake Chad potash for Hausaland, while forest products, especially kola nuts, were brought from Kano and sent north to the Sahara and east to Darfur.

During the Fulani invasion trade was broken up and one of al-Kanami's urgent tasks was to restore Bornu's commercial supremacy. Born and brought up at the important caravan stopping point of Murzuk, he used his connections in the Fezzan to get the caravans moving again. But, although Kukawa became a busy commercial centre attracting fifteen to twenty thousand traders on market days, Bornu never regained its eighteenth-century commercial monopoly. The development of the Kano-Tripoli route into the major caravan route of the early nineteenth century made Zinder, which was located on it, an important vassal of the Bornu empire. But when, under Umar, the friendship of the Teda was not cultivated and Zinder revolted, Bornu's commercial position deteriorated. Also the practice of the Shuwa families of making fortunes in currency speculation, meant that the value of the Maria Theresa dollar changed from day to day, and traders began to prefer the Kano market where the state maintained a stable currency.

It was thus during Umar's reign that Wadai became a serious commercial competitor. Kolak Sabun, 1803-13, had opened a new caravan route through Teda country to Benghazi, and trade later expanded rapidly during the political stability provided by three outstanding and long-reigning Kolaks, al-Sharif 1835-58, Ali 1858-74, and Yusuf 1874-98. The Kolaks also sought to give a further stimulus to trade by establishing industry in Wadai. For, while the leather workers, weavers and smiths of Kano attracted traders, Wadai, like Bornu, lacked artisans. To overcome this weakness the kolaks sought artisans in Bagirmi. Kolak Sabun in 1806 and Kolak Ali in 1870 sacked Messenya, capital of Bagirmi, and carried into slavery thousands of artisans, who were settled in Wadai and given special privileges in the royal court.

The Sanusiyya became the major religious brotherhood of Wadai under Kolak al-Sharif, who was converted to the order before he ascended the throne in 1835. In the 1840's the Sanusiyya headquarters was established in Cyrenaica. Enterprising missionary activity spread the zawiyas or lodges of the order though the oases of the Fezzan, Borku and Tibesti, converting the Teda by the 1870's. In 1874 the head of the Sanusiyya arbitrated in a succession dispute and placed his own candidate – Kolak Yusuf – on the throne of Wadai.

By the mid-seventies the Sanuisiyya had created a trading and religious 'empire' uniquely suited to the desert people it controlled from Cyrenaica in the north to Bagirmi in the south. The zawiyas acted as local government centres, carrying out the orders of the Grand Sanusi, subordinating the nomadic chiefs to their judicial authority, and maintaining peace and order. Wadai under Kolak Yusuf, was like a vassal state of the 'empire'. Since the Sanusiyya financed its activities through trade, and every zawiya head was a trader, the brotherhood was vitally concerned with providing the conditions under which the caravan trade could flourish. The co-operation of the Teda and Wadayans under Sanusiyya leadership raised the Wadai-Benghazi route from being the most obscure to being the most profitable by the late nineteenth century.

There was a close relationship between brotherhoods and empires in the central Sudan. In the caliphate the Qadiriyya was the dominant brotherhood. In Bornu, possibly because of the Fulani connection with the Qadiriyya, the Mai and Kanuri belonged to the Tijaniyya. The Sanusiyya, who spread around Lake Chad with the rise of Wadai, made it a policy to emancipate slaves, teach them in the zawiyas of the Fezzan and Cyrenaica, and send them back to the interior to establish zawiyas as trader-missionaries. In Bagirmi and Kanem the zawiyas tended to bolster the political supremacy of Wadai.

The Wadai invasion of Bornu in 1846 was the beginning of the decline of Bornu and the rise of Wadai. The crisis of 1846 had been on one hand a struggle between factions for control of Bornu and on the other a struggle between Bornu and Wadai for control around Lake Chad. Between 1846 and 1890 Wadai steadily brought Kanem and Bagirmi within its commercial and political orbit, under the overriding shadow of the Sanusiyya. Bornu, in 1800 the undisputed master of the central Sudan, was by 1890 little more than a small state between the two empires, the caliphate and Wadai.

Rabeh 1893-1900

The weakness of Bornu became apparent when, in 1893, it fell prey to a new conqueror. This was Rabeh, who was born in the eastern Sudan of slave parents, had served in the Egyptian army, and later commanded the private troops of Zubair Pasha, an Egyptian slave trader in the Nile Valley. With the expansion of the Mahdist state along the Nile, Rabeh marched his army to the west and defeated Wadai, conquered Bagirmi and Bornu, burnt Kukawa and established the capital of his empire at Dikwa.

Since the European conquest of Africa was in full swing, and European-led armies were advancing into the heart of Africa, Rabeh's major concern was organizing united resistance. He had supported the Mahdist opposition to Europeans along the Nile and uniformed his troops in Mahdist style; he now called for a jihad against the Europeans. However, neither the caliphate nor the Sanusiyya, who controlled his supply of firearms, was eager to join his jihad; the former because Rabeh had been joined by a pretender to the throne of Sokoto, the latter because he had seized Bagirmi from Wadai.

The British at one time considered allying with Rabeh to check the French, who were winning the race to the interior. But then Bagirmi went over to the French, and in 1900 Rabeh was defeated and killed by a French army. Eventually, the arrival of a British column placed a descendant of al-Kanami on the throne, whose descendant reigns today as Shehu of Bornu.

4 The Mandinka empire of Samori Touré, 1870-98

The Mandinka and the rise of Samori

The Mandinka inhabit an area of the western Sudan bounded on the west by the Futa Jalon, on the south by the forests, on the north by the Tokolor empire and on the east by the Mossi and Asante kingdoms. They possessed no central political authority nor sizeable states in 1800, but were organized in hundreds of towns or village groups. They did, however, possess a pride in a common origin and the greatness of their past under the empire of ancient Mali.

One group of Mandinka – the Diula – were long-distance traders. Because of the foreign goods they sold and their skill as craftsmen – weavers and blacksmiths – they moved freely throughout Mandinka country and beyond, trading among the Mossi, with French merchants on the Senegal and on the coast at Monrovia and Freetown. The Diula were Muslims. They settled in villages, some of which grew into towns and insisted on their independence from the local people. They built mosques and schools and attracted a scholar class to their towns. Kong, one of the famous Diula towns was noted not only for its trade, its weavers and dyers, but also for its mosques, schools and scholars.

The Diula towns were Muslim islands in a sea of Animism. However, since the Diula were Mandinka like their Pagan neighbours they compromised, inter-married and practised Pagan rites along with their Muslim faith. The circle of Muslims widened around them but they were not missionaries, far less jihadists, for they were unwilling to upset their commercial activities by rousing Pagan hostility. They were the 'nominal Muslims', 'compromisers' and 'sacrificers to many gods' condemned by the Islamic reformers of the nineteenth century.

By mid-nineteenth century some of the Diula towns were expanding into sizeable states. While the Muslim reform movement sweeping the Sudan may have begun to rouse these contented Muslims to a more vigorous spreading of their faith, Diula traders may also have begun to see the commercial advantages of large political units. Kong's expansion was commercial. In its efforts to control the horse trade from the northern savannah and the kola nut trade from the southern forests it had by 1860 became the largest of all the Mandinka states. Kankan's expansion on the other hand, was motivated by religious fervour under Mamadu, a Mandinka, and former disciple of al-Hajj Umar. Two other Diula towns, Odienne and Sikasso, had also expanded into sizeable states by 1850.

Samori's rise was part of this same Mandinka movement towards larger political units. He was a Diula, trading in gold from Wassulu, and cattle from Futa Jalon in the course of which he probably visited Freetown and the Tokolor empire. He was not born a Muslim but was converted to the faith under a scholar-chief of Wassulu. He must also have been well aware of the teachings of al-Hajj Umar. Indeed a number of disciples and a nephew of Umar were later to hold high positions in Samori's empire.

By about 1870, with surprising speed, Samori had brought the small states of the Wassulu area under his authority. He made his capital at Bisandugu, took the title 'Almami' and captured Kankan. By 1886 his empire (115,000 sq. miles) was the third largest political unit of the western Sudan, following the Sokoto caliphate (180,000 sq. miles) and Tokolor empire (150,000 sq. miles).

It was more than Samori's diplomatic and military genius that brought about the unification of the Mandinka. Although divided into a multitude of political units the Mandinka, as we have noticed, possessed a kind of national spirit through their common pride in the illustrious empire of ancient Mali. To the Mandinka, Samori appeared ready to do what Mansa Musa had done for their fourteenth-century ancestors.

Samori stood not only for political unification and revival of Mandinka greatness but also for the spread of Islam as the bond of unity in the new state. His ruthless destruction of Animism was less resented than might have been expected. This suggests that his action was approved by many and that al-Hajj Umar's preaching tours in Mandinka country had at least partly prepared the way for Samori. The activities of his disciple at Kankan indicated that Umar's message had been effective. The Tijaniyya brand of Islam, with its emphasis on equality, which Umar preached and Samori favoured, made a special appeal to the Mandinka whose traditional culture emphasized the dignity and equality of men.

Samori was the commonest of common men, unlike the other great nineteenth-century reformers who had been born into the scholar class. He was born poor and he went much further than Umar in attacking and destroy-ing the worldy position of the chiefly class. Neither did he antagonize his people by going to the extremes of Umar and Hamad Bari in enforcing the moral prohibitions of Islam (except the 'no liquor' rule); rather he stressed

The Almami Samori

A Mandinka fertility doll. Carvings like this which were a part of the traditional religion have almost completely disappeared because of the deep penetration of Islam begun by Samori education. In newly conquered villages his first concern was for the mosque, the school and the teacher. He took a personal interest in the schools and made education compulsory for the children of state officials. The army too, was an instrument of conversion and education in which the faith and basic literacy were taught.

Since the Diula commercial states of Kong and Sikasso resisted Samori it is often supposed that the merchant class opposed him. On the other hand the commercial towns of Kankan and Odienne supported him, Odienne being his most faithful ally. By destroying the great number of customs charges among the small states, his empire removed many obstacles to trade. The merchants may have resented the tight economic control which Samori exercised over agriculture and markets but at the same time they must have benefited from his export drive designed to pay for the importation of war material. Lastly it was the widespread network of long distance Diula traders acting as his spy system among the French in the Futas, the British in Freetown and the Tokolor on the Niger which helped to make his international diplomacy the success that it was.

Samori's political organization

The Mandinka empire was divided into 162 cantons each of which consisted of twenty or more villages. The cantons were grouped together to form ten large provinces. The empire was governed by three parallel lines of authority, the traditional, the military and the religious leading up to the Almami and his state council. Village heads were chosen by traditional methods. Their power was limited by the village Imam's judicial rights and Samori's appointee, who was responsible for raising troops and supplies for the army and the harvesting and sale of produce from the Almami's field farmed communally in each village. Canton chiefs were also chosen by traditional methods, but held purely honorary positions. Real authority lay with the sofa (professional military officer) administrator and the qadi. The provinces were headed by relatives or close friends of Samori assisted by a war chief who had 200 to 300 sofas under his command, and a scholar. The Almami was the supreme political, judicial and religious head of the empire as well as its military commander. He was assisted by a state council composed of the provincial heads of the three lines of authority: political, religious and military.

The Mandinka empire was probably the most effectively governed of the larger west African empires of the nineteenth century. It was much more united and centralized than the Tokolor empire and may, in fact, have been more closely modeled on the Bambara states of Segu and Kaarta. The political organization incorporated two traditional techniques, chiefs at the village level and higher offices distributed among Samori's friends and relatives. Both groups were checked and reduced in power more than was usual by the religious leaders and sofa administrators, the latter being especially important as direct appointees of the Almami with no traditional claim to office and therefore subject to his will in promotion, transfer and dismissal. The importance of the sofas in administration have led some to call the empire a military state. Since the empire was at war for most of its existence the predominance of military officers could be expected. It was in this branch of the administration that Samori could reward merit and call the best talent to the service of the state. Since education, discipline and national rather than tribal loyalty were stressed in the army it was a fine training ground for political officers.

The major aim of Samori's administration was to destroy tribalism and promote national loyalty among the Mandinka. He did this by placing less emphasis on the village groups and more on the canton which brought villages together irrespective of their past relations. At each level of government he saw to it that men of different families and tribes worked together. More than that, he tried to abolish distinctions between privileged and non-privileged classes by giving everyone the chance to rise through the army to the highest places in the state.

Mandinka unity was to be based on the law, way of life and thinking of Islam. Religious leaders took their place at every level alongside the political and military. Images, ancestor houses and sacred groves were replaced with mosques and schools, the major agents in creating the new values and goals of the younger generation. Taxation and law were according to Islamic practice. Judicial matters were usually settled in the alkali's courts at the village, canton or provincial levels but grave matters could be brought before Samori and his state council.

Samori was an innovator, not a preserver of old customs and institutions. He created the essential ingredients of a modern state, a complex administration with an appointed political service and an efficient and loyal army to carry out the will of the central government. Most important he fostered a quite recognizable national spirit without which the existence of a state is not likely to last for long.

Samori's diplomacy

Between 1885 and 1889, while Samori felt that French efforts were directed against the Tokolor empire, he followed a policy of playing the British off against the French, hoping thereby to preserve his independence. As he realized the full might of French military strength and their ambition to conquer the whole Sudan he began to court the British for an alliance. Two years later, on the eve of his seven-year war with the French, he was offering his country to the British, almost begging them to send their troops and raise the Union Jack.

Both the Creoles of Freetown and the British in Sierra Leone were ready to ally with Samori. Their efforts and friendliness misled Samori into believing that he could expect British help. However, the British government in London merely bargained the Mandinka empire for French concessions elsewhere in Africa. Sierra Leonians could not change the British attitude and when the Franco-Mandinka war opened in 1891 Samori faced the French alone.

Samori did succeed in preventing the British from agreeing with the French to ban the export of arms from Freetown. The French requested a ban on exports to Samori but the British delayed until 1893. Indeed it would have been difficult to stop the export of arms from Freetown where everyone from the Governor down was sympathetic to Samori. In 1884 Samori launched a campaign south towards Freetown to open and control the trade routes. In addition he sent messengers to the British governor hinting that he would be willing to discuss a British alliance. When his activities began to frighten Sierra Leone he promised to advance no farther but suggested that the British advance up to his borders to maintain peace and keep the trade routes open.

In Sierra Leone the government and merchants advocated British advance into the interior to increase trade. By the mid 1880's they became worried that the French planned to encircle Sierra Leone, as they had the Gambia, cutting off for ever its hopes of prosperity. Edward Blyden, who had visited the Mandinka empire and was much impressed with the revolution Islam created in African life, became Samori's champion in Freetown. He pressed the British to support Samori, to promote the spread of Islam and check the French.

In 1886 the French approached Samori for a boundary settlement which resulted in the Treaty of Bisandugu. By its terms Samori gave up to France all of his territory north of the River Niger in return for French friendship. He hoped that by satisfying French demands he would either remove future sources of conflict or delay conflict long enough to strengthen his own position. He wanted to gain time to conclude an alliance with the British and build up his military strength by the importation of arms from Freetown. Lastly he hoped to eliminate the state of Sikasso on his north-east frontier and secure control of the trade route supplying horses from the north which was controlled by Tieba, the king of Sikasso. The French signed the treaty because they also wanted to gain time in order to destroy the Tokolor empire before challenging Samori. In order to check a possible Anglo-Mandinka alliance the French gave out that by the treaty of Bisandugu, Samori had ceded his empire to France.

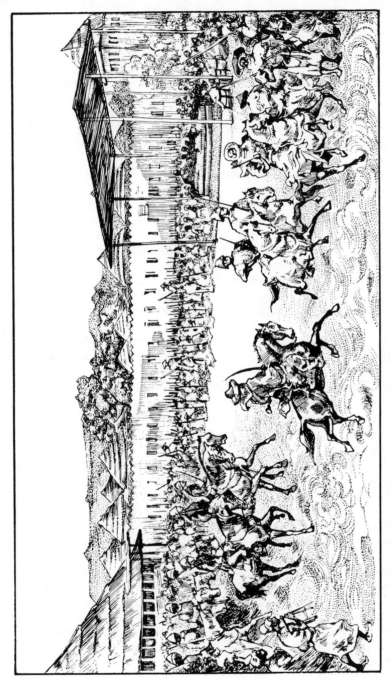

French deputation to Samori's court at Bisandugu. From a contemporary print

Samori's agents in Freetown denied this. The British, fearing that Samori, with the goodwill of France, might sweep up to the boundaries of Freetown, sent an envoy to Bisandugu to ascertain the truth. Samori welcomed the envoy, denied having ceded his empire, assured the British of his goodwill, requested an alliance and offered a railway concession as an inducement.

This show of British interest gave Samori a false sense of security and he made one of his greatest blunders. In 1887-88 he laid siege to Sikasso, probably the best-fortified city in the western Sudan, and for eighteen months he threw his forces against its walls, losing 10,000 men and all his horses. Until then Sikasso had been undecided as to policy. Tieba, jealous of Samori's spectacular rise to power, in control of a lucrative trade and not yet menanced by the French, held back from alliance. Now Samori's siege of Sikasso induced Tieba to sign a treaty of protection with the French.

Although not aware of it, until his ambassador visited London in 1892, Samori was losing his hoped-for British alliance. Even though Ahmad was softening in his attitude to Samori, the French capture of Segu in 1890 drove a wedge between the Tokolor and Mandinka empires, making an alliance difficult. In addition, the French had been secretly urging Tieba to attack Samori while laying their own plans for advance. When Samori discovered this treachery he repudiated the treaty of friendship and sent it back to the French. The seven-year Franco-Mandinka war had begun.

Realizing the unequal nature of the coming struggle Samori sent word to Freetown that he was willing to cede his empire to the British. The Sierra Leone government sent an envoy to Bisandugu. Samori repeated his offer and warned that if Britain did not send troops to occupy his empire, France would. Without authority the envoy hoisted the British flag in Samori's southern towns. The Sierra Leone governor then did his best to make London change its mind. But the British had accepted the French version of the treaty of Bisandugu and felt it was dangerous to recognize Samori's repudiation in case it should encourage African kings in British spheres of influence to do likewise.

Although the British decision was final, Samori was still given reason to hope. Alfred Jones, head of Elder Dempster Shipping Lines, was enraged at his government's abandonment of Samori to the French. In January 1892 he sent his private envoy to Bisandugu. Samori offered to cede his empire and promised the envoy that if he could get British support, Jones would be allowed to build roads and railways, coin money and collect taxes in the empire. But the British government remained firm. It prohibited Jones from sending a second envoy and banned the export of arms from Freetown. In 1892 Samori sent his envoy to London to clear up the mystery of British policy. While a succession of British envoys eager for co-operation had visited his capital and his agents in Freetown reported the unanimous desire there for alliance, yet these promising signs never led to an actual treaty. The facts were that Britain was now only interested in her Freetown naval base. There were few British merchants in Sierra Leone and the British Government was not willing to anger Paris for the sake of Creole prosperity. Samori was abandoned to the French.

Mobilization and military tactics

The professional standing army even in peacetime was from 2,000 to 3,000 strong and made up of the 200 to 300 sofas in each province plus Samori's special guard. In addition there was a regular call up of a different set of men from the villages for military training every six months. It has been estimated that this gave a total military strength of 100,000. However, to remove these men from the land at one time would have disrupted farm production to the point of famine. Furthermore, Samori had not enough guns to arm so many men. Only about 20,000 were ever under arms at one time and of these only half actually fighting. At the height of the struggle about 4,000 sofas, one-quarter being cavalry, were armed with repeater rifles and engaging the French. The non-combatants were used in the carrier corps or the supply division. Each regiment was supported by a carrier corps which transported baggage and ammunition or tended the horses. Carriers could hope that some day they would earn a gun and uniform and become a sofa. The supply division brought in the food and ammunition. At Sikasso a daily food convoy of 200 porters carried 100 tons of food per month for the eighteen-month siege.

Since he lacked artillery (which caused his failure at Sikasso) Samori avoided being bottled up in fortified cities and also any large-scale massing of his troops, where the French artillery could be especially effective. It was typical of the conquest of Africa that large ill-equipped African armies were defeated by small heavily-armed European-led forces. Samori, however, seldom threw more than 1,000 soldiers at the French at one time. Indeed the French occasionally outnumbered the Mandinka. Samori realized that in modern war numbers did not count as much as quality, discipline, organization behind the lines, adequate arms and food.

The military effort was sustained by the sale of the produce from the Almami's field in each village, the ten per cent tax on the gold miners was used to buy arms from Freetown, and the sale of slaves to buy horses (an estimated yearly requirement of 2,000) from the north. At the height of the struggle the state completely took over direction of all markets and agriculture in order to regulate prices and assure a steady food supply. There were also state controlled workshops where blacksmiths repaired and copied all makes of guns and manufactured gunpowder. Some writers claimed that their products were inferior and unreliable and credit Samori's long resistance to the arms purchased in Freetown. But Samori was almost totally dependent upon the state workshops for five years after the Freetown market was closed.

Due to lack of artillery Samori avoided pitched battles, preferring small engagements, followed by a slow retreat to the east. It was at this stage that he divided the army into three divisions: the first armed with repeater rifles engaging the French and retreating; the second organizing the population, evacuating them, leading and protecting their exodus; the third conquering and organizing the new area in preparation to receive the people. As they retreated they carried out a 'scorched-earth' policy, burning villages, crops and everything of value, leaving the French not a grain of maize nor a single man, woman or child to work for them. The French took over dead and deserted country. Their food problem became acute and supplies had to be brought from farther and farther away. This slowed the French advance as much as did the actual fighting.

Most West African resistance to European aggression tended to consist of one sharp encounter followed by collapse of the local organization. This was the case in Ijebu-Ode, Dahomey and Bornu under Rabeh. But although Samori lost almost every battle, his forces remained intact, ready to fight another day.

By 1896 the Mandinka empire had entirely abandoned its first area and was located far to the east in what may be called the second Mandinka empire.

The second Mandinka empire, 1894-98

Samori established his new capital at Dabakala, the centre of the second empire. This was really the first empire which had moved slowly towards the east, coming to rest when further retreat was impossible. Samori's new location was not as good as that of the first empire. He had lost the goldfields and the wealth they provided. To compensate he had to increase the export of slaves to the north. He was cut off from Freetown and had to depend entirely upon his workshops for his military supplies. While his southern frontier had been protected by Sierra Leone and Liberia it was now open to attack from French forts on the Ivory Coast. To the north-east was Kong, suspicious and watchful for commercial advantage, to the south-east Asante ready for an alliance. Beyond were the unpredictable British along the Gold Coast.

Kong's main concern was commerce and Samori, desperate for horses and slaves, could be easily squeezed to enrich its merchants. Kong felt secure

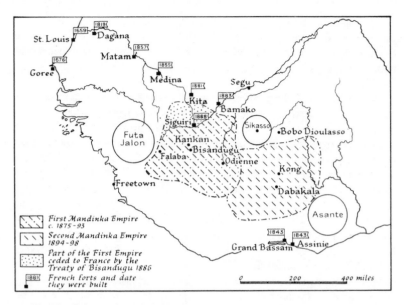

12 The Mandinka empires, 1870-98

because it had signed a treaty of protection with the French. Furthermore, the clerics of Kong were Qadiriyya; educated and sophisticated, they looked down upon Samori as an upstart Tijaniyya with no claim to the scholarship in which they gloried. As relations with Samori deteriorated Kong invited the French to send troops to its defence. Samori defeated the relieving French column and in 1895 turned on Kong and destroyed it. This shocked his army and Muslim subjects generally because Kong had been the respected centre of Islamic learning among the Mandinka. Samori's attack upon Kong was, however, as justified as Umar's on Macina or Bello's on Bornu, for Kong had allied with the infidel against brother Muslims.

Samori now shared a common frontier with the Asante who were eager for an alliance against the British. But there was little advantage in such an alliance because Asante could supply neither of Samori's urgent requirements: horses or guns. Nor was Samori anxious to add the British to his enemies. In 1896, having taken over Asante, a British force left for the north and invaded the Mandinka empire, hoisting the Union Jack in a number of towns. Samori's commander, anxious to avoid a clash, asked the British lieutenant to withdraw. When he refused he was taken prisoner, his force routed and Samori's army captured the first two cannon it had ever possessed. Anxious that this incident should not arouse British hostility, Samori set the lieutenant free with gifts for the British governor of the Gold Coast.

The French captured Sikasso and Bobo Dioulasso in 1898, which cut off the northern trade route and opened another front against Samori. With food, guns and horses in short supply, French armies advancing from the north, west and south and the British in Asante blocking further retreat to the east, Samori evacuated Dabakala. When the French offered him safe conduct and a quiet retirement in his home village he accepted and gave himself up. In spite of this promise, Samori Touré was deported to Gabon where he died in 1900.

Since the Mandinka offered the longest and most coherent resistance to invasion in West Africa they have been looked upon as the only group which might have maintained African independence during the scramble and partition of Africa. They tried to do for the west what Ethiopia did for the east of Africa. The major obstacle was the unwillingness of the African leaders either to combine in a formal alliance or co-ordinate their attack upon the French. Few grasped the extent of French ambition until it was too late. This was aggravated by jealousy and suspicion among the African leaders of Futa Jalon and Sikasso. This national antipathy between Tokolor and Mandinka was made even more serious by minority groups such as Kong who sought to preserve their identity through alliance with the French.

Playing upon these jealousies and antipathies the French prevented an all-African alliance. As early as 1881 they had signed a treaty of friendship and protection with Futa Jalon promising not to interfere in the state's internal affairs. In 1886 they signed a similar treaty with Samori. In the following year they guaranteed Ahmad never to send their army against the Tokolor empire. In that year they agreed to the same terms with Sikasso. By 1887 the French were in treaty relations with all the major African powers and therefore able to strike them down one by one in turn. Not one African state broke the terms of its treaty except Samori, who repudiated it and sent it back to the French. Not until he was in flight did Ahmad consider an African alliance. Once the French had pushed Samori to the east and isolated Futa Jalon and Sikasso, they dealt with each in turn. In 1896 they invaded Futa Jalon, killed the Almami, installed a puppet and then deposed him on the charge of being sympathetic towards Samori.

Next they turned on Sikasso. Tieba died in 1893 and his brother Ba Bemba succeeded him. The new king's sympathy for Samori was well known but the opportunity for an African alliance had passed. The Tokolor empire and Samori's first empire had just fallen. Ahmad was in retreat towards Sokoto, Samori towards Dabakala. Sikasso was isolated. Once Samori's resistance was broken the French demanded that Sikasso accept French soldiers and a resident.

On 18 April 1898 French cannon began the destruction of the walls. The Sikasso cavalry in repeated sorties failed to dislodge the French. After twelve

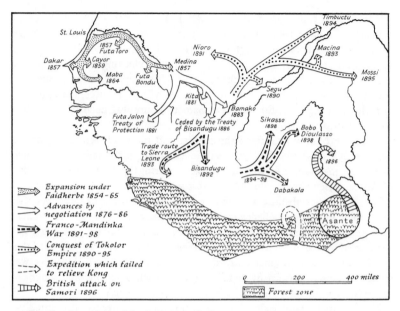

The map legend reads:

- Expansion under Faidherbe 1854–65
- Advances by negotiation 1876–86
- Franco-Mandinka War 1891–98
- Conquest of Tokolor Empire 1890–95
- Expedition which failed to relieve Kong
- British attack on Samori 1896

Forest zone

Map labels: St. Louis; 1857 Futa Toro; Dakar 1857; Cayor 1859; Maba 1864; Futa Bondu; Medina 1857; Nioro 1891; Kita 1881; Futa Jalon Treaty of Protection 1881; Ceded by the Treaty of Bisandugu 1886; Trade route to Sierra Leone 1893; Bisandugu 1892; Bamako 1883; Segu 1890; Sikasso 1898; Macina 1893; Timbuctu 1894; Mossi 1895; Bobo Dioulasso 1898; 1894–98; 1896; Dabakala; Asante; 0 200 400 miles

13 The French conquest of the far western Sudan

days of cannonading, French forces went through the walls. The fighting continued hand to hand and street by street, house to house and over two interior walls. As the struggle neared its end Ba Bemba and the captain of his bodyguard retired into the palace. Minutes later French soldiers entered the throne room to find Ba Bemba slumped over the throne, his captain sprawled at his feet. They had committed suicide.

Considering that the French were trying to conquer the Mandinka empire so that they could rule and trade with the people, their diplomacy was crude rather than clever. Divide and conquer was not a new idea to Africans or Europeans. The French violated every treaty of friendship they signed, overthrew every friendly monarch and by the execution of their puppet, the Bambara king of Segu, indicated that the 'oppressed minorities' had nothing to gain from their leadership. After the capture of Segu in 1890 it should have been clear to all that the French had no intention of co-operating with African governments. Only Samori grasped the significance of Segu, the rest waited to be eliminated at French convenience.

The Franco-Mandinka war was the first 'modern' war in Africa. Samori waged total war, mobilizing the whole population. His tactics were modern: ambush, surprise, scorched earth and the mass-movement of people. The results too, in their scale, were modern: thousands died, the land was devas-

54

tated, depopulated and left a charred and smoking ruin. It has been estimated that the population was reduced to one-third of its original size.

The tendency has been to blame Samori. Some groups claim that they were an important and populous people reduced to a remnant as a result of the war. Others maintain that Samori was so ruthless and callous to human suffering that many turned to the French as the lesser of two evils, that an African alliance was impossible because of the fear of Samori and that this fear drove many to sign alliances with the French. There is truth in all this.

However, the French share blame for the devastation and depopulation. They were the aggressors. They also burnt down towns and fields. Since they suspected everyone, even their own soldiers, of sympathy for Samori they mercilessly destroyed villages and people, many of whom were their genuine friends. Suspicious of their soldiers as possible Mandinka agents, their harshness and brutality caused as many desertions as Samori's propaganda. Gallieni, certainly no friend of Samori's, blamed the French when he wrote: 'In pursuing the war by these methods the French army will leave only desolate solitude for our merchants.'

While some look back on Samori with bitterness, to others his name is magic, 'the greatest West African of the nineteenth century', 'Napoleon of the Sudan', and the finest example of the African personality in its struggle to retain independence. Finally, it should be noted that people do not usually adopt the religion of people that they hate. Though Samori converted at sword point the conversions were permanent. Even in the second empire which existed for only five years it was estimated that about forty per cent of the people accepted Islam as a result of his rule.

5 Changing trade patterns

Sahara caravans of the early nineteenth century

Long-distance trade in West Africa has always had two branches. The first, which is much the older, flowed northwards to the western Sudan, and then across the Sahara to the countries of North Africa – Morocco, Algeria, Tunisia, Libya and Egypt – and even across the Mediterranean to southern Europe and the Middle East. The second branch ran southwards to the Guinea coast, and from the second half of the fifteenth century extended across the Atlantic to Britain, western Europe and the Americas. Until about the end of the sixteenth century the trade with the north, usually known as the caravan trade, was of far more importance to the peoples of the Sudan and the Guinea forest than the coastal or Atlantic trade. But from the seventeenth century onwards, with the fall of Songhai and the consequent anarchy in the area of the Niger bend on the one hand, and the development of the trans-Atlantic gold and slave trade on the other, the Atlantic trade steadily gained on the caravan trade. By the beginning of the nineteenth century the former was of much greater importance than the latter. The caravan trade retained some of its importance during the first half of the nineteenth century, but during the second half it steadily lessened and finally stopped completely during the first two decades of this century.

What were the main routes of the caravan trade during the nineteenth century? What were the important centres for the trade? What commodities were involved in the trade? Why had the caravan trade virtually stopped by the end of the nineteenth century, and what, by then, was the nature and pattern of trade in West Africa?

By the beginning of the nineteenth century, the caravan trade across the Sahara had become concentrated on four main routes. One route began in Morocco and ran through Taodeni to Timbuctu on the Niger. The second route began in Tripoli, and passed through Ghadames and the oasis of Air to the Hausa states of Katsina and Kano. The third route also began in Tripoli, then trailed through the oasis of Fezzan to the kingdom of Bornu and eastern Hausaland. The fourth route linked eastern Tripoli (or Cyrenaica) through Kufra with the kingdoms of Wadai and Darfur. The main centres for these four routes in the western Sudan were Timbuctu, Katsina and Kano, Birni Ngazargamu, and Wara and Abeche respectively.

From these centres other routes began which passed through the savanna to towns and cities of the forest areas to the south. For instance, from Timbuctu, in modern Mali, routes ran south-westwards to Labe and Kankan in Guinea, and southwards to Wagadugu in Upper Volta, Kong and Bonduku in Ivory Coast, and to Kintampo and Kumasi in Ghana. The route which began at Katsina in Nigeria then passed through Sokoto, crossed the Niger at Gaya and continued to Sansanne-Mango, in modern Togo, then to Yendi, Salaga and Kumasi. Another well-beaten track ran from Kano through Zaria, crossed the Niger at Bussa, then ran on through Nikki and Djougu in Dahomey, and Sokode in Togo, before continuing to Salaga and Kumasi in Ghana. At Zaria an important route branched off southwards through Nupe to Ilorin and Oyo, in Nigeria, and Abomey in Dahomey. From these towns in the forest further routes continued to the coast. As Bowdich noted when he visited Kumasi in 1812, the town was not only the meeting point for the routes from Timbuctu and Hausaland, but was also the nerve centre for four important routes to the coast. The first route passed through Sefwi to Nzima and Grand Bassam in Ivory Coast; the second went through Denkyira and Wassa to Axim and Sekondi; the third through Twifu and Assin to Cape Coast and Elmina, and the fourth through Akyem to Accra. Similarly, routes radiated from Abomey to Ouidah and Grand Popo, and from Oyo and Ilorin to Badagri and Lagos.

It is thus clear that at the beginning of the nineteenth century the towns of the forest and Guinea coast were linked to those of the Mediterranean by a complicated network of caravan and trade routes which had been established for centuries. However, a single caravan or band of traders hardly ever travelled the whole length of any single route from, say, Tripoli to Kumasi. The trade was carried on in the form of a relay. The caravans and traders from North Africa and the Sahara usually ended their journey in the market centres of the western Sudan, where they sold their goods or exchanged them for local produce. Some of the traders from North Africa even ended their journey in the centres in the Sahara, such as Ghat and Arawan. From the Sudanese towns, not only a new set of traders, but even different beasts of burden took over. The beasts of burden used across the Sahara were camels – animals especially fitted for travel across wide sandy stretches of desert. From the Sudan southwards the beasts of burden were mainly bullocks and asses, and from the forest centres to the coast the principal means used was human porterage. The western Sudan, or the savanna belt, was thus the commercial watershed for Africa north of the equator. It was from there trade flowed both north and south, as well as east and west.

Furthermore, these routes were not all used to the same extent either before

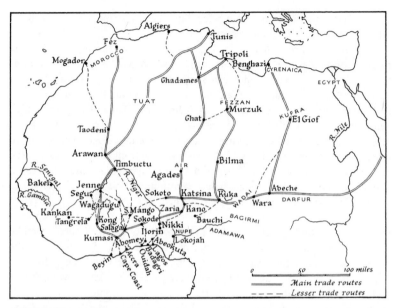

14 Changing patterns of trade

or during the nineteenth century. Throughout the eighteenth and at the beginning of the nineteenth centuries, trade along the two routes from Tripoli to Hausaland and Bornu was more brisk than that along the Morocco-Timbuctu or Cyrenaica-Kufra-Wadai routes; and, of the two routes from Tripoli, by the middle of the century the Tripoli-Ghat-Kano route was easily the more active, as the European explorers of the period – Denham, Clapperton, Richardson and Barth – reported. However, by the 1880's, while trade along the Morocco-Timbuctu route had virtually stopped altogether, and that along the two Tripoli routes was on the verge of extinction, trade was still relatively brisk on the Kufra-Wadai route. By 1900, in fact, the traditional caravan trade had ended on all the routes, but it continued on the Wadai-Kufra route for another fifteen years or so.

Traffic at the Sudanese and forest ends of the routes, on the other hand, never dried up, though it suffered the same changes in fortune. For instance, by the beginning of the nineteenth century it seems that very little export trade was flowing northwards from Ghana, Ivory Coast or Guinea to Timbuctu, and beyond to Morocco and Tunis. Nor did this ever revive; on the contrary, the little there was declined steadily, and by the 1860's, if not earlier, trade in those areas had become a one-way affair, the produce being sent mainly from north to south, and, in the region of the Senegal and the Gambia, from east to west; there was little traffic in the reverse directions. By the

58

1860's, the regions of Timbuctu, Walata and Jenne had stopped being a commercial watershed. On the other hand, the two-way traffic along the north-eastern routes from Ghana and Togo continued throughout the century, and during the first half of the nineteenth century it became particularly brisk and valuable. Indeed, according to a recent authority, trade between Hausa and Salaga reached its peak during the nineteenth century. For reasons to be discussed presently this trade has been continuing to this day, the only difference being that, instead of bullocks and asses, lorries are used in the transportation of goods.

Commercial centres of the western Sudan

The main important commercial centres of the western Sudan at the beginning of the nineteenth century were Timbuctu, Katsina, Kano, Zaria, Birni Ngazargamu, Wara, and Abeche in the western Sudan. Timbuctu, which had been the main commercial and educational centre of the region of the Niger

Timbuctu, from a drawing by the French traveller, René Caillié, in 1828

bend in the sixteenth century, had declined by the beginning of the nineteenth century. The French explorer, Caillié, who entered that town in 1827, reported that he found it 'neither so large nor so populous' as he had been led to expect. Barth, who visited Timbuctu in 1853, reported that it did recover some of its former position as an entrepôt (trading centre) in the 1840's; he estimated its population at 10,000. Though this figure appears to have been exaggerated, it was none the less only a fraction of what it was in the days of Leo Africanus in the sixteenth century. Nor did this very limited recovery last. In fact the fortunes of Timbuctu steadily lessened throughout the second half of the nineteenth century; when Felix Dubois, a French writer, entered it in 1894, Timbuctu was a ghost of its former self. Its role as an entrepôt for goods from the north and south had long ceased, and Dubois found its once famous market, the meeting place of traders from Morocco and Egypt, and from Ghana and Hausaland, attended only by 'women with little baskets, little calabashes and little mats, selling insignificant little things, red, green, white, drab and black spices and vegetables for infinitely little sums of money, just as in any, no matter what little market, in no matter what little town of the Sudan'.

In Hausaland, Katsina was the main commercial centre at the beginning of the nineteenth century. But the town received a blow from which it never recovered during the wars of the Fulani jihad. From about 1815 onwards, Kano became the main commercial and industrial town of Hausaland, as well as its chief entrepôt. The population of Kano was estimated by Clapperton, who visited it in 1824, at between 30,000 and 40,000. Barth, who was there in 1851, estimated it at 30,000, but added that the figure doubled itself during the main caravan season between January and April each year. The markets of Kano were reported by both travellers also to be crowded 'from sunrise to sunset every day', and some of the traders came from as far as Tripoli and Tuat in the north and modern Ghana and Togo in the south. Kano was also at that time the main depot for goods from the south as well as the north, and it was there that these goods changed hands and began their transportation in the opposite direction. But what particularly impressed the nineteenth-century European explorers about Kano was the fact that it was not only a market town and an entrepôt, but also an industrial centre. As Barth put it, 'the great advantage of Kano is that commerce and manufactures go hand in hand, and that almost every family has its share in them'. Its main manufactures were the famous Kano cloth woven on looms from locally-grown cotton and usually dyed blue, as well as sandals, and tanned hides. And these manufactures, particularly the cotton goods, were exported as far north as Ghat, Fezzan, Tripoli and Morocco, as far west as Timbuctu and the shores of the Atlantic, and as far south as Kumasi and Lagos. Towards the end of the nineteenth century, Kano, unlike Timbuctu, lost only its role as entrepôt;

but it remained as it has been ever since, an important commercial and industrial centre of the northern region of Nigeria.

In the area of the Chad, the old capital of Bornu, Birni Ngazargamu, was destroyed in the wars of the Fulani and Kuka or Kukawa, the town built by al-Kanami in 1814. It had, by the middle of the nineteenth century, become the main commercial centre as well as an entrepôt. It was mainly from there that the states of Bagirmi, Bauchi and Adamawa were supplied with goods brought from North Africa.

What were the commodities involved in this trade? From very early times the caravans from the north brought to the commercial centres of the western Sudan goods made not only in North Africa and the Middle East, but also in western Europe. The imports from North Africa and the Middle East consisted mainly of items of clothing (such as shawls, red caps, red sashes, trousers), carpets, silk (mainly from Tripoli), spices, perfumes and cowries (the currency of western Sudan), books – especially the Koran and other religious books – and horses, which were in great demand throughout the western Sudan as well as in Oyo for military purposes. The goods imported from Europe consisted of cloth, especially bleached and unbleached calicoes and cotton prints of various colours, mostly from England; silk, muslins and linen from France, writing paper, mainly from Italy (especially Venice); beads of different sizes and colours, and sword blades, looking-glasses and needles from Germany. Other articles from Europe included files, chisels, snuff boxes, razors, scissors and trinkets. In the Sahara the caravans from the north picked up further goods which consisted mainly of provisions – dates, tobacco and the most important and most valuable Sahara exports of all, salt and copper. All these goods were deposited in the main commercial centres of western Sudan where special houses or magazines had been built for the purpose, and exchanged for goods from the western Sudan, as well as from the Guinea forest.

The products of the western Sudan included the manufactures of Kano already discussed, as well as ivory, gum, natron, ostrich feathers and slaves.

Cowrie shells, formerly important currency in West Africa

Natron, a product obtained only in the Chad basin, was a commodity in great demand throughout the western Sudan, the forests, and the Guinea coast. It is a carbonate of soda which was used as medicine, and also for dyeing leather and cloth and for making snuff; it could also be used instead of salt.

These commodities from the north as well as from the western Sudan were sent farther southwards by caravans starting or returning from the western Sudan, where they were once again exchanged for the commodities of the forests and coastal regions. The latter consisted mainly of gold, obtained mainly in modern Ghana, kola nuts, ivory and slaves. Thus it was possible to find salt, a piece of cloth or a piece of Turkish carpet in the market of Kumasi or Salaga, which started its journey from a warehouse on the Mediterranean coast, or in an oasis of the Sahara; while kola nuts and gold dust from an obscure Asante village or from Ivory Coast could be seen in Morocco or Tripoli.

Decline of the traditional trade

While all these traditional commodities were still involved in this trans-continental trade at the beginning of the nineteenth century, those that were being exported to and from the Sahara and Northern Africa were in relatively small quantities, and they declined steadily throughout the nineteenth century. Gold, gum and ivory from the forest and savannah, and European manufactured goods from North Africa were good examples. By the 1820's there was no gold being exported northwards along the Hausa-Bornu-Tripoli routes, and, as Barth found when he visited Timbuctu, only a very small quantity of gold was going northwards to Morocco. Exports of ivory and gum northwards also became negligible. Nearly all these commodities were being sent southwards or westwards to the Atlantic coast. Indeed, in the nineteenth century the main exports from the western Sudan and the Guinea lands northwards were kola nuts, Kano cloth and above all, slaves. The traffic on the route from Ghana to Hausaland remained brisk throughout the nine-teenth century mainly because of kola nuts, which, while not needed by the Europeans on the coast, were in constant demand throughout the western Sudan and the Sahara.

The demand for slaves in North Africa and in the Muslim states of the Middle East also continued throughout the nineteenth century. The number of slaves exported from the Sudan was, however, relatively small, not exceed-ing an average of about 10,000 per year during the first half of the century. Of these, about 5,000 were exported to Tripoli alone, and from there about 2,500 were re-exported to Turkey, the Dardanelles, Cyprus and Albania. Slaves were virtually the only commodity that was exported along the last of the routes that remained in use at the end of the nineteenth, and the first ten years of the twentieth, century. And, incidentally, they were exchanged mainly for guns and ammunition which began to be imported in large quantities into the Sudan for the first time at this period.

It seems clear from the above that the story of the internal transcontinental trade in the nineteenth century was, by and large, one of steady decline, leading eventually to a complete change in the pattern of trade. By the end of the century the Saharan or caravan end of the trade had all but ceased, and the principal products of the western Sudan and the forest regions, namely the traditional ones of gold, ivory and gum, as well as the newly established ones of ground nuts, rubber and palm-oil, were being sent southwards and westwards to the Atlantic and Guinea coasts. How then can this revolutionary change be accounted for?

The ending of this pattern of trade, which had gone on for well over a thousand years, was due to three main factors. The first was the changing political conditions in the Sahara and the western Sudan; the second was the abolition and eventual suppression of the trans-Saharan as well as the trans-Atlantic slave trade; and the third was the successful commercial and later political drive by Europeans into the western Sudan from the west coast.

The flow of traffic along trade routes anywhere is controlled largely by political conditions in the area through which they pass. The more unstable and disturbed the area is politically, the less the volume of its trade. And there is no doubt that, owing to the overthrow of the famous Songhai empire by the Moroccans at about the end of the sixteenth century, and the subsequent rivalry for the political control of that area which ensued between the Moroccans, the Songhai, the Tuareg and the Fulani, chaos and insecurity were common in the region of the Niger bend, and continued common throughout the seventeenth and eighteenth centuries. The disorders continued, particularly in the western Sahara, during the nineteenth century. The result was that trade along the western routes was steadily diverted to the eastern routes leading from Tripoli.

The supremacy of the Tripoli-Hausa routes during the first half of the nineteenth century was also the direct outcome of the establishment of law and order in most of the regions of Hausaland – especially in the Sokoto half of the empire – by the new Fulani rulers. The Tripoli-Fezzan-Bornu route became particularly active during the first thirty years of the nineteenth century, when the Karamanli dynasty of Tripoli and al-Kanami of Bornu were able to maintain peace and order throughout the entire length of that route. However, with the overthrow of the Karamanli dynasty in 1835 by the Turks, and the subsequent wars in southern Tripoli, and with the death of al-Kanami in Bornu in 1837, conditions on that route began to get worse, and the caravan trade declined also.

Farther to the east, however, the Cyrenaica-Tripoli route enjoyed more stable and peaceful conditions throughout the nineteenth century than had ever been known before. This was mainly due to the expansion of Wadai in the Sudan during the first half of the century, and the spread of the Sanusi order, which was a puritanic Islamic order from Cyrenaica, along the route to Kufra and Wadai, during the second half of the century. By establishing zawiyas (lodges or headquarters) along the route, by ensuring friendly relations among the different peoples who lived along it, and by actively encouraging trade, the Sanusi gave a great boost to trade on the Tripoli-Wadai route; it is not surprising, therefore, that in 1905 the great French travellers and scholars, Gautier and Chudeau, saw large caravans still leaving Benghazi, the main town of Cyrenaica, for Wadai, whereas traffic on all the other three routes had ceased. Indeed, it was the French occupation of Wadai and Tibesti and Borku between 1906 and 1914, and the Italian occupation of Cyrenaica in 1911-12, that finally snapped the last of the commercial links between the Mediterranean, the western Sudan and the Guinea coast.

The second factor in the ending of the transcontinental route during the course of the nineteenth century was the abolition of the slave trade from Africa to the Americas and the Middle East. As is well known, the slave trade was legally abolished by most of the European powers between 1807 and 1820. The attack on the slave trade across the Sahara and the Mediterranean, however, was not begun until 1840. By 1857 the slave trade had been abolished, on paper at least, throughout the Ottoman empire and the Barbary States except Morocco; it was partly with a view to seeing to the effective suppression of the trans-Saharan slave trade that the British government established two vice-consular posts at Murzuk in Fezzan in 1843, and at Ghadames in 1850, and maintained them till 1860 and 1861 respectively. The laws against the slave trade were not fully enforced in the Barbary States or the Ottoman empire, and the trade went on illegally until the Italian and French occupation of Tripoli and Morocco during the last years of the century; but there is no doubt that the attack and pressure on the governments by the British, from 1840 onwards, greatly reduced the trade in slaves, and was certainly one of the factors that ended the traffic on the Tripoli-Ghat-Hausa and the Tripoli-Murzuk-Bornu routes, during the last forty years of the nineteenth century.

European traders on the Niger and on the Senegal

However, what dealt the final blow to this centuries-old commercial link between the Mediterranean and the Guinea coasts was the successful drive of European traders and their political influence inland from the west coast during the nineteenth century. Though one of the main motives for beginning the exploration of the west coast was to gain direct control of the sources of the supply of gold reaching the North African countries across the Sahara, the European nation confined themselves entirely to the coast after the failure of a few early attempts to push inland, mainly from the regions of the Senegal and the Gambia, in the sixteenth and seventeenth centuries. Indeed, so ignorant did they remain of the areas a few miles inland from the coast that, for instance, they did not know until 1830 that the rivers which emptied themselves into the Bight of Biafra together formed the mouth of the Niger. Had this confinement of European activities to the Guinea coast continued, the overland trade routes would most probably have remained in use also. From 1788, however, under the auspices first of a private scientific society, the African Association, and then from 1805 onwards, under those of both the British and French governments, a series of systematic exploratory activities were begun, aimed at ending the ignorance about the interior of Africa. The first phase of these activities ended in 1830. By that time, the entire western Sudan and the Sahara had been explored and reported on by Europeans approaching them from North Africa, as had the areas of the Senegal, the Gambia, and the west coast; the problem of the mouth of the Niger, and of its connection with the Nile of Egypt, which had haunted geographers and historians for well over a thousand years, had also been solved.

The exploration of the Senegal and Niger rivers raised great hopes among traders and imperialists in Europe. As one of them, Laird, wrote, on hearing of the solution to the Niger problem, 'The long sought for highway into central Africa was at length found. To the merchant it offered a boundless field for enterprise, to the manufacturer an extensive market for his goods.' The solution of the Niger problem also coincided with the abolition and suppression of the trans-Atlantic slave trade and the search for new commodities and new markets to replace the lost ones. Naturally, therefore, both on the Senegal and on the Niger, attempts were begun to push European commerce along the trails left by the explorers. Between 1817 and 1840, for example, the French attempted to push up the Senegal and promote the establishment of plantations, and between 1818 and 1821 they built forts on the River Senegal at Bakel, Dagone and Richard-Toll. In 1832 the British and the Americans also each sent out an expedition to travel up the Niger and set up trading stations on its banks 'for the purpose of collecting the various products of the country'. Other expeditions by British merchants followed in 1836 and 1840; and in 1841, largely urged on by the abolitionists, led by Fowell Buxton, the British government sent a carefully prepared expedition to establish legitimate trade and set up experimental farms as a means of overthrowing the slave trade. All these efforts by the French, the

British, and the Americans to push up the Senegal and the Niger failed, mainly because of the opposition of the African rulers and middlemen, traders, and above all because of the high rate of mortality suffered by the crews of the ships. Indeed, the British government became so convinced of the fatal nature of the climate of the west coast and the lower Niger basin that from the late forties onwards they turned their attention northwards to the Sahara. And it was partly with a view to seeing to the suppression of the slave trade, and partly to develop legitimate trade that, as we have seen, they established two vice-consular posts in the Sahara. They followed this step up with a dispatch of the now famous Richardson-Barth expedition from Tripoli to Bornu and Timbuctu in 1849.

However, in the 1850's both the French and the British resumed their drive from the Guinea coast inland, up the Senegal and the Niger respectively, and this time both of them were successful. Mainly as a result of the energy and drive of General Louis Faidherbe, the governor of the Senegal from 1854 to 1861 and 1863 to 1865, the French had gained full control of the Senegal River by 1865. French traders followed their armies, and were soon able to divert such little trade at trickled northwards from the regions of Timbuctu down the Senegal to the coast. It was only the strong resistance of al-Hajj Umar (see chapter 2), in the 1860's, and the defeat of the French in Europe by the Germans in 1870, that temporarily halted French political expansion inland; but this was resumed in 1879. Four years later they occupied Bamako on the Niger and pushed on from there to Timbuctu, which they captured in 1894.

Equally decisive advances were made by the British on the Niger from the 1850's onwards. The greatest stumbling block in the way of the British on the Niger was, it may be recalled, the high rate of mortality, caused mainly by fever. However, this obstruction was removed when Baikie, the commander of the expedition sent up the Niger in 1854, discovered that by taking regular doses of quinine, Europeans could become immune to fever. Moreover, the British government not only agreed to subsidize the development of trade up the Niger, but also to send warships to break down the opposition of the African coastal traders and middlemen to the development of inland trade. Led by Laird, British merchants began, from 1857 on, to establish trading stations up the Niger, and by 1859 had pushed up as far as the confluence of the Niger and the Benue and established a station at Lokoja. Indeed, so successful were these early traders that by the late 1860's as many as five British companies were operating on the Niger. What now threatened this growing trade was the keen rivalry that soon broke out among the traders. But this was ended in 1879 when Goldier Taubman (later Sir George Goldie) amalgamated all of them into the United Africa Company. This company was given a charter in 1886 under the name of the Royal Niger Company, and it was its activities that won northern Nigeria for Britain during the scramble for Africa in the last twenty years of the century.

Once European goods began to reach the markets of Hausaland, and, from the late fifties onwards, at relatively cheaper prices, and in greater quantities, it was obvious that the caravan trade was bound to collapse. The camel was obviously no match for the steam vessel! It was this steady penetration of manufactured goods via the waterways, in steadily increasing quantities from the late 1850's onwards, and the occupation of the entire western Sudan as well as the Sahara by the French and the British, that finally put an end to the northern or Saharan section of a commercial link that had been maintained for well over 2,000 years.

6 The suppression of the slave trade

For the coastal kingdoms and ultimately for all of West Africa, the British action in abolishing the slave trade, and forcing other European and African states to abandon it as well, ranks with the Islamic revolutions of the western Sudan and the later partition of Africa by European powers as one of the three most significant events in the nineteenth-century history of West Africa. The end of the slave trade brought revolutionary changes in the social structure of many African states. The abolition led to the establishment of Sierra Leone and Liberia which besides being the nucleus of two present-day West African states, exerted an influence far beyond their immediate borders. The replacement of the slave by palm-oil trade brought Europeans slowly but steadily into the political life of the coastal kingdoms, which led on ultimately to the partition of West Africa. In this chapter, slavery, the slave trade and the causes of, and attitudes to, abolition, are discussed, while in following chapters the significance of abolition for the coastal states, including the events leading to partition, is one of the major themes.

Slavery and society

Before the twentieth century many societies practised some form of slavery which was upheld by religious belief. As King Pepple of Bonny said, slavery was ordained by God and sanctioned by the juju priests. The Old Testament command that 'thy bondsmen . . . shall be of the heathen . . . and ye shall take them as an inheritance for your children' had become accepted in both Christianity and Islam. Neither Christ nor Muhammad attempted to change it.

Prisoners of war were often enslaved. They might be political opponents, like the supporters of Monmouth's rebellion in England who were given to the Queen for sale, or like the people of Ketu who King Glele put to work on the royal plantations of Dahomey, or they might be people of different religious beliefs, so that, while Cromwell's Irish and Scottish Catholic prisoners were sold to the West Indies, non-Muslims who opposed the Sokoto jihad were sold to North Africa.

Criminals in Europe and Africa might be executed, transported, or sold.

Europeans favoured execution; Africans favoured sale. In the eighteenth century there were 300 different offences in Britain for which one could be executed. In Dahomey there were only two, for the king preferred to sell rather than execute his troublemakers. Those who could not pay their debts were sold for life or until the debt was paid. Among the Yoruba debt slaves (pawns) were called *Iwofa*, among the Asante *Awowa* and among the Europeans *indentured servants*. About a quarter of a million white debt slaves entered America before the nineteenth century. Islamic law, however, forbade the selling of debtors.

Frequently in African societies slaves with special talents or skills were purchased to supply special needs. In the Oyo empire Hausa slaves were especially valued for the care of the cavalry horses upon which the military power of the empire was built. Wadai sought skilled artisans, weavers and blacksmiths to enhance its trading position.

Designed to provide cheap labour, slavery in many societies was the beginning of a process of absorbing foreigners into the community. Once the slave learned the language, and practised the religion and customs of the new society, he or his children gradually achieved a status as free commoners. In Asante it was state policy to increase the population by absorbing people like this. Slaves could give evidence in court against their masters, change masters or inherit their property and, once a free member of society, it was a legal offence to speak publicly of their slave origins. In the Niger Delta the marriage system was designed to encourage rapid change from slave to free. To ensure that all their grandchildren were freeborn, merchants married their sons to slave women by large dowries and their daughters to slave men by small dowries.

Slaves had many privileges in African kingdoms. In Asante, Oyo and Bornu they held important offices in the bureaucracy, serving as the Alafin's Ilari in the subject towns of Oyo, as controller of the treasury in Asante, and as Waziri and army commanders in Bornu. Al-Hajj Umar made a slave emir of Nioro, one of the most important of the emirates of the Tokolor empire, and in the Niger Delta states slaves rose to become heads of Houses, positions next in rank to the king. Jaja, who had once been the lowest kind of slave, became the most respected king in the delta, and was no exception; one of the Alaketus of Ketu, and Rabeh of Bornu, rose from slave to king.

In Muslim states slavery was a method of converting Pagans to Islam. Masters had a duty to seek their slaves' conversion, and manumission (the freeing of one's slaves) was believed to bring a reward in paradise. Slaves might engage in trade and buy their freedom by instalments. Upon conversion a slave became the ward of his master and could inherit his property; this put him in the last stage before he entered society fully as a free commoner.

In Spanish America the system operated much as in Muslim states.

Slavery was a preparation for becoming a full member of society, and conversion to Christianity; slaves were prepared for baptism, and marriages which could not be broken by sale were encouraged. Slaves could give evidence against their masters in court, could acquire property and could purchase their freedom. Manumission, as in Islam, was a virtue. Under this system, and without special acts to set them free, almost half of the slave population of Spanish America had gained its freedom by the beginning of the nineteenth century.

Slavery was never under any conditions an ideal institution, and slaves often revolted against oppression and cruelty, as under Afonja in the Oyo empire. Another example was the Koranko slave revolt in 1838 against the Susu of Sierra Leone; led by Bilale, the Koranko ex-slaves built a fortified town which, because it offered freedom to runaway slaves, was a constant threat to the slave-holding society of the Susu. In Calabar the slaves united in a society, the Blood Men, and forced the freeborn to respect their human rights. The history of the New World is filled with slave revolts. There were nine in Bahia between 1807 and 1835, while in the province of Pernambuco, Brazil, the revolting slaves set up the Negro Republic of Palmares, which lasted for a hundred years before it was destroyed in 1694. Palmares was a constant threat to Portuguese slave-holding society since it offered a refuge for runaway slaves. In Jamaica the ex-slaves, known as Maroons, also maintained their independence for a hundred years in their mountain stronghold, while in Santo Domingo in 1803 the slaves revolted under Toussaint Louverture, massacred their French masters, and proclaimed the independent state of Haiti, a successful revolt which frightened the entire slave-holding society of the New World. In the British West Indies one revolt followed another; British Guiana 1808, Barbados 1816, British Guiana again in 1823, Antigua and Jamaica 1831. It was evident that if the British government did not free the slaves by decree they would soon seize their freedom by force. If freedom had not come from above it was only a matter of time until it came from below. However, regardless of its merits or demerits, the traditional slavery of Africans, Arabs and Americans might have faded away, as it had in Europe under the impact of machines and industrialization, without particular notice, had not a new and degraded kind of slavery developed, between the sixteenth and nineteenth centuries, in West Africa, the West Indies and in North America.

In West Africa a number of kingdoms organized state monopolies for the shipment of slaves overseas in return for European firearms, with which they built empires. Some people, like the Vai of Guinea, resisted this change; but, once neighbouring kingdoms possessed guns, it was a choice between enslaving others to secure guns for protection, or being enslaved oneself. In bringing this change political rulers often had the willing co-operation of the priests and their oracles, as for example with the Agbala and Arochuku oracles among the Ibo. There was a tendency for African rulers to pervert traditional law and make slavery the punishment for all crime, large and small, and so, for example, on the Gambia River a man was sold into slavery for the theft of a tobacco pipe. Furthermore, in the nineteenth century, with the increasing demand in Europe for palm-oil, Africans – especially in Calabar and Dahomey – sought to bring large oil plantations into production. As in America, plantations meant a kind of slavery where slaves were valued only for their labour, where an eventual entry into society as a free man was not encouraged, and where there was little chance for the slave to improve his or his children's status.

In the West Indies and southern United States traditional ideas of slavery were swept away in the desire to bring vast acres of land under cultivation. Originally both white and black slaves had been sold in America as 'indentured servants', or debt slaves, who after a term of slavery secured their freedom. Gradually white slaves were brought into the society by a series of laws such as that masters could not kill their white slaves, whip them without a court order, or even sell them.

As white slaves became free members of society conditions worsened for the blacks. Since the church taught that Christians could not be permanently enslaved, laws were passed making it a crime to teach Christianity to the blacks, on the justification that Africans did not originate with Adam and Eve and therefore were not included in Christ's plan of redemption. When some slaves became Christian the Bishop of London proclaimed that conversion to Christianity did not bring freedom. By the early eighteenth century slave codes (special slave laws) had been created in the West Indies and Southern States whereby Africans and their children were condemned to eternal slavery; marriages and manumission were discouraged; slaves could not give evidence in court; and their masters held the power of life and death over them. Under the slave codes Africans lost their status as persons and became the master's property, in the same relationship to him as his dog or horse. This was the degenerate slavery of America which made it almost completely evil by the nineteenth century.

The Atlantic slave trade

In the eighteenth century sugar was a luxury food of high price. The British West Indies, because they produced sugar for Europe and America, were the most valuable possessions of the British empire. The wealth of England was made in the Atlantic triangular trade in which the West Indies played a key role. Cloth was shipped to West Africa and exchanged for slaves, who were carried to the West Indies and sold for sugar; the sugar was shipped to England where it was refined and sold to Europe for silver and gold. This profitable trade was almost entirely monopolized by English merchants. The West Indies plantations were worked by slaves and owned by aristocrats who lived in England and used their immense incomes to bribe and purchase seats in the British Parliament. During the eighteenth century between fifty and seventy of these sugar barons controlled the government, regardless of which political party won the election.

In the last quarter of the eighteenth century the French West Indies, by producing cheaper sugar, won the European monopoly from the English and, when the American colonies revolted, they also bought cheap French sugar which, as British possessions, they had been forbidden to do. The British West Indian plantations were now only able to sell in the British market and as they declined thousands of slaves were abandoned by their masters and died of starvation. As a result, by the early nineteenth century, the West Indian colonies were of much less importance to Britain than they had been in the eighteenth century, and in the middle of the nineteenth century the British themselves stopped buying the high-priced sugar from their own West Indies

15 The Atlantic triangular trade of the eighteenth century

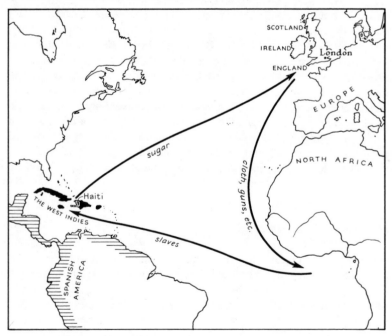

islands and turned to the cheaper sugar of Brazil. Thereafter the West Indies became more of a burden than a source of profit to Britain.

The sugar barons lost their wealth and political power; their place was taken by a new class of industrial barons, and profits from the triangular trade were spent on the newly invented machines for the manufacture of cotton cloth and other products in Britain. The cloth factories needed raw cotton as the basic requirement and oil to lubricate the cotton-producing machinery; the first was shipped from the southern States and the second from West Africa. These manufacturing profits created a new class of industrial barons who challenged the power of the sugar barons in the British parliament.

The industrial barons argued that the slave trade and slavery, out of which England had created her wealth in the eighteenth century, were limiting her further development. Firstly, if Britain stopped the slave trade, it would deny labour to the French West Indies and thereby raise their sugar prices so that the British islands might once again compete with them. Secondly, the triangular trade was out of date. Instead of a triangular trade they wanted ships loaded with English cotton cloth to go to West Africa and return with

16 British Atlantic trade in the nineteenth century

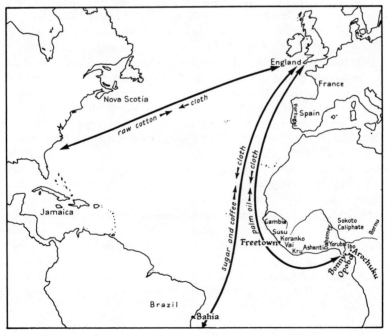

palm-oil; to Brazil and return with sugar and coffee; to the United States and return with raw cotton. Thirdly, the slave trade interfered with the palm-oil trade in West Africa. Since slavers paid higher prices than oil traders, African kings often made oilers wait as long as a year for a cargo, while they rushed to meet the slave trader's requirements. This pushed up the cost of oil to the industrial barons, and reduced their profits.

It was by no means certain that the industrial barons would be able to force their policy on the British government in the early nineteenth century, for the sugar barons and suppliers of the slave trade were still powerful in the political parties. However, in the last quarter of the eighteenth century, a new concern arose for the welfare of mankind, and this new spirit of humanitarianism came to the support of the industrialists. The evangelical revival associated with Methodism in the Christian church created a sharper conscience among Christians and greater concern for non-Christian peoples. In addition both the French and American revolutions proclaimed the radical principles of the equality and brotherhood of men, neither of which could comfortably co-exist with slavery.

In 1772 Granville Sharp secured a judgement in the courts making slavery illegal in England. In 1787 he, along with others, formed a society for the abolition of the slave trade. While Thomas Clarkson gathered the facts and stories of brutality to arouse public opinion, William Wilberforce conducted the anti-slave trade campaign in parliament. The Abolitionists, as these men were called, waged one of the most brilliant propaganda campaigns in British history until, through clergymen's sermons, newspapers, pamphlets, and books, the public were being informed of the inhumanity of this trade in men.

An aroused public opinion demanded and achieved the abolition of the slave trade in 1807. Had it not been for the Abolitionists the government would not have acted as quickly as it did, and industrialization would have been slowed down, losing for Britain both the advantages of her early industrial leadership and the moral superiority over Europeans, Americans and Africans which her early crusade against slavery gave her. In addition, the Abolitionists set a pattern of humanitarianism which, though often weak, especially in the first half of the twentieth century, has nevertheless always been a part of British colonial policy.

A further result of the humanitarian movement coupled with the evangelical revival was the missionary movement, which brought about the formation of Missionary societies in Britain at the end of the eighteenth century to carry Christianity to the world. A tiny settlement of free Negroes from England, Nova Scotia and Jamaica had been established at Freetown, Sierra Leone, and this became a logical place to begin missionary work.

Suppression of the slave trade

British abolition of their own part in the slave trade in 1807, and of slavery itself in British possessions in 1833, did not stop the slave trade. Other nations merely rushed in to take over where the British left off, and between 1807 and its suppression in 1861 the trade flourished as never before. However, the British government, backed by industrialists, humanitarians and missionaries, was determined that the slave trade should end entirely. A British naval squadron was therefore stationed off the coast of West Africa, to seize all slavers and set their cargoes of slaves free in Sierra Leone, where the missionaries could teach them Christianity.

The missionaries supported the Anti-Slavery Squadron, because Africans could hardly be impressed with a religion whose priests taught brotherhood and whose traders carried them into slavery. The industrialists supported it in order to deny labour to the American and French sugar plantations in the West Indies, and to encourage Africans to labour in Africa at harvesting and preparing palm-oil for the factories of Britain.

It was hoped that West Africa would eventually supply Britain with raw cotton, as well as palm-oil, and thus free her from dependence upon the United States. Englishmen had not yet discovered the secret of keeping alive successfully in West Africa and therefore could not directly exploit its resources as they had done in the West Indies. But although African kings organized the palm-oil trade, they did not take to the production of cotton. It was hoped that the missionaries could produce a class of Christian and educated African merchant who would become British partners in trade, and would supervise the growing, collecting and preparation of raw cotton for British traders.

The Anti-Slavery Squadron could not seize the ships of other nations without risking war with the European nations and the United States. Neither could Britain approach the nations for co-operation by saying that the slave trade interfered with her trade and plans for West Africa. So she appealed to them to join her in a great act of humanitarianism. The French, Americans and Portuguese did not require palm-oil or raw cotton because they had few factories. And furthermore, they were making big profits from slaves. Accordingly they accused the British of hypocrisy, of trying to enhance her own prosperity while destroying theirs under a mask of humanitarianism.

Britain's monopoly of machine-made goods was bringing her tremendous wealth and power and few nations dared oppose her openly; when they did, the British bribed or bullied them. Britain began by asking the nations to forbid their subjects to trade in slaves and to give the British navy the right to search their ships in West African waters and seize them if they carried slaves. The United States declared the slave trade piracy, for which the

Toussaint Louverture, Liberator of Haiti.

penalty was death, and the French followed. After bribes to Spain and Portugal the British secured permission to search their ships. But no one had any intention of enforcing these laws, and slaves continued to land in the United States, while slave ships openly sailed from France, Spain, and Portugal. At sea slavers threw their cargoes overboard when the British squadron approached, in order to destroy the evidence which would convict them of slaving.

Since the old treaties were useless the British negotiated new ones which included an 'equipment clause' by which, if ships possessed slave-carrying equipment, they could be seized. France and Spain signed, but Portugal, Brazil and the United States would not. Slavers therefore hoisted the flag of one of the nations which had not signed and continued to trade in slaves without fear of British interference. Since Portugal and Brazil were weak nations the British squadron began seizing their ships illegally and this compelled them to sign treaties in the 1840's. Slavers now took refuge under the American flag and since the United States would not be bribed and was too big to bully, the slave trade continued almost entirely under the American flag.

The British tried new tactics. Between 1841 and 1850 the navy forced

The Anti-Slavery Squadron capture a slave ship. A contemporary engraving

African kings along the West Coast to give it the right to seize slavers while they were loading in port, hoping to stop the trade by blockading the major slave ports. But ports such as Kalabari, Nembe or Ouidah, located on a maze of creeks with numerous exits, could still load the slavers who slipped away to sea unnoticed.

If a slaver flying the American flag possessed a captain and crew who spoke nothing but Spanish, Portuguese or French the squadron often seized it, on the chance that it was not really an American registered ship; frequently they were right, but when they were wrong the Americans were bitterly annoyed. Both the French and Americans claimed that the British were stopping not only their slaves but also their palm-oil ships, in order to delay them and discourage their merchants from cutting-in on the British oil trade. They claimed the British were using the navy to collect their merchant's debts and making puppets out of African kings in their plans to create a West African empire. Both the French and Americans sent anti-slavery squadrons to West Africa to protect their interests, but neither was very active in stopping slavers. The American squadron was instructed that its first duty was not to stop the slave trade but to protect American palm-oil traders against the British and to help collect their debts from the Africans, and its first action in West Africa was to kill an African king and burn four of his villages for mistreating an American merchant. It was obvious that, without honest American co-operation which could not be secured short of war, the British were unable to stop the slave trade.

In 1861 war broke out between the states in America, the southern States desiring to break away to form an independent country. In the hope that the slaves would rise against their southern masters, Abraham Lincoln, President of the northern States, proclaimed their freedom in 1863. The British, contrary to what one might expect, sympathized with the desire of the slave-owning southern States for independence. The northern States, who were hoping to blockade southern ports and win over British friendship, therefore signed a treaty permitting the British navy to seize American ships which carried slaving equipment. In the same year the first American was hanged for trading in slaves. Almost immediately the slave trade ended.

Resistance to suppression

In the early nineteenth century the slave trade had become unnecessary and even a hindrance to British trade, economic expansion and prosperity. On the other hand, the Portuguese, French and Americans had only just begun to industrialize. They were where Britain had been in the eighteenth century and they clung to the profits of the slave trade exactly as Britain had done then. They had colonies, and vast stretches of land in them which required cheap labour to cultivate. It was the United States and Brazil, the two countries with the most land and greatest need of labour, which were the last importers to give up the slave trade and slavery. As the nineteenth century wore on, both France and the United States followed Britain's industrialization, and once these nations reached the stage where their own class of industrial barons dominated their respective governments, they too took steps to stop the slave trade.

The majority of the coastal kingdoms of West Africa, even more than the European states, stood to be ruined by the suppression of the slave trade. Yet while most European nations and the United States abolished the trade when they had found a more profitable substitute for it, African states, as well as Portugal and Brazil, had abolition forced on them before they had found a substitute. Although abolitionists talked about finding a substitute for the slave trade in Africa, there was none; cotton, upon which so many hopes were based, never flourished anywhere along the coast; and the little money from groundnuts in Senegal, gold in Asante, and shea butter, indigo and ivory elsewhere, did nothing to replace the income lost through abolition.

Palm-oil was one commodity for which a steady and expanding market existed in Europe, but the area of suitable soil and climate for oil-palms in West Africa was limited. Not only was the return on palm-oil smaller than on slaves but it was costly to produce as well, requiring huge gangs of slaves for harvesting and head porterage to the coast. Thus one of the unexpected results of the suppression of the Atlantic slave trade was that, at least in parts of West Africa, the trade in slaves increased due to the search for cheap labour for the production of palm-oil. It was therefore not surprising that African kingdoms which could find no adequate substitute for the revenue of the Atlantic slave trade resisted abolition with every weapon at their command.

On the other hand, those who had found substitutes were as actively abolitionist as the British. Neither the people of the Ivory Coast, nor the Kru of Liberia, had ever engaged in the slave trade to any degree. The Kru were boatmen who worked everywhere along the coast manning the canoes which carried first slaves and later palm-oil across the bar to the European ships; since they thus found employment and income for the purchase of firearms, the Kru were never tempted to enter the slave trade.

Again, Calabar and the Cameroons, who were unable to compete with Bonny, had never prospered on the export of slaves. When the British began looking for oil, the Efik of Calabar quickly organized plantations for its production, so that Calabar was exporting palm-oil before British abolition in 1807. Like Britain, Calabar found that the slave trade interfered with the palm-oil trade, and the Efik became vigorous abolitionists, acting as informers to the British navy in reporting the movement of slave ships. In 1843 the Efik refused to supply a cargo of slaves to the French even though a French warship threatened to bombard Calabar. It was therefore apparent that among Africans, Europeans and Americans the degree to which national prosperity was dependent upon the slave trade was a very important factor in the national attitude to abolition.

A second important factor was national pride, and the extent to which the British considered this in persuading other nations to abolish the trade. Brazil, Bonny, the United States and Dahomey resented the manner in which the British disregarded their sovereignty, seized ships, entered and bombarded ports, created puppet kings, used naval action to defend British troublemakers, and overrode the authority of the national courts. The British seldom acted solely because of opposition to slavery; in Brazil and Bonny especially they were concerned to secure a privileged position for British traders as well. This gave the slave traders the support of people who, although they had no monetary interest in the trade, nevertheless resented British interference in their domestic affairs; the issue thus became one of sovereignty and independence, rather than the rights and wrongs of the trade in slaves.

Brazil, newly independent from Portugal, was particularly sensitive over any threat to its sovereignty. When Britain, seeking to take over the privileged position formerly held by Portugal in Brazil's trade, also seized ships illegally inside Brazil's territorial waters, all Brazilians, whether opposed to slavery or not, were united in opposition against her. Thus although a Yoruba slave revolt in Bahia in 1835 led to a public outcry demanding abolition, continued British naval arrogance turned attention away from abolition to considerations of sovereignty. The contempt in the British prime minister's statement that 'the Portuguese are of all European nations the lowest in the moral scale and the Brazilians are degenerate Portuguese' did not encourage Brazilian co-operation.

In Bonny as well the British so mismanaged the situation that the division in the state was not between slave traders and abolitionists, but between Alali and supporters committed to a policy of forcing the British to respect Bonny sovereignty, and the king and party who stood for co-operation with the British from the practical point of view that they were too powerful to resist. The British squadron assisted King Pepple to the throne in 1837 and thereafter he was a British tool, although an unwilling one; but since the squadron could sail into Bonny harbour and direct its guns on the palace, it was difficult for any ruler to refuse to do its bidding.

The British negotiated four treaties with King Pepple – similar to those signed with European and other African states – promising compensation to Bonny in return for the abolition of the slave trade. Britain never ratified the treaties nor paid the compensation. When Pepple tried to force them to live up to their promises in 1854 they deported him, but, finding no one to take his place, brought him back in 1861. These actions indicated clearly that Bonny had lost its sovereignty. While events in America were ending the slave trade, Alali was succeeded by Jaja, who, though he ultimately re-established African sovereignty, only did so at the expense of ruining the Bonny kingdom.

Neither Dahomey nor the United States would sign an anti-slave trade treaty with Britain. Dahomey regulated trade so that foreign merchants looking for slaves or palm-oil could not interfere with the politics of the state, and since the palace and capital were far inland, and the port of Ouidah was on the lagoon rather than the open sea, the British squadron could not turn its guns on either. The lesson of Lagos was not lost in Dahomey. The King of Lagos had signed a British treaty and banned the slave trade, but in spite of this he was the first on the coast to lose his independence; this convinced Dahomey that a British treaty was the first step to subjugation.

The United States also felt very touchy about its sovereignty. She had only recently fought for independence and now it appeared as if the British, by searching and seizing her ships, were continuing to treat her as a colony. In

1812 Americans had gone to war with Britain to defend the principle of the freedom of their ships at sea, and thereafter the British had more respect for Americans and the American flag. They did not refer to Americans as degenerate Englishmen. As in Bonny and Brazil, abolitionist sentiment was submerged by concern for American sovereignty. The famous American, John Quincy Adams, said that there was one thing worse than the slave trade and that was allowing American ships to be searched at sea, 'for that would be making slaves of ourselves', a statement which would have been approved by Alali and Jaja in Bonny, by Gezo and Glele of Dahomey and by the Brazilians.

While stressing the resistance to abolition it is well to remember that there were sincere abolitionists in all societies where slavery was practised. Every European and American nation had its counterparts of the Wilberforces and Clarksons of England, men who held ideals which they believed should not be sacrificed to economics or considerations of sovereignty. Neither should outstanding New World Negro abolitionists such as Frederick Douglass, Martin Delany and Alexander Crummell, be forgotten. Olaudah Equiano, an Ibo escaped from West Indian slavery, pointed out in his autobiography in 1789 the profit to British merchants if they treated Africans as customers rather than merchandise. Ottobah Cugoano, a Fanti ex-slave, in his *Thoughts and Sentiments on the Evil of Slavery* (1787) called upon the British to station a fleet in West Africa to suppress the slave trade. Africa also produced abolitionists. In Sierra Leone a Muslim Mandinka scholar, Momodu Yeli, opposed slaving among his own Muslim brethren and the Christians of Freetown, and suffered the persecution of both communities for his convictions. Had it not been for his assistance the Freetown courts would have found it difficult to check secret slave trading in the city. At about the same time Sidi Muhammad al-Sanusi, founder of the Sanusiyya Brotherhood, began a programme of buying and manumitting slaves from the trans-Saharan caravans. Some of the freed slaves settled down around his headquarters in Cyrenaica, while others, after conversion and training, returned to the central Sudan as Muslim missionaries, in much the same way as slaves liberated in Sierra Leone by the British squadron became Christian, and returned to their homeland as Christian missionaries.

Slavery and the slave trade are still emotional subjects. Europeans and Americans frequently display a guilt complex about their eighteenth-century participation in the slave trade; then, turning to abolition, they overstress the humanitarian and noble role of the Wilberforces and Lincolns, and assume a moral superiority over Africans in their nineteenth-century history by pointing out that Africans were the greatest opponents of abolition and only stopped shipping slaves when compelled to do so. On the other hand Africans are also ashamed of the role they played and tend to blame all the ills of their continent on the 'European-sponsored' slave trade, defending themselves

John Clarkson

Granville Sharp

Olaudah Equiano

Abraham Lincoln

by saying that if Europeans had not purchased slaves, Africans would not have sold them.

Slavery even in its mildest form has always been a social evil, but at times it appeared to be a necessary evil designed to do what no other social institution appeared capable of doing. Few peoples of the world can claim they have never practised slavery or traded in men at some point in their history. While the slave trade of the eighteenth and nineteenth centuries was a crime committed by humanity against humanity, and abolition a beneficial reform of human society, to apportion blame or praise between European and African or between one nation and another is to deviate from the spirit and purpose of history.

Part **two**

Coastal kingdoms in
the nineteenth century

*A bronze figure of
an Oni of Ife in
coronation dress
(right) A devotee of
Shango, one of
the Yoruba major
deities worshipped by
the people of the
Oyo empire*

Mende carving of
the Yassi society

Temne carving

7 Collapse of the Oyo empire and Yoruba civil strife

West African states are often divided into two groups according to geography and culture. There are the states of the western Sudan in the area of savannah vegetation and distinguished by their attachment to Islam, particularly following the revolutions of the nineteenth century. There are the coastal kingdoms situated in the tropical forest and Pagan in their religious beliefs and organization of society. This division has value as long as its limitations and distortions are clearly realized. It does not, however, fit all the facts; the Mossi kingdom, like many others, remained a non-Muslim state in the heart of the western Sudan and Dahomey, a coastal state, is not in the tropical forest. Both areas were influenced by many of the same historical events. The best examples are the Yoruba states, usually classed as coastal, yet with some situated in the savannah, some in the forest. Like the western Sudan generally, the Yoruba country was profoundly influenced by the Islamic revolution in the Hausa states inspired by dan Fodio and many Yoruba came within the political and spiritual sphere of the Sokoto caliphate. At the same time the Yoruba like other coastal peoples were greatly influenced by European activities on the Guinea coast, the change from the slave to palm-oil trade, the availability of guns and powder and the missionary and cultural influences emanating from Sierra Leone and Liberia, Europe and America.

The Yoruba people lived in a number of states clustered round the centrally located mother kingdom of Ife. These states were bounded on the north by the Niger, on the east by Benin, on the south by the Gulf of Guinea and on the west by Dahomey and Borgu. Inter-state relations were governed by the principle that Ife, the mother state, must not be attacked. Due to the central location of Ife, and the prestige of its Oni (king), a considerable degree of peace was thus maintained among the daughter kingdoms. Oyo and Ketu were situated in the savannah, the other kingdoms within the tropical forests.

In the sixteenth century Oyo began to rise from a junior kingdom to a position of commercial prosperity and military power. Oyo's prosperity was the result of its fertile soil and its position as the leading trade centre south of the Niger. Its market was the pivot of three trading systems; one from Nupe and the Hausa states to the north, another from the Yoruba forest kingdoms to the east and south and yet another from the coastal ports on the Gulf of Guinea. Oyo also developed as a manufacturing centre; its high quality cloth, leather and iron products finding ready sale.

Commercial wealth was necessary to Oyo to maintain its military power which was built around a fast striking cavalry force. Horses imported from the Hausa states were expensive to maintain and, because of the tsetse fly, their life span was short, possibly as short as two years. Horse breeding was difficult and importation depended upon a continual ability to pay. Since cavalry was most effective in the grasslands, Oyo's main expansion was west as far as Asante and north to Borgu and Nupe. In the mid-eighteenth century, when Oyo reached the peak of its splendour, riches and power, it maintained correct relationships with the other Yoruba states and with Ife from which, like other Yoruba states, it received the beaded crown of its monarch.

The Oyo empire began to crumble in the late eighteenth century and collapsed in the early nineteenth, not only from external pressure, the revolts of restive vassals and from the loss of its commercial supremacy, but because of its failure to find a governing formula which would combine effective leadership with popular checks upon unbridled autocratic power. In addition Oyo failed to find a symbol or principle which would command the loyalty of the masses in its empire and the personal sacrifice and respect of its leaders.

Political weakness of Oyo

The Oyo political system was built on a system of checks and balances centring around four powerful figures; the Alafin, the Bashorun, the Oluwo and the Kakanfo. Theoretically all power came from the Alafin who was considered semi-divine. His administration was headed by three lieutenants; the Ona Efa, the chief judge in dispensing imperial justice, the Otun Efa, the administrative head of Shango, a cult which worshipped the Alafin's deified ancestors, and the Osi Efa, the controller of palace finances who set and received the tributes and tolls of the empire as well as heading its intelligence service.

In each subject town the Alafin was represented by an *Ilari* who either acted as, or was assisted by, the chief priest of the local Shango shrine, and who used both political and religious sanctions to enforce obedience to his judicial decisions. Watching over all, including the Ilaris, were the Alafin's many wives who acted as the eyes and ears of the monarch, and as his secret service in the course of their trading activities throughout the empire. In earlier centuries the Alafin used to associate his chosen son, the Aremo or heir apparent, with his rule so that the succession might pass to him smoothly and without dispute.

Next to the Alafin was the Bashorun, leader of the Oyo Mesi or Council of Notables, comprising seven prominent lineage chiefs of the capital. The Oyo Mesi acted as a check upon the Alafin's power in several ways. They were lineage-appointed office holders and the Alafin had little control over their appointment. They, as well as the Alafin, held judicial power in the capital, they acted as mediators for provincial and vassal chiefs in their dealings with the Alafin, and were therefore a check upon the authority of the Ilaris, and, finally, the army was responsible to the Oyo Mesi who appointed and promoted its officers.

The Bashorun, whose decisions were final, dominated the Oyo Mesi and also held an ultimate check upon the Alafin. As high priest controlling all the cults except Shango and Ifa, he could proclaim that the ancestors and heaven had lost confidence in the Alafin and could command his suicide.

The third power in the empire was the Ogboni headed by the Oluwo. The Ogboni chiefs like the Oyo Mesi were elected by the various lineages or great families. They too had judicial functions, especially in cases involving the spilling of blood. The Alafin's representative sat on the Ogboni Council and his opinion carried considerable weight in its decisions. The Oluwo in his position as chief Ifa priest controlled the Ifa oracle which could accept or reject the Bashorun's decision to command the Alafin's suicide. Since the Alafin had immense influence in the Ogboni this provision checked ambitious Bashoruns.

17 The Oyo empire and its neighbours in 1800

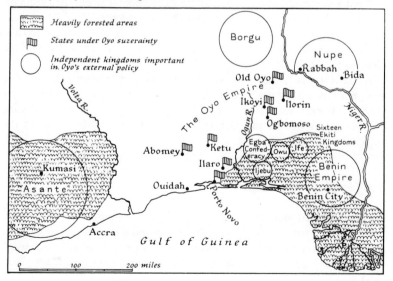

Theoretically the army had no political role but in practice it could enforce its will at a time of civil deadlock or dispute. While the Kakanfo, or field marshal, and his seventy war chiefs (the Eso) were expected to be loyal to the Alafin, their promotion depended upon the Oyo Mesi. Civil authority feared the potential power of the Kakanfo and in order to isolate him from politics he was usually of humble origin and was forbidden to enter the capital city.

The political system was thus a complex and delicate balance with checks and counterchecks against concentration of power in one man's hands. However, changes took place which upset this balance. The succession rule was altered so that the Aremo did not succeed but died with the Alafin, after which the Oyo Mesi chose a successor from a number of candidates. This increased the Bashorun's power since he could now virtually choose his own favourite for the throne. Ambitious Bashoruns passed over the strong and pushful and chose weak, poor and insignificant candidates. Furthermore, since the Bashorun could choose the Alafin, he became increasingly tempted to command the death of a troublesome monarch.

In the third quarter of the eighteenth century the political system became so unbalanced that it brought about a civil war. Bashorun Gaha raised five Alafins to the throne and destroyed four of them while he and his family ruled despotically and unchecked until the empire groaned under his iron hand. Finally, Alafin Abiodun while prostrating daily before Gaha secretly plotted with the provincial chiefs and the Kakanfo. The chiefs rose and massacred Gaha's family and followers while the Kakanfo marched into the capital, besieged Gaha in his compound and burnt him at the stake.

Taking advantage of the civil war the Egba under 'Lishabi the Liberator' murdered the Alafin's Ilaris and proclaimed their independence. To compensate for the loss of the Egba territories and to help exercise control over the trade route south to Porto Novo, Oyo strengthened its authority over the Egbado people.

Alafin Abiodun proved a strong ruler and his reign following the civil war was remembered as a golden age, but decay set in again after his death. Six Alafins followed one another in rapid succession, an Oyo invasion of Nupe met disastrous defeat, and Dahomey assaulted Ketu without fear of the imperial Oyo army.

Collapse of the empire

In 1817 the final blow fell. Kakanfo Afonja, a slave-born child of the royal family, disappointed in his bid for the throne and discovering a plot against his life by the Alafin, raised a revolt in Ilorin, a town founded by his great-grandfather. Had all been healthy in the empire Afonja would have been quickly brought to his knees, but important provincial chiefs sympathized with him. Encouraged by Mallam Alimi, Afonja's Fulani advisor, warriors from dan Fodio's jihadist armies in the north, as well as certain Muslim Yoruba from Oyo itself, came to the Kakanfo's support. In addition thousands of Hausa and Fulani slaves in the empire revolted and fled to Ilorin.

Ojo, the only suriving son of Bashorun Gaha, returned at the head of an army from exile in Borgu to support the Alafin and crush Afonja. At Oyo he carried out a bloody purge of pro-Afonja sympathizers and of those who had turned against his father in the civil war of the previous century but few were anxious to see the empire again ruled by a man from the family of Gaha. The Onikoyi of Ikoyi, the largest provincial town of the empire, marched with Ojo on Ilorin but changed sides in the battle that followed and gave the victory to Afonja.

Afonja's ex-slave supporters roamed the country pillaging and taking vengeance on their former masters. Because their excesses were turning the Yoruba against him, Afonja ordered them to stop. This action was interpreted as being hostile to Islam and as a result Afonja was killed. Abdul Salami, son of Alimi and his Yoruba wife, then mounted the throne as emir of Ilorin and gave his allegiance to the Sokoto caliphate.

Neither the emir nor the Alafin could rally enough united force to triumph. The major concern of the provincial chiefs was their independence from both. Like slippery fish they fought on one side and intrigued with the other, accepted bribes from both, made promises they never intended to keep and like the Onikoyi changed sides during battle. Finally the Alafin allied himself with the king of Borgu.

This, however, lost him the support of the many Yoruba who preferred the Fulani to the Borgawa. As a result of the advantage that this gave to Ilorin, the capital city of the illustrious Oyo empire was sacked, abandoned and totally destroyed in 1837.

The refugees

In the twenty turbulent years before the destruction of the capital almost every major city of the empire had been sacked. Farming was difficult and famine and disease swept the land. Armies pillaged everything of value and carried hundreds into slavery. Each new defeat or destruction of a city in the north sent waves of refugees pouring south into Ogbomoso, Oshogbo, Ife, Owu and Egbaland. Although the southern kingdoms sympathized with these fleeing homeless exiles, because of their numbers and lawlessness they frequently threatened to overwhelm the indigenous people, seize their lands and behave as overlords rather than guests.

Some of the southern kingdoms began to look upon the refugees as potential slaves for farm work or sale at the coast. Prior to this, the Yoruba had not been in the habit of selling their brethren to the Atlantic slave traders but now the slave markets of the coast became glutted with Yoruba for sale. Ife and Ijebu were accused of capturing Oyo. Owu, supported by the Oyo refugees, attacked Ife, thus violating the ancient tradition of the sacredness of the mother kingdom and destroying the principle by which peace had been maintained among the Yoruba states. In the war the kingdom of Owu was destroyed, sending forth new hordes of refugees. The victorious Ife and Ijebu armies swept into Egbaland turning the Egba into refugees as well. The refugee problem and the chain reaction of wars of which it was a product created bitterness and suspicion between the branches of the Yoruba family, which soured future inter-Yoruba relations and prevented the Yoruba from uniting against external foes.

Civil authority had collapsed and in a search for security the refugees began to cluster around talented warriors. This marked the beginning of the great

18 Yorubaland, 1840-60

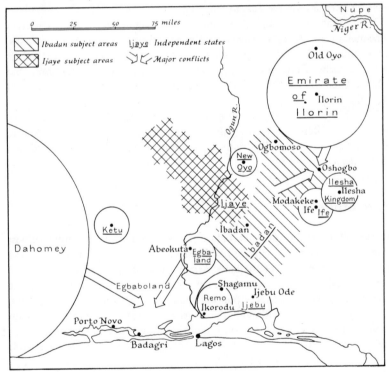

cities which arose in the 1830's. A band of refugees from Oyo under Atiba founded New Oyo while other bands moved into Egba territory where one under Kurunmi founded Ijaye, and another, led by a group of warriors, made a settlement which became the city of Ibadan. The Egba fled south under Shodeke and established Abeokuta where they later welcomed Owu refugees. The Oyo refugees at Ife were at first kept in servile positions but later were allowed to establish their own city of Modakeke. Incoming refugees turned Ogbomoso from a minor town of the old Oyo empire into a populous city, but although the refugees formed the majority of its population, they were excluded from political power. Oshogbo, originally a small outpost of the Ijesha kingdom accepted so many refugees that it took on the character of an Oyo rather than Ijesha city.

Since Ibadan had attracted the largest number of refugees, the organization of the resistance to Ilorin fell to her. The problem was one of military technique. The old Oyo army had been built on the strength of its cavalry but Ilorin now controlled the northern routes and monopolized the horse trade. Somehow Ibadan infantry had to stop Ilorin cavalry. The Ijebu had introduced firearms to the Yoruba but it was the Ibadan Baloguns who perfected their use in warfare. In 1840, at the battle of Oshogbo, Ibadan infantry armed with long Dane guns decisively checked Ilorin cavalry and Ibadan was hailed as the saviour of the Yoruba.

The Ijaye war, 1860-65

The major aim of Ibadan's policy was the restoration of Yoruba unity and in 1855, with the eager support of the Alafin, Ibadan called a conference of the Oyo towns. Resolutions were passed rejecting war as a method of settling disputes between each other, recommending the voluntary payment of tribute to the Alafin and proposing peace and friendship with the Egba and Ijebu.

Meanwhile, Ibadan had acquired an empire, partly by conquest, partly by the voluntary submission of cities desiring protection and partly by the reconquest of some of the Ekiti states from the Ilorin. Ibadan paid nominal tribute to new Oyo and encouraged others to do likewise, but Kurunmi in Ijaye and the Egba and the Ijebu still suspected that Ibadan's real intention was to create an empire of her own. For Ibadan continued to accept tribute from her own subject towns while she encouraged towns subject to Ijaye to send their tribute to the Alafin.

In an effort to strengthen the monarchy and prevent the growth of chiefly power as in old Oyo, Atiba's son succeeded to the throne upon the death of his father in 1859. Ibadan supported this action as likely to ensure a continuation of pro-Ibadan policies in Oyo. Kurunmi, however, opposed it on the grounds that the succession of the Alafin's son was contrary to tradition, hoping in this way to secure the election of a candidate more favourable to himself. When he failed he withheld his allegiance.

In Ibadan the conviction grew that Kurunmi must be brought back to allegiance to the Alafin if another disintegration of Yorubaland was to be prevented. After all Kurunmi held the title of Kakanfo, and was acting very much like a second Afonja. Anxious to prevent Ibadan from becoming undisputed master of the interior the Egba supported Kurunmi who also had the support of the Ijebu. For some time Ibadan, in order to secure a route to the coast, had been encouraging a movement in Remo against their Ijebu overlords so that the Ijebu were quick to join any movement hostile to Ibadan. Once the war began Ibadan was also harassed by her old enemy the Emir of Ilorin who saw Ibadan as the principal obstacle to his intention of carrying the jihad to the sea.

Once the Egba joined the war it became really a struggle between two powers with conflicting policies in Yorubaland, Ibadan who aimed at unification and the Egba who sought to prevent this. In this conflict Ijaye was no more than a pawn, as the Egba, with their greater numbers, dominated their side of the alliance. By supporting Ijaye and bringing the Ijebu into the alliance the Egba hoped that they could hold Ibadan in check and create a balance of power among the Yoruba states.

Once the war began the allies blockaded Ibadan to cut off her supply of arms from the coast. This angered the British merchants in Lagos who encouraged the Remo merchants of Ikorodu to smuggle arms to Ibadan. The Ibadan armies closely blockaded Ijaye to starve her out. The town fell in 1862 and Ibadan stood astride the Yoruba country like a colossus.

The Egba and Ijebu turned upon the Remo and the smugglers of Ikorodu who were openly proclaiming their independence from Ijebu. When the allies sought to punish Ikorodu, British forces intervened, and in 1865 massacred the Egba army. This was the beginning of an unsigned British-Ibadan alliance against the coastal kingdoms. Egbaland retaliated in 1867 by expelling the missionaries and all those of her Christian community suspected of pro-British sympathies. Thereafter the Ijebu forbade Europeans to enter their country.

The western frontier

Having secured Dahomey's independence from Oyo between 1818 and 1822, King Gezo turned his attention to solving his country's economic problems. Dahomey was not well situated for securing control of either of the exports – palm-oil or slaves – which the coastal traders demanded. Beginning in 1839

Gezo had established palm plantations around his capital but the country was dry and infertile and the trees grew with difficulty. To the north and west the slave raids of the seventeenth and eighteenth centuries had depopulated the country. The most promising area for expansion was to the east among the Egbado people from where Dahomey could tap both the slave and oil markets of the Yoruba.

Gezo therefore watched with some misgivings the establishment of Abeokuta on the edge of Egbadoland in 1830 and was even more apprehensive when the Egba welcomed European missionaries in the 1840's. The Egba began to penetrate Egbado country with the aim of securing Badagri as a port under their exclusive control. Gezo determined to stop Egba expansion and marched against Abeokuta in 1851. Both the English merchants who considered the Egba their trading partners, and the missionaries who believed that Abeokuta was the hope of Christianity in Yorubaland, urged the British government to supply arms and ammunition to the Egba. Following the defeat of Dahomey's army before the walls of Abeokuta the Christians were highly popular and gained considerable influence in the Egba government.

The regimental emblem of the 'Wild Antelopes', a famous Dahomean regiment. A wall decoration from Abomey

The following year the British navy and the Egba army co-operated to oust Kosoko from Lagos and enthrone the friendly Akitoye. Gezo claimed that, as he had predicted, European alliances were leading to African subjugation. The British replied by describing Dahomey as a barbarous state fattening on its trade in Yoruba slaves. Gezo's fears were confirmed when the British seized Lagos in 1861 while the Egba were engaged in the Ijaye war. In 1864 Glele, son of Gezo, again failed to capture Abeokuta but did succeed in keeping Badagri out of Egba hands.

From the moment the British seized Lagos their partnership with the Egba began to break up. Anxious for all Egba trade to flow through Lagos, the British navy checked Egba influence in Badagri. The British were not satisfied with Lagos island and continued to expand their power at the expense of the Egba and Ijebu.

The Yoruba kingdom of Ketu remained neutral in the Egba-Dahomey wars. Two factions dominated Ketu politics: the farmers who desired to unite with their Yoruba brethren, and the traders and the Muslims who preferred to remain neutral and to trade with both sides. There was a profitable trade in the ransom and exchange of Egba and Dahomey prisoners of war in the Ketu market and Muslims could see little between the contestants in these wars between non-Muslims. Furthermore, cut off from the sea, Ketu could not secure firearms and so could not match either the strength of Dahomey or of the Egba.

Ketu passed through a series of crises over her policy of neutrality. When the Alaketu invited missionaries to visit the city his palace was burnt down by those who felt this was a pro-Egba policy and likely to anger Gezo. S. A. Crowther, whose mother was from Ketu, received a tumultuous welcome when he visited Ketu in 1853, but again opposition was bitter and the palace and city were burnt to the ground.

In 1858, when Gezo was killed by a Ketu sharpshooter, his death was kept secret but the Dahomey army sacked a Ketu town in revenge. As the refugees poured into Ketu, mobs demanding war and accusing the Alaketu of pro-Dahomey sympathies, gathered around the palace. The king's ministers sided with the populace and the Alaketu had to commit suicide. When the news of Gezo's murder became public, popular sympathy swung back in favour of the dead Alaketu and the ministers were publicly humiliated. The political atmosphere was so heated that it took three months to select a new Alaketu. Thus, as the internal divisions deepened, it became more and more difficult for Ketu to retain its neutrality.

Furthermore, neutrality must be preserved by military strength. Both Dahomey and the Yoruba violated Ketu's sovereignty. In 1883 Ibadans occupied Ketu's eastern territory from where they hoped to worry the Egba. While Balogun Hungbo was leading the Ketu army to the east to chase the

Ibadans, King Glele of Dahomey, who had hitherto appeared friendly to Ketu, suddenly attacked the city, killed the Alaketu and marched home with thousands of prisoners leaving the city a blazing ruin. Hungbo hurriedly returned, took civil and military power into his own hands and rebuilt the city and its walls. Glele led his army back to Ketu in 1886 and settled in for a long starvation siege. Finally, as hunger and disease stalked Ketu, Glele offered peace with honour while at the same time he was negotiating secretly with Hungbo's Muslim advisor. Hungbo suspected the offer but, bowing to the will of the people, went out with all his baloguns to negotiate. Glele seized the baloguns, had them put in chains and stormed the walls of the city. Refugees fled to Lagos, Abeokuta and Ibadan while Glele returned for a triumphant march through his capital leading Hungbo captive with the largest catch of slaves in Dahomey's history. Balogun Hungbo and his people were humiliated and mocked in street scenes much like the victory parades of the Roman emperors.

The war to end all wars, 1877-93

While Dahomey and Ketu were fighting out their destinies to the west, the entire Yoruba country to the east was locked in a sixteen-year struggle which Balogun Latosisa of Ibadan described as a war to end all wars. After its foundation, Ibadan developed a form of government radically different from anything seen before among the Yoruba. Ibadan turned its back on blood connections, a common ancestor, Oduduwa and divine monarchs – everything which the traditional Yorbua held sacred. Her doors were opened to all willing to give their loyalty exclusively to her cause, and Ibadan became a republic of warriors where promotion was based upon military service to the state. These revolutionary principles attracted young men to the republic from all over Yorubaland and when Ibadan stopped the Fulani in 1840 she was hailed as the saviour of the Yoruba. More flocked to her standard until she became by far the most populous city of Yorubaland. She then took up the cause of Yoruba unity in partnership with Oyo; Ibadan providing the military force and the Alafin the religious and social prestige of a traditional king. Ibadan's prestige continued to rise, for unity was a popular cause among the common people.

The Ijaye war was, however, a turning point. After its outbreak jealousy and fear began to replace admiration and Ibadans became pictured as upstart outcasts, and as ruffians who had no right to dictate to crowned heads. It did not pass unnoticed that Ibadan had created an empire for herself in Ekiti. Fear became widespread that Ibadan's policy of Yoruba union was really a cloak for imperialism and many were shocked at the excesses of Ibadan's militarism. Had not Ibadan baloguns boasted after the fall of Ijaye, the 'Egba and the Ijebu are next'?

Ibadan leaders for their part felt that the Ijaye war proved the hopelessness of union through negotiation, consent and the Alafin. Becoming arrogant, the warriors of the republic turned to naked force as the only path to Yoruba unity. From being the saviour of Yorubaland Ibadan was fast becoming its scourge.

The Ijebu and Egba continued to fear the growing British friendship with Ibadan. As the most populous city in tropical Africa, surrounded by fertile soil, with a constant supply of slave labour from its wars of conquest, Ibadan was potentially profitable to British merchants, both as a market, and as a supplier of palm-oil. Ibadan manufactured its own cloth, superior, in quality to Manchester cotton and, due to the cost of head porterage, cheaper as well, so that she needed only one product which British merchants had to sell – guns. The Egba and Ijebu were ready to allow any trade except that in guns, but as far as Ibadan was concerned no guns meant no trade.

19 Yorubaland, 1877-93

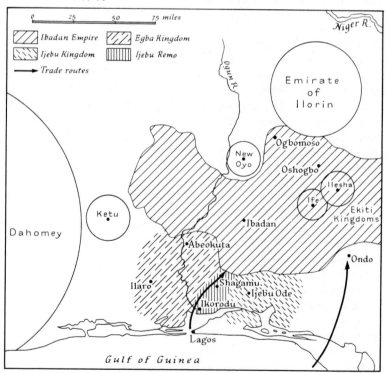

Ibadan, 1854, from a drawing by the missionary Anna Hinderer

The Ijebu and Egba, later joined by Ilorin, declared war in 1877, setting out their war aims as (1) the capture of Ibadan, (2) the forced suicide of Latosisa, its famous balogun, and (3) the neutralization of the republic under the joint administration of the Egba, the Ijebu and the Oyo.

In 1882 the allies received unexpected aid from a revolt of the Ekiti states, within Ibadan's empire. The rebels formed an alliance, the Ekiti-Parapo, to which both Ilesha and Ife adhered and chose the Ibadan-trained, Ijesha general, Ogedengbe, as its leader. An Ekiti-Parapo Committee was formed in Lagos which provided the confederacy with Schneider rifles, superior and faster loading than the guns used by Ibadan forces. The revolt was proof of the allies' contention that Ibadan imperialism was not enlightened. Ibadan had exploited the Ekiti states as a source of wealth and cheap labour, had become callous to local feelings, had imposed unpopular rulers and had permitted her representatives to enjoy privileges that had become intolerable.

Since Ibadan was now totally ringed with foes, even the Alafin having lost his enthusiasm for the alliance, her enemies had a better chance of blockading her than during the Ijaye war. But Ibadan had to trade to survive and, because of the high prices she was able to pay, traders from the enemy kingdoms continued to smuggle arms to her. Ibadan paid for them by selling Ijesha and Ekiti slaves in her southern markets to the Egba and Ijebu, and Egba and Ijebu slaves in her eastern markets to the Ijesha and Ekitis.

In these circumstances the war could not be fought to a conclusive finish.

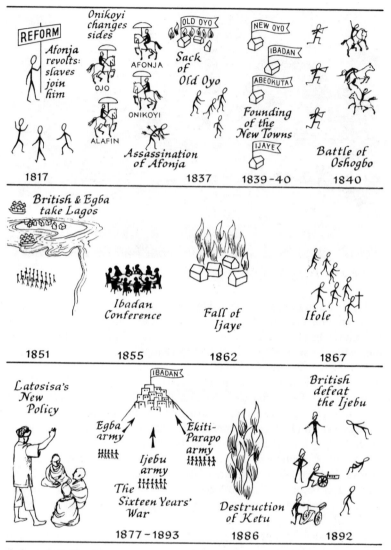

REFORM

Afonja revolts: slaves join him

Onikoyi changes sides

OJO

ONIKOYI

ALAFIN

AFONJA

ONIKOYI

Assassination of Afonja

Sack of Old Oyo

OLD OYO

1817

1837

NEW OYO

IBADAN

ABEOKUTA

Founding of the New Towns

IJAYE

1839-40

Battle of Oshogbo

1840

British & Egba take Lagos

Ibadan Conference

Fall of Ijaye

Ifole

1851

1855

1862

1867

Latosisa's New Policy

IBADAN

Egba army

Ijebu army

Ekiti-Parapo army

The Sixteen Years' War

1877-1893

Destruction of Ketu

1886

British defeat the Ijebu

1892

A chart of the Yoruba wars

In 1886 two Anglican clergymen, S. Johnson, an Oyo, and C. Phillips, an Egba, sponsored by the British, concluded a cease-fire whereby Ekiti independence was recognized and the roads opened for trade. In 1890, when the Egbado appealed to Lagos for protection and a British garrison was stationed in Ilaro, an Egba subject town, the Egba and Ijebu responded by again closing the roads.

The scramble for Africa was now well advanced. Governor Carter of Lagos manufactured an incident with the Ijebu, and in May 1892, by means of repeater rifles and cannon, smashed the Ijebu army with such force that the remaining war-weary Yoruba states negotiated treaties which placed them under British protection. The Egba secured treaty recognition as a semi-independent state while Ilorin remained arrogantly independent until humbled by force in 1897.

8 Dahomey: a centralized and planned economy

The history of Dahomey is especially fascinating, for it throws light on one of the major themes of West African history in the nineteenth century, the deliberate attempts of a state to change from economic dependence on the slave trade to an economy centred on the production of palm-oil. Dahomey was a rare case in West Africa of the extensive development of plantation agriculture and the effects this had upon the institution of domestic slavery are clearly shown. Dahomey was also remarkable for the development of one of the few absolute monarchies of West Africa with a highly organized central government. This made possible the economic planning necessary to cope with the crisis produced by the forced abolition of the trade in slaves.

Dahomey was one of the smaller kingdoms of the Aja group of states whose leading member, Allada, held a position similar to that of Ife among the Yoruba. Early in the eighteenth century, King Agaja conquered the Aja states and Ouidah and amalgamated them into the kingdom of Dahomey. The Aja states had been tribute payers under the Oyo empire and despite Agaja's efforts he was still unable to secure his country's independence, and Dahomey's tributary status to Oyo was confirmed in the treaty of 1730. This provided for heavy annual payments to Oyo and in certain ways restricted Dahomey's sovereignty but, in return, Dahomey was permitted to keep its army and was not subject to the supervision of resident Oyo officials like other sections of the empire. In the late eighteenth century particularly Dahomey was not closely bound to the economic system of the Oyo empire, for Oyo had developed a major trade route through Egbado country, by-passing Dahomey, to the port of Porto Novo in another of its tributaries, the kingdom of Ajase-Ipo.

It is in many ways surprising that one of the great states of West Africa should have arisen in this area at all, for Dahomey is situated in one of the poorest of the West African coastal areas. It had neither the gold resources of its western Asante neighbours nor the advantages of the forest-savannah economy of Oyo to the north and east. It is located in poor savannah and its capital was on a plateau which frequently suffered from drought and famine.

Dahomey's achievements are thus something of a triumph of man over geography.

Dahomey was one of the few states of West Africa which owed her rise and splendour to the profits of the slave trade. She organized the trade efficiently and built up a well-drilled and well-led army which raided north and west, in search of captives to be sold at Ouidah for guns and powder which, in turn, kept the army in the field. In the last quarter of the eighteenth century it became necessary for King Kpengla to organize slave-worked plantations to feed the growing population of the capital and its army regiments. The slave trade, the conscription of men, the full time army and the plantations led to a growing centralization of power in the hands of the Aladaxonu dynasty of kings.

In 1818 Gezo overthrew King Adandazan and seized the throne of Dahomey. The Oyo empire, split by internal strife, the defection of Afonja and the subsequent civil wars, was unable to prevent Gezo declaring his

20 *The Kingdom of Dahomey (i)*

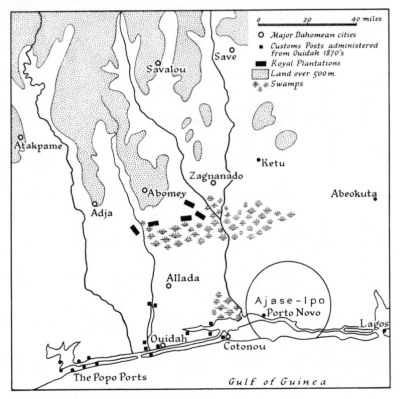

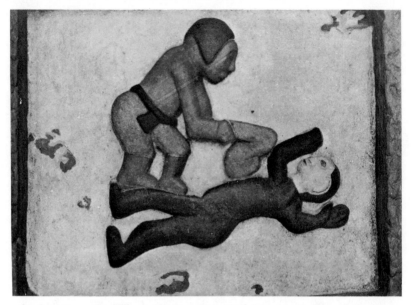

An Amazon warrior killing a Yoruba soldier. Wall decoration in King Glele's palace, Abomey

independence and conquering Ajase-Ipo, a former vassal of Oyo. Dahomey's nineteenth-century history begins with Gezo's revolution and Dahomey's independence, which was nurtured by a strong national sentiment, developed under the long subjection to Oyo imperialism.

The Dahomean army increased in size and efficiency until the mid-nineteenth century when the economic crisis caused by British action against slave exports reduced state revenues. In 1726 the army was estimated to consist of 3,000 regulars and 10,000 militia who could be called upon at short notice. In 1820 the regulars had increased to between 5,000 and 6,000 and by 1845 to 12,000, about 5,000 of which were in the women's corps, plus a militia of 24,000.

The regulars were uniformed in blue and white tunics, short trousers and caps decorated with distinctive regimental emblems. Each regiment possessed its own drum band and officers with umbrellas in regimental colours, designed to encourage regimental pride and rivalry which was particularly intense between the male and female corps. The march past of the army was a spectacular sight which invariably impressed visitors to Abomey. The combat units were supported by a carrier corps of young men in training from which replacements were drawn. Arms, ammunition, food rations and uniforms were provided by the state.

The kingdom was small, with a population of possibly a quarter of a million, and the army was also small though well-drilled and famous for its strategy. The poorly organized peoples of the north and west, who were denied firearms by Dahomey's rigid monopoly, were no match for it. However, Dahomey was wise enough not to challenge either Asante or Ibadan, both of which were larger and had the use of firearms. In the attack upon Abeokuta in 1851 the Dahomean army was probably outnumbered by as much as two to one.

For all the central position of the army in the kingdom it did not appear to wield substantial political power. The army was subject to the king and his officials like most other Dahomean institutions. Dahomey was not a military state, even though many leading official positions were filled from among the army generals.

The social classes

Dahomean society was divided into three, the leisured, the commoner and the servile classes. The leisured class comprised the relatives of the king and earlier kings. Those furthest removed from the reigning monarch held the prestige but few of the privileges of the aristocracy and gradually merged back into the commoner class. However, royal blood was recognized through both males and females and thus the extended royal family was large. Royalty might hold minor but seldom high state positions. This lessened the temptation to seek popularity and power and reduced intrigue against the throne. The royals were essentially a class who lived off others, thus the term leisured rather than aristocratic. They were supported by the state and this, combined with the army, was a growing burden on the revenue of the kingdom.

At the opposite end of the social scale was the servile class made up of slaves, who worked the plantations and could be sacrificed or sold, and serfs, those born in Dahomey of slaves or slave and freeborn parents. The latter could not be sold and a portion of what they produced was their own but they did not enjoy the same freedom of movement or choice as the freeborn. Just as there was a tendency for royals to fall back into the commoner class, so there was also the tendency for the descendants of slaves to move up into the commoner class as they became Dahomeans.

Next to the king the state officials were politically the most powerful group in the kingdom. They were drawn from the commoner class and were appointed, transferred or dismissed by the king. Their offices were not hereditary although a son might reasonably expect to follow his father if the father had proved efficient and loyal. The officials were the instruments of the monarch's power. As commoners they could never attract a following of potential rebels nor hope to gain the throne. When called to office they were ennobled by chieftaincy titles and given in marriage to royal princesses. Top officials were provided with large estates and they possessed residences in the major cities and occasionally rest-houses along important roads. These officials held all positions, from councillor-ministers and provincial administrators to village chiefs and customs officers.

The king was advised by a council whose members were in charge of specific aspects of government. Among the councillor-ministers were the Mingi, chief magistrate and superintendent of police; the Meu, collector of revenue; and the Tokpe, minister of agriculture. The kingdom was divided into the metropolitan area of Abomey and six outlying provinces. The provincial administrators were almost equal to the councillor-ministers in the power they wielded and in their influence on state policy. The Mingi, Meu

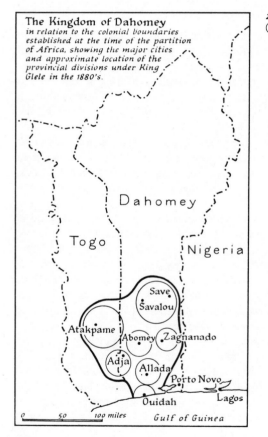

The Kingdom of Dahomey
in relation to the colonial boundaries
established at the time of the partition
of Africa, showing the major cities
and approximate location of the
provincial divisions under King
Glele in the 1880's.

21 The Kingdom of Dahomey (ii) in about 1880

and Yevogan, the provincial administrator of Ouidah province in charge of overseas trade and European relations, formed the inner core of the council and on state occasions they occupied positions next to the king.

A second group of officials as influential, if not more so, than those already mentioned were called the Nayé, often referred to as the king's wives. A few may have been so, but mainly they were older women past child bearing, or slave women of exceptional ability. Each Nayé was assigned an official whose department she was expected to know as well as the official himself. The Nayé in charge of Ouidah province and its administrator, the Yevogan, was called the Yevogana. Every official was thus paired with a corresponding Nayé in the palace. When an official reported to the king the Nayé was always present. In addition, the Nayé had a large number of workers directly under her control to check upon the reports of the official. For example, the sale of salt was a royal monopoly. The Yevogan was required to send one pebble to the royal court for every bag of salt produced in the salt pans of Ouidah province. The Yevogana not only kept record of these pebbles but also sent her inspectors to check the salt pans and stored salt to ensure that the Yevogan was honest and efficient. Since the Nayé were close to the king and knew as much about the administration as the officials it would not be surprising to find that they exercised more influence over the king and therefore possessed more power than the officials themselves.

Despotism

The Aladaxonus were a rare example in West Africa of absolute monarchs. They commanded respect bordering on awe. They appointed and dismissed all officials in the state. They licensed the chief priests of all religious societies. Conquered peoples' gods were either absorbed into the Dahomean group of gods or identified with those already there. All the religious societies recognized the place of the king in the order of human society just as the supreme God was responsible for order in the universe. Beyond this the king did not interfere with religious thinking. The paradox of Dahomey was that while on one hand it was the most controlled society in West Africa, on the other it gave unusual scope for individual and independent thought which resulted in religious beliefs of great complexity.

The king forbade secret societies because they might prove a threat to royal power. This was also unique since all Dahomey's neighbours possessed them. The ancestors were important to the well-being of each Dahomean family, while the royal ancestors were especially significant for they were important to the well-being of the whole nation. The royal ancestors were honoured annually and in this celebration important officials and people gathered at the capital from the entire nation. This celebration was not only a religious but also a political occasion when the monarch displayed his wealth, power and splendour and the people renewed their allegiance and loyalty to the throne.

The law of Dahomey often appeared severe but there was an honest effort to make it impartial rather than arbitrary (which is frequently a cause of bitter complaint in human society). Although the king's word was the law of the land yet he was not above the law. Dahomeans like to recount how King Glele was fined for breaking the law. When gangs of men were working co-operatively either on state roads or building a house for one of their members, it was the law that a passer-by must approach the leader and make an excuse as to why he could not break his journey to assist in the work. Permission was almost inevitably given, the law being largely designed to reinforce courtesy. King Glele's procession passed one such group without asking to be excused. He was stopped by the headmen and fined many cases of rum and pieces of cloth for breaking the law. This oral tradition along with that concerning the levy of regular tax on the royal plantations are often brushed aside as mere stories because they do not fit the picture of royal despotism. However, the fact that the kings of Dahomey were prepared to obey the laws they themselves created was the difference between arbitrary despotism and a despotism which realized that its power and position rested ultimately, no matter how indirectly, upon the will of the people. The success of the Aladaxonus can be measured from the way the people voluntarily supported the royal family, as well as institutions either not recognized or forbidden by the French in the colonial period. Many Dahomean citizens even today look back to the 'great century', their golden age under the Aladaxonus, and this suggests there was good government under the dynasty.

Although the king himself was the 'state', and particularly the administration, in some ways he stood apart from it. The Royal Court of Appeal was often presided over by the Mingi. Severe judgements were given so that the king, if he wished, could reduce or commute sentences on the principle of tempering justice with mercy. The king was the commander of the army and often accompanied it to war but he did not dictate military tactics and was not responsible for defeat. The Gao (general) was fully in charge and fully responsible. On the battlefield this relationship was symbolized by the Gao occupying a higher stool than the king and by his being permitted to smoke in the king's presence, normally the height of disrespect in Dahomean manners and etiquette.

Little is known about the relations between the king and his council. Most visitors felt that the king was all-powerful, a few believed that he required the consent of his council before deciding on new policy. However, even if he can act alone, it is a foolish ruler who appoints officials and

Emblem of His Majesty, King Glele, from the palace Abomey

ignores their advice. Both Gezo and Glele appeared too astute for this and it seems likely that they sought a consensus of opinion in their councils on major issues.

Dahomey has been noted for the strength of its national feeling of which the monarch was the symbol. Unlike many African states, citizenship was not based entirely upon blood relationships. Foreigners, mainly Yoruba and Europeans, could become citizens in a symbolic ceremony which had something in common with modern ideas of nationalism. The state was represented by a perforated calabash filled with water which represented the national spirit or the king. Each citizen symbolically had a finger in a perforation and a candidate for citizenship actually placed his finger in such a hole during the citizenship ceremony. The responsibility for the nation was laid upon each individual, for it was stressed that should even one citizen withdraw his finger by an act of treason the spirit of the nation would drain away. During ennobling ceremonies the same concept was stressed by the words, 'Dahomey is great and must come before all else . . . a country must be loved by its people'.

From slaves to palm-oil

It is difficult to say how far the centralization of government in Dahomey had gone before the accession of Gezo in 1818 and how far the centralization which observers reported in the nineteenth century was the work of the two monarchs, Gezo, 1818-58 and his son Glele, 1858-89. Certainly the eighteenth century witnessed growth in the monarch's power and a consequent elaboration of the bureaucracy. The population censuses from 1680, the standing army, the royal plantations from about 1775 and the efficient organization of trade at Ouidah required a highly developed bureaucracy under the king's control. However, there is also evidence that officialdom was expanding in the nineteenth century and that the monarch was increasing his powers especially through the Royal Judicial Court of Appeal.

The greatest encouragement to further centralization in the nineteenth century was the British action in putting a stop to the export of slaves, the tax on which was the major financial support of the kingdom. The king had to find, and quickly, other sources of revenue and a new export product to pay for foreign goods, especially arms and ammunition. In 1807 the British stopped trading in slaves and abandoned their depot at Ouidah. The slave trade, however, continued almost uninterrupted until the British added the equipment clause to their slave-trade treaties in 1839 and began to seize Portuguese and Brazilian slavers.

1840 to 1850 was a period of economic uncertainty for Dahomey. Two oil firms, Regis (French) and Hutton (British), established themselves in Ouidah while the Brazilians and Portuguese were still smuggling out slaves to the new world. There was some doubt as to whether the oil or slave interests would ultimately triumph. It was not until the British were established in Lagos in 1851 and closely blockaded the Dahomey coast that Gezo began to be convinced that the economic future lay with palm-oil. At this time, when the British were offering him only £400 compensation, their envoy had estimated that Gezo's yearly revenue on the slave trade was £60,000. Gezo then stated his difficulty clearly. He said that while palm-oil was promising it was slow and brought only a small amount into the state treasury, while his army and state organization were expensive and could only be changed at the risk of revolution, overthrow of the dynasty and anarchy.

As elsewhere in West Africa slavers and oilers were hostile, each seeing a victory for the other as a defeat for themselves. The pro-slave faction for a time pressed Gezo successfully to continue the trade and not divert the nation's energies. But in the forties Gezo began simultaneously to encourage palm cultivation on his own plantations and those of his officials and to divert slaves from export to plantation labour. At the same time his army was directed away from the slaving grounds of the north towards securing a hold upon the Yoruba palm belt in Egbado and Egbaland. This was the major aim behind Dahomey's attacks upon Ado in 1844 and Abeokuta in 1851 and 1864. During the sixties King Glele sought to extend his customs posts along the Porto Novo beach up to the British posts in the Badagri area. However, the Egba foiled Dahomey's designs on the palm belt and the kings had to solve their economic problems by internal organization rather than external aggression. The army continued to be important, firstly because hostile European activities increased with the palm-oil trade, and secondly because the economy required more and more cheap labour. This probably accounts for the destruction of Ketu in the 1880's when the entire population was led into slavery.

Once Britain began, after 1839, to seize Brazilian and Portuguese ships, Ouidah rapidly declined as a slave port and the slave trade degenerated into smuggling activity spread along the coast. However, prices were high and Dahomey's annual exports were still estimated at £160,000, of which the state's share was about £60,000. Prior to 1850 Regis and Hutton shipped only about £16,000 worth of oil annually, of which the state's share was less than £1,000. Oil, therefore, was not a substitute but only a supplement to the slave trade.

In the fifties, as the slave trade shrank into insignificance, Lagos, Porto Novo and Ouidah began to ship oil in quantity. Prices were high but as more oil reached the world market there was a steady decline up to the 1880's. In the severe competition which followed, Lagos, because it was situated in the palm belt and in spite of the hold-ups due to the Yoruba civil wars, shipped more oil than Porto Novo, Ouidah and the Popo (Togo) ports combined.

Porto Novo on the edge of the palm belt could tap the Egba oil markets but its harbour facilities were poor. Oil had to be shipped either via Lagos where British customs duty had to be paid or via Cotonou where Dahomean duty was paid. Porto Novo became a pawn in the trade war between Britain and Dahomey. To break out of this squeeze the king of Porto Novo accepted French protection in the 1860's. French firms followed the French flag and tried to load from the Porto Novo beach but Dahomey completely sealed the city off from the sea by a string of customs posts. The French were then forced to withdraw and their firms dispersed to Cotonou, Ouidah and Lagos.

The Dahomey ports – Ouidah and Cotonou – were badly sited since they could not tap the palm belt but depended upon plantation oil with its higher costs of labour and lower yields. However, by the 1870's it was estimated that Dahomey was shipping palm products worth about £500,000 annually, which suggests that she had fully and successfully made the transition from a slave to an oil-centred economy. But some observers argued that this success was more apparent than real and that in the late nineteenth century Dahomey was a hollow shell, that the kings sought to hide the economic crisis which they were unable to cure by the creation of an image of ferocity to check invasion from the French, British or Yoruba.

In spite of the change over from the slave to the oil trade the army's raids for manpower continued. The slaves were concentrated within the country more than ever before, and there was a tendency for the character of domestic slavery to undergo serious changes on the plantations. The profit motive was strong and the king and officials were absentee landlords. The landlords demanded maximum yields from their overseers who in turn drove the slaves harder. Thus slavery in Dahomey in the last half of the nineteenth century became more like slavery in the new world or Calabar, and changed from slavery as it was known in neighbouring West African societies.

Household slaves or those in the employ of small farmers were likely to be treated in the traditional manner. In the royal household, for example, the king often chose as his heir one of his sons by a slave wife, because it was felt that she must be greatly endowed and superior to her freeborn colleagues to have risen so high. It has also been pointed out that slaves born in Dahomey – second generation slaves – moved into a half-way position between slave and free and were on the way to being assimilated into freeborn society. This process depended upon acceptance of Dahomean ways but the plantations, as in Calabar, must have slowed down the opportunities for slave children to grow up with the same language and customs as Dahomean citizens.

By mid-nineteenth century Gezo felt that slaves required more legal protection. All deaths in the kingdom had customarily been reported to the capital in order that the census might be kept up to date. Gezo placed officials in the provinces charged with reporting whether deaths were natural or violent. Since the violent death of a freeborn would be taken up by the family through normal processes of law this innovation was designed to protect the slaves from brutal owners and overseers. The result was that all cases of violent death, slave and freeborn, were brought before the Royal Judicial Court in Abomey.

A planned economy

One of the spectacular achievements of Dahomey in the nineteenth century was the planning of agricultural production by the state. Originally begun in a small way to feed the growing population, army and leisured class it became the central feature of state policy once the slave trade ended. Experiments were carried out on various export crops but palm-oil was the most successful. Plantation owners and small farmers were encouraged to produce oil. All palm trees in the kingdom were counted and a constant check kept on their annual yield. Taxation was about one-third of the total production. The tax oil – the largest single source of state revenue after the 1850's – was sold at Ouidah for guns and powder.

The production achievements of Kings Gezo and Glele may best be seen in comparison with the later French colonial period. The general trend of production in the twentieth century has been static or downward. At the French conquest there were forty million palm trees in Dahomey. In the 1950's there were only thirty-two and a half million most of which were old, having been planted before the conquest. In addition to the neglect of production by the colonial government the prices offered by the French middlemen firms were often so low that the people preferred to grow food crops and use the palms for production of wine rather than oil. In 1946, for example, the firms were buying oil for 3,500 francs per ton and selling it in France for 38,000 francs, thus making ten times more than they had paid the producers.

Livestock and food crop production were as closely controlled and regulated as palm-oil. The basis of planning was the annual census which provided figures for the total population and its distribution by sex, occupation, province and village. Originally designed for conscription and other military needs – for instance all blacksmiths were licensed and each forge had its trade mark registered in the capital because of the importance of the industry to the army – the census came to be employed for other purposes, an important one being taxation.

For livestock, keeping the balance between production and consumption was a major concern of the state. There was a census of all goats, cows, sheep and pigs and a strict account of slaughtering. In the case of pork each village chief reported the number of pigs slaughtered. The butchers' guilds kept all the skulls of pigs sold in the market. Both reports went to the Tokpe and Nayé in Abomey. The Nayé, in addition, sent out market inspectors to make periodic checks. If sales were running ahead of production the king might forbid the slaughter of sows or all pigs for a year. During the ban pigs could not be taken past the toll gates on the public roads.

Food crops were similarly controlled. Each province of the kingdom concentrated upon certain crops. Abomey specialized in beans and maize, Zagnanado in millet, Allada in maize and cassava, Save in groundnuts and maize and Adja in maize. During a shortage of one crop the Tokpe could order one or more districts to switch cultivation to the crop in short supply. Condiments – honey, red and black pepper, and ginger – were royal monopolies produced in restricted areas under supervision. Pepper, for example, was grown by only seven villages near Allada.

The result of centralized planning, as elsewhere in the world, was greater taxation, and Dahomeans were the most heavily taxed West Africans in the nineteenth century. There were the export and annual agricultural and palm-oil taxes. Livestock were taxed every three years. Artisans paid an income tax and the wealthy paid death duties. In addition there was a market tax and toll charges on all major roads.

'He who makes the powder'

Whether Dahomey was a hollow shell or not in the last half of the nineteenth century may be debatable but after the French took over Porto Novo in 1883, they began to demand privileges in Cotonou and to squeeze the trade away from Ouidah. The poverty of Glele's court was then unmistakable and contrasted sharply with the rising splendour of the court of the king of Porto Novo. French firms moved away from Ouidah. This formerly flourishing port exported less than £100,000 of goods in 1887, became negligible between 1890 and 1893 and dropped to nothing in 1894 on the break-up of the kingdom. Meanwhile exports at Porto Novo and Cotonou under French control rose rapidly to record heights in 1894. Ouidah collapsed with the kingdom of

Statues of Gezo, Glele and Behanzin

Dahomey and has never recovered, while Cotonou flourished and became the commercial centre of the French colony also named 'Dahomey'.

As the tempo of the partition of Africa mounted in the 1880's French pressure on Dahomey increased. Dahomean policy towards France included everything short of force though they would not actually fight, following King Glele's advice that 'he who makes the powder must win the battle'. Yet every year that passed after 1883 saw a drastic decline in exports which caused a deepening financial crisis at Abomey. Unsuccessful overtures were made to the Portuguese and British for alliance and in 1888 negotiations were opened with German firms in Togo for credit and supplies of guns and ammunition. In 1889 a French mission arrived in Abomey demanding that Dahomey renounce all rights to Cotonou. While the mission was in the capital King Glele poisoned himself rather than live to watch the ruin of his kingdom. Factions arose in the court as whether to surrender or resist. Behanzin, the son of Glele, favouring a policy of resistance, was enthroned and crushed a revolt of those who wished to surrender. Thereafter it was only a matter of time until France marshalled her forces and in 1892 Behanzin was conquered, captured and exiled to the West Indies, an ironic fate for the last representative of a dynasty which, with the exception of the Pepples of Bonny, had been responsible for the greatest shipment of slaves to that very part of the world.

However, regardless of the actions of his distant ancestors, Behanzin's grandfather and father had shown themselves capable rulers, quick to change and adapt to the economic crisis of the nineteenth century. They may rightly be remembered as the innovators of the most original administrative and economic techniques of any of the coastal rulers of West Africa in the nineteenth century.

9 The Asante empire
in the nineteenth century

At the beginning of the nineteenth century the Asante empire had expanded to include virtually the whole of modern Ghana and parts of modern Ivory Coast and Togo. The only state of modern Ghana that had not been incorporated into the empire by that time was the relatively small kingdom of Fante which stretched along the coast of Ghana from the mouth of the Pra to the borders of the Ga kingdom and about twenty miles inland. But even within this stretch was the state of Elmina which was directly under Asante. The rise and expansion of Asante between about 1680 and 1750 was due firstly to the state building genius and military skill of Osei Tutu and Opoku Ware whose joint reigns covered the period; secondly, to the martial ardour and bravery of the Asante people; and thirdly, to their desire to free themselves from the political control of Denkyira and to control the trade routes to the coast and the western Sudan.

The government of the Asante empire

The empire consisted of two parts, each with its own system of administration. The first part was metropolitan Asante, and the second was provincial Asante. Metropolitan Asante consisted of the Kumasi state or division directly under the Asantehene, and all the states within about thirty to forty miles' radius of modern Kumasi. All these states recognized the Golden Stool created by Osei Tutu as the symbol of their soul and unity, looked on the King of Kumasi state or division (Oman) as their paramount chief or Asantehene, and recognized the great oath '*Ntam Kese Miensa*' as their supreme oath. The central government of metropolitan Asante consisted of the Confederacy Council made up of all the kings or Omanhene of the various divisions, presided over by the Asantehene. It also had an executive council or cabinet, made up of a few of the principal wing chiefs of the Kumasi division and some of the divisional kings. Each of the states of metropolitan Asante had its own king or Omanhene, and its own State Council. It must be noted that though all these Councils were advisory rather than policy-making bodies, neither the Asantehene nor any Omanhene enjoyed uninhibited dictatorial powers. On the contrary, each of them could be destooled whenever he was considered to have abused his powers. During the first half of the eighteenth century, membership of the Asante inner council or cabinet, as well as succession to most of the stools, was hereditary. However, the last two rulers of the century, namely Osei Kwadwo and Osei Kwame, embarked on some constitutional changes by which they began to convert the hereditary offices or stools of the Kumasi division into offices held by appointment, and created new stools with the aim of increasing the personal powers of the king.

Provincial Asante consisted of all the outer circle of states conquered and annexed by the Asante during the eighteenth century. Until about the middle of that century, all these states continued to govern themselves in exactly the same way as they were doing before their conquest and annexation. All

22 *The Asante empire*

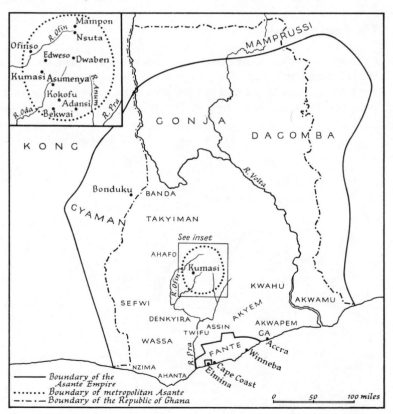

that they were expected to do was to accept one of the wing chiefs of Kumasi, who seldom visited the provinces, as a friend at Court, to pay annual tribute and contribute a contingent to the army when called upon to do so. The Golden Stool had practically no significance for them. In the government of provincial Asante, Osei Kwadwo and his successors also attempted to introduce some changes. For instance, they tried to tighten their control over the provinces by stationing regional and district commissioners in these states, in addition to the proconsuls who were seldom or never there. In 1776, for instance, Osei Kwadwo established a regional commissioner in Akwapem to be responsible for Dutch, English and Danish Accra. However, these changes in the provincial system did not go far enough, and throughout the eighteenth century most of the states made a bid for their independence, either singly or at times in alliance. It was the superior military techniques and the bravery of their army that enabled the Asante to crush all these rebellions and to preserve the empire intact.

The Fante kingdom

The only state within modern Ghana that had been able to dam the tide of Asante imperialism was the Fante kingdom. By the beginning of the nineteenth century, this kingdom in fact consisted of about seventeen states. It seems that the founders of most of these states lived in Mankessim for

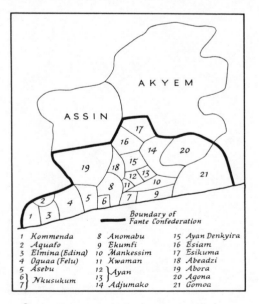

23 The Fante states

1 Kommenda	8 Anomabu	15 Ayan Denkyira
2 Aquafo	9 Ekumfi	16 Esiam
3 Elmina (Edina)	10 Mankessim	17 Esikuma
4 Oguaa (Felu)	11 Kwaman	18 Abeadzi
5 Asebu	12 } Ayan	19 Abora
6 } Nkusukum	13 }	20 Agona
7 }	14 Adjumako	21 Gomoa

centuries. However, during the last three decades of the seventeenth century, as a result of population pressure, they moved out to carve out kingdoms for themselves in the areas left virtually empty by the decimation or assimilation of its original inhabitants, the Etsii. Between 1700 and 1730, partly to ensure their 'middleman' position, but mainly to provide a united front against the Asante and the Akyem (who were driving towards the coast and would thus be able to control the flow of arms and ammunition inland) these states jointly conquered the non-Fante states to the east and west of them, namely Asebu, Fetu, Aguafo and Agona, though they failed to take over Elmina. Thus, by the middle of the eighteenth century, this vital stretch of the coast of Ghana from the mouth of the Pra to the borders of the Ga kingdom had, with the exception of the state of Elmina, come under the control of the Fante. A clear and accurate picture of the government of this kingdom, or rather Confederation of states, has not as yet emerged. It appears that up to the 1730's they formed quite a closely knit group under the joint rule of the Brafo, who was probably the King of Mankessim, and the High Priest of the national god, referred to in the European records as '*Bora Bora Weigya*', or in Fante as '*Nnanom Mpow*'. But during the second half of the century, the Confederation broke up into two parts, western or Bore Bore Fante, and eastern or Ekumfi Fante, each half with its own government. By 1750, the only authority recognized by the two Fante states was their national god, and the only decisions binding on both of them were those of the Chief Priest.

Relations between Asante and Fante

Throughout the eighteenth century, relations between the Asante and the Fante remained by and large hostile. There are numerous references in the records to threats of Asante invasion of Fante, and on three occasions – in 1727, 1765 and 1776 – the Asante did in fact attack the Fante. The main reason for this state of enmity between the two was the persistent refusal of the Fante, in spite of the pressure of both the British and the Dutch, to allow Asante traders direct access to the European forts and castles situated in their kingdom. Wars between them in the eighteenth century were not as frequent as might have been expected for a number of reasons. The first was that during the first half of the century, the Fante were more united and therefore sufficiently powerful to keep the Asante out of their territory. The second reason was that during the second half of the century, when the Fante became disunited, the Asante kings were preoccupied at home with their constitutional reforms, while Wassa acted as an effective buffer state. The third reason was that throughout the century, the British adopted the policy of preventing any direct clash between the two powers, and of backing the Fante in the event of an Asante attack. The fear of the British, as one of their Governors wrote in July 1765, was that, 'Should the Ashantees become masters of the Fantee Country, the forts and settlements on this coast would be greatly endangered as the king of Ashantee, being an absolute Prince, might upon the slightest provocation, and from mere caprice, so effectively block up any fort as to oblige the garrison to surrender.'

The Great Osei Bonsu

Such then was the state of Asante and Fante, and of the nature of the relations between them when Osei Bonsu was enstooled as Asantehene at the beginning of the nineteenth century. What policies did he pursue during his long reign from 1801 to 1824, and with what consequences?

Firstly, Osei Bonsu adopted the policy of continuing the constitutional reforms begun by his predecessors, secondly, of maintaining intact the empire that he had inherited, and, thirdly, of extending its frontiers even farther.

On the constitutional front, Osei Bonsu began by filling the vacant stools or offices, as his immediate predecessors had done, by young men of his own choice. Secondly, he created three more stools or departments in the Ankobia Stool or Ministry of Home Affairs established by Osei Kwadwo, and he improved on the machinery of the Gyasewa Stool or Ministry of Economic Affairs by co-ordinating the activities of the various sections and employing literate Muslims. It appears that, during his reign, Osei Bonsu developed a real chancery whose records were kept in Arabic. Thirdly, he completed the conversion of the Cabinet or Privy Council from a fixed body of hereditary members to an *ad hoc* Council to which members were invited according to the nature of the business to be transacted. Similarly, during his reign, the diplomatic service, which, before the reign of Osei Kwadwo, had been in charge of the Akyeame or linguists who occupied hereditary stools, became fully appointive. Finally, he also continued the changes in the system of provincial administration by appointing more district and regional commissioners. We know for certain, for example, that as soon as he conquered Fante, he stationed a regional commissioner at Abura, a district commissioner at Cape Coast and another at Elmina.

As a result of this successful continuation of the constitutional reforms of his predecessors, the powers of Osei Bonsu in Kumasi and the provinces greatly increased. As Dupuis observed, 'The king rules with unrivalled sway; every king, chief, viceroy or caboceer, being his absolute and unconditional vassal as tributaries or not and most of them holding their governments by virtue of an appointment from the Court.' It should be added, however, that this is true of the king's powers in the Kumasi state or division only since all these reforms did not affect other divisions of metropolitan Asante. Furthermore, since membership of the new administrative class or bureaucracy depended now on talent and ability rather than on birth, the administration became more efficient than before, and peace and order reigned in the Kumasi division in particular, and in metropolitan Asante in general. As one European observer wrote in 1816, 'Law and order is just as great in the Ashantee kingdom as with Asiatic peoples. There exist no palavers between one town and another, and panyarring finds no place.'

His second policy was to preserve intact the empire that he had inherited from his predecessors. This meant that he had to suppress all revolts, and, as he told Dupuis, 'to eradicate the seeds of disobedience and insubordination'. It should not be forgotten that in spite of the considerable improvement in the system of provincial administration, revolts and rebellions aimed at independence continued in the nineteenth century, nor did the vassal kings always obey the orders of their sovereign. Indeed, at the time of his accession, Gyaman or Abron was in revolt, and shortly after his accession, Gonja also rebelled. In 1806, the Assin rulers Otibu and Aputae openly defied the Asantehene, killed his messengers and took refuge in Fante. In 1809, Fante attacked both Elmina and Accra, the two vital Asante footholds on the coast; Akyem and Akwapem also raised the standard of revolt in 1811, Gyaman again in 1817, and Wassa, Denkyira and Assin in 1823. Fortunately Osei Bonsu was able to execute his policy. He quickly suppressed the first two revolts, and after a series of appeals to the Fante to surrender the fugitive Assin chiefs had failed, he launched a campaign under his own personal command against the Fante, which ended in 1808 with, as we shall see presently, the defeat of the Fante, an attack on the British fort at Anomabo and the capture and execution of Otibu. He next turned his attention to the Akwapem, who put up a spirited fight, and it took two campaigns, in 1811, and from 1814 to 1816, to suppress their rebellion and relieve Elmina and Accra. Gyaman proved an even tougher nut to crack, but it was cracked in 1818.

The final campaign of Osei Bonsu was launched against the Wassa and the Denkyira in 1823; this ended with the defeat not only of the rebels but also of the British contingent sent to their aid under the command of Sir Charles Macarthy, the then Governor-in-Chief of the forts. Indeed, during the final and decisive battle of this campaign near Akantamansu on 21 February 1824, Macarthy was himself killed by the Asante.

But Osei Bonsu did not aim merely at preserving what he had inherited, but at adding to it also. He accomplished this by conquering and annexing the hitherto independent Fante Confederation in the series of expeditions already referred to between 1806 and 1824. Though the refusal of the Fante to hand over the Assin chiefs was what immediately led to the first of Osei Bonsu's expeditions against the Fante in 1806, that episode was more of an

An Asante captain in war dress. From a British print of 1819

excuse for the war. The roots of the main causes of the Asante-Fante wars are to be found in the eighteenth century.

The first and foremost of these was the refusal of the Fante to allow the Asante to come and trade directly with the Europeans on the coast. The Asante never abandoned their determination to gain direct access to the Fante coast, and the conflicts between them over trade routes in the eighteenth century continued into the nineteenth. Indeed, the latter century opened on a note of Asante-Fante dispute. In October 1800, the British governor reported that 'the trading paths have for many months past been shut up by a misunderstanding between the Fantees and Ashantees'. And his successor also stated in 1807 that the Fante had 'always thrown impediments in the way of the Asante so as to prevent their intercourse with us'. What worsened the situation was that the Fante added insult to injury by not being particularly honest in their dealings with the Asante traders. As Osei Bonsu told the Bowdich Mission in 1817, the Fante obtained pure gold from the Asante and mixed it with other base metal before selling it to the Europeans on the coast.

As is evident from the European sources, this practice had been going on throughout the eighteenth century, and this gold was referred to as 'Cracra' gold as distinct from the 'Akannes' gold, or pure gold.

The second main Asante grievance against the Fante was political. First of all, to defend their huge empire and suppress all internal revolts the Asante needed a regular supply of firearms. And, as was the case in the eighteenth century, one of the main reasons for the drive of the Asante to the coast in the nineteenth century was precisely to ensure a regular flow of firearms to Kumasi, especially from the Dutch and the Danes in Elmina and Accra respectively. It was also for the same reason that they steadfastly maintained their hold on, and persistently defended Accra and Elmina, their two principal coastal outlets.

The third grievance of the Asante was also political. It was that throughout the eighteenth and the nineteenth centuries, the Fante assisted their southern tributary states such as Denkyira, Twifu and Akyem whenever any of them rose up in rebellion. In the 1740's and the late 1770's, the Fante for instance, assisted the Wassa; in 1806, they granted sanctuary to the Assin; in 1812 they backed the Akyem and Akwapem, and Wassa and Denkyira in 1823. Here the motives of the Fante were mainly to safeguard their 'middleman' position and to ensure that there were strong buffer states between them and the Asante.

Besides these economic and political considerations, which have their roots in the eighteenth century, there was another factor which was of nineteenth century origin, and this was the personal ambition of Osei Bonsu himself. Two of his predecessors whom he admired most and whose actions he obviously sought to emulate were Osei Tutu and Opoku Ware. The former conquered Denkyira and thereby acquired the note for the rent of Elmina Castle. The latter conquered Akyem and the Ga kingdom and won the notes for all the European castles in Accra. The acquisition of the notes then held by the Fante rulers must have proved an irresistible attraction for this ambitious and proud descendant of Osei Tutu and Opoku Ware. The very fact that in all his negotiations with the British, Osei Bonsu insisted on being given the notes held by the Fante rulers, and also that he sent out administrators to Fante to ensure its full incorporation into the empire, shows that he was indeed following in the steps of his two great predecessors.

Shortly after the arrival, in February 1824, of the news of the final and decisive victory of his army over the combined forces of Wassa, Denkyira, Fante and, for the first time, a British contingent, Osei Bonsu died in Kumasi after a short illness. His death coincided with the pinnacle of Asante power and greatness, due largely to his own organizing ability, diplomatic skill and bravery. He certainly deserves the title of 'the great', and was easily the foremost of the nineteenth-century Asante kings – a most worthy successor of Osei Tutu and Opoku Ware.

Decline of Asante power

However, by 1874, only fifty years after the death of Osei Bonsu, the Asante empire had completely broken up. All the southern states had first reasserted their independence and then lost it again to the British who formed them into a Crown colony; the northern states had also declared themselves independent. Indeed, the Asante empire had shrunk to that area formerly occupied by metropolitan Asante alone, and even that was in a very much weakened and totally demoralized condition. What then brought about this unexpected turn of events? The collapse of Asante between 1824 and 1874 was due mainly to the weakness of the Asante provincial system of administration and above all to the intervention of the British.

It seems clear that despite the work of Osei Kwadwo and Osei Bonsu, the Asante system of provincial administration never became effective. The vassal states were never fully incorporated into the empire. The Golden Stool never acquired any significance in their eyes; and their desire to regain control over their own affairs remained as strong in the nineteenth century as it was in the eighteenth. The continued allegiance of all of them to the Asantehene depended, therefore, as it always had, on the military strength of metropolitan Asante. Unfortunately for Asante, this force binding the two parts of the empire together was destroyed between 1824 and 1874, and with it the empire itself.

A drawing of the British mission to the Asantehene's court in 1824. This drawing is, of course, not accurate but was done to please British magazine readers before photography was invented

The main reason for the destruction of this military strength was the series of defeats inflicted on the Asante by the British and their allies in 1824, 1826 and 1874. Indeed, from 1824 onwards, the wars between the Asante and their southern subjects became primarily wars between the Asante and the British. It is necessary to examine the causes of these wars.

As far as the Asante were concerned, their main preoccupation after 1824, as before, was to preserve their great empire. Osei Yaw Akoto, who succeeded Osei Bonsu, launched the expedition of 1826 with a view to crushing the rebellion of the southern tributary states. Though, as a result of the Maclean treaty of 1831 which will be discussed later, Osei Yaw was compelled to agree to the independence of all the southern states except Elmina, neither he nor any of his successors ever abandoned the hope of winning these territories back. Indeed, in March 1873, almost half a century later, Kofi Karikari, the then Asantehene, told the British that the only step that would appease him would be the restoration of the Denkyira, the Akyem and the Assin back to their former position as his subjects. Particularly uncompromising was the Asante hold on Elmina, and this was for sentimental as well as political reasons. Elmina was the only one of the southern states whose acquisition was associated with the revered Osei Tutu, and for that reason, no Asantehene was ever prepared to abandon it. This sentimental attachment was strengthened by the more practical consideration that it was only their hold on Elmina that ensured them a regular supply of guns and powder on which, in turn, depended the very survival of even metropolitan Asante. There is absolutely no doubt that the Asante invasions of the coast between 1869 and 1873 were primarily to stop the British from taking possession of Elmina from the Dutch. From the Asante point of view, then, these wars were for the revival and preservation of their empire.

What about the British? They became directly involved in these age-long conflicts between the Asante and their southern subjects for three main reasons. The first reason was precisely the same eighteenth-century one of self-preservation and security already discussed. The Asante did in fact occupy the entire coastal area during the first two decades of the nineteenth century. But this was not because the British welcomed it, but because they were too weak to resist it. However, in 1821, partly to see that the slave trade was effectively suppressed and that trade in natural products was developed, and partly to ensure the promotion of western education and civilization, the British government assumed direct responsibility for the administration of the forts in Ghana. Because of this, the British felt strong enough – or thought they were – to drive the Asante from the coast, and therefore began their active campaigns in 1824.

The second reason was economic. The British merchants on the coast had become convinced by the third decade of the nineteenth century that if

An imaginary British drawing of an Asante chief receiving warning of British approach. British illustrators of this period wanted to excite their public with such things as skulls and 'Juju'. They were not troubled if these things did not exist in fact !

Asante power could be broken, a vast field for commerce would be open to them. As one of them wrote to his brother in London in April 1823, 'We could then have direct and free access and intercourse with the Bontookos in fact with Kong and leading from there, with Timbuctoo, Houssa, etc.'

The third reason was humanitarian. Most of the British officials and traders who were interested in the introduction of western education and Christianity into Ghana were also convinced that necessary measures could never be put into effect until Asante power was destroyed or humbled.

The fourth and last reason for the active intervention of the British was the contempt that most of them on the coast had for the Asante and their institutions. It was, for example, the contempt that Sir Charles Macarthy had for the Asante, whose king he constantly referred to as 'barbarian', coupled with the pressure on him by the local British merchants that led to his rash and ill-fated entry into the Asante-Denkyira wars of 1823-24. Similarly it was the contempt that the British Governor had for Asante law and custom that led him to refuse to hand over an Asante refugee to the Asantehene, an action which precipitated the Asante invasion of the coast in 1863.

It was certainly with a view to driving back the Asante from the southern districts, of humbling the Asante and of gaining access to the markets beyond Asante that the British took to the battlefield in 1824, 1826, 1863 and in 1874.

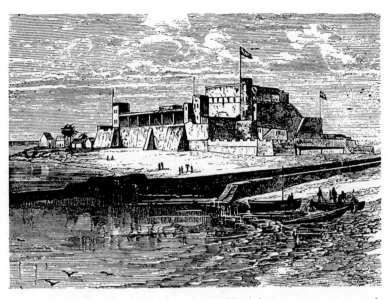

A general view of Elmina Castle from the sea in 1873. This is from a contemporary engraving

As we have seen, the first expedition of February 1824 ended disastrously, but in July 1824 and again in 1826, the British inflicted decisive defeats on the Asante. In 1873, they not only beat back the Asante invasion but also drove them right back to Kumasi which they entered and burnt in 1874. These defeats definitely gave the Asante military power a blow from which it never recovered. It is significant that as soon as news of the Asante defeat of July 1824 reached Cape Coast the southern vassal states began to assert their independence, and the Asante defeat at Dodowa ended their vassalage. In the Maclean treaty of 1831 and the Fomena Treaty of 1874 signed between the Asante and the British, the former were compelled formally to recognize the independence of all the states south of the Pra. The Brong states to the north and north-west as well as Dagomba and Gonja also took advantage of the weakened power of the Asante to break away. In addition these defeats shook even metropolitan Asante. Some of the member states like Dwaben and Adansi asserted their independence of Kumasi, while Kokofu, Bekwai and Nsuta became disaffected. It was quite clearly a dismembered, disunited and demoralized remnant of an empire that Mensa Bonsu inherited in 1874.

However, far from despairing and reconciling themselves to the collapse of their empire, Mensa Bonsu and his two successors Kwaku Dua II (1884) and Agyeman Prempe (1888-1931) set themselves the task of reuniting metropolitan Asante and even winning back provincial Asante. Mensa Bonsu, as one would expect, tackled the problems of metropolitan Asante first. By diplomacy and personal appeals, he soon won back Kokofu and Bekwai. However, the Dwaben, who were being supported by the British, rejected these peaceful overtures, and even went on to persuade the neighbouring states of Afigyaase, Asokore and Oyoko to join them. In October 1875, therefore, Mensa Bonsu invaded Dwaben and routed her forces. As a result of this defeat, the Dwaben and their allies migrated for the second time to Akyem. There, on a stretch of land bought for them by the British, they founded new towns which they named after their old towns in Asante – hence the present towns New Dwaben or Koforidua, Afigyaase, Asokore and Oyoko in southern Ghana. This victory greatly strengthened Mensa Bonsu's position as well as the authority of Kumasi and the Golden Stool. However, in 1875, probably with a view to winning the friendship of the British, Mensa Bonsu abandoned the use of force in favour of diplomatic missions. He dispatched one to Adansi, sent another to Gyaman in 1878 under a European, Karl Neilson; the next year he supported Banda in her struggle against Gyaman. Banda was defeated in 1882, and it was Mensa Bonsu's refusal to raise an army to assist the Banda and reconquer Gyaman, coupled with his avarice, that led to his deposition in February 1883.

Prempe I

The rule of Prempe I

This deposition led to a series of civil wars among the metropolitan Asante states and the Kumasi chiefs which were not brought to an end until Kwaku Dua III or, as he became better known, Agyeman Prempe I, was sworn in as the Asantehene in March 1888. By the time of his accession the fortunes of Asante had clearly reached the lowest possible ebb. Taking advantage of the anarchy in Kumasi, the Brong states had consolidated their independence; farther south, the Dwaben were still in Akyem though a member of their royal family, Yaw Sapon, who was captured during the war and sent to Kumasi, had been recognized as the Dwabenhene; the Adansi had been chased south of the Pra after their unsuccessful war with Bekwai in 1886 and, as if to add to Prempe's problems, the states that had not supported him during his contest for the Stool, Kokofu, Mampong and Nsuta, rose up in rebellion soon after his enthronement. It looked, then, as if even the very creation of Osei Tutu, the hard core of the former Asante empire, was at long last really cracking up.

However, this did not happen for two reasons. The first was that the magnetic pull of the Golden Stool proved irresistible in the end. It should not be forgotten that most of the troubles and civil wars that raged in Kumasi were the result of clashes of personalities and interests rather than of withdrawal of allegiance to the Golden Stool. The second and even more important factor, however, was that Agyeman Prempe, the last of the nineteenth-century rulers of Asante, like the first, was a real political genius, a natural leader of men and an able commander, and he was able to avert the coming disaster.

How did he accomplish this? He used two main weapons: diplomacy and war. His first concern was to repair the cracks in the core of the confederate states, and he began this by attacking and defeating Kokofu with the assistance of Bekwai. He then turned his attention northwards and in November 1888 his army successfully crushed the Mampong and Nsuta revolts. The Mamponghene sought refuge in Atebubu but most of his subjects deserted him and returned home. With the support of the Asantehene, they deposed him in favour of his younger brother who promptly returned to Prempe's fold. Nsuta also joined Prempe. It seems then that within a matter of months of his accession, he succeeded in repairing most of the cracks in the Confederacy, and no sooner had he done this than he turned his attention outwards. He wrote a letter to the British governor in November 1889 objecting to the extension of British protection to Kwahu which he claimed was his. He followed this letter up in July 1890 with a large mission to the governor to ask for the governor's assistance in re-establishing his authority over the old outer ring of states, and demanded the repatriation of all the Asante refugees in the British Crown colony. He also appealed directly to those Dwaben and the Kokofu who had also moved across the Pra after their defeat in 1888, to come home, and most of the Dwaben people began to return. The British had by this time become so alarmed by this steady revival of the Confederacy and by French activities in modern Ivory Coast that in 1890 they declared a protectorate over Atebubu and, in March 1891, sent an officer to Kumasi to invite the Asantehene to place his country under British protection. Prempe, as one would expect, rejected this invitation politely but firmly. To quote his own words, 'My kingdom of Asante will never commit itself to any such policy. Asante must remain independent as of old, at the same time to be friendly with all white men. I do not write this with a boastful spirit but in the clear sense of its meaning.' After dispatching this reply to the British, he turned his attention to the north-west with the view of subduing the Brong states. In 1892 and 1893, he attacked and defeated the Nkoranza and their allies the Mo and the Abease, and only the timely arrival of a British contingent under Sir Francis Scott saved Atebubu. In the south, the Kokofuhene Asibe also decided in 1893 to return to Asante but significantly he was prevented from doing so by his arrest and detention in Accra by the British. In March 1894, Prempe felt that he was so firmly entrenched, and that the cracks in the Confederacy were so fully sealed, that he even rejected the British request for the establishment of a resident in Kumasi for fear that it would inevitably lead to the establishment of a British protectorate over his rapidly reviving empire. Three months later, full of hope and confidence, Prempe was formally installed on the Golden Stool with great pomp and pageantry.

The exile of Prempe and establishment of British rule

This ceremony, however, marked the height of Prempe's achievements. Barely twenty months later, in March 1896, he, his mother, his father and uncles, together with a number of the amanhene and the Kumasi divisional chiefs, were arrested in Kumasi by the British, detained first in Elmina Castle and then exiled to Sierra Leone where they arrived in January 1897. As soon as Prempe was out of the way, Asante was declared a British protectorate and a resident was stationed in Kumasi as the representative, under the governor, of the Queen. This effectively forestalled the French and the Germans who were closing in on Asante from the modern Ivory Coast and Togo respectively.

Deprived of their leader but still confident of his restoration in the very near future, the Asante would not have reacted very quickly had Governor Hodgson not added insult to injury by demanding the surrender of, and instituting a search for, the Golden Stool in March 1900. The Golden Stool was, and still is, the one sacred object that the Asante cannot part with, and their answer to the governor's demand was an armed rebellion in April under the leadership of Yaa Asantewaa, the Queen Mother of Edweso, and the siege of the governor in the Kumasi fort. But this rebellion was crushed and though the British failed to gain possession of the Golden Stool, Asante was formally annexed to the British Crown. In August 1900, with a view to quenching the last embers of hope of the restoration of Prempe and of resistance in Asante, the British removed Prempe and his party of fifty-five away from Freetown on the West African Coast to the far away Seychelles Islands, whence he was not to return to Ghana until 1924.

Thus the nineteenth century, which opened with the Asante as the rulers of virtually the whole of Ghana, closed with both Asante and all her former subjects firmly under the yoke of British imperialism.

10 Sierra Leone 1787-1914: mother of British West Africa

A black settler colony, 1787-1807

The colony of Sierra Leone was inspired by the humanitarian opposition to slavery and was nurtured by the British determination to end the slave trade in West Africa. Sierra Leone was founded in the late eighteenth century by three groups of black settlers from England, Nova Scotia and Jamaica. During the American Revolution a number of Negro slaves and freemen fought for the British empire. Following the defeat of the British, black loyalists along with their white compatriots fled either to England or Nova Scotia as refugees from American persecution. In England and Nova Scotia life was hard for both black and white loyalists but particularly so for the blacks, because of the unwillingness of the white population to permit their entry into society or recognize in practice the freedom and equality which British law granted them in theory. Granville Sharp in co-operation with the British government undertook to send 400 of the unwanted blacks of England to establish a colony in Africa. In 1787 the colonists settled on the Sierra Leone peninsula and named their pioneer camp, Granville Town, in honour of Granville Sharp. The expense of the new colony was too heavy for Sharp to bear personally, and a group of merchant-humanitarians organized the Sierra Leone Company of which both Sharp and Wilberforce were directors.

Once the black loyalists of Nova Scotia (nicknamed Nova Scarcity because of the hardships of pioneer life) heard of the new colony, they sent one of their number to England to interview the directors of the Sierra Leone Company. Their delegate was Thomas Peters, an Egba who had been sold into slavery in America, escaped and joined the British army in the revolution and fled with the loyalists to Nova Scotia. Peters met the company directors who promised his people freedom from discrimination and free land in the new colony. As a result about 1,000 black loyalists left Nova Scotia and arrived in Sierra Leone in 1792. The third pioneer group were the Maroons, free Negroes from Jamaica who had revolted from slavery a hundred years before and maintained their independence in the mountains, until conquered in 1796 by the British who deported a large number to Nova Scotia. They requested transfer to Africa and arrived in Sierra Leone in 1800.

The problems of survival were those usually experienced by pioneer colonists whether in Canada, Australia or Africa plus others unique to the west coast. Some of the colonists arrived at the beginning of the rains. Many died of malaria. They did not know how to farm in Africa. The food crops they knew would not grow and they did not know how to eat the crops Africans planted. Initially most of their food was imported from England. Many thought in terms of the large American-type plantations but neither would the local people – the Temne – part with large tracts of land nor could the necessary labour be found to work plantations without introducing a slave system which was distasteful to the colonists. The Napoleonic wars between Britain and France resulted in the destruction of the supply ships from Europe and, in 1794, the French navy destroyed the new settlement of Freetown. In addition, the Temne, like most West Africans, feared settlers. They did not intend to sell their land permanently and gave it to the settlers 'for use only' which by Temne law made the settlers mere tenants. The settlers believed they owned the land outright. As a result of this dispute

24 *The founding of Sierra Leone*

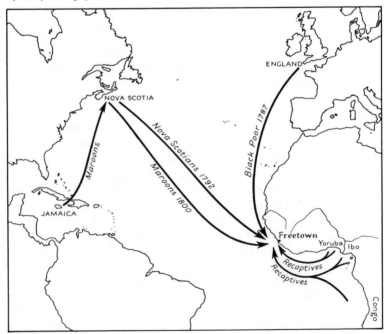

25 *Land allotment in the colony of Sierra Leone*

the Temne almost wiped out the colony in 1789. In 1800 when British soldiers arrived with the Maroons, the Temne began to realize the seriousness of the threat and again tried to uproot the colony.

The settlers had many complaints about company rule. British officials, soldiers and sailors were either patronizing or racially discriminating and this enraged the colonists. They had hardly suffered so much for the sake of freedom in America only to allow the British to establish a master-servant relationship in Africa. The company governor was autocratic, failed to provide the land promised to each family and imposed land rents where the settlers had been promised free land.

In 1800 a section of the Nova Scotians rebelled. A larger section, while opposed to force, remained neutral and unwilling to support the company because of their grievances against the administration. The rebels put up a public placard declaring a new code of laws which meant, in effect, the founding of a rival and virtually independent government. The governor and his few supporters were in serious danger of being overthrown when a large shipload of settlers, the Maroons, who came originally from Jamaica, arrived with an escort of soldiers and overpowered the rebels. When the company found that profits were not what it expected, it welcomed the British government's action in taking over Sierra Leone as a Crown colony in 1807. Although 3,000 black settlers had landed in Sierra Leone only half of them were alive in 1807, the rest having died, the victims of pioneer life.

The recaptives, 1807-50

When the British navy decided to patrol the West African coast to stop the slave trade, the colonists' new settlement of Freetown became its headquarters. The captured slavers were brought to Sierra Leone and their cargoes of slaves when freed became known as liberated Africans or 'recaptives'. The little colony began to receive an annual influx of hundreds and occasionally thousands of recaptives. Altogether 40,000 were settled in Sierra Leone and the population grew rapidly from 2,000 in 1807 to 11,000 in 1825, and to 40,000 in 1850. Sierra Leone became one of the great cultural 'melting pots' of the world, its population being a blend of peoples with different customs, religions and languages originating from every people and state in West Africa from Senegal to Angola.

Governor Charles Macarthy (1814-24) saw an opportunity to spread western education and Christianity among the recaptives who were uprooted and cut off from their own societies. The settlers were to be the models of educated Christians which the recaptives were expected to imitate. The British government would provide the money and the missionaries would be the agents of this cultural and religious change. Macarthy began systematically to settle the recaptives in villages in which the school and church were the prominent institutions. Most of the villages were given English names. Nothing could be more British than Leicester, Regent, Bathurst, Charlotte, Kent, York and Wellington. Two villages founded by discharged West

Landing the recaptives at Freetown. From a contemporary print

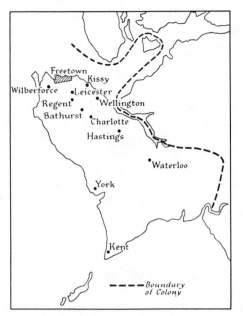

26 *The colony of Sierra Leone during the 1830's*

Indian soldiers, Waterloo and Hastings, recalled British military history. Africa, however, was remembered in Kissy (named after the Kissi people), Kru Town and Congo Town. Not all the recaptives were settled in the farming villages. Some were either recruited into the army, the Royal African Corps, or apprenticed (adopted) into the homes of the settlers who educated them and gave them their own surnames.

Initially the settlers looked down upon the recaptives as crude and illiterate heathens. However, the recaptives took to education and Christianity with zeal, left the village farms, moved into Freetown and built their mud houses alongside the elegant storey houses of the settlers. At first they were lowly pedlars, hawkers, tailors, barbers, carpenters or masons, but soon they began trading in the interior, operating respectable shops and buying or building storey houses like the settlers. By 1839 two recaptives were wealthy enough to purchase auctioned slave ships for their coastal trading operations. The recaptives worked hard, lived cheaply, co-operated in wholesale purchases and soon were out-selling both European and settler merchants. Many became wealthy and educated their children in secondary schools in Freetown and even in universities in England. As the children of both groups inter-married the distinction between recaptive and settler slowly disappeared. The recaptives were not assimilated by the settlers, rather the Creoles, who emerged as a distinct group by 1850, were a blending of settlers and recaptives, the proud inheritors of European, American and numerous African cultures.

The Creole culture which flowered after 1850 was Christian but with an emphasis upon the events of the life-cycle, birth, baptism, circumcision, marriage and death – reflecting the influence of African religions. The Creole social system was built on monogamy like European society but ties of relationship in the extended family were strong, the wealthy sharing their money, food and home with the less fortunate as in African societies. Creole food was a blend of West Indian, French and African cookery. The Creoles developed their own language, Krio, which has been aptly described as the English language Africanized. It is particularly suited to describe African society and life and has a melodious liquid tongue which eliminates the harshness of English. The numerous cultural strands which make up the Creoles are best seen in Krio, which is English and Yoruba enriched by Portuguese, Spanish and French vocabulary and containing elements of Temne, Mandinka, Ibo, Susu and Arabic.

The apogee of Creole civilization, 1850-98

By 1860 a greater percentage of children were attending school in Sierra Leone than in England. This magnificent effort was achieved by the co-operation of the government, the missionary societies and the Creoles, many of whom went into debt to educate their children. The school system was completed by the addition of secondary schools for boys (1845) and girls, and a teacher training college, Fourah Bay (1827), which in 1876 achieved University College status. The educational system poured forth a stream of teachers, clergymen, doctors, lawyers and writers producing many of the 'firsts' of the professional class of West Africa; John Thorpe the first African lawyer 1850, J. B. Horton the first doctor 1859, S. A. Crowther the first bishop 1864, Samuel Lewis the first knight 1896, as well as the first newspaper editor and owner and the first to be granted Cambridge and Oxford degrees.

In the church and government Creoles pioneered the path which future generations of West Africans would follow. In 1861 the Anglicans withdrew their missionaries from Sierra Leone and turned the entire work over to Creole clergymen under the semi-independent Native Pastorate Church. Creoles had always sat in the Governor's Council but in the 1850's the growing maturity of the society brought forth agitation for increased representation. In 1863 a new constitution introduced executive and legislative councils in both of which Creoles were represented. In 1872 when Creoles held almost half of the Senior civil service posts, Governor Pope-Hennessy maintained that there were enough qualified Creoles to replace the entire European staff. In 1893 Freetown was made a municipality with its own

Freetown, c. 1851

mayor. By the end of the century Creoles formed an educated society, proud of their achievements, who voiced their views in a vigorous and flourishing press and took a prominent part in religious and secular government.

Agriculture was an exception to the story of success. The original settlers worked hard growing pepper, cotton and cinnamon on a large scale. The two commodities Europe wanted, however, sugar and cotton, did not grow well nor could the settlers really compete in the world market without the use of slave labour. The recaptives first turned to farming but although they understood African agriculture, they could not achieve a respectable standard of living. The recaptives like the settlers were ambitious and like them turned from farming to trade. The villages declined as the young people left for Freetown which became a city of shopkeepers.

Neither Europeans nor settlers understood tropical agriculture. New techniques introduced were those practised in Europe which proved disastrous under tropical conditions. The soil was poor and land limited. The best method was shifting cultivation but this required more land than the colony possessed and as recaptives continued to arrive the acreage per farmer decreased. Lack of capital was not a vital cause of failure, for a number of wealthy Creoles invested in plantations which failed. The choice was either trade, the professions or descent into dismal poverty. The Creoles chose to overstrain their resources in educating their children and to search for new commercial opportunities far from Freetown, north to Senegal, up the Niger to Nupe and south to the Congo either as independent merchants or as agents for European firms.

Necessity made the Creoles an adventurous and exploring race. Their

The Sierra Leone senior civil service, 1885, showing its inter-racial composition

traders first spread out into the northern rivers, the interior and the Sherbro. They purchased condemned slave ships and traded farther down the coast. In about 1839 recaptives began to return to Egbaland in search both of their relatives and work so that by 1851 there were 3,000 Egba recaptives living in Abeokuta. By the 1880's Creoles were operating businesses in Bathurst, Monrovia, Cape Coast, Accra, Lome, Porto Novo, Lagos, Abeokuta, on the Niger and in the Cameroons. These 'sons abroad' called upon Sierra Leone to send missionaries and teachers. Some Europeans were sent but it was the Creole teachers and clergymen far more than the Europeans who, in responding to these appeals, were the pioneers of education and Christianity along the coast. In the Niger Delta Bishop Crowther led an all-Creole staff which christianized the city states and created a self-supporting, self-governing Delta Church before the end of the century. Creoles were pioneers among the Ibo and Yoruba. In 1875 the Lagos Anglican churches were organized into a pastorate on the Sierra Leone model almost totally operated by Creole clergy. Even as late as 1900 Creole clergy formed the majority of the missionaries among the Yoruba. Everywhere Creoles held the prominent church positions, an Anglican bishop, superindendents in Anglican and Methodist churches, a colonial chaplain in the Gambia, archdeacons on the Niger. It was the Creoles who pioneered the independent African churches among the Yoruba.

As the British expanded their empire in West Africa they were dependent upon the Creoles to fill the junior and many of the senior civil service posts. Creoles sat in the executive and legislative councils of Ghana, Gambia and Nigeria. In Ghana Creoles were judges of the supreme court, Colonial Treasurer, Solicitor-General, Postmaster General, Chief Medical Officer, district officers and once acting-Governor; in Nigeria the Registrar of the Supreme Court, Colonial Treasurer and Postmaster General were Creoles.

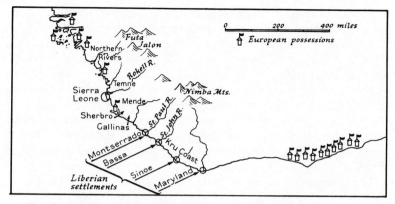

27 *The colony of Sierra Leone and the Liberian settlements, about 1865*

In the Gambia two successive Chief Justices and in Abeokuta both the President and Secretary-General of the Egba United Board of Management were Creoles. In Liberia one Creole was elected mayor of Monrovia and another, President of the Republic. Under the Niger Company and in Lagos and Dakar they held responsible positions as marine engineers. In Fernando Po a Creole prospered as a cocoa plantation owner. Everywhere along the coast they were the first or among the first clergymen, lawyers, doctors and newspaper owners. As late as 1925, forty-four of Nigeria's fifty-six barristers were of Creole descent.

Freetown became the hub of the West Coast. The Creole 'sons abroad' came and went on leave, and returned to Freetown to marry. Freetown newspapers were read all along the coast, more copies being sold outside than inside Sierra Leone. The 'sons abroad' sent money back to their relatives. The wealthy endowed charities, built schools, churches and public buildings which gave Freetown the appearance of comfort and wealth. Freetown was the centre and the Creoles the agents of a unique fusion of European and African culture which inspired Africans to imitate them. Thus Sierra Leone was the mother of Christianity, western education and culture, and the English language in British West Africa.

Although the major Creole group was Christian there were Muslims as well. Muhammad Shitta Bey, born in Waterloo of Yoruba recaptives, was typical, except in his religious conviction, of hundreds of other Creole sons abroad. As a child he emigrated to Badagri with his parents. As a man he traded on the Niger from his business headquarters in Lagos. When he made his money he did not forget Freetown but gave generously towards the rebuilding of Fourah Bay mosque in 1892. In Lagos he spent £4,000 in building a mosque which still bears his name. Shitta Bey was the outstand-

139

ing Muslim Creole of his day. The Sultan of Turkey in recognition of his good works awarded him a decoration and the title 'Bey'.

Freetown was also an intellectual centre in the nineteenth century, the 'Athens of West Africa'. Sierra Leone's 'sons abroad' sent their children back to Freetown for their secondary education until grammar schools were established closer to home. Some, as in Lagos and Accra, were founded by the Creoles themselves. Creole children along with the children of the rising African educated class along the coast still returned to Freetown for teacher training, divinity and university degrees. As a result the largest proportion of the student body of Fourah Bay College was drawn from outside Sierra Leone.

Creole culture was creative. In linguistics J. C. Taylor's work on Ibo, C. Paul's on Nupe and P. J. Williams on Igbirra are less well known than Bishop Crowther's *Grammar and Vocabulary of the Yoruba Language*, 1843. In medical research Dr. J. B. Horton wrote a number of books on tropical medicine, the most important of which, *The Medical Topography of the West Coast of Africa*, was published in 1860. Dr. J. F. Easmon, head of the Ghana Medical Service, researched on blackwater fever and Dr. Oguntola Sapara studied the Sopono smallpox society of Lagos. In history, in 1868 A. B. C.

Shitta Bey mosque, Lagos

Sibthorpe published his *History and Geography of Sierra Leone*, and J. B. Horton his *West African Countries and Peoples*. Samuel Johnson, son of a pioneer Creole missionary, completed his classic *History of the Yoruba* in 1897.

Between 1850 and 1898 the Creoles (called Sierra Leonians by Africans along the coast), although a very small community, excelled in every field of endeavour open to them, trade, religion, the professions, administration and the creative arts. The small Creole settlements spread far along the coast were the pioneers of Christianity and western education, the interpreters of western culture to Africans and of African culture to Europeans. They found their focal point and unity in their common attachment to Freetown, which in the last fifty years of the nineteenth century shone with a brilliance and held an importance quite out of proportion to its small size. These were the golden years, the apogee of Creole civilization.

The Temne-Mende war of 1898

Freetown, the city of shopkeepers, depended on the interior trade for its prosperity. During the nineteenth century Creole merchants had frequently requested that the British government extend its authority in the interior. In 1885 when the French were beginning to expand, the Freetown merchants' association petitioned the British government to save the city's hinterland. The government was reluctant because of the expense and because there were few English merchants involved. Sierra Leonians pleaded unsuccessfully for support for Samori, but once he was driven east there was little of the hinterland not under the French flag. In 1896 Governor Cardew proclaimed a protectorate over the area which is modern Sierra Leone and established an armed police to keep the peace.

Sierra Leone had to bear the full expense of the new administration because the British government gave no subsidy as it did for Northern Nigeria. Governor Cardew (1894-1900) established the cheapest administration possible, indirect rule, where the chiefs continued to govern, supervised by district commissioners and financed by an annual five shillings tax on every house in the interior. The house tax caused war. Cardew blamed the Creoles in the interior for it, accused them of disloyalty and called it the Hut Tax war. The Creoles blamed it on misgovernment and called it Cardew's war. Although the special investigator sent from London condemned Cardew and agreed with the Creoles, the British government supported Cardew and his suspicions of Creole loyalty.

To the Temne and Mende it was a war of independence. They had grievances against Cardew's police, occasionally recruited from runaway slaves, who took vengeance on their old masters. Chiefs were installed who held no traditional right; one police officer installed his mistress. Chiefs were not respected but were imprisoned, handcuffed and publicly flogged. The people suspected the merchants of price-fixing. They resented missionary teaching, which undermined respect for their institutions, and looked upon both Creole and white missionaries as government agents because they urged them to pay the tax. While these things indicated that British rule was unlikely to be enlightened they were not the real issue. When the chiefs had promised Cardew friendship in return for protection they had not suspected this meant the surrender of independence. They saw the tax as tribute which meant subjection. Thus the tax was the symbol of their loss of sovereignty and the 'revolt' of 1898 was a war to preserve their independence.

In 1898 the Temne chief, Bai Bureh, refused to pay the tax and the police opened fire on his people. Bai Bureh fought a 'gentleman's war', attacking the police and army but not molesting European or Creole civilians. The Mende were organized in small political units with no chiefs of the stature of Bai Bureh. Their military effort was directed by the Poro, a secret religious, educational and trading society with headquarters at Bumpe. The Poro waged 'total war', killing anyone connected with the Freetown government, Creoles, whites or Mende who wore European-style dress. The Creoles suffered most, over 1,000 men, women and children being slaughtered until the Poro ordered that women be spared.

The Temne-Mende war indicated the impossible position of the Creoles as interpreters between Africans and Europeans. While Cardew was blaming them for encouraging rebellion, they were being slaughtered in the interior for supporting Cardew's administration. The Creole-owned Freetown press had repeatedly warned Cardew about his interior policy and tax. When Bai Bureh gave himself up and was brought as a prisoner to Freetown he was welcomed by the Creoles as a conquering hero. While Cardew interpreted these actions as disloyalty they were in fact Creole efforts to be spokesmen for the grievances of the Temne-Mende people. Meanwhile, in the interior the Mende considered Creoles 'black Englishmen' as arrogant and as much a threat to their independence as the whites. The Mende were less impressed by the efforts of the Freetown press to plead their cause than they were by Creole advice in the interior to pay the tax. In the interior the Creoles were killed because they tried to interpret European actions to Africans while in Freetown they were despised because they sought to interpret African feelings to Europeans.

It was a sad irony that as a result of the war the government began to support the interior chiefs and to encourage them to despise Creole culture. The war of 1898 became the excuse for the British to begin systematic discrimination against the Creoles in all fields. It was the end of the Anglo-Creole partnership in the exploitation and development of West Africa.

Decline of the Creoles, 1898-1914

It was Cardew's policy to keep Creoles out of the protectorate. He rejected J. C. Parkes' (Creole head of the Department of Native Affairs) plan for a scheme of indirect rule to be supervised by Creole officers. Supported by the London government he laid down the policy that only Englishmen should administer the interior. The Colonial office felt it was not unfair that Englishmen should benefit from the fruits of their conquest. Creole influence was to be kept out, the Mende and Temne were to remain uncreolized, unsophisticated and unspoilt, and for the first forty years of British rule they peacefully stagnated. As late as 1931 there was not even a road connecting Freetown with the interior over which modern ideas might pass. Education was 'not to be that given to Creoles' nor were Creole teachers to be employed. It was designed to train the Mende and Temne for tribal life, not for senior posts nor as leaders of protest or nationalist-type movements. It was to strengthen tribal not national loyalties. Rather than narrowing the gulf which history had already created between the Creole and interior people it sought to make it wider and deeper, delaying the time when Sierra Leone could hope to emerge as a nation and follow Canada, Australia, New Zealand and South Africa into 'dominion' status.

Creole merchants began to lose their place in commerce. French conquests diverted the nineteenth-century caravans of ivory, gold dust and cattle from Freetown to Conakry. The railway, begun in 1895, reached Pendembu in 1908 and opened up a large palm-oil bearing area. Prices rose under the heavy demand in Europe before 1914 for palm-oil to make explosives and margarine. Individual European traders were replaced by large European firms with which Creoles could not compete. Originally wholesalers, the firms moved into retailing and with their capital resources drove the Creoles out of a sector of the economy they had controlled for seventy years. In the interior Creoles were treated as foreigners and forbidden to buy and invest in land, the customary starting point of any commercial class. In the 1890's Syrians and Lebanese appeared as hawkers of imitation coral on the streets of Freetown. Soon the 'Corals', as they were called, set up small stalls and later larger shops which displaced the smaller Creole traders. Had the Creoles controlled their government they would have adopted protective measures against the firms and probably banned the Syrians and Lebanese just as Canada and Australia in the same years and for similar reasons, were banning oriental immigrants. By 1914, with European firms all over West Africa moving down from the top and Syrians and Lebanese moving up from the bottom of the economy, Creole merchants were squeezed out.

Once the partition was complete the French and Germans expelled the Creole traders from their West coast colonies on the excuse that they were

British sympathizers. Creole merchants in the northern rivers (Guinea), Togoland, Dahomey and the Cameroons lost their businesses. As early as the 1880's Creoles had been eliminated from the middle Niger where they had operated as independent merchants or as commercial agents of the Royal Niger Company. The independents were excluded by the licensing laws of the Company and the employees by the Europeanization of its staff.

Creoles began to meet similar troubles in the missions. Anglicans and Methodists replaced their Creole archdeacons and superintendents by Europeans. A European succeeded Bishop Crowther and no Creole or African was again consecrated to this high office for sixty years. On the middle Niger the entire Creole staff was dismissed and similar action prevented in the Delta only when the Christians of the city-states threatened to leave the Anglican Church if it was attempted.

It was Cardew's policy that every government department in Sierra Leone must be headed by a European assisted by a European. Creoles were replaced upon death or retirement. While in 1892 fifty per cent of the senior service posts were held by Creoles, in 1917 the percentage had dropped to ten. Now that malaria was controlled the 'white man's grave' which had earlier killed 109 Anglican missionaries in twenty-five years, became rather pleasant,

28 *Sierra Leone's 'sons abroad', 1840-1914*

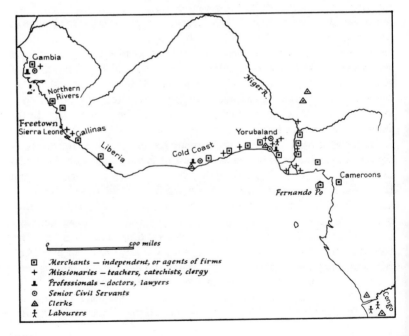

29 *Sierra Leone: the colony and protectorate after 1896*

especially with a pension after only twenty years' service. Sitting high and cool on their reservation on the mountain above Freetown the British began to talk of their imperial mission, shunned social mixing with the Creoles and were placed above the law by being exempted from trial by Creole juries. The European population rose steadily and although many office holders were capable men, others got jobs because they were unemployable at home.

Cardew's policy became general practice throughout British West Africa. By 1911 there was not one Creole left in the judiciary or executive council of any British colony. In 1902 when up to twenty Creoles had qualified in medicine African doctors were excluded from the government medical services. When the military forces of British West Africa were united it was policy that the men were to be illiterate, the officers European. There was no place for the Creoles. It could not be disguised that by 1914 the majority of Europeans viewed with disfavour, jealousy and hidden fear the Creoles who were the product of their own nineteenth-century efforts. Europeans were extremely irrational, some despised the Creoles because they were not completely English, because they clung to certain African customs and beliefs, others advised them to go back to the bush and become 'real' Africans.

Sierra Leone's decline was rapid. Cut off from an extensive hinterland, with the large European firms and Syrian-Lebanese traders sending their profits out, rather than investing them in the colony, the economy decayed. With few prepared to employ the graduates of the school system the incentive to sacrifice for education disappeared. Economically weakened the Creoles could not maintain their elaborate educational system; the number of schools and scholars and their standards declined. Enrolment at Fourah Bay dropped so much that by 1910 the Anglicans considered closing it down.

The Creoles became bitter and defensive, clinging to their culture but losing faith in their own moral and spiritual worth. Very critical of themselves among themselves, they became super-sensitive in front of Europeans, attempting to defend the indefensible because Europeans used the weakness of the individual to condemn the race. A distinguished Creole, for example, from a respectable family and head of a government department embezzled £1,000 of government funds. Although his guilt was clearly evident, two successive Creole juries acquitted him. The Europeans, who made little effort to understand the society with which they were dealing, used such incidents to 'prove' the inability of the Creole to hold responsible positions or to govern themselves.

Creoles became keenly aware of the weaknesses of their society in dealing with Europeans. This bred insecurity, the insecurity of the knowledge that anyone who sought a high and responsible position under colonialism must be ten times better than his European competitor. Furthermore, ·Creole society which applauded the man who spent lavishly, was ill-prepared to compete in commerce with European society which applauded the man who saved carefully. Family fortunes did not pass from generation to generation and coupled with their inability to co-operate as partners to pool or accumulate capital they could not compete with European family concerns or companies whose capital was built up over generations. To this was added the educational and charitable burden of the extended family which often impoverished the wealthiest merchant or drove the successful professional into debt.

In spite of it all, the rising western-educated class in Nigeria, Ghana, Gambia and in the protectorate of Sierra Leone began to develop in ways which resembled the fusion of European and African methods and thought which was the basis of Creole culture. The Europeans treated the new group as they had the Creoles, and it was the reaction against this treatment which nurtured the nationalist movement and forced the British to give up political control in West Africa. Unfortunately the Creoles did not have the nationalist alternative, for as a small group of probably never more than 100,000 scattered all over British West Africa they could always be ignored or labelled as agitators and malcontents, unrepresentative of the millions of Africans 'happy' and 'content' under the Union Jack.

11 Liberia 1822-1914: the love of liberty kept us free

Foundation; independence; survival

Liberia, like Sierra Leone a product of the efforts to abolish slavery and the slave trade, was founded in 1822 when a few free American Negroes negotiated for land at Cape Mesurado and began the pioneer settlement, later named Monrovia. Within the next fourteen years more pioneers settled at Grand Bassa, Sinoe and Cape Palmas. But the idea of an American Negro state in Africa dated back to the foundation of the American Colonization Society, formed in 1816 by a few white Northern American clergymen and Southern slave owners, whose inspiration was a mixture of religion, economics and politics. The return of American Negroes to Africa was expected to lead the continent to Christianity, begin the expansion of American trade along the West Coast, and rid the United States of the free Negroes, who were considered undesirable citizens. Therefore among the early settlers a number were clergymen such as the Baptist, Lott Carey, and others were representatives of American firms.

For free Negroes there were two alternatives: segregation in America or repatriation to Africa. The majority of free Negroes opposed repatriation, determined to fight the battle for equality because 'America is more our country than it is the whites. It was built by the sweat of our labour.' A small minority were ready to leave. 'We love this country and its liberties if we could share them, but our freedom is partial and we have no hope that it will ever be otherwise.' The genuine supporters of Liberia were thus few. It became the Lone Star Republic, not only because its flag carried a single star but because it had few friends, either white or black. White Americans who supported the Colonization Society were not many and their aims contradictory; quarrels followed, the branch organizations broke away, and the funds of the Society dried up. Particularly after the civil war, leading American Negroes and their organizations were hostile, because they looked upon emigration to Liberia as a white excuse to banish them from the

United States. When Liberia sought independence many in the Colonization Society were happy to rid themselves of an unprofitable and embarrassing burden.

The pioneers, like their Sierra Leonian neighbours, faced African hostility, and did not get the land promised them. The death toll was frightening, especially among Mulattos (those of mixed race) and those from non-malarial areas of the United States who possessed no natural immunity. About 12,000 emigrated to Liberia, many more than the 3,000 who pioneered Sierra Leone, and, while the British navy freed 40,000 Africans in Freetown, the American navy freed only 2,000 in Monrovia. Thus, after the joining of

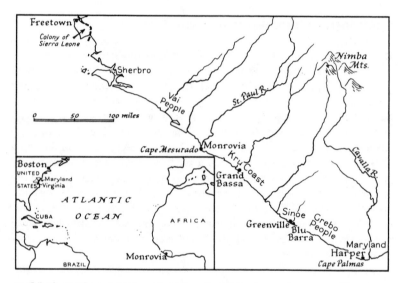

30 Liberian settlements in the early nineteenth century

the two groups of pioneers and freed slaves, the Creoles of Sierra Leone were much more African than the Americo-Liberians, who combined the culture of the American South with the puritanical religious ideas of New England, the rugged individualism of the American pioneer and a passionate desire for liberty reflected in Liberia's national motto: 'The love of Liberty brought us here.'

Almost immediately, as in Sierra Leone, the settlers complained of the arrogance and despotism of the white officials sent to govern them, and of the constitution forced on them on board the ship while crossing the Atlantic. By the constitution they swore an oath of allegiance to the Society, whose officers were given power to permit entry or deport anyone from the colony

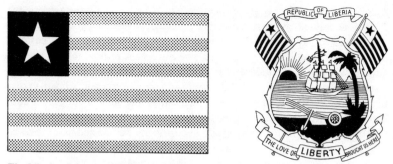

The Liberian flag and seal of the Republic

and to appoint and dismiss all officers of government. The settlers 'had seen enough of slavery', and from the first resented the Society's paternalism and the arrogance of its white officers.

Nor were the white governors particularly successful; and when they visited America and left the Negro, Elijah Johnson, in charge, the colony was quiet and peaceful. A major complaint was that the governors favoured Mulattoes over Negroes in the distribution of land. But petitions of grievance to the Society were answered by expressions of shock at the ingratitude of the colonists, and by calling them 'deluded, depraved and deserving banishment'. While Elijah Johnson sought to be a moderate and tried to compromise, Lott Carey led the agitation for reform. Since the Society did not possess a navy it could not prevent reform. A governor's advisory council and the elected lieutenant governor became more and more powerful until 1839 when a conference in Monrovia drew up a constitution of self-rule. The Society rejected it and imposed their own, whereby the governor held a veto over acts of the council and full control over land distribution. And, because all land acquired from Africans was vested in the Society, it continued

31 The growth of Liberia, 1847–1911

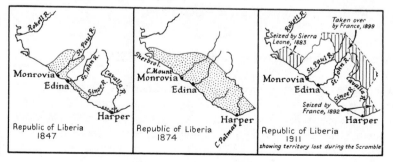

to hold final control over the settlers. But in 1841, to pacify the settlers, the Society appointed the first non-white governor, a Mulatto, Joseph Roberts.

In order to pay for its administration expenses Liberia imposed customs duties on ships trading in her ports. Some Europeans refused to pay, because Liberia was neither an independent nation nor an American colony and held a status unknown to international law. This gave Roberts a legitimate excuse to press towards independence; in a referendum the settlers supported him, and at the Monrovia Convention of 1847, a constitution, national flag and declaration of independence were adopted. Roberts was elected first president of the Republic of Liberia in 1848.

To stop the continued evasion of Liberian customs, President Roberts sought to strengthen Liberian control along the coast. When a British merchant (Harris) in the Sherbro refused to pay customs dues the Liberians seized two of his trading ships; but the British governor of Sierra Leone dispatched a gunboat to Monrovia and recovered the ships. Then, when Harris later came into conflict with the Vai people, the Liberians sent a military force to their aid. On this occasion the governor of Sierra Leone sailed into Monrovia with four gunboats and demanded a large indemnity.

During the scramble for Africa, European powers operated on the convention that areas claimed must be effectively occupied. Although Liberian travellers had 'explored' the interior as far as the Nimba mountains and had negotiated treaties with the chiefs, due to their country's slowness to react she lost the Sherbro to the British, and the coast east of Cape Palmas and a large section of the interior to the French. In 1908 Liberia belatedly began to organize a military force under the command of an Englishman; when the French demanded that she employ a Frenchman as well, the Liberians dismissed the Englishman and asked for American officers. These experiences developed in the ruling class a deep suspicion of the European powers. Consideration of the losses, however, should not obscure the fact that Liberia, weak and poor, saved a larger and richer hinterland for future development than did the British who were directing Creole affairs in Sierra Leone. In this regard, independence, even for a weak country, proved more effective than colonial status under a great power.

Americo-Liberian merchant princes, 1830-1900

The settlers, or Americo-Liberians, were building up a substantial foreign trade by the 1830's in palm-oil from the Kru coast, camwood, used for dyes, from the St. Paul River and fibres from the raphia palm. By the 1850's plantations of coffee and sugar were flourishing, and Liberian coffee was considered the finest in the world, while sugar and molasses were manufactured in quantity for the export market. Liberian merchants entered the overseas trade and their merchant ships manned by the skilled Kru carried the Lone Star flag of Liberia into European and American ports. Merchant princes like R. A. Sherman, Joseph Roberts, Francis Devany and E. J. Roye owned ocean transports, coastal vessels and trading posts along the coast and in the hinterland. Prosperity was reflected in the affluence and southern American style mansions of Monrovia. Roberts willed £2,000 to the cause of public education, newspapers flourished – the first being the *Liberia Herald* of 1826 – and Liberia College, founded in 1862, became the second institution of higher learning, next only to Fourah Bay, in West Africa.

Americo-Liberians never shone with the brilliance of the Sierra Leone Creoles in the professional fields but they did produce such outstanding men as the traveller, Benjamin Anderson, whose *Narrative of a Journey to Musardu*, published in 1870, ranks with the best of traveller's accounts in its understanding of African society; the missionary writer, Alexander Crummel, with his *The Future of Africa*, 1862; and probably the most outstanding educated West African of the nineteenth century, E. W. Blyden, whose writings influenced two or three generations of Africans. Of his many published works five major ones concerned Liberia, the first in 1862, *Liberia's Offering*, and the last in 1909, *Problems Before Liberia*. In addition, the Liberian Vaughan family were pioneers of the Nigerian Baptist Missions, and the Jackson family's newspaper, the *Lagos Weekly Record* (1890-1930) was a powerful advocate of the right of Africans to self-determination and a bold and influential champion of the African race. When the French occupied Abomey and the king of Dahomey fled, the *Record* took up his defence, the editor leading a delegation to Paris to plead his cause. Lastly, the famous Liberian evangelist, William Wade Harris, brought about one of the largest numbers of conversions to Christianity ever credited to one man in West Africa, in his preaching in the Ivory Coast between 1914 and 1916 (see chapter 16).

Between 1880 and 1900 Americo-Liberian plantations collapsed and their merchant princes were swept from the oceans at the same time as the Creoles of Sierra Leone began their decline. Both groups were badly affected by the changes which accompanied the partition of Africa. The world-wide depression of the 1880's and 1890's which bankrupted many European traders hurt the Liberian merchant princes as well. Then, as the European powers partitioned West Africa, they developed their own colonies to the exclusion of others, and their own trading patterns which ignored Liberia. Both French and British West Africa developed palm-oil and raphia fibre production, and, while the United States might have been expected to provide a market for Liberia, in fact once the partition was complete the large and important nineteenth-century American trade was abandoned. Liberia was too small a supplier by herself to attract a large American business, and Americans therefore abandoned West Africa to the Europeans and turned to exploit Latin America for their tropical requirements.

The Liberian coffee plant was introduced into Brazil, which quickly monopolized the American market. Prices fell and Liberian plantations were ruined. As far as sugar was concerned, American developments in Cuba, British developments in Brazil, and the discovery of beet sugar in Europe, ruined the Liberian plantations. Then around 1900 the German synthetic dyes destroyed the camwood industry. Thus between 1880 and 1900 a series of disasters hit Liberian exports of palm-oil, raphia, coffee, sugar and camwood. British and French ships passed by Liberia for their own colonies and American traders stopped coming so that Liberia sank into economic insignificance.

To offset their losses Americo-Liberians turned to a more vigorous exploitation of the interior, although even at the climax of their prosperity this had proved difficult. The major obstacle was the power and domination of internal trade by the Poro society and Diula Mandinka. In 1856, for example, when the government had financed an expedition to the interior, the Mandinka and Poro demonstrated their power by a trade boycott of Liberian settlements. Liberian rivers were not navigable, yet they were so numerous that road building was more costly than anywhere else in West Africa except the Niger Delta.

Since Germany's colonial empire was unable to supply her tropical needs, her merchants moved into Liberia before 1900 until they monopolized Liberia's trade; by 1914 twenty German firms were doing business and two out of every three ships calling in Liberian ports were German. The sons of the Liberian merchant princes became agents of German firms, and not independent traders as their fathers had been. Caught between the Mandinka and Poro in the interior and the Germans on the coast, many Americo-Liberians retreated into a dependence for their livelihood upon the civil service, teaching and the priesthood.

The years 1880 to 1914 demonstrated the growing isolation of Liberia from the American, European and African worlds, caused by her exclusion from the world trading systems and reduced contact with Africa after the partition. This forced Liberians to set up standards beholden only to themselves and become timid and defensive regarding foreign inquiries. Isolation was particularly harmful to the intellectual elite and the educational system, which did not evolve sufficiently to meet the development needs of the country.

The chronic economic problem

Liberia's twentieth-century problems were the direct result of the post 1880 economic stagnation, for this delayed Liberia's effective occupation of the interior and resulted in her subsequent loss of territory; it also increased friction with Africans as the Americo-Liberians, having been forced out of the export trade, entered into greater internal competition with Africans; and it slowed the growth of education for the African peoples. Economic competition and poor education became the causes of repeated revolts, especially among the progressive and ambitious Kru, and this resulted in overstaffing the civil service in an effort to provide jobs, and a fear that Africans educated enough to seek government employment would overrun the last stronghold of Americo-Liberians, and thus their last hope of survival.

Government revenues fell below expenditure. In 1906, with the assistance of a British firm called the Liberian Rubber Corporation, the government negotiated a loan in London. Part of it paid off the Roye loan of 1870, which will be discussed later, and the remainder was given to the Rubber Corporation to develop plantations in the interior. Rubber prices fell and the corporation had nothing to show for the money, and, with interest payments to meet, the financial situation was even worse. The Rubber Corporation began to work for a British take-over and Britain suggested that Europeans be employed to supervise Liberian finances and the army. Liberia turned to America in desperation, and in 1912 American bankers offered a loan to pay off the British, on condition that an American be placed in control of Liberia's customs collection; with Americans in control of her finances and army Liberia had become a semi-colonial state.

In 1914 the British navy cut off German trade with Liberia and refused to allow British goods to be imported by German firms; since there were no other firms this put a total stop to Liberian trade. In 1917, when the United States entered the war against Germany, Liberia had little choice but to follow and much to her own loss confiscated the German firms and bank. This left the Bank of West Africa as Liberia's only financial institution, which attempted through its monopoly to bring about the financial collapse of the government and thus to establish a British take-over. By 1918 Liberia had reached the lowest point in her national history, tottering on the verge of collapse and full British or American colonialism.

Liberian politics, 1839-83

In the pre-independence period the major political division had been between the commercial elements of Monrovia and the agricultural groups in the other coastal settlements. Between 1839 and 1847 Joseph Roberts led the Monrovia group while Rev. John Seys headed the opposition. The opposition opposed the total break with the Colonization Society at independence, in some areas boycotting the referendum and in Grand Bassa threatening to break away and form a separate state. In the first presidential election Roberts, on a Republican Party ticket, defeated the opposition candidate but immediately named him first Chief Justice of the Supreme Court. The technique of giving opposition leaders government posts became typical of the way in which the opposition was absorbed into Liberian politics.

Although the Republicans dominated Liberian politics from independence to 1877, the two-party system continued to function. Roberts was a capable administrator, politician and statesman, who extended the nation's boundaries, maintained fairly peaceful relations with the local Africans and won international recognition for Liberia. He had the advantage that his presidency coincided with the era of the merchant princes and prosperity. However, Roberts, himself a light-skinned Mulatto, fostered a caste system based on skin colour; the light complexioned Mulatto governing class kept socially apart, contending that since the climate took a greater toll of their numbers than of full blooded Negroes, they should be favoured in administrative positions. This was a philosophy which the Negroes would not accept; yet it was not surprising that the Mulattoes adopted it since they were fighting for their lives, eight out of ten Mulatto colonists dying against four out of ten of the Negro colonists. The Society in America aggravated the situation by favouring Mulatto emigrants, who supported the Republican Party when they arrived; but after the American Civil war emigration to Liberia sharply declined, and with the high death-rate among Mulattos it was only a matter of time before the Republicans fell from power.

In 1869 the victory of E. J. Roye brought the opposition, the True Whigs, to power. Roye was a full-blooded Negro who had arrived in Liberia in 1846, became Speaker of the House of Representatives in 1849, published a newspaper and was nominated Chief Justice in 1865. A merchant prince, he was a typical example of the opportunities for advancement in Liberian society which the economic prosperity of the times encouraged.

Even at this stage the Republicans continued to give offence by their racial arrogance: Joseph Roberts, after retiring from the presidency, became principal of Liberia College and made it a policy to admit only Mulatto students; the Masonic secret society became an exclusive Mulatto club whose members enjoyed government patronage; the Republicans had no policy for opening the interior; and finally they used the courts to suppress the opposition.

Opposition grew around Roye and Blyden. Blyden at Liberia College argued a racialist theory praising the superiority of persons of pure blood, whether white or black, as against the inferiority of the 'unhealthy' and 'unnatural' Mulatto mixture. Roye gained immense prestige when, as Chief Justice, he resigned in protest against the government attempt to bring treason charges against True Whig leaders.

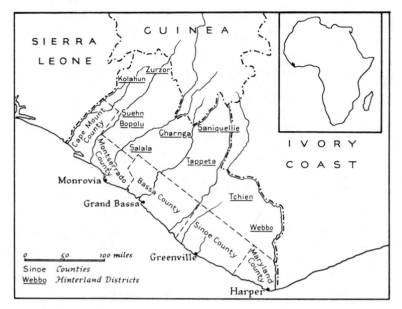

32 Administrative divisions of Liberia

When Roye became president he inherited a Republican civil service which not only resented his Negro pedigree and his rapid rise to wealth and power but, also, that he was not descended from one of the founding fathers of the Republic. With advice from Blyden, Roye advocated the opening of the interior; he tried to get American money for a railway, and welcomed foreign investments. To secure money for road building he negotiated a loan from London bankers, who handled the transfer in such a way that only two-thirds of the amount reached Liberia, where most of this amount was pocketed by government officials, until less than one-tenth of the original sum was available to the Liberian treasury. Aware of his growing unpopularity Roye unconstitutionally extended the presidential term from two to four years.

Although Roye's aims were enlightened, his lack of control over his officials and his fear of standing for re-election in the normal two years aroused fears among the people; he was charged with planning to sell the country to foreigners and set up a personal dictatorship. In 1871 an angry Republican mob attempted to lynch Blyden, stormed the presidential mansion and imprisoned Roye, who died shortly after in mysterious circumstances. Joseph Roberts came back for two more terms as president. In 1877 the True Whigs again won an electoral victory and they have never since lost power, although the Republicans continued strong in the civil service.

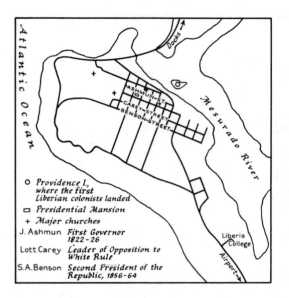

33 Monrovia: a plan of the city

In 1883 H. R. Johnson, son of the pioneer Elijah Johnson, was endorsed by both political parties because of his immense popularity. However, on his election he declared for the True Whigs and removed the Republicans from the civil service. The emergence of the one-party state in Liberia dates from Johnson's election in 1883.

The True Whigs were able to create a one-party state because of the urgent need for unity against aggression and intrigue by Europeans, and repeated revolts by Africans. The frontier encroachments by the British and French and financial intrigues by British, Americans and Germans made Americo-Liberian solidarity essential if their independence was to be preserved. Even with this solidarity established a constant threat to survival remained in their attempt to impose their rule over Africans. Wars of resistance and independence were fought with the Grebo in the 1880's and 1890's and with the Kru and Gola in the early twentieth century. There was always the possibility that European intrigue and African revolts would combine to topple Liberia into one or other of the huge empires around her.

Although the colonists had arrived in small American-type family groups, like the Creoles they developed extended families, until, by the end of the nineteenth century great dynastic families had emerged through intermarriage and consolidation. Government became the art of balancing the number of civil service jobs held by each family, and if a great family became

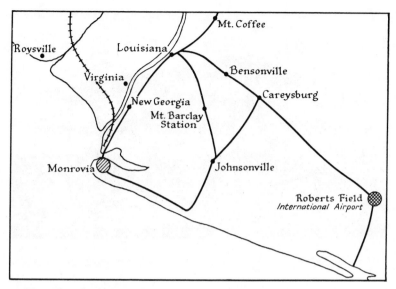

34 Monrovia and environs

aggrieved it was conciliated by the offer of more positions. Since opposition was thus absorbed by offers of government posts the civil service was overburdened with staff; the Justice Department for example absorbed nine per cent of Liberia's revenue compared with two per cent in Sierra Leone. The cost of maintaining the one-party state was a major cause of the continuous shortage of finance, because every time government revenue increased, the struggle began among the family dynasties as to how it was to be shared.

One-party rule was sustained because all positions were in the patronage of Whig politicians, including the staff of Liberia College, judges, heads of church denominations, and newspaper owners, all of whom were bound together in the Masonic secret society. The system was not the invention of the Whigs. The Republicans had introduced it between 1848 and 1877; while under the Republicans Liberia College was all Mulatto, when Roye came to power Blyden was given the principalship and it became almost all Negro. Following Blyden, principals were either politicians on the rise or politicians being quietly pushed into retirement. The result was that thirty years after its foundation Liberia College had produced only eight graduates. This was why an intellectual class did not arise to challenge the ruling oligarchy. Because of the fear that it might get out of control, the True Whigs did not encourage a Liberian merchant class, preferring to leave commerce in the hands of Europeans.

157

Liberia College, 1900

Relations with African peoples

From the arrival of the first pioneers at Cape Mesurado, when the African chiefs were forced to sign away their land at gun point, the competition for land disturbed relations between the settlers and the Africans. At Cape Palmas the Grebo were prepared to exchange land for education and welcomed the pioneers on condition that settlers and Grebos be treated alike, particularly in the matter of education. Successive governors unsuccessfully attempted to persuade the Grebos to move back and leave the coastal strip to the colonists, until, in 1855, the militia from Monrovia, supported by an American warship, drove 2,000 Grebos out of Cape Palmas.

Compared with the later period, the era of prosperity from 1850 to 1880 was one of relative peace between settlers and Africans. Merchant princes operated interior trading posts and, by co-operating with the chiefs, maintained Liberian influence, while the government occasionally paid subsidies to the chiefs to keep the trade routes open to the coast. The depression and collapse of the merchant princes in the 1880's brought a decline in government revenue, yet the patronage policy of the one-party state and European border encroachments· necessitating effective interior rule called for large government expenditure. To meet this need Africans were taxed, and taxed heavily; most were willing to pay if in return they were provided with teachers and schools.

The Americo-Liberian had to deal with progressive and ambitious African people. The commercial ability of the Mandinka has been already noted. The Vai had developed their own system of writing, created by Momolu Daolu in the early nineteenth century, so that by mid-century a majority of adult Vai males could read and write the Vai script. The Kru, and related Grebo, had a passionate desire for education and English was widely spoken along their coast when the pioneers arrived; they were also devoted to their country, their institutions and their freedom, which was symbolized by their facial mark, called the 'mark of freedom' because the Kru were never sold as slaves. They enthusiastically embraced Christianity, becoming teachers, catechists and clergy in the missions operated by American churches. The Kru were commercially aggressive in fostering trade along their coast, and many worked on European merchant ships where they were praised for their dependability and efficiency as deck hands, stevedores and firemen. When in 1884, President Johnson permitted groups which paid more than a specified amount of tax to send members to the House of Representatives, only the Kru and Grebo had the wealth and ambition to qualify.

The Vai script, showing vowels and the words 'small boy'

dehñ   bese
small boy

ENGLISH LETTER OR SYLLABLE	ORIGINAL SYMBOL	MODERN SYMBOL
a		
e		
i		
ō		
u		

There were similarities between Americo-Liberian treatment of Africans and the earlier attitude of the Mulatto settlers towards Negro settlers, which included the same cultural arrogance and an effort to restrict education. In order to exclude Africans from the already over-burdened governing class, the Americo-Liberians proposed technical rather than literary education for the Kru, but there was little scope for the technically trained in a non-industrial society. The Kru, who with mission help were trained in technical subjects overseas, had difficulty in securing employment, and even those who qualified in literary education were discriminated against in government jobs.

The normal path into Americo-Liberian society was via the apprenticeship system whereby African children worked in Americo-Liberian homes, became familiar with their customs and way of life, adopted their names and later married among them. This system was distasteful and offended the pride of the Kru and they seldom took part in it.

In addition to their grievances over education, the Kru complained of economic discrimination. They were energetic trading people, and when the government had declared six Americo-Liberian cities as international trading ports, Kru cities declined into villages, the ultimate result being to make the Kru economically subservient to the Americo-Liberians. Repeatedly the Kru asked that their city, Settra Kru, should be made an international port of entry. In 1905 the president of the republic agreed but when the Americo-Liberians of the area prevented the erection of the necessary customs post and forcibly refused to allow customs officials to take up their duties in Settra Kru, the Monrovia government made no effort to compel obedience to the president's order. This was typical of the political paralysis at Monrovia in enforcing unpopular measures on the Americo-Liberians, especially in disputes with Africans. The Monrovia government was a settler government ultimately enforcing settler policies. A further example of this paralysis occurred when the senator of Sinoe county lynched six Kru chiefs and imprisoned a number of others, demanding 2,000 dollars apiece for their freedom; the senator personally pocketed this money and despite repeated Kru petitions the Monrovia government did not interfere.

Under these conditions Africans frequently revolted against Americo-Liberian rule; there were major revolts among the Grebo and Gola and also the serious Kru revolt of 1915. In 1912 the Kru presented the American ambassador with a petition of grievances in order to persuade them to stop supporting Americo-Liberian policies. When the Americans ignored this, the Kru turned to the British, asking for guns and ammunition. There had been a long connection and trading partnership between the Kru and the British, who were the best customers of Kru palm-oil exports, while thousands of Kru worked on British warships and merchant vessels along the West Coast. Kru colonies had developed in Freetown, Takoradi and Lagos and they felt that advancement and education would be quicker under British than under Liberian rule. Once the revolt began the Kru hoisted the British flag. Although British merchants and the British press were sympathetic, the British ambassador in Monrovia was even more hostile than the Americans had been. Nevertheless the Monrovia government disguised the real causes of the revolt – oppressive and intolerant rule – by claiming that it was provoked by the British as an excuse to bring Liberia within their empire.

In 1900 there were about 12,000 settlers and 60,000 Africans in the counties where Americo-Liberian law, custom, institutions and religion prevailed. The Monrovia government pursued a policy of assimilating these Africans. In order to become assimilated, Africans had to give up their language for English, their traditional religion or Islam for protestant Christianity, their rights in communal land for private ownership and their loyalty to African institutions for loyalty to the Monrovia government. A sharing of the two cultures was not intended, but instead total African assimilation was required, which was a slow and often painful process. The Americo-Liberians, although they were settlers with all the arrogance, feelings of superiority and cultural blindness typical of settlers, permitted progress towards assimilation which, had it occurred in settler communities elsewhere in Africa, would have been hailed as revolutionary. In the 1920's, of a school population of 9,000, only 600 were Americo-Liberians. A prominent lawyer and Secretary of state married a Grebo in 1881, a Chief Justice married a Vai in 1910, a Kru had risen to be Secretary of State for education in 1915, and in 1925 a Grebo held the second highest position in the Republic, Vice-President.

The Monrovia government policy in the hinterland, however, was indirect rule, which was developed under Presidents Barclay (1904-12) and Howard (1912-20). Chiefs were to govern according to tradition, assisted by Liberian district commissioners and backed by the frontier police. African law was administered in the chiefly courts, with appeals to the courts of the district commissioners. President Howard, an Americo-Liberian with a broad national outlook, a graduate of Liberia College and fluent in two African languages, brought a new sympathy into the hinterland administration. He appointed five travelling superintendents responsible to the president to check and supervise the district commissioners. The powerful Poro Society was banned but when a number of proto-nationalist underground movements developed the Poro was revived as an instrument of government control and discipline.

In traditional society it had been the Poro, not the chiefs, which had exercised the most significant political power. The Liberian government appointed paramount chiefs over numerous clan chiefs and this, coupled with the Poro ban, fundamentally altered the form of traditional government in just the same way as the British recognition of the Calabar chiefs undermined the power of the Ekpe society.

A mask of the Poro society

Usually indirect rule was introduced because it was cheap, but this was not the case in Liberia. The hinterland civil service enlarged the patronage available for distribution by the True Whigs and multitudes of officials soon overburdened the hinterland administration as it had in earlier days over-staffed the county administration. It did, however, provide an opportunity to employ educated Africans – Kru, Vai, Grebo – and thus became an avenue for them into the governing class. Since indirect rule was not economical and since, in any case, it altered African traditional government, it appears unfortunate that the policy of assimilation was not applied throughout the country in the interests of national unity.

FOUNDATION – SURVIVAL – INDEPENDENCE

Colonisation Society

Cape Mesurado

Constitution

Monrovia Conference

Governor Roberts

Referendum

Declaration of Independence

Monrovia Conference

| 1816 | 1821 | 1839 | 1841 | 1848 |

1848 THE REPUBLICAN ERA 1877

Grebo War

AMERICO-LIBERIAN TRADING COMPANY

raffia
coffee
sugar
palm-oil
camwood

Roye

LONDON £

AMERICO-LIBERIAN TRADING COMPANY CLOSED

| 1855 | 1871 |

ONE-PARTY STATE OF THE TRUE WHIGS

President Johnson

LONDON £

AMERICA $

GERMAN TRADING COMPANY CLOSED

Kru Revolt

| 1883 | 1906 | 1912 | 1914 | 1915–16 |

A pictorial chart of the history of Liberia

Conclusion

Americo-Liberian history is a record of struggle for survival, suspicion of the imperialistic aims of the great powers and a passionate devotion to independence. The struggle began with the throwing off of the Colonization Society's paternalism and the establishment of recognition as a sovereign state. It continued in the effort, first to save Liberian territory during the partition of Africa, and then to survive the intrigues of foreign bankers.

Internally it was a struggle to develop a national loyalty in the interests of national unity. At first the division was between the Mulatto and Negro settlers, followed in 1883 by the division between the settlers and the coastal peoples, the Kru, Grebo and Vai, and later between the people of the counties and the people of the hinterland. Credit for survival was largely due to the one-party state but it was achieved at a high cost to the development of the country.

Unity had its price. The patronage policy of the True Whigs multiplied civil service posts and overburdened an already economically weak nation. When the party brought the courts, press and schools under its control this weakened independent thought and action. The Americo-Liberians set the standards and fixed the rules by which Africans might assimilate, which often required that they conceal their origins and pretend to be of settler pedigree. Discovery of this concealment brought shock and scandal. Americo-Liberians also sought to monopolize national politics, which was the main road to success and wealth, while business and commerce were spurned.

Yet it would appear that Liberia's basic weakness was economic, after her plantations and merchant class were destroyed, following a brief but brilliant beginning, and she was isolated outside the world's major trading systems. Liberia's continuous lack of revenue left her exposed to imperialism, widened the gulf between settlers and Africans, made the full application of assimilation impossible, accounted for the abuses of the administration of the hinterland, drove every ambitious man into seeking a government job and left the economic development of the country to foreigners. The significance of Liberian history for West Africa lies in the fact that modern independent African states face many of the problems and in many cases are following similar paths to those pioneered by Liberia between 1821 and 1914.

12 Iboland: a segmentary political system

The Ibo people live in the area between Benin and Igala, the Cross River and Niger Delta city-states. They were divided into five major cultural groups: the western or Riverain, northern or Awka, Owerri, Cross River and Ogoja Ibo. These cultural groups could be considered the 'tribes' of the Ibo nation but since they did not possess a central government nor act together politically they were not 'tribes' in the sense in which that word is used to describe, for example, the Egba or Ijebu 'tribes' of the Yoruba people.

Regardless of cultural differences between the groups there were certain characteristics typical of Ibo society. The Ibo respected age and leadership

35 The Ibo and their neighbours (early nineteenth century)

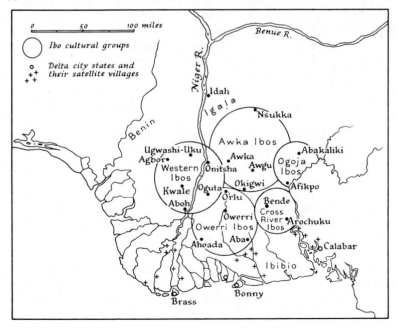

came from the elders. Respect was not servility and was balanced by the belief that birth did not confer advantage on any man. The Ibo were individualistic and egalitarian, every man considering himself as good as everyone else and demanding a voice in his local affairs. Since everyone had a right to rise in the society Ibo culture emphasized competition; competition between families, between lineages and between clans. Competition was promoted by Ibo national sports, wrestling and mock battles. Although men were born equal they could rise to positions of prestige through a combination of wealth and a record of service to the clan. Ibo society was, therefore, intensely democratic with a vigour characteristic of competitive, egalitarian societies. With this it also had the failings of wasted uncoordinated effort, slow decision-taking and a lack of unity typical of such people and which was underlined in facing more disciplined and autocratic societies. The Ibo were not unique in the type of government which they created. In West Africa the Kru of Liberia, Tallensi of Ghana, Konkomba of Togoland and Tiv of Nigeria to mention a few, possessed political organizations closer to those of the Ibo than to the Yoruba, Dahomey, Asante or Mossi systems. The following discussion of a segmentary political system can be applied to both the Ibo and Ibibio.

Segmentary is the word used to describe the political organization of

Ibo diagram 1: Clan organisation

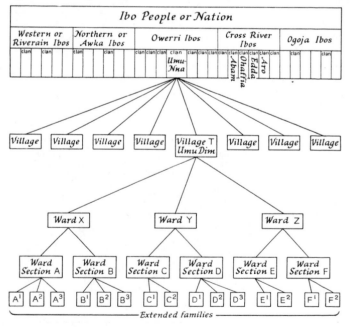

societies without a central government which, in pre-colonial Africa, was usually headed by a single person (king, emperor, sultan, almami, etc.). Segmentary societies are distinguished from 'stratified' societies which usually have royal and noble families who pass high political office from generation to generation. In segmentary societies stable government is achieved by balancing small equal groups against each other and by the ties of clanship, marriage and religious association; these institutions therefore have special significance.

Among the Ibo each cultural group was divided into a number of clans (diagram 1). Usually the clans in one cultural group spoke a similar dialect and had certain customs, traditions and institutions which distinguished them from clans of other cultural groups. There were hundreds of patrilineal (tracing descent through the father) clans in Iboland averaging in population between 5,000 and 15,000 people. (Consult diagram 1 frequently as you read on.) Of the hundred or so clans which make up the Owerri Ibo, let us say that

Ibo diagram 2: 'T'. A typical Ibo village

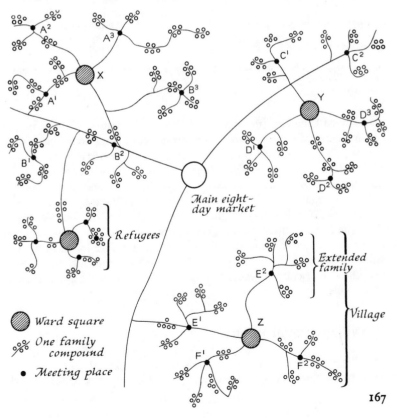

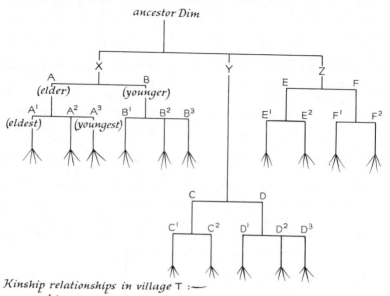

Kinship relationships in village T :—

     Lineage = all who trace a relationship to ancestor Dim

Major segment =   „ „ „ „   „   „ great-grandfather X

Minor segment =   „ „ „ „   „   „ grandfather A

Extended family = „ „ „ „   „   „ father A¹

Ibo diagram 3: Kinship relationships in Ibo village 'T'. This and the two preceding diagrams should be discussed in class. How far can you find similar groups of relations among your own people?

one is called Umu Nna (the children of Nna). This means that all the people of Umu Nna claim descent from their ancestor Nna. They do not claim relation any farther back. All within one clan are considered relatives.

Umu Nna is made up of eight villages. In Iboland there were no large cities but thousands of villages, so closely packed that Iboland had an overall density of population greater than anywhere else in West Africa. The eight villages were founded by the eight sons of Nna. One of the sons was called Dim who founded village 'T' (diagram 2) whose people call themselves Umu Dim (the children of Dim). Umu Dim is called a lineage (diagram 3). The village is the political unit of Iboland. There is no governmental organization over the clan or cultural group. We will therefore look at the government of an Ibo village and see its relationship to the lineage.

Ibo village government

Ibo village government, described as a segmentary political system, operated in its purest form among the Owerris. The segmentary system reflected the structure of the Ibo village and lineage. The Ibo village was divided into wards. The wards were grouped around the large village market which operated every four or eight days depending on its size and importance. Each ward was made up of sections and each section of a number of extended families whose compounds were close together. A meeting of the village would be held in the main market, of the ward in the ward square and of the extended family in a cleared area near its compounds or inside an elder's compound. Diagram 1 shows a 'typical' Ibo village composed of three wards X, Y and Z which in turn were made up of a number of extended families.

The people of village 'T' claimed descent through their fathers from a common ancestor, Dim (see diagrams 1 and 2) and called themselves Umu Dim, 'the children of Dim', and the family of Dim is called a lineage. Dim had three sons, X, Y and Z, the three villages of the town being descended from them, and called the major segments of the lineage. While the village coincided with the lineage, its wards represented the major segments which in turn were divided into sections representing minor segments. For example, X, the oldest son of Dim, had two sons, A and B, each of whose descendants formed a minor segment. The minor segments were made up of the extended families such as A1, A2, and A3. Thus a man from C2 family would describe all other members of C2 as his brothers. But if he was talking to someone from Z major segment he would refer to everyone from Y segment as his brother. If he was talking to someone from a neighbouring village he would describe everyone from village 'T', all Umu Dim, as his brothers.

Occasionally if Umu Dim became very large the major segments might quarrel. If the quarrel was not settled the major segments might break away and in future only claim descent from X, Y or Z. Thus three lineages would be created out of one. This tendency to fission (break-up) kept Ibo groupings small. If the Ibo system of pure democracy, in which every man had a say in what happened to him, was to operate the groups could not be too large.

On the other hand there was also a tendency towards fusion (union) of smaller groups for protection. Two or more smaller lineages might decide to organize a larger lineage. Or a refugee group might be given land and permission to settle in village 'T' by the major segment X, particularly if X felt weaker than the other two major segments (see diagram 1). The refugees would ultimately call themselves Umu Dim and establish a mythical relationship with Dim. This assimilation of strangers also applied to slaves brought into the town to labour on the farms. In time they would be given land and if they prospered and founded their own extended families they would take up a place in the lineage and after a few generations their slave origins were forgotten. Thus through a process of fission and fusion Ibo and Ibibio lineages tended to keep to average sizes, not too big, not too small.

Village government consisted of two basic institutions, the Ama-ala (Council of Elders) and the village assembly of citizens. In village 'T' the Ama-ala consisted of the fifteen heads of the extended families. However, any adult male held the right to sit on the council. Normally this right was not exercised but if a decision was to be taken which vitally affected an individual he could insist on his right. This was an important check upon elders who inclined to take decisions without proper consideration. In routine matters the elders ruled by decree and proclamation but where decisions likely to produce disputes were to be taken the Ama-ala could order the town crier to announce a village assembly in the market place or in a ward square.

At the assembly the elders laid the issues before the people. Every man had a right to speak, the people applauding popular proposals and shouting down unpopular ones. Decisions had to be unanimous and it was here that young or wealthy men with records of service and dedication to the village could influence policy. If the elders tried to enforce an unpopular decision the young men could prevent any decision through the operation of the unanimity rule. If the Ama-ala acted arbitrarily and refused to call the assembly the people could demand it by completely ignoring them and bringing town life to a halt. An unpopular elder would be ignored and no one would speak to him. This social pressure would compel the elder to bend to the popular will. The village assembly was considered the Ibo man's birthright, the guarantee of his rights, his shield against oppression, the expression of his individualism and the means whereby the young and progressive impressed their views upon the old and conservative.

The administration of justice possessed the same democratic quality. Quarrels between individuals of different families in the ward were settled before the people, the ward elders acting as arbiters. Quarrels between major segments or wards or serious crimes such as theft would come before the full Ama-ala and village assembly. The danger of the system was that the people, acting as a mob, occasionally took justice into their own hands and the accused did not have a proper opportunity to defend himself. However, this was balanced by the deeply-rooted conviction that it takes two to make a quarrel. The elders, therefore, seldom acted as judges pronouncing guilt and innocence but as arbiters assessing the degree of guilt of each party and punishing both accordingly.

The Ibo judicial system was noted for its flexibility. A man might attempt to settle with the individual who had aggrieved him. If this failed he could appeal to a respected elder to intervene or call members of the two families together. He could also appeal to the ward or village elders. There were no set rules as to where he should begin his appeal for redress but he could appeal against the decision of the families to the ward elders and finally to the Ama-ala of the village.

Individuals always conducted their own case. They might call witnesses, or anyone in the assembly might speak. If an elder who was a powerful and persuasive speaker could quote history or an earlier similar case for either side it had an influence on the assembly. If, however, there was suspicion that the elder was in any way connected with the individual he was speaking for, instead of helping, he might hurt the case for which he spoke.

Once both sides of the case had been heard the two men withdrew and the Ama-ala and assembly argued the pros and cons. When the decision had been taken, one elder was asked to give judgement when the two parties to the case had returned. It is important to note that in arriving at a decision the assembly acted like a large-sized jury which had to agree unanimously. The Ama-ala could not push a decision against the will of the assembly.

Respect for the elders was not entirely the result of their age but also because of their priestly functions. The family, segment and lineage heads were responsible for rituals and sacrifices to the founder of the family, segment or lineage and this helped to maintain the peace, prosperity and happiness of the group concerned. The rituals reminded the people of their common origin and helped maintain their unity and group awareness.

Characteristic features of the cultural groups

The segmentary political system so far described was fairly typical of the Owerri Ibo. Others employed the same basic system but added certain features which distinguished them from the Owerris and from other Ibo cultural groups. Almost all groups had age-set organizations. Age-sets varied from one group to another but only in a few areas such as Ogoja were they important elements in village government. Every so many years young people of a certain age were initiated into an age-set in which they remained all their lives so that the whole population was arranged in two parallel male and female age-set organizations. Each age-set chose a leader and after it had proved its service to the community, it was given a distinctive name by the elders, signifying that it had passed from boyhood to manhood. The age-sets competed among themselves in sports and in rendering service to the village and they promoted and strengthened the competitive element in the society.

Age-sets besides being societies for mutual help and for discipline were convenient for organizing public works. Younger age sets were responsible for keeping the village tidy, older ones for clearing the bush for new markets, providing night watchmen, guards or market police. There was a tendency for each segment of a lineage to think of itself as a unit and this, if unchecked, could lead to the break away (fission) of that segment. The age-sets brought

An Ibibio Ekpe mask

together people of similar ages from all the segments of the lineage. Through working together, helping each other and competing with other age-sets the members developed a loyalty to the age-set leader which was a strong bond of unity in the village, which cut across the loyalty to the segment and thus reduced the tendency to fission.

In Ogoja the age-set leaders occupied equal positions on the Ama-ala with the lineage elders which gave the younger men a formal and constant voice in government. In Asaba the oldest age-set was retired with an honorary advisory status, the next age-set providing the members of the Ama-ala. By retiring the oldest group, government came into the hands of younger, more progressive elements.

Among the Awka and some Niger Ibo such as Onitsha, graded title societies were more important than age-sets in government. In Awka town and Onitsha the title societies were called Ozo while in Nsukka they were called Ama and their meeting places Ozo or Ama lodges. Any freeborn male who could afford the initiation fee might take a title. Upon further payments he proceeded up the grades to the top where he shared in the fees paid by lower grades, a kind of pension scheme for the highest ranking members. The Ozo or Ama members shared seats on the Ama-ala with lineage elders or occasionally replaced them as makers of policy and arbiters of justice. To a greater degree than the age-sets, title societies encouraged competition and individualism, brought government into the hands of ambitious men and made wealth an important mark of success.

The Cross River clans and Ibibio were distinguished by their secret societies, the Ekpe being the most popular. Like the Ozo and Ama they conferred titles, were graded with initiation fees and provided pensions, but unlike the title societies they possessed a secret ritual which they maintained gave them special powers from the gods. Major political decisions were taken by the top grades of the Ekpe while the lower grades carried out administrative duties along with the age-sets which were also well organized among the Cross River clans. The will of the ordinary people, expressed through the village assembly, was reduced and a small ruling group resulted which

Ozo title holders with ivory trumpets

Spirit cult mask representing a female ghost

gave these clans more cohesion and greater direction and may have been one of the reasons why the Aro, in co-operation with other Cross River clans, were able to achieve trading leadership over much of Iboland.

Possibly through the influence of Benin and Igala the Ibo living on the river as well as at Nri near Awka had kings who were in some ways considered godlike. They ruled over centralized states rather than villages under segmentary political systems. The king was chosen by and from a royal lineage and his Council might either be Ozo title holders, lineage elders or age-set leaders appointed by him. In Onitsha the Obi (king) was chosen by and from the royal lineage of Eze Chima while his council consisted of the Ndichie (Red Cap chiefs), all senior Ozo title holders.

The weakness of the Ibo system is found in the thousands of small independent villages, each jealous of and competing with others, quarrelling with each other, going to war and disturbing the·peace. However, this aspect of the segmentary political system can be over-emphasized because there were in practice many links which promoted clan co-operation over a wide area.

A major link within the clan was that many Ibo were forbidden by custom to marry within their lineage and thus Ibo men sought their wives in neighbouring lineages which created a complex interlocking web of marriage relationships throughout an entire clan. Men thus married would be unwilling to engage in war with their wives' relatives. Age-sets were frequently co-ordinated over a number of villages and age-set loyalty could be as strong as the bonds of the lineage. Among the Ada the age-sets were uniform over about 42,000 people, who were divided politically among many villages. Ozo, Ama and the Ekpe operated the same way. An Ozo might travel far outside his own clan and receive hospitality and respect from his brothers in other Ozo lodges.

One of the major forms of inter-clan co-operation was the oracle system. Some clans possessed an oracle for the settling of disputes when evidence of guilt was inconclusive. A dispute between two villages might be referred to the oracle or elders of a third but this did not always assure impartiality because the surrounding villages were linked to the two quarrelling villages by marriage, age-sets, title or secret societies. The farther away the oracle was located from the immediate area the more chance there was of impartial justice. Thus a system of nationally famous oracles developed in Iboland which specialized in the settling of inter-lineage disputes.

The Arochuku oracle

Oracle consultation was a method of strengthening the segmentary political system. Although there were many oracles only a few became nationally famous for the impartiality of their judicial decisions; there were those at Awgu, Umunoha, Ozuzu, the Agbala oracle at Awka and, what became the oracle of highest appeal in all Ibo and Ibibio land, Arochuku (map 36).

Awka was famous for its blacksmiths whose guilds took turns touring Iboland, settling temporarily in various places and manufacturing iron farming tools, swords and spears. Because of their superior products they were welcomed in all the clans. If an inter-lineage dispute arose, the visiting Awka blacksmith might suggest that it be referred to Agbala and would offer, for a fee, to conduct the contestants to his home town. Most well-known oracles possessed travelling agents but the Awka and the Aro were so widely

*An Ibo altar piece
for the Yam spirit*

spread throughout the country that they drew the largest patronage to their respective oracles.

More famous than Agbala was the oracle at Arochuku, 'the voice of Chukwu', the high god, and its agents the Aro who traded over three-quarters of Ibibio and Iboland. An Aro trader might recommend his oracle, conduct the contestants and house them in his family compound at Arochuku for which service he received a fee. Since he had been a trader among the people of the disputing villages he was able to provide the oracle priests with a detailed and impartial view of the dispute. When the oracle delivered its decision it was able to show an intimate knowledge of the history, state of public opinion and the conditions of the two villages which impressed the contestants with the oracle's supernatural insight.

Since Arochuku was far away, with little direct interest in the dispute, its impartiality was an important element in its popularity. The guilty party or both sides were fined so many slaves according to their degree of guilt. The slaves were supposedly sacrificed to Chukwu to appease his wrath for the offence committed. In fact the slaves were not sacrificed. They were taken into the oracle and then sold which, although deceptive, was more humane than execution. The Ibo and Ibibio generally believed the slaves were sacrificed but whether the Aros as a whole or whether just the priests and highest grades of Ekpe knew the truth is not certain.

To ignore the verdict of Chukwu or any other oracle was believed to bring down the displeasure of the gods in the form of famine, disease or other disasters. Naturally in every society there were those prepared to test and defy the gods and it was the weakness of the other oracles that they possessed no concrete way of enforcing their decisions except through religious sanctions. The Aro, however, employed mercenary troops (professional soldiers) from other Cross River clans, as Chukwu's agents, who swept down upon any village which refused to obey the oracle, burnt it and carried the offenders into slavery. Although carrying a dispute to Arochuku was expensive it was popular, not only because of impartiality and the powerful religious sanctions, but also because its decisions were final and enforced by the mercenaries. However, even the wealthy and powerful kings of the Niger Delta city-states who were beyond the range of Chukwu's mercenaries carried their disputes to his oracle, thus indicating the strength of the purely religious sanctions.

The Aro trading system

The Aros' main concern was not their oracle but the organization of a complex trading system. They held a monopoly of the sale of slaves to the traders of the Delta city-states, especially Bonny and Calabar, in return for which they secured firearms to equip their mercenaries. Under the protection of Chukwu's mercenaries the Aro opened up long-distance trade which the numerous small Ibo political units normally made very difficult.

The Aro organized three major trade routes from the north over which the slaves were brought to the central market at Bende from which they were marched to the Bonny markets on the Imo River. When the British

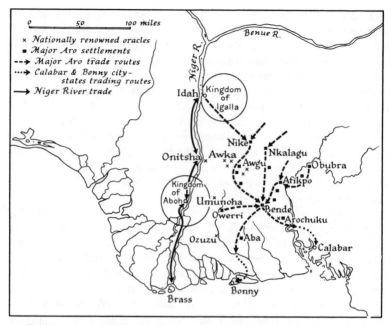

36 Trading systems of Iboland in the nineteenth century

decided to buy only palm-oil in Bonny and, by blockading the city-state, stopped its export of slaves, it was the Aros, at least in part, who helped to organize the new oil trade among the Ibo and Ibibio so that Bonny quickly became the largest African exporter of palm-oil. Moreover, although slaves were no longer in demand for overseas export, they were required in larger numbers within Iboland for the harvesting, collection and transport of palm-oil to market.

Along the trade routes the Aro settled in colonies which were used as resting and feeding stops for the slave and goods caravans and the mercenary troops. By the end of the nineteenth century there were four times as many Aros living in the colonies as in Arochuku. The Aro seldom engaged in the actual slave raiding. They kept the routes open and safe, purchased in the markets, transported the slaves southward often by sale and re-sale, the slaves frequently changing hands until their arrival at Bende.

People have assumed that most of the Aro slaves came through the oracle. The oracle and the slave trade were two distinct businesses both carried on by Aro agents. The majority of slaves were brought via the trade routes not via the oracle. However, it was the status of the Aro people as oracle-protected persons, backed by oracle mercenaries, which gave them the freedom to establish colonies, trade in the markets and travel unmolested over long distances through numbers of jealous, hostile clans. In this sense the oracle was a vital part of the Aro trading system.

Another important trading system to the west of the Aro on the Niger was organized by the Ibo kingdom of Aboh. Traders from the city-state of Brass came as far as Aboh market from where they carried slaves or palm-oil in their canoes to be sold to Europeans at the coast. The Ibo of Aboh, like the Aro, were in the strategic position of middlemen between the interior producers and the delta buyers. As a result the kingdom of Aboh was the largest Ibo political unit of the nineteenth century.

The Aro set up a kind of rule over clans along the trade routes. They sought no more political domination than was absolutely necessary for the pursuit of their commercial interests. They were wise enough to see that domination was likely to run counter to the strong democratic feelings of the Ibo and Ibibio and cause no end of strife and war which would be bad for trade. Furthermore, indirect rule, through creation of puppet chiefs, the customary beginning of political domination, was virtually impossible in a segmentary political system as the British, also carrying on trade and with the sanction of another high god, were later to discover. The Aro were content to secure a voice, often a dominant one over strategic markets using their oracle and mercenaries to keep the peace in the interest of profits. Otherwise the Ibo and Ibibio villages were left as far as possible to govern themselves.

One of the Aro strengths was that it was not the village which was the political unit but rather the clan (diagram 1). The Aros were in fact one of the few Ibo clans to operate as an effective political unit. Unity certainly gave them an advantage over other Ibo. However, it should be remembered that the Aro were merely a clan of the Ibo people. They had basically the same political system and it was little suited for political imperialism. Imperialism requires highly organized central rule by a single person or group. It is very difficult for a thoroughly democratic system to adjust to the holding of other people in subjection.

It should also be noted that the mercenaries which came from neighbouring Cross River clans – the Abam, Ohaffia and Edda (diagram 1) were neither merely servants of the Aro, nor were they in any way subservient to them. They also had their own ambitions which occasionally clashed with the Aro. The Edda for instance at one time virtually sacked Arochuku. In addition it was not only the Aro who employed them. Ohaffia mercenaries in the mid-nineteenth century were hired by a village in the Onitsha area to fight a neighbouring village.

The Aro were not exclusive. Ambitious Ibo of ability were taken into trading partnerships, acted as oracle agents and intermarried with the Aro.

The Aro had trading agreements with some Ibo groups especially the Ozo title-holders of Awka with whom they also intermarried. Whether there was an informal division of Iboland into Awka and Aro spheres of influence or whether the Aro had agreements with the agents of other national oracles is unclear but it appeared that the Aro trading system penetrated very little into the areas of the other major national oracles.

The British claimed to have 'destroyed' the Aro oracle in 1901-2. They did destroy its setting but since it was believed to be supernatural not even British guns could destroy it. Many Ibo believed that it had fled and taken refuge in a cave in Okigwi where as late as the 1920's it was still being consulted.

Part **three**

West Africa and Europe, 1800-1900

An Elem Kalabari shrine for the dead of the Ekine secret society

Urhobo sculpture

A messenger of Ekpe

13 City-states of the Niger Delta: social revolution and collapse

For a hundred years the Niger Delta city-states had been the leading West African participants in the slave trade. In the nineteenth century, due to British naval insistence and their situation in relation to the palm-oil belt, the city-states quickly converted to the palm-oil trade and by the middle of the century had become the leading African exporters. This conversion of the economy was not accomplished without social disruption of revolutionary proportions which occasionally went so far as to replace the freeborn aristocracy of the state by the ex-slave classes. Thus the change brought about by the suppression of the slave trade was the major factor in the history of the Niger Delta in the first half of the nineteenth century.

The history of the city-states also illustrates how the suppression of the slave trade led to a greater European involvement in and encroachment upon African politics, and thus to the partition. The late nineteenth-century trade war between the city-states and European firms throws considerable light on the economic background to the partition and the unfortunate consequences of European commercial dominance for the city-states.

In 1800 the Niger Delta area was dominated by five city-states: the Itsekiri kingdom to the west, the kingdoms of Brass, Elem Kalabari and Grand Bonny to the east and the state of Calabar at the mouth of the Cross and Calabar rivers. Each city-state was composed of three parts; the capital, its heart and nerve centre, its colonies of satellite villages and its trading empire in the oil-palm belt of the interior. Since the capital cities were located in the mangrove swamps, land there possessed little value for agriculture or transportation. As the European demand for slaves had grown in the seventeenth and eighteenth centuries, the capital cities had reached out, ignoring the land but striving to control the harbours and creeks, the fishing grounds, and the waterways to the interior. Satellite villages, like tiny colonies, settled from the capital, grew up along these waterways. Beyond the colonies was the trading empire where citizens of the city-state enjoyed a monopoly of trade, and where hundreds of them lived during the buying season. The city-state protected, advanced credit to, and intermarried with the people of its trading empire. King Pepple had an Ibo wife from the Bonny trading empire; Nana of Ebrohimie married a number of Urhobo women from the Itsekiri trading empire.

Grand Bonny was ideally located and organized for trade. It was closer to the palm belt than any other state except Calabar. It possessed an excellent river transport system, the Imo, which tapped a densely populated Ibo area. Bonny and to a lesser degree Brass and Calabar had developed a partnership with the Aro who had created a trading system over much of the territory of the Ibo and Ibibio. As a result Grand Bonny was the largest Delta exporter of slaves in 1800 and of palm-oil by 1850. Elem Kalabari, the second city-state of the Delta had its trading empire along the Sambreiro river. The kingdom of Brass, with its capital at Nembe and its port at Twon, was in trading partnership with the Ibo kingdom of Aboh. The Itsekiri kingdom had its capital at Warri, its ports on the Benin river and its trading empire among the Urhobo along the Ethiope and Warri rivers. Calabar's trading empire stretched up the Cross and Calabar rivers.

The House system

Originally the city-states, like the Ibo and Ibibio clans, possessed a segmentary political system based on lineages, but important changes had taken place in order to organize their export trade and their trading empires effectively. The lineages developed into Houses each with a head, who once elected became an absolute ruler with the power of life and death over the members of the House, and who was the custodian of its property and finances. The Houses were like trading corporations and were in fierce competition with each other. The weak were driven into bankruptcy and thus absorbed by the strong. A House was judged by the size and quality of its fleet of trade and war canoes. Its commercial success depended upon its trade canoes for transporting goods from its trading empire to the coast. Its prestige depended upon the number of war canoes it could put at the service of the city-state in wartime. Every House maintained at least one war canoe mounted with cannon, manned by about 50 paddlers and carrying 80 to 140 soldiers, and most Bonny Houses could boast of ten or more such canoes. A war fleet was a vital necessity because loss of control of the waterways could cut off the capital from its empire and bring immediate ruin. The Houses also established villages and markets which depended on them, employed their own trading agents and advanced credit to their interior partners.

There was a continual process of fission and fusion of Houses. A large House, through mismanagement or poor leadership, economic disaster or political quarrels, might split up into a number of small separate Houses. On the other hand a successful House often became the head of a House group, either through alliances, or by paying off the debts of weaker Houses and thus getting control of them, or by wealthy men from within creating their own Houses which they controlled. As a House prospered it needed more men to man its war and trade canoes and to act as buying and selling agents. Slaves were purchased in order to increase the population of the House and often they ultimately outnumbered the freeborn. King Amakiri I almost doubled the population of Elem Kalabari by the purchase of slaves.

Originally only royal princes could found or head Houses, but in the commercial competition of the eighteenth century a House either chose its ablest man as leader or collapsed before its rivals. As a result, except in Itsekiri, capable and energetic businessmen among the slaves rose to prominence in the Houses. In Elem Kalabari and occassionally in Calabar they rose to the head of subordinate Houses, and in Bonny and Brass they often became the heads of House groups, positions which were next in rank to the king.

There was a royal family in each city-state – the Pepples of Bonny, the Amakiris of Kalabari and the Mingis of Brass. By the beginning of the nineteenth century the Bonny monarchy was 400 years old. The king ruled through a state council of House heads, was responsible for relations with the European traders, collected the comey (customs dues) and settled inter-House disputes. He was considered semi-divine, his person was sacred and he performed rituals to the God who protected the state, while each House head performed similar duties to the ancestor-founder of the House.

In 1800 House heads were still royal princes and when the king died they acted as kingmakers, choosing one of their own number, usually the wealthiest, to succeed. If a man had organized a prosperous House he was likely to have the qualities of a good king. Upon coronation the king received the divine power associated with kingship and this, combined with his wealth and augmented by the comey he now received, made him the most powerful individual in the city-state.

House society was organized in layers; the royal princes at the top, freeborn commoners and slaves who had been born in the state and could not by custom be sold outside it in the middle, and purchased slaves, who could be sold in times of financial stress, at the bottom. In the nineteenth century freeborn commoners and slaves were becoming House heads but there remained a strong prejudice against their election as kings. By the mid-nineteenth century House heads who had been born slaves were electing kings and were therefore kingmakers although they were never kings. The result was, particularly in Bonny, that the wealthiest could no longer be chosen as king. The monarchy was weakened and had to rely on the support of European merchants and on a policy of playing the powerful House heads off against each other. In Bonny and Kalabari this led to civil war and to the division of Bonny into two, and of Elem Kalabari into three, separate city-states.

House organization was a much altered segmentary political system. The capital city and villages round it were internally organized into Houses and represented the major segments of the lineage in the Ibo village, House heads replacing lineage elders. Although the principle of election was kept the democratic element had been weakened by the concentration of power in the hands of the House heads and the king. The emphasis upon competition and wealth was greater than in the lineage system and the strangers and slaves became more quickly full members of society. Respect for age and blood relationship was less important but House heads continued to perform the ritual functions of lineage elders, the king having become responsible to and for the original clan deities. The idea of a royal family and of a partly divine king were new ideas added on to the segmentary system. Every city-state had its secret society but only in Calabar did it possess political powers comparable to those among the Cross River Ibo clans. Splitting apart and joining up again kept altering the political balance between Houses as it did in Iboland between lineages. The division of Grand Bonny into two, and of Elem Kalabari into three separate states was also similar to the sort of things that happened under the Ibo segmentary political system.

Commercial rivalry, 1807-56

After the slave trade had become illegal for British subjects, former British slavers began coming to the delta city-states in search of palm-oil for the rapidly expanding factories of Britain. Calabar, the only city-state situated within the oil palm belt, and which had never been able to compete successfully against Bonny in the export of slaves, had begun even before 1800 to develop plantations and to convert to palm-oil exports. Bonny sought to supply oil to the British at the same time as supplying slaves to other Europeans, who rushed in to take over the trade which the British had abandoned. Initially Elem Kalabari, Brass and Itsekiri were little affected and continued to ship slaves as before.

As the American, Brazilian and Cuban plantations expanded the price of slaves rose, and the palm-oil merchants found they could not compete with the slave merchants, because the city-states naturally concentrated principally on the more profitable trade. Oil ships often waited on the coast for up to eighteen months for a cargo, which increased their costs in lives, salaries and insurance rates, and lowered their profits. In the late 1830's the Anti-Slave Trade Squadron of the British navy began to prevent the export of slaves by blockading the city-states. Bonny, close to the open sea, was easily watched and had to convert her exports rapidly from slaves to oil. Bonny's misfortune brought prosperity to Brass, which became a major slave exporter for the first time as it was surrounded by a maze of creeks and slave ships could slip away unnoticed by the British navy. Bonny, traditional ally of Brass, diverted its supply of slaves to Brass for sale. In Itsekiri slave captains were afraid to be caught inside the dangerous bar of the Benin river and stopped coming. Oil merchants failed to take their place even though Itsekiri oil prices were the lowest on the coast, and a long depression followed which ultimately caused the collapse of the Itsekiri monarchy.

The palm-oil trade, like the slave trade, operated on the trust (credit) system. European merchants advanced goods on trust to House heads who in turn gave them out on trust to their buying agents in the interior. When a ship arrived the captain expected that the merchants to whom he had given trust would have a cargo of oil ready to load so that there would be little delay in returning to Europe.

Trust was not only a source of friction but also a weapon of commercial rivalry. Everyone accused everyone else of cheating yet no one would give it up because it was an effective weapon against rivals. An African was compelled to sell all his oil to the European whose trust he held. The European never wanted his trust totally repaid by a reliable African merchant because the African would then be free to sell to the European's rivals. Europeans tried every method, honest and dishonest, to keep Africans in debt to them. When a new firm arrived it found that all House heads were under trust to the old firms. To break the monopoly the new firm would offer either higher prices for oil or trust on easier terms which tempted Africans to break their original trusts. If Africans supplied the new merchant with oil the old firms would forcibly seize it. The king would then declare a boycott of all trade until the dispute was settled. The king might also proclaim a trade boycott if the European firms combined to fix prices. In this case one or two of the firms could usually be bribed to buy above the fixed price so that the European combine would collapse.

Between 1830 and 1850, when twelve Liverpool firms were buying in Bonny, the price and demand for palm-oil kept rising steadily. In the 1850's two factors combined to cause supply to run ahead of demand and prices to fall. The first was the regular steamship service between West Africa and Europe, started in 1852, which greatly increased the number of European buyers (200 in the delta in 1856), many of whom were now small men who could not afford their own ships. The other was that Bonny, Kalabari and Calabar, the major exporters, were joined after 1850 by Lagos, Brass and Itsekiri. In addition to these two factors all the city-states were busy extending their trading empires deeper into the interior in order to increase their oil exports, which caused rising costs at a time when prices were falling.

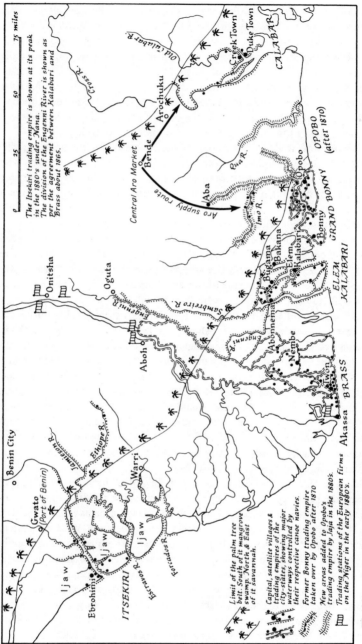

The Itsekiri trading empire is shown at its peak
in the 1880's under Nana.
The division of the Engenni River is shown as
per the agreement between Kalabari and
Brass about 1865.

Central Aro Market

Aro supply route

*Limit of the palm tree
belt. South of it mangrove
swamp. North & East
of it savannah.*

*Capital, satellite villages &
trading empires of the
city-states, showing major
waterways controlled by
their respective canoe navies.*

*Former Bonny trading empire
taken over by Opobo after 1870*

*New areas added to Opobo's
trading empire by Jaja in the 1880's.*

*Trading stations of the European firms
on the Niger in the early 1880's.*

37 *The Niger Delta in the mid-nineteenth century*

The fifties were years of bitter commercial rivalry as the weaker European firms and African Houses were forced into bankruptcy by the squeeze between falling prices and rising costs. There was rivalry among African Houses, between city-states as they overlapped each other's trading empires, between African Houses and European firms, and between the European firms themselves. In 1855 and again in 1857 the Efik of Calabar sought to ship their oil direct to Europe by chartered ships, thus by-passing the English middlemen and raising their profits by one hundred per cent. The British had no intention of allowing this kind of trade and the navy threatened to bombard Calabar so that the scheme was dropped. Without British naval support British firms were hardly the commercial equals of the House trading corporations. But once Africans lost political control they lost their economic prosperity as well.

The rise of the new men: Bonny

Bonny reached the height of its power between 1792 and 1830 under Opubu the Great. At his death the heir to the throne, Prince Dappa Pepple, was still a minor. The headship of Opubu's House, Anna Pepple, passed to Alali, who was one of the first and most capable of the new men – men not of royal or even freeborn ancestry – who were beginning to feature in Delta society. Alali was not a royal prince, not even a freeborn commoner, but an assimilated slave; he was appointed regent in 1833. Had Bonny overcome its remaining prejudices against men of his origin and elected Alali king the state might have avoided some of its later troubles.

In 1836 the British navy, without warning, violated Bonny's policy of allowing all nations to trade with her, and entered her territorial waters to seize a Spanish slave ship in her harbour. In retaliation for this outrage against international law, Alali imprisoned the British merchants. The British navy in its turn then threatened to destroy Bonny unless the merchants were released. Prince Dappa, anxious to rid himself of Alali and take over the throne, offered co-operation. In return for a promise never to touch British subjects again, Prince Dappa persuaded the British to force Alali to sign his own deposition. As a result British subjects became an arrogant and often criminal element, a privileged caste above the law of Bonny. Alali thus gained the support of those who resented British privilege and felt that Prince Dappa had sold Bonny's sovereignty to further his own personal ambition.

King Dappa was not wealthy and his power was challenged, both from without by the British who expected his subservience since he owed them his throne, and from within by Alali who was prospering and increasing his political power by absorbing Houses into the Anna Pepple group. Dappa tried to build up his power at the expense of both the British and Alali but in the end he was crushed between them. He signed an anti-slave trade treaty with the British whereby they promised to pay him a subsidy for five years to enable him to switch from slaves to oil; but Dappa's real need for the subsidy was to build up his House to compete with Anna Pepple. To check Alali he passed a law forbidding further absorption of Houses and ruled that Europeans might only give trust to, and Africans hold trust from, the king. These policies were universally unpopular. In 1854 Pepple seized a British merchant ship, in place of the payments they owed him under the treaty, which they had four times signed and four times refused to ratify; thereupon Alali and his supporters signed a proclamation for the king's deposition and the British consul, backed by the navy and the British merchants, deported the king. A civil war followed in which Alali, leading a combination of the new men, who were mainly ex-slaves, destroyed the royalist and freeborn supporters of the ex-king.

Alali was now the real power in Grand Bonny. He might even have overcome the prejudice against his servile origins, but the British were too much aware of his hostility to their privileged position to favour him as a replacement on the throne. They supported instead a Regency Council of four; and although three of these were new men, the British were careful to see that only one was from the Anna Pepple House group. Since this government ignored the realities of political power, chaos and confusion followed, until the British merchants called for the return of King Dappa.

Dappa returned in 1861, now only a shadow of his father Opubu the Great. At British insistence he was forbidden to engage in trade and forced to rely upon comey (the customs dues paid by foreign traders). His deportation had undermined his divinity, the civil war had destroyed his fortune and the trade ban prevented the rebuilding of his wealth. The British wanted a king who held absolute power over his subjects and who would do their bidding and be able to command his people to do likewise. This was impractical, for although control of trade was the key to wealth and wealth was the source of a monarch's power, the British were determined to control trade. Following the civil war it became true that whether there was a king or not real power lay with Anna Pepple House under Alali and Manilla Pepple under Oko Jumbo, both new men of servile origin. King Dappa Pepple died in 1866 and was succeeded by George Pepple, who in external affairs did what the British wanted, and in internal affairs did what Oko Jumbo wanted.

When Alali died, Anna Pepple House elected Jaja, a purchased Ibo slave, to succeed him. Jaja had risen to prominence in the House, was popular in the interior markets, had a quick eye for the promotion and advancement of capable men and like Alali continued to build up the Anna Pepple group and absorb other Houses. In 1868 the Manilla Pepple House under Oko Jumbo attacked the Anna Pepple House with the support of the king. Rather than engage in a civil war Jaja withdrew his House group and established it at Opobo, carefully placed so as to cut off Bonny from its trading empire on the Imo river. Jaja invited British firms to establish themselves in Opobo and made it clear that they must operate under African law without special privileges.

Bonny and the British firms called upon the British consul to force Jaja to return. The consul advised a boycott of Opobo until Jaja's ammunition was exhausted when it was believed he would collapse. But Jaja had what everyone wanted, palm-oil. A couple of firms moved to Opobo, the boycott failed, and in 1872 the British consul recognized Opobo as an independent city-state. While Grand Bonny and the British firms who remained loyal to her declined, Opobo and her commercial allies prospered as never before.

As the greatest king of the Delta, Jaja represented the triumph of the new men of servile and common origin; these men had risen with the palm-oil trade at the expense of the nobility who had declined as the trade in slaves came to an end. In all the city-states the pattern was the same, with the lower classes challenging the upper; but in none was the social revolution so complete or dramatic as that led by King Jaja of Opobo.

The rise of the new men: Calabar

Since Brass and Elem Kalabari were farther from the sea and thus from the pressure of the British consul and navy, their royal families – the Mingis and and Amakiris – lost neither their power nor their wealth to the same degree as did the Pepples of Bonny. Nor in those states did the new men rise beyond headships of subordinate Houses. In Itsekiri, however, the monarchy collapsed after the cessation of the slave trade and, following a period of anarchy, the new men represented by Nana, 'the uncrowned king of the Itsekiri', rose on the profits of the palm-oil trade. Nana was not of servile origin but a freeborn commoner who by tradition could not be chosen to rule.

The rise of the lower classes in Calabar took a different form because of the unique political and economic organization of that state. Calabar was organized in Houses but was divided politically under two kings. Real political power, however, lay neither with the kings nor with the House heads, but with the Ekpe secret society, which was divided into grades, the highest being the Nyampa or governing grade. The Nyampa were the real rulers of Calabar and its supreme judicial authority, through which the British merchants collected their debts. Ex-slaves became House heads, but since they were normally forbidden entrance to the top Ekpe grades they were politically powerless.

Unlike the other city-states, Calabar's economy was based on palm plantations which, like the plantations in America, bred a new and more oppressive
type of slavery. The freeborn and slaves were more segregated than in the
eighteenth century, the former living in Calabar town, and the latter on the
plantations along the Cross and Calabar rivers. There was less opportunity
for assimilation, promotion or inter-marriage. Except for those privileged to
be employed in the House trading activities in Calabar, the slaves were
looked upon as no more than a source of cheap labour by their absentee
freeborn masters.

It was Efik custom that upon the death of a king or prominent person the
House concerned displayed its wealth by the number of slaves it sacrificed
to accompany and render service to the dead in the next world. House
competition in sacrificing greater and greater numbers became a terrifying
abuse of the slave class. Ultimately runaway slaves established their own
community on the Qua River where they founded the Order of Blood Men,
which was organized in grades like the Ekpe, and was formed as a protection
against the oppression of that society. Slaves from the plantations as well as
from Calabar town joined the Order for protection. It undertook its first
defensive action in 1851. When the Ekpe arrested some slaves, thousands of
Blood Men poured into Calabar threatening to destroy the town utterly if
their brethren were harmed. Although the British consul and merchants
tended to favour their trading partners in the Ekpe, without an army they were
helpless against the slaves. In 1852 when King Archibong I died the Blood
Men again poured into Calabar, standing around the town, watchful but
non-violent. No funeral sacrifices took place either then or later as the Order
repeated these tactics upon the death of every prominent freeborn man in
Calabar. In 1857 when a freeborn man killed his slave the Blood Men
demanded and got the offender delivered up to justice. Many of the poorer
freeborn began to join the Order as a protection against Ekpe oppression.

The Order of Blood Men, through non-violent methods, secured a measure
of equality for the new men (both freeborn and slaves) so that by 1863 they
were able to win court cases against the nobility and Nyampa. The Order
sought justice and equality but not domination. It neither attempted to set up
its own king nor to destroy the Ekpe. The social revolution it created did
not replace one class by another. Rather it compelled the nobility to govern
in the general interest rather than for the advantage of one class. This
revolution in Calabar was perhaps the most remarkable non-violent revolution
in nineteenth-century West Africa.

Commercial war, 1856-86

At the same time as the city-states were preoccupied with the internal dislocation and strife arising from the clash between the rising new men and the traditional ruling classes, the commercial rivalry of the earlier period changed after 1856 to commercial war. Three new competitors entered the palm-oil trade, Brass, Opobo and the Royal Niger Company. Until the Anglo-Brass treaty of 1856, by which Brass promised to stop shipping slaves, Brass had continued slave smuggling in co-operation with the Brazilians and Portuguese. Following the treaty Brass began to exploit the oil markets up the Engenni river to Oguta and at Aboh and Onitsha.

Opobo, having taken over the Imo river market from Bonny in 1870, began to develop the Qua river. Bonny, squeezed out of its traditional markets, invaded Kalabari markets to the west and the Kalabari were thus compelled to push up the Engenni and began to fight Brass for control of Oguta. The resulting wars put a heavy strain on the finances of the city-states especially at a time when they were attempting to increase their exports of oil to make up for the lower prices.

It was in these circumstances that British firms broke through the Delta and established themselves on the middle Niger at Aboh, Onitsha and Lokoja. The beginning of this process was the discovery in 1830 by the Lander brothers that the Delta was the mouth of a large river. Early efforts to establish trade on the Niger failed due to the hostility of the city-states and the death toll from malaria. In 1854, however, Baikie, a medical doctor with a British expedition to the Niger, kept everyone alive by the use of quinine, a discovery of momentous importance to the subsequent history of tropical Africa.

Immediately a British merchant, Macgregor Laird, with the aid of a British government subsidy, opened trading posts in and behind the Brass trading empire, at Aboh, Onitsha and Lokoja. Brass in reply fortified the river and encouraged the destruction of Laird's factories at Aboh and Onitsha. Insurance rates rose for ships bound for the Niger, and Kru stevedores refused to work on them. Again it was the British navy which decided the issue. Laird's ships were given naval escorts through the Delta, and Aboh and Onitsha were bombarded to punish them for their attacks on Laird's factories. As long as warships were on the Niger, trade flowed; when the dry season reduced the water level so that they could not ascend the river, trade ceased. By 1878 four British firms were trading on the Niger. British merchants in the Delta who had originally opposed Laird began to surrender to the inevitable and to transfer to the Niger where oil could be bought more cheaply.

The British effort to take over the middleman's position and increase their profits was a serious threat to the very existence of the city-states. On the Niger a price war raged between British and French firms, African merchants from Lagos and Freetown, and Brass and Kalabari traders. In 1879 an Englishman, George Goldie, aiming 'to paint the map red', united the British firms on the Niger into the United Africa Company, established up to one hundred trading posts supported by twenty gunboats, and offered very high prices for oil until the French firms were made bankrupt. The only effective competition that continued to stand in Goldie's way now came from the Lagos and Brass traders.

In 1886 Goldie secured a royal charter for his company now renamed the Royal Niger Company, by which the company became the government of the Niger. Immediately it eliminated its last opposition by imposing heavy licences and taxes on the Lagosians and Creoles, by refusing to allow Brass or Kalabari traders to enter its area, and by confiscating the trade canoes of those caught smuggling. The Company went so far as to threaten Ibo traders who tried to pay their debts to Brass merchants. The kingdom of Brass was thus economically strangled by the most severe and rigid monopoly of middlemen that the Niger had ever witnessed.

Collapse of the city-states, 1880-95

Elem Kalabari was the first victim of the commercial struggle of the 1880's. The state was already exhausted in wars fought to preserve its trading empire against its powerful neighbours, Bonny and Brass, and by the necessity of transporting oil in convoys escorted by war canoes. Inside the state the new men were challenging the traditional nobility and the Barboy House was threatening the authority of the Amakiri dynasty. In the early eighties civil war brought disintegration, the Amakiri supporters moved to Buguma and the Barboy House split, one section settling at Abonema and the other at Bakana. Thereafter Kalabari was no longer significant in Delta trade and politics.

Opobo was fortunate in having control of the Imo and Qua markets and in having good trading relations with the Aros. Within the state Jaja was not threatened by internal divisions and was not much affected by the British break through into the Niger, which was too far to the west to tap his oil markets. British traders tried to smuggle oil out of the Qua valley, which they refused to recognize as Jaja's trading empire, but Jaja more than made up for this by shipping oil direct to England and by-passing the European middlemen.

In 1884 when the partition of Africa was under way Jaja signed a treaty of protection with the British but specifically refused to include a free trade clause. In the same year the British firms at Opobo combined to fix the price of oil but Jaja persuaded the firm of Miller Bros. to break the combine and buy on his terms. If British merchants were to secure a trade monopoly here it would have to be imposed by force. In early 1887 the consul asked Jaja to insert a clause which would allow British traders access to any part of his kingdom and when he refused the consul asked for a meeting, promising that after it Jaja 'would be free to go'. At the meeting, however, Jaja was informed that, if he left, British naval guns would destroy Opobo. To save his capital and people, who had no hint of the disaster which hung over their heads, Jaja left peacefully with the consul and was tried at Accra and deported to the West Indies. He died in 1891, his corpse being brought back to Opobo for a royal funeral and burial within the palace walls. Much has been made of British duplicity, and certainly 'consul' was for a long time synonymous with treachery in the eastern delta; but even had the British been honourable and met Jaja in open war, the end result would have been the same because the British were determined to monopolize the middleman position of the palm-oil trade.

The collapse of the Itsekiri monarchy in 1848 following the effective stopping of the slave trade in the 1820's caused the Itsekiri capital of Warri to fall into insignificance as many Itsekiri moved to the Benin river where a couple of British firms were buying palm-oil. The oil trade here developed slowly and it was not until the early 1870's that it really got under way. The Itsekiri Houses in co-operation with the British consul and merchants elected an Itsekiri 'Governor of the Benin River', to deal with inter-House and Anglo-Itsekiri trade disputes.

The governors of the river were usually new men, not from the royal family, but commoners who were rising to prominence through the palm-oil trade. Such a man was Olomu, the wealthiest Itsekiri merchant in the 1870's, who established his own town Ebrohimi, and served as governor of the river for four years before his death in 1883. Upon his death his son Nana inherited Ebrohimi and the family fortune and was elected Governor of the River. By this title he was recognized by the British as head of the Itsekiri people, and in practice therefore was an uncrowned king.

Among the Itsekiri merchants only Nana was big enough to deal with the European firms as equals. Nana did not require large trust and most Itsekiri traders held trust from him rather than from the Europeans. This prevented the quarrels and accusations which elsewhere were a convenient excuse to call in the navy. Nana maintained law and order, and by a combination of force and friendship cemented by marriage alliances, brought the Urhobos along the Jamieson, Ethiope and Warri rivers into his trading empire.

In 1885 Nana signed a treaty of protection with the British but like Jaja rejected a clause which would have allowed British traders to operate anywhere in his empire. Anglo-Itsekiri commercial relations were smoother than elsewhere in the Delta and when the consul urged the oil firms to agitate against Nana they showed little interest. The consul then turned to stir up trouble among other Itsekiri traders. He found assistance from Dore Numa, who was an ambitious merchant from a rival Itsekiri House. Fearing treachery Nana refused to meet the consul and in 1894 a British naval expedition destroyed Ebrohimi. Nana gave himself up and was deported to Accra.

In 1893 Goldie tightened his customs controls so severely that the Brass smuggling trade was stopped. Brass merchants appealed to the consul, Claude Macdonald, who repeatedly asked the British government to give up its support for the Niger Company. However, Goldie was as ruthless in Britain as in Africa. In addition prominent members of both British political parties held shares in his company, which was the most profitable British charter company in Africa. Furthermore the scramble for Africa was now at its height and Goldie was in a position to threaten the British government that, if his monopoly was broken, he could withdraw and let the whole Niger fall to the French or Germans. In 1894 Macdonald was forced to admit that he could do nothing to help Brass.

In 1895 King Koko of Brass made a desperate bid for survival. With about 1,000 soldiers in thirty war canoes he destroyed the Royal Niger Company's headquarters and port at Akassa. Although Brass insisted that it had no quarrel with the British government, the Royal navy together with Company troops retaliated by blowing up Nembe and Twon, the capital and the port of Brass, confiscating all Brass war canoes, fining the king £500 and driving the people into the swamps, where starvation and a smallpox epidemic killed more people than did British bullets. Brass was broken.

King Koko's war canoe on the way to attack Akassa in 1895

Goldie called the Brass attack on Akassa a 'wild unprovoked act of savages'. Macdonald, however, pointed out that Jaja had been deported because he had been a monopolist (he could have mentioned Nana as well) yet 'now we have wiped the floor with the Brass men because they have endeavoured to go for the biggest monopolist of the crowd – the Royal Niger Company'. He pointed out that in the vast territories of the Niger there was no trader white or black except the Company, which could therefore close any market and offer any price. However, the real issue had never been monopoly and free trade, but rather whether the monopoly should be enjoyed by Delta merchants or by British firms. Partly as a result of the Akassa war the British government forced Goldie to give up his charter in 1900. But this was no victory for Brass, whose people sank into poverty and subsistence fishing while the Niger Company emerged as the largest and wealthiest British firm in West Africa.

Conclusion

The first major theme of nineteenth-century Delta history was the effect upon the city-states of the suppression of the slave trade and of the change over to palm-oil exports. The British, particularly in Bonny and Calabar, not only tried to abolish the trade in slaves but also employed the navy against the city-states to gain for British oil merchants a privileged position above African law. The result was to weaken the power and authority of the kings and traditional ruling classes of the states, and to make them less able to maintain law and order and to deal with the social upheaval in their states.

As the city-states tried to change from exporting slaves to exporting palm-oil, the nobility and the freeborn traders hung on too long to slave trading, while the new men, either freeborn commoners or ex-slaves, found opportunity for advancement in the oil trade. As the slave trade declined it carried the nobility down with it, and as palm-oil became important it carried the new men to wealth and power. In the city-states there was a social upheaval of revolutionary proportions as the lower classes, led by men like Alali, Oko Jumbo, Jaja, Nana and the Blood Men, struggled upwards against the prejudice and oppression of the nobility.

Delta history was a century-long battle of middlemen. There were three sets of middlemen between the oil-producers in Africa and the factory consumers in Europe; these were the European merchants who bought oil in the city-states and sold it in Britain, the Delta merchants who bought oil in the interior and transported it to the coast, and the interior organizers of the trade such as the Ibo of Arochuku and Aboh. The commercial rivalry within these sets – English firms against French, Bonny Houses against Kalabari, stronger firms and Houses absorbing the weaker – prepared the way for the final battle for survival in the 1880's and 1890's between the Delta traders and the British middlemen. The British firms won because the British government was ready to back their expansion with military force. Goldie's amalgamation of the firms on the Niger, his skilful use of economic and political weapons, and the steady support he received from the British government, brought about the end of the battle of the middlemen, the end of the power of the city-states, and the beginning of the colonial period.

Once the city-states were economically ruined British forces destroyed the Aro system, leaving British firms as the sole middlemen of the Niger trade. Africans were excluded from this key sector of the economy, in which profits were largest, where capital could be accumulated and from where the economic development of the country could be stimulated. The people of the city-states sank into dismal subsistence-level poverty, where they remained throughout the colonial period.

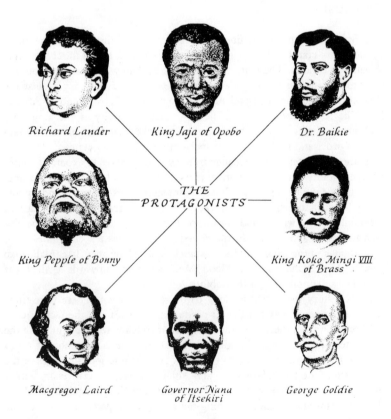

Richard Lander

King Jaja of Opobo

Dr. Baikie

King Pepple of Bonny

THE PROTAGONISTS

King Koko Mingi VIII of Brass

Macgregor Laird

Governor Nana of Itsekiri

George Goldie

14 The fall of southern Ghana

The British conquest and annexation of Asante between 1900 and 1901 was, of course, not a sudden and isolated event. It was the final stage in the growth of British power and jurisdiction in Ghana, which began with their direct and active entry into the wars between Asante and her southern vassal states. It is this development of British power and jurisdiction in Ghana which culminated in the annexation of southern Ghana in 1874 that forms the theme of this chapter.

When the nineteenth century began, the British were by no means the only European traders on the coast of Ghana. The Dutch and the Danes were also quite active. Though openly and officially they were all neutral in the affairs of the local states and merely acted as referees, secretly the British and the Danes supported the coastal and southern states, while the Dutch were on very intimate terms with the Asante. The Danes and the Dutch stuck to their official policy of neutrality mainly because they were too weak to do otherwise. But the British, for reasons already discussed, came out openly in support of the southern states from 1821 onwards, when the Colonial Office assumed direct responsibility for the administration of the forts. As we have seen, their first real clash with the Asante ended disastrously, but in August 1826 the British fully avenged that defeat by a decisive victory over the Asante. However, instead of strengthening their position, the British government decided to withdraw from Ghana altogether; this was because they found the administration too expensive and too difficult, while trade was in fact declining, and no headway had been made in the promotion of Christianity and western education. The British merchants who were active in Ghana vehemently opposed this decision. As a compromise, the British government decided to hand over the administration of the forts to them and grant them an annual subsidy of £4,000. But they were specifically asked to exercise their authority and jurisdiction only over the people living within the British forts, and not in any way to interfere in local politics. The forts were to be administered by a committee of three members in London and a council in Cape Coast elected by British merchants resident at Cape Coast and Accra who had been there for more than a year. The Council was to be under a president elected by its members.

A general view of Cape Coast Castle from the sea

Administration of George Maclean

The Company administration, which began in 1828, continued until 1843, and instead of British jurisdiction being confined to the forts, it had by the end of the period been extended over all the states along the coast, with the exception of Elmina, and for about forty miles inland. This great extension of British power and influence was mainly the result of the work of George Maclean, who was appointed as President of the Council in October 1829. He arrived in Cape Coast in February 1830 and remained in Ghana until his death in May 1847. How, then, did he accomplish this?

Maclean was realistic enough to see that unless peace and order were established in Ghana, neither legitimate trade nor missionary activities would flourish. Therefore he deliberately ignored the British government's instructions and actively interfered in local politics. Indeed, no sooner had he arrived than he began to negotiate with the Asante. These negotiations

Governor
George Maclean

were successfully concluded and a peace treaty was signed by the Asante and the British and their allies in April 1831. According to the terms of this treaty, the Asantehene recognized the independence of his former vassal states to the south – Denkyira, Assin, Twifu, Wassa, Fante, Cape Coast, Nzima, etc. – and agreed to refer all disputes between himself and the southern states to the British for peaceful settlement. He also agreed to deposit 600 ounces of gold in Cape Coast Castle, and to hand over two young men of the royal family to the British government for six years, as security that he would keep peace with the British and their allies. The allied states, on their part, undertook to keep the paths open and free to all persons engaged in lawful traffic, not to force them to trade in any particular market, and not to insult their former master. Finally, all parties to the treaty agreed to stop 'panyarring', that is, forcibly seizing debtors or relatives and imprisoning them or selling them. This treaty was a very clever piece of work, since it satisfied both principal parties. The allied states at long last regained their independence, while the Asante also gained the direct access to the forts that they had been fighting for since the eighteenth century.

Maclean did his best to ensure that the terms of this treaty were strictly observed by all parties. Furthermore, in order to win the full confidence of the Asante, he first of all sent the two princes, Owusu Ansa and Owusu Kwantabisa, to England for education, after which they returned to Kumasi in 1842. Secondly, he returned the entire 600 ounces of gold, in the very bags in which they were sent to Cape Coast in accordance with the terms of the treaty, an action which greatly impressed the Asante. Thirdly, he protected all the Asante traders who came to the coast, and made it a point to return all fugitives and criminals who escaped to the coast from Asante. As a result of Maclean's policy, peace and friendship continued between the British and the Asante throughout his long tenure of office.

Maclean also sought to maintain peace and order among the chiefs of the southern states, to stop human sacrifice, panyarring, attacks or raids on peaceful traders, and slave trading. He did this by peaceful means, though he did not hesitate to use force when necessary. Thus in 1833, he stepped in when war broke out between Wassa and Denkyira, and fined the chief of the latter, Kwadwo Tsibu, whom he blamed for the fight. In the same year or the next, he arbitrated between Akwapem and Krobo; in 1836 and 1838 he tried to settle the long-standing dispute between Upper and Lower Wassa, that is Wassa Amenfi and Wassa Fiasi. In 1835, on the other hand, he sent an army to Nzima against Kwaku Ackah, the famous chief who was accused of slave trading, human sacrifice, panyarring and attacks on peaceful Wassa traders. Further expeditions were sent to Wassa in 1836 and 1842, and to Asikuma in 1837. However, it was only in Nzima that actual fighting took place.

The other method by which he established order and peace was by administering justice impartially among the peoples of southern Ghana. At first Maclean and the Council left the local authorities to deal with all their criminal cases. But from 1836 onwards, Maclean attended the courts in person or sent a member of the Council to watch the actual process of the trial and to see that justice was really done. Maclean also later on allowed the chiefs, as well as their subjects, to bring cases of all kinds to his court, and he tried the cases, and imposed sentences of fines or imprisonment on the guilty. He also stationed magistrates in Dixcove, Anomabo and Accra, and he supervised their judicial activities closely by paying regular visits. By 1841 there were ninety-one prisoners in the Castle prison: fifty of them were debtors, sixteen were suspected of murder, seven were sentenced for theft, and some were political prisoners. Furthermore, he used the soldiers of the forts as police, and stationed them singly or in groups in various towns in southern Ghana, to see that order was maintained and that any outbreaks of violence, or infringement of regulations, were promptly reported to Cape Coast.

As a result of the work of Maclean in the political and judicial fields, order was established in southern Ghana; peace also existed between Asante and her former allies throughout the 1830's and 1840's, and the external slave trade was effectively suppressed. The inevitable result was that traders and farmers were able to go about their activities, and trade therefore boomed. The growth of trade that occurred during Maclean's administration is borne out by the figures for imports and exports to and from Cape Coast. The value of exports from Cape Coast increased from £90,000 in 1831 to £325,000 in 1840, and that of imports from £131,000 to £423,000. The main exports from Ghana at this time were palm-oil, gold, ivory, pepper and corn. The production of palm-oil, coffee and corn greatly increased, particularly due to the extinction of the external slave trade, and to the encouragement of British traders and, later, missionaries. Imports consisted of the usual commodities of the seventeenth and eighteenth centuries, the principal ones being rum, brandy, gin, tobacco, cotton goods, guns, gunpowder and Indian cloth.

Besides traders, missionaries also received encouragement from Maclean's administration. Although the Basel Missionary Society had started operations in Ghana in 1828, not much had been accomplished when Maclean began his term of office. But, taking advantage of the peace and order, the Basel missionary, Riis, was able to abandon the coast, which was considered to be unhealthy, and settle inland at Akropong in 1835; from that time the work of that mission began to take root, and to spread northwards and southwards. By 1843 Riis had established a school at Akropong, and soon opened others in Accra and Aburi. In 1848 a catechists' training college was established at Akropong, and another at Osu in 1850. Six years later, the latter was amalgamated with the one at Akropong. The Wesleyan Missionary Society also began operations in Ghana in 1835, and the work made rapid strides with the arrival in Ghana of the Mulatto missionary, Thomas Birch Freeman, in January 1838. He not only established churches in the coastal areas, but also began the missionary drive into Asante with a visit to Kumasi in 1839. By 1843 twenty-one missionary stations had been established in Ghana by the Wesleyans, and there were 360 children attending their schools. The Methodists expanded their missionary and educational activities during the second half of the nineteenth century, and even founded a secondary school, the now famous Mfantsipim school, in 1876. Maclean did not establish any schools himself, for want of funds, but he gave the missionaries every encouragement, and his relations with Freeman were particularly intimate. Though several attempts had been made to establish Christianity and western education in Ghana ever since the Portuguese set foot there in the 1470's, it was not until the time of Maclean that these attempts began to take firm root and yield any fruits; these fruits not only lasted but have been multiplying ever since.

Britain assumes direct responsibility

It should be clear, then, that by the early forties, peace had been established in Ghana, and British power and jurisdiction had completely replaced that of the Asante; a British protectorate had in practice come into existence. But however successful Maclean's jurisdiction was, it had no legal basis whatsoever. Moreover, reports reached England that Maclean was conniving at slavery and was not preventing ships which took part in the slave trade from buying goods at Cape Coast. It was mainly for these reasons that, on the recommendation of the Parliamentary Select Committee of 1842, the British government in that year once more assumed direct responsibility for the administration of the forts, and appointed Captain Hill as Governor, and Maclean as Judicial Assessor.

Hill arrived in Cape Coast in February 1844 charged with three main duties. First, he was to gain a formal acceptance from the African chiefs of the jurisdiction exercised by Maclean; second, he was to establish a machinery for administration in place of the Council of Merchants that had been abolished; and finally, he was to continue the promotion of trade and western civilization in Ghana. It was with a view to placing Maclean's former jurisdiction on a proper legal basis that, shortly after his arrival, Hill got a delegation of Fante chiefs, who had called on 6 March to pay their respects and to ask about the intentions of the new government with regard to domestic slaves, to sign a document now known as the Bond of 1844. The document contained three clauses. The first clause set down that the signatory chiefs recognized the power and jurisdiction that had been exercised in their states, and declared that 'the first objects of law are the protection of individuals and property'. The second clause stated that human sacrifices and 'other barbarous customs, such as panyarring, are abominable and contrary to law'. The third clause stated that murders, robberies and other crimes were to be tried before British judicial officers and the signatory chiefs, and that the customs of the country were to be 'moulded in accordance with the general principles of British law'. This document was originally signed by eight Fante chiefs, but between March and December 1844 Hill got eleven more rulers to sign it, including those of Dixcove, Wassa Fiasi, Gomoa and James Town (Accra).

It should be clear from the clauses that the Bond is not as important as has been supposed. First, it merely recognized Maclean's former administration of justice, and did not create it. Secondly, the new jurisdiction that it granted to the British was limited only to criminal cases, and even this limited power was to be exercised in co-operation with the chiefs themselves; in other words, the sovereignty of the signatory chiefs was fully recognized. Finally, contrary to the general belief prevalent in Ghana before and soon after independence, there was no clause in the Bond to the effect that the British were to rule Ghana for a hundred years.

Since Maclean was appointed as the Judicial Assessor, the exercise of British jurisdiction continued very much as before; that is, in close co-operation with the chiefs. In August 1846, for instance, a murder case was tried before him and four chiefs. However, after his death in 1847, the system of administration of justice began to change to the disadvantage of the African rulers. In 1851, a Chief Justice was appointed, and in 1853 regular courts were formally established by the Supreme Court ordinance to deal with civil and criminal cases in the British forts. Jurisdiction in the Protectorate continued to be exercised by the Judicial Assessor. But in 1856 jurisdiction of the British courts was extended to the Protectorate in certain cases such as bankruptcy, which would have been better dealt with by the Judicial Assessor and the chiefs. From the late 1850's onwards, a single person tended to act as the Chief Justice as well as the Judicial Assessor, administering English law. Thus, by the 1860's, English law, and English law courts with attorneys, had in many cases entirely replaced customary law and the courts of the chiefs, especially in the coastal states.

The problem of administration, however, was not satisfactorily solved until 1850. In that year, Ghana was again separated from Sierra Leone and given its own Executive and Legislative Councils, consisting of the governor, British officials and merchants.

The other task that Hill and his successors tackled between 1843 and 1865 was that of promoting western civilization and trade, and, as is evident from the Poll Tax ordinance, they had in view the construction of roads, hospitals and schools. These measures, as well as the great extension of British power and jurisdiction already discussed, were costly. And it was partly with a view to raising revenue to meet these costs that in 1850 the Danish forts were bought by the British government, and two years later the Poll Tax ordinance was passed. With the acquisition of the Danish forts, it was hoped that increased custom duties could be imposed; but these hopes were frustrated because the Dutch authorities refused to co-operate, in spite of all the efforts of the British between 1857 and 1866. The Poll Tax ordinance, passed by the Assembly of chiefs which met in Cape Coast in April 1852, and ratified by a similar body of chiefs that assembled in Accra, imposed a tax of one shilling per year per head on every man, woman and child in the 'Protectorate'. This attempt at raising revenue through direct taxation also failed. Instead of the estimated annual revenue of £20,000 from this tax, only £7,567 was collected in the first year, and even this yield fell steadily to £1,552 in 1861 when, for reasons to be discussed, the tax was abandoned.

While the failure of these attempts to raise revenue prevented the carrying out of what we might today call the development plan of 1852, it did not end British power and jurisdiction in the southern states. What did really threaten the latter was the Asante invasion of 1863, immediately caused, as we have seen, by the refusal of the British governor to restore two fugitives to the Asantehene. The Asante army routed the allied forces in a series of engagements and returned to Asante in triumph. In the following year, the British launched a counter invasion and moved a strong contingent to the banks of the Pra, but such was the heavy rate of mortality among the soldiers owing to the rainy season, that the expedition had to be abandoned. The mishandling of the counter-attack by the British officials on the coast led to the setting up of the Parliamentary Select Committee of 1865 to go into the affairs of the British West Africa settlements. One of the major recommendations of this Committee was that there should be no further extension of British power and jurisdiction, nor any more treaties offering protection to African states, and that the objects of British policy in West Africa should be 'to encourage in the natives the exercise of those qualities which may render it possible for us more and more to transfer to them the administration of all the Governments, with a view to our ultimate withdrawal from all except probably Sierra Leone'. Had this recommendation been carried out in Ghana, all would have certainly been different. But it was not. On the contrary, far from preparing to withdraw, the British began to entrench themselves even further. In 1866 they deposed and exiled Aggrey, the king of Cape Coast, and they revived their negotiations with the Dutch; this led first to an agreement in 1867 to exchange their forts, and four years later (February 1871) to the purchase of all the Dutch forts on the coast of Ghana. Three years later the British went on to annex the whole of southern Ghana as a Crown colony.

The Fante confederation

The seal of the Fante Confederation

We must now examine the reaction of the traditional authorities to this steady growth of British power and jurisdiction, and the reasons for the Colonial office's final decision to annex southern Ghana, a demand that they had been resisting since the 1840's.

The answer of the Ghanaian rulers to the steady growth of British power and jurisdiction was the formation of the Fante Confederation based at Man-kessim. Though this movement crystallized in 1868, after the report of the Select Committee of 1865 and the Anglo-Dutch exchange of forts, its roots go much deeper into the past, as far back as the period of Maclean's admini-stration. The first of these roots was political. It seems clear that the southern states were not prepared to see their newly won independence from Asante being encroached upon by any other power, African or European, and therefore, right from the time of the Company administration, they protested against this. Owing to the enlightened way in which Maclean exercised his power, and the respect he showed to the local rulers and their customary law, there were not many instances of resistance to his rule. But a few did in fact occur.

As early as 1834, the king of Denkyira sent a petition to the Secretary of State for the colonies, protesting against the treatment he had received at the hands of Maclean. Kwaku Ackah, that notorious Nzima king, also steadily resisted any attempt to lessen his power, and, as a scholar has recently shown, in spite of the expedition of 1835, Maclean's influence was never really effective in Nzima. In 1846, the people of Tantum released their chief, who had been arrested on the orders of Maclean, and beat up the policemen. In the same year, the king of Gomoa also refused to obey the summons for repeated extortion served on him by a policeman sent by Maclean.

In the 1850's and 1860's, as British judicial power became wider and its exercise more direct, resistance increased. Early in the 1850's, the king of Assin rebelled and began to negotiate with the Asantehene to return to his former ally. But even more significant was the reaction in the 1850's to the Poll tax. Resistance to it broke into the open in the eastern districts in January 1854, when protest meetings occurred and the chiefs and people refused to pay. Though this protest was suppressed, it broke out even more violently later in the year, when an army of more than 4,000 men, not only from Accra but also from Akyem, Akwapem and Krobo, attacked the Christiansborg Castle after a British bombardment of Labadi, Teshi and Osu. This move-ment was again crushed, but in Krobo a fierce civil war broke out four years later between pro- and anti-British parties over the tax. When the latter were defeated with the help of a British force, and a fine of £8,125 was imposed on them to meet the cost of the expedition, they refused to pay the fine by refusing to sell their palm-oil from 1858 to 1860. Similar protests also broke out in the western districts from 1854 onwards, centring on Cape Coast, and only the threat of the use of force compelled the chiefs and people to con-tinue to pay. But even here, so reluctant were the people, and so strong the spirit of resistance that, as we have seen, the money from the tax continued to get smaller until 1861 when it was so little that the collection was stopped.

It should be noted that the main reason for the failure of the tax was that the chiefs had neither a say in its collection, nor, which infuriated them even more, in the expenditure of its proceeds. In fact the assembly of chiefs which passed the ordinance was not summoned again. In other words, the British officials did not follow the principle which the chiefs and people of the southern states were insisting upon, the well-known principle of no taxation without representation. But the end of the Poll tax did not mean the end of British jurisdiction in the country; in 1864 the new governor, Richard Pine, even passed an ordinance making it compulsory for all traders in wine and spirits to obtain a licence of £2 per annum; this was to be enforced not only in the British forts, but 'over the whole of the British possession and to a distance two miles inland'. The chiefs of Cape Coast protested strongly against this, mainly on the grounds that since they and their people were not British subjects, they could not be taxed without first being consulted.

This steadily growing protest against the extension of British power and jurisdiction came to a head in 1865 when John Aggrey was elected king of Cape Coast. Two months after he became king he clashed with the government when he objected to appeals against the decisions of his court being sent to the British court; he went on to criticize Maclean who had, he said, 'in a very peculiar, imperceptible and unheard-of manner, wrested from the hands of our kings, chiefs and headmen their power to govern their own subjects'. And, to strengthen his claims, he sent a delegation of two (Martin and Carr) to England, who gave evidence before the Select Committee of 1865. His opposition to British jurisdiction became even fiercer after the recommendations of the Select Committee, and finally, in December 1866, he sent a letter to Governor Conran in which he expressed this opposition in very strong terms. 'The time has now come for me,' he wrote, 'to record a solemn protest against the perpetual annoyances and insults that you persistently and perseveringly continue to practise on me in my capacity as legally constituted king of Cape Coast.' And he reminded the Governor that, 'the government in England has expressed its desire that we, the kings and chiefs of the Gold Coast, are to prepare ourselves for self government and no protection'. He followed this letter up with a petition to the Colonial Secretary. The governor felt so angry and his power so challenged that, a day or two after receiving this letter, he arrested Aggrey, declared him deposed, and deported him to Sierra Leone; he was not allowed to return to Cape Coast even as a private citizen until March 1869, and he died later in the same year. But neither Aggrey's deportation nor death ended the explosive situation created by years of resistance to the growth of British political and judicial power, and the demand for self-government. What was needed was a spark to touch this off, and this was provided by the Anglo-Dutch exchange of forts.

However, the growth of British jurisdiction and the reactions to it were not the only deeper causes of the rise of the Fante Confederation. The other equally important force pulling the southern states together, particularly in the 1850's and the 1860's, was the old Asante problem. Just as the Asante never abandoned the hope of reconquering their former subject states to the south, so the coastal and southern states never gave up their desire to regain their middleman position and safeguard their independence. Politically, too, the Asante neither surrendered their traditional hold on Elmina in the west, nor their strong alliance with Akwamu and the Anlo in the east. Thus, relations between the Asante and their former subjects never became smooth. With his reputation and tact, Maclean was able to maintain peace between them, and settle all disputes that arose in a friendly way. But after 1843, when he ceased to be in sole control of affairs, the old abuses, insults and attacks on traders began again. In 1844, for instance, the trade paths were closed when an Asante female trader was murdered in Assin. This was amicably settled when the murderer was executed, but an even more serious dispute broke out again in 1845, which once more led to the closing of the trade routes and the seizure of the Fante traders in Asante, and Asante traders in the southern province. This crisis also passed, only to revive again in 1847 over an abuse of the Asantehene by an Anomabu woman. With the death of Maclean, relations between the two sides got worse, and in 1853 only a last minute change of heart by the Asantehene prevented an invasion of the Protectorate. But this eventually did occur in 1863 for reasons already discussed. The early victories won by the Asante, the absolutely ineffective help given by the British, and the disastrous end of their counter-invasion in 1864 once more showed the southern states the need for a strong united front for the preservation of their independence. Indeed in 1863 the wealthy Fante gentleman, Hutchinson, formed the Rifle Volunteer Corps for the defence of their land, and though the British broke up the Corps, the formation of a national army was one of the programmes of King Aggrey.

With their sovereign power being steadily curtailed by the British from the south, and their very existence, as well as their economic interests, threatened by the Asante, the formation of a united front was only a question of time. The recommendation of the Select Committee about the eventual withdrawal merely strengthened and accelerated the drive towards the formation of some sort of a union or unions in Ghana. It did not create it. What finally did lead to the formation of the Fante Confederation, which, in spite of its name, consisted not only of the Fante states but also of the Denkyira, Twifu, Wassa and Assin, was the agreement between the Dutch and the British for the exchange of forts which was drawn up in March 1867, and was to come into force in January 1868. According to the convention, all the Dutch forts and settlements and 'rights of sovereignty and jurisdiction', east of the mouth of the Sweet river, near Elmina, were to be taken over by the British, while the

Dutch were to take over those of the British to the west. The news of this agreement, which came out in January, infuriated the Fante because they were not consulted. It also alarmed the rulers of the western districts because, since they knew that the Dutch were the traditional friends of the Asante, they expected their states would soon be overrun by the Asante. In fact it was the Denkyira who hurriedly sent ambassadors to the Fante kings to ask about their response to the news, and followed this with another delegation to Mankessim where all the Fante chiefs, as well as the other delegations from the western districts, assembled. And it was at this meeting at Mankessim in January 1868 that the delegates present refused to accept the Anglo-Dutch agreement, and significantly decided to form a government which would 'be to ourselves a head, having no king under the British'.

The Confederation continued to be active until 1871, and from then on it began to decline until 1873 when it ended altogether. What did it achieve during its brief spell of life and why did it fail? First and foremost, it succeeded in setting up administrative machinery. At their first meeting in January 1868, they set up a council in which each state was to be represented by seven elected members, they elected three joint-presidents to head the Council, and also elected a magistrate and a secretary. In 1869, however, they elected Ghartey of Winneba as King-President. Finally, in November 1871, after discussions among the educated Africans led by the Sierra Leonian scholar and nationalist leader, J. (Africanus) B. Horton (who, as early as 1868 wrote a book entitled *West African Countries and Peoples*, in which he

38 *The Fante Confederation 1868-73 and British Crown Colony, 1874*

Surgeon-Major J. (Africanus) B. Horton

discussed how the self-government recommended by the Select Committee in 1865 could be implemented), Dawson and the traditional rulers, the Confederation successfully worked out a written constitution and adopted it. There was to be an executive council of ex-officio members and others appointed by the Confederation; a representative assembly was to to established consisting of two delegates from each state, one of whom must be a chief, and the other an educated man; there was to be a national assembly of kings and principal chiefs which would meet annually to confirm the proceedings of the Legislative Assembly, to elect the ex-officio members of the Executive, and also to elect the King-President, the constitutional head of the Confederation. And the Confederation did in fact elect officers to the Executive. J. F. Amissah was elected as secretary, J. H. Brew as under-secretary, F. C. Grant as treasurer, and J. M. Abadoo as assistant treasurer. However, because of the rivalry between the kings of Abora and Mankessim, it was not until a year later that the latter was elected as King-President (July 1872). The Confederation also adopted a national seal which consisted of the now familiar elephant standing against an oil palm tree, encircled with the words 'The Government of the Fante Confederation, Mankessim.'

Secondly, the Confederation set up a national army which was able to send military assistance to the Kommenda and the people of Dixcove, who were resisting an attempt to take them over by the Dutch; the army also besieged Elmina and the Dutch headquarters. Indeed, it was mainly the strong action taken by the Confederation which made things so difficult for the Dutch that they finally decided to leave Ghana altogether.

211

Thirdly, the Confederation did impose and collect a Poll tax as well as export duties, though it is clear that the money from these began to decline in 1871. Fourthly, it set up a Confederate court in December 1868 at Mankessim under the presidency of King Ghartey, and many cases were referred to this court by some of the chiefs.

It should be clear from the above that the Confederation was not just a paper scheme, but a movement that did come into existence, that did draw up plans, and did attempt to execute them. However, by 1872, it had lost its real drive and it had ceased to exist by the early months of 1873. One of the main reasons for its failure was undoubtedly the rivalry among the chiefs, especially the rivalry between Edu, the king of Mankessim, and Otu, the king of Abora. This rivalry did not allow for sincere and complete co-operation between these two kings, who were by then the most powerful of the kings of the western district. But the second and more decisive cause was the hostile attitude of the British officials on the coast. Both Ussher and Salmon, who acted as administrators during the period, saw the Confederation as a real challenge to British power and jurisdiction in southern Ghana, and did everything possible to crush it. And they did this first of all by playing off the chiefs against the educated Africans and then, as Ussher himself confessed in 1872, by detaching the chiefs one by one from the Confederation.

The British determination to crush the movement became greater when the agreements for the transfer of the Dutch forts was at last signed in 1871, and the Confederation adopted a full constitution nine months later. Indeed, the Acting Administrator, Salmon, felt that developments at Mankessim were such an irritating threat that he had all the members of the Executive arrested early in December 1871, on the ridiculous charge of treason. Though the Colonial office condemned the action and ordered the immediate release of the officials, the Confederation never recovered from it. And, indeed, so successful had the British become in spreading disunity among the states of the western districts by the end of 1871, that not even the possible invasion of the Asante could bring them to act together. Had the Confederation movement received the blessing and support of the British officials, it would most probably have succeeded.

The establishment of British rule

Having killed the Confederation the British went on to annex not only the states of the Confederation but all the states of southern Ghana in July 1874. Why then did the British take a step that they had been refusing to take, in spite of the demands of the traders and some local officials, since the 1840's? The final annexation of southern Ghana was due to three main factors. The first was the withdrawal of the Dutch from the coast of Ghana in 1872. The second was the beginning of the new imperialism in England, and the third was the decisive defeat of the Asante in 1874. One of the main reasons why the Colonial office constantly objected to any great extension of British power in Ghana was the fear of increased cost of administration. Since the attempt to raise revenue through direct taxation failed with the failure of the Poll tax scheme, the only other obvious source of revenue were customs duties. However, not much could be gained from this source because of the refusal of the Dutch to agree to any increase in these duties. But with their final departure from the Ghanaian scene in 1872, the British were in a position to raise greater revenue than before from increased custom duties, and they could therefore extend their power.

The second factor was the changing attitude in England towards the acquisition of colonies. Until about 1860, the attitude in Britain had on the whole been anti-imperialist and anti-colonial. Preference had been given to informal empires and protectorates while formal empires and increased responsibilities were frowned upon. But in the 1870's public opinion began to change in favour of the acquisition of colonies. This change was caused mainly by the need for markets and raw materials, as international trade became more and more competitive. Indeed, in 1873, when the Colonial Office considered the question of whether the British were to withdraw from Ghana, one of the under-secretaries cautioned against withdrawal on the grounds that British public opinion would be against it. 'In the present tone and temper of the British mind,' he wrote in February 1873, 'no abandonment of territory would be permitted by Parliament or sanctioned by public opinion.' Nevertheless, the Colonial office would most certainly not have annexed southern Ghana at the time it did, but for the Asante war of 1874. Before news of the war reached England, the Colonial Secretary had already decided against withdrawal in favour of the continuation of the old moral protectorate but with the powers of the British now clearly defined and considerably strengthened. However, the decisive defeat of the Asante by the British in 1874 put them in a position to do whatever they liked with Ghana. The choice open to them was either total withdrawal or complete annexation; and with the recent victories and prospects of increased revenue, and the changing mood in England, and since the Confederation was by that time destroyed, annexation was the obvious choice.

In July 1874, therefore, the British issued an edict formally annexing southern Ghana as a British Crown colony. The Anglo-Asante war of 1874 thus not only finally destroyed the military power of the Asante and thereby sealed the dissolution of their empire, but it also brought about the conversion of the British moral protectorate of southern Ghana into the British Crown colony of southern Ghana.

15 Partition

'a forcible possession of our land has taken the place of a forcible possession of our persons'

The partition is so important for subsequent history that, for West Africa, it can be said to have begun the twentieth century. For most Africans it divides independent sovereignty from subjection to foreign rule. Almost every event since partition results from it or is in some way closely connected with it; it was as revolutionary in its effect upon West Africa as were the Islamic or abolitionist movements. Like these earlier movements it affected people unequally, some being only slightly touched and others being driven almost into chaos. Just as the abolition of the slave trade led the way to partition, so partition in turn stimulated the rise of modern nationalism, the fourth great theme of West Africa's two revolutionary centuries.

European powers for a long time showed little interest in creating empires in West Africa. But during the nineteenth century a gradual increase in foreign authority occurred until by the 1880's the entire coast with the exception of Dahomey was dominated by one or other European nation. This domination either involved formal government of the coastal area, as was the case with the French in Senegal, the British in Sierra Leone and Ghana, and the American settlers along the Liberian coast or it involved the ownership of strategic points such as Boke and Isles de Los in Guinea, Grand Bassam and Assinie in the Ivory Coast and Lagos on the Yoruba coast, through which the foreign powers controlled the export-import trade of African states.

In other areas European merchant firms backed by European navies were dominating the ports and coastal states almost as completely as if they possessed formal power. In Bonny, Onitsha, Brass and Calabar they possessed their own courts, which placed them above African law. The British in Calabar and the Cameroons and the French in Cayor and Futa Toro decided the succession to the throne. Although, in order to reduce expenses, both the British and French governments had at various times in the nineteenth century withdrawn from sections of the coast, these withdrawals were often the beginning of even greater advances. Thus, though in 1828 the British government abandoned Ghana, their merchants remained and their missionaries arrived, and this increased their influence so much that in 1843, when the British government returned, it took over a larger area than it had left in 1828. Again, in 1869 the British closed their Lokoja consulate but in the following decade British control of the Niger-Benue was confirmed. The

French gave up Porto Novo in the sixties and the Ivory Coast in the seventies but in both cases their merchants enlarged the sphere of French influence and prepared the way for the return of the French government.

In the seventies and early eighties European positions were strengthened. The Dutch sold out in Ghana, and the French sold out on the Niger-Benue, leaving both entirely to the British. The French took over the Dahomey coast and squeezed the Sierra Leone Creoles out of the rivers of Guinea. Only in Senegambia, where the British clung to the Gambia river although surrounded by French traders, was the establishment of power in the hands of one nation incomplete. The position of African kingdoms weakened, for they were no longer able, in their own interests, to play one European group against another. European merchants of one nationality found it easier to combine together and pay lower prices or to control or ban the importation of firearms and ammunition.

In the 1850's Europeans began to penetrate the interior via West Africa's great water highway, the Niger, and while the British entered from the Delta, the French came from the Senegal. Goldie's amalgamation of British firms on the Niger-Benue in 1879 and French activity on the Senegal in 1878 showed that a new phase of expansion was beginning in the interior. While European expansion before 1880 was slow and steady, though with a quickening pace in the seventies, after 1880 it developed into a feverish rush or scramble. The causes of this change in the pace of European expansion were due to important developments in the internal politics of Europe, to new economic conditions, and to a fundamental alteration in European attitudes to non-European people.

39 *Alien domination of the import-export trade of West Africa in 1880*

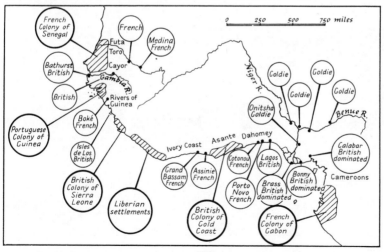

The European balance of power

The scramble was partly the result of European rivalries resulting from the rise of Germany. Before 1870 the German people were split up into numerous small states dominated by their powerful neighbours, France and Austria. In a rapid military campaign the German states were united by Bismarck and a humiliating defeat inflicted upon Austria and France. In 1870 Bismarck captured Paris and dictated terms to the helpless French, whereby two provinces, which were rich in the coal and iron upon which French industrialization depended, became part of a the new German nation.

Before the rise of Germany, France and Britain had been the two great rival powers of Europe. Since Britain dominated the seas and France the land neither could overcome the other. With the rise of Germany this balance of power became more complicated. Since Germany was a land power she was the greatest threat to France, and it was a constant German fear that France would be reconciled with her old enemy, England, and begin an Anglo-French alliance against her. While seeking friendship with Britain and France, Germany was willing to encourage disagreement between them during which she would hold the balance of power. An opportunity arose over Egypt.

In 1882 Egypt was on the verge of bankruptcy with debts owing to a combination of French, German and English bankers. Paris bankers held the largest bloc of Egyptian debts and French teachers, technicians, merchants

40 The British commercial lifeline of the late nineteenth century

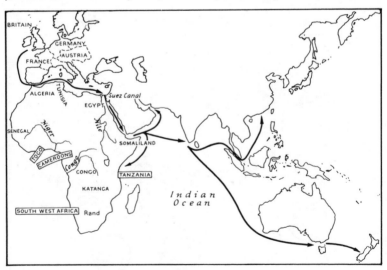

and military officers far outnumbered other Europeans in Egypt. Egypt was considered to be in France's sphere of influence and it was expected that her fate would be decided in Paris. However, the British moved first.

After the collapse of England's triangular Atlantic trade and sugar monopoly in the eighteenth century, the centre of her trade, empire and wealth had shifted to the Indian ocean. Once the Suez canal opened in 1869 it became a most important link in Britain's trading connections with India. Britain was happy if Suez was in the hands of a weak Egypt but not if it was in the hands of a strong France. Britain therefore risked French anger not because she was interested in Egypt itself but in order to protect her interests in Asia. British occupation of Egypt was one of the factors which led to the scramble and partition; for while Germany supported British occupation on the one hand, on the other she encouraged the French to make up for their two lost provinces in Europe, and for Egypt, by seeking empire elsewhere in Africa.

Quite unexpectedly both Bismarck of Germany and King Leopold of Belgium showed their imperial ambitions in Africa. Bismarck personally disapproved of overseas empire but he began to see that if Germany was to play England against France it would help to possess territory in Africa at least for bargaining purposes. In a surprise move in 1884 he sent warships to declare German sovereignty over the coasts of Togoland, Cameroons, South West Africa and Tanganyika, which were areas of British influence where their missionaries and traders were at work. This was designed to reassure the French and warn Britain that German support and friendship

The opening of the Suez Canal, 1869

were not automatic. Leopold of Belgium, described as a 'big-minded king in an insignificant kingdom', having failed in his search for empire in Asia, then created an International Association; this was supposed to promote scientific knowledge about Africa, but was in fact established to conceal his imperial ambitions in the Congo.

The French were not opposed to enlarging their African empire. They might yet strike a blow at Britain in Egypt by linking up their existing colonies, namely Senegal on the west, Somaliland on the east, and Algeria and Tunisia on the north. Britain's success in forcing Egypt to pay her debts depended upon her ability to make use of the Nile waters. Thus if the French could get control of the upper Nile they would be in a position to turn Egypt into a desert and force the British out. Furthermore, the first modern censuses were showing the French military commanders that Germany possessed a larger and younger population with a higher birth-rate than France. In an age when battles were decided by foot soldiers it became obvious that every year the balance of manpower in Europe was turning against France. One way of reversing this was to create an empire from which to recruit soldiers.

Britain was quite content to leave the African situation alone. Her traders dominated African trade because their cheaper prices assured them of an advantage over any rivals. Another important factor was that the system cost the British tax-payers little. However, German, French and Belgian manœuvres were a challenge to British supremacy; if she did nothing Africa would go behind the customs barriers erected by other nations in their colonies and her own traders would be excluded.

While the British occupation of Egypt may have been vital in starting the scramble elsewhere on the continent, its importance for West Africa was much less. Long before the British occupation of Egypt in 1882 there were many signs in West Africa that a new imperial advance could be expected. There was the British defeat of Asante in 1874, renewed French activity on the Senegal in the late seventies, British and French manœuvring on the Niger and French and Belgian activity on the Congo. It was, in fact, the rivalry on the Niger and Congo which prompted the Berlin conference.

Once it became evident that the carving up of Africa was to begin, the European powers met in 1884 at the Berlin West African Conference, 'a memorably absurd gathering' because it achieved nothing but to proclaim what was quite obvious, that certain powers had imperial ambitions in Africa. While it resolved that the Niger and Congo should be open to the trade of all nations, Goldie and Leopold promptly created monopolies which excluded other traders on these rivers. While it declared that a coastline must be 'effectively occupied' before it could be declared a colony, most of the West African coast was already occupied by one or other of the European powers.

Regardless of the absurdities, the Berlin Conference did establish that, despite rivalries, the occupation of Africa was to be a co-operative European effort. In pursuance of this, conventions grew up to control and regulate European rivalries and to ensure that they did not lead to open conflict. Treaties signing away their sovereignty by African chiefs were accepted as valid claims for colonies, even though everyone suspected the treaties were fraudulent, misunderstood, purposely mistranslated or repudiated. The major concern was to keep Africans out of the scramble which was to be a strictly European affair. There was to be no temptation for a European power to ally with an African state against another European power; such an alliance might be the means whereby an African state could get modern firearms, with which it might save its independence. Regardless of the jealousies and divisions among Europeans, the striking thing for Africans was the force and reality of European unity in their assault upon the continent.

Economic imperialism

The diplomatic manœuvring of nations can often be traced to what they believe to be their economic interest. Merchant groups were among the most powerful pressures upon European governments, who accepted that what was good for the merchants was good for the nation. In the late seventies and early eighties, for example, German trade with West Africa had been growing rapidly and the merchants engaged in it were clamouring for colonies. Bismarck's surprise move in 1884 was therefore not purely diplomatic; as a politician needing support he decided to win the merchant's favour with an African empire. Similarly Britain's occupation of Egypt in 1882 may have been strategic but it was nevertheless her economic interests in Asia which led to it.

Until the middle of the nineteenth century the British held a near-monopoly of the manufactured goods of the world. Among the European nations the British thus had the greatest need for the raw materials of Africa. But by the eighties France and Germany were industrializing, and they resented depending on British sources for their tropical products. Since their industrialization was in an earlier, less mature stage than Britain's they found it difficult to compete with British merchants in the credit they could offer, in the quality and cheapness of their products for sale, or in the price offered for raw materials. Their merchants therefore wanted colonies from which they could exclude British and other traders and which would provide raw materials for their factories and markets for their goods.

The idea that the imperial objective is commercial profit is the theory of economic imperialism. Although colonies are not always such profitable trading partners as independent nations, it was nevertheless a theory in which many Europeans put their faith. Travellers and missionaries continued to stress the value of Africa's raw materials and markets; and politicians such as Germany's Bismarck or England's Gladstone, whether they believed in the theory or not, could not long resist the pressures which merchants, through the press, brought to bear on them.

Between 1873 and 1893 the world passed through a severe economic depression. Trade was slow, prices low and profits small. Some companies went bankrupt while others joined together both to reduce competition, and to drive down prices of raw materials so as to increase their profits. In the seventies the strengthening of European positions on the coast, and renewed activity in the interior, were a response to depression conditions. During times of prosperity European merchants often resisted any extension of colonial authority over their trading areas, in order to avoid paying colonial customs taxes. When they got into trouble with African authorities they would call upon their navy or consul, but only in desperate circumstances would they press for annexation of their trading area.

As the depression continued more and more firms looked to their governments to cut out the African middlemen, for if they could be brushed aside, and European traders could deal direct with the producers, prices could be driven lower and profits thereby increased.

By such methods large firms could often make greater profits in times of depression than in times of prosperity, as is indicated by the history of the Royal Niger Company. By the 1880's West Coast firms were loudly calling for the help of their governments in crushing coastal states and middlemen. As one colonial governor said, 'The commercial world are insatiable; they say "we want territorial expansion, open roads and interior markets for our wares and for the overflow of the produce in return". They seem no longer satisfied with the sandbeach policy of past years ... The middlemen are the obstacles to our ... development in West Africa.'

Compared with Europe's trade with America or Asia, her trade with Africa was small and it has been argued that it was hardly worth the expense of partition. However, it was often not present trade but future prospects which lured Europeans forward, for travellers stressed the great potential and the vast opportunities. In 1886 the largest gold deposits in the world were discovered on the Rand in South Africa and there were rumours of Katanga copper. Few nations felt they could sit idly by and see undiscovered riches fall to their rivals. Even if a nation had no immediate need for African products and markets it was believed to be both good business sense and insurance to take as large a slice as possible for future use.

Thus the European partition of Africa was as much the result of the fear that undiscovered wealth might fall into the hands of rival nations, as of the desire to own new land, or to control and govern peoples outside Europe.

Racialism and nationalism

The political and economic causes of the scramble can best be understood against the background of the changing European attitude to non-European peoples in the late nineteenth century. Early in the century it was widely believed that African inferiority to Europeans was due to the effects of centuries of the slave trade. Commerce, cultivation of export crops, Christianity and education could raise Africans to the European level. Coupled with the short European life expectancy on the West Coast, this belief fostered the view that West Africa could best be exploited by a European partnership with an educated Christian African middle class of merchants, farmers, clergymen and teachers which would ultimately fashion modern Christian states in West Africa. Originally these partners were the Creoles of Sierra Leone, the 'Habitants' of Senegal or the Americo-Liberians; but eventually educated Yoruba, Efik, Fante, Ga and Wolof people joined the small but growing middle class.

The flourishing churches of Freetown, Cape Coast, Lagos and the Delta showed African initiative in religion. Liberia, the Fante Confedereration and the Egba United Board of Management indicated the possibilities of educated African political leadership. In commerce a number of Anglo-African partnerships were created such as that of Christie and Davies, with the Englishman, Christie, running the business in England, and the African, Davies, handling it in Lagos and on the Niger.

Once quinine was discovered and the industrial revolution gave Europeans vast technical and military superiority over all other peoples of the world some Europeans began to propound an absurd doctrine of absolute superiority inborn in European peoples. Writers such as Richard Burton and Winwood Read argued that the races of the world were at different stages of evolution, the white having evolved the furthest, the black the least. Neither Christianity nor a university degree could overcome inborn African inferiority. Europeans were therefore not only born to rule and dominate commerce, religion and government, but it was their duty or divine mission to do so, since only they could so order the world to lead to universal happiness. Some fought against this new doctrine but in the end it triumphed among most Europeans and provided an ideology for the partition, that subjugation to their rule was the greatest privilege which Europeans could bestow upon Africans.

Nationalism had been growing in Europe and towards the end of the nineteenth century had developed to fanatic excesses in which each nationality claimed superiority over others. The possession of an empire became a test and proof of a nation's superiority. This fantastic nationalism easily led to the slogan 'my country right or wrong' which was used to justify any action against foreigners as long as it glorified the motherland. Flags and national anthems became sacred, almost mystical symbols. The churches guaranteed a life after death in paradise for those who died for king and country, and service to one's country and the defence of its honour were believed to be the greatest of virtues. Poets, composers and novelists glorified the empire builder far out on the frontiers, bringing the so-called 'savages', 'heathen' and the 'lesser breeds' within the sway of their European 'benefactors'.

'Painting the map red' became the driving force behind the Goldies and Lugards, the men who tramped, sweated and fought across Africa because it was the noblest cause their generation understood. Nationalistic imperialism was intense among the lower classes. Though they counted for little in European society except as wage-slaves tending the machines of the industrial revolution imperialism made them feel they possessed an assurance of their superiority over the rest of mankind. They took pride in 'our empire' even though they might not quite know where it was. They could take out their anger on any politician who appeared ready to barter it away. Thus the partition and subjugation of Africa may be viewed as one of the great crises of European nationalism which reached its climax a few years later in the First World War.

The causes of the partition were various and complicated. The long, steady process of European expansion in West Africa seemed likely to increase in speed in the late seventies even without the host of new factors which appeared in the eighties. The upset in the European balance of power, which reflected the challenge of France and Germany to British industrial supremacy, together with the prolonged economic depression, drove the European nations

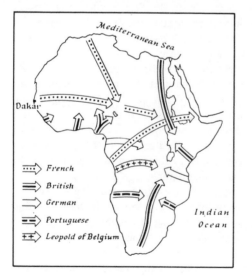

41 The major directions of European ambition during the scramble for Africa

to work out their political and commercial rivalries in Africa. These rivalries were exaggerated by the excessive growth of nationalism in European nations, while the doubts held in the mid-nineteenth century about the wisdom of overseas empire were swept away by the growth of racialism which, by emphasizing the duty and mission of Europeans to peoples whom they believed to be inferior, provided the ideology to move the masses to support the demands of the merchants and to force their governments into the scramble. In addition the British occupation of Egypt in 1882, the personal ambitions of Leopold, and the discovery of the Rand gold fields in 1886 all contributed to the haste and hurry.

The pattern of the partition

Some historians argue that the pattern of the partition was partly determined by the British occupation of Egypt. Once France decided to strike a blow at the British in Egypt by creating a west-east empire from Dakar to the Red Sea, Britain was determined to block French aims and protect Egypt by securing the entire Nile Valley. In the diplomatic moves and counter-moves Britain concentrated on the Nile and she neglected her West African empire, allowing it to be cut into four separate colonies surrounded by French territory. Even though West Africa was likely to contribute more to British trade and wealth than the Nile Valley of the Egyptian Sudan and Uganda, yet it was to these areas that Britain was committed by her occupation of Egypt.

Other historians reject the idea of the importance of Egypt in determining the pattern of partition in West Africa. They suggest that Britain took those parts of West Africa which were paying profits to her traders and ignored the rest; that Britain built her colonies around the rivers – the Niger, Volta and Gambia – which gave access to the products of the interior. The same historians argue that French ambitions to link up their colonies in Senegal and Algeria with their trading posts on the Guinea coast go back as far as Faidherbe and had little to do with the British occupation of Egypt.

By and large Britain left the governors of the colonies in West Africa to enlarge their territories as best they could with their own soldiers and finance. The poverty-stricken Gambia got almost no more territory. Governor Cardew of Sierra Leone did the best he could with the resources he had. To fight Cardew's war in 1898 the Sierra Leone government had to borrow the money from Britain, paying it back over the following years. The Gold Coast colony was bigger and financially stronger and so was able to carve out a larger area inland. Governor Carter of Lagos was fortunate in being able to bring the Yoruba states under protection after one decisive victory over the

Ijebu. On the Niger it was the revenues of Goldie's Royal Niger Company which defeated Nupe and Ilorin and laid the basis of Northern Nigeria. Otherwise the lands north of the joining of the Niger and Benue would probably have fallen to the French.

Almost every colonial border presented its absurdities. The geographical and cultural area of the Lake Chad region was split up especially in the division between the related Kanuri and Kanembu. The Nigerian-Dahomey border separated Ketu from the main Yoruba kingdoms and split the people of Borgu. In Ghana the Mossi and Dagomba were cut off from related groups in French territory. The Mende people were divided between Sierra Leone and Liberia, while the Susu and Koranko were on both sides of the border of Sierra Leone and Guinea.

However, it was not the separation of kindred people which was the main disadvantage, but rather the fact that none of the imperial powers established a colony of sufficient area or population to enable it to become a major or first-class power by mid-nineteenth-century standards. Educated Africans like E. W. Blyden repeatedly urged upon Britain the necessity of creating a mighty empire in West Africa. He was not thinking in terms of its value to the British, but rather, convinced that European empires would be temporary, he looked forward to the day when African colonies would emerge as independent states. British imperialism in the past had created large states such as Canada, Australia and India. Blyden desired that the British should repeat this process in West Africa.

The views of educated Africans

Blyden's support for imperialism raises the question of the reaction of educated Africans to the partition of Africa. Many of the educated merchant princes of the coastal cities, like their European counterparts, were suffering from the depression and hoped to benefit from colonization of the interior. G. W. Johnson condemned merchants 'who in this our world of haste to be rich' were willing to sacrifice African national interests. Devout Christians, both clergy and laity, cautiously welcomed British colonialism as a substitution of Christian for non-Christian government. Since they believed that Christianity was Europe's greatest gift to Africa, they were ready to make sacrifices for it. Others did not have the same faith in the virtues of Christianity and were particularly angered by those who supported subjection as a step to conversion. Missionaries possibly suffered the greatest abuse, because Africans expected more of them than of traders and consuls, as the following parody of a Christian hymn in a Gold Coast newspaper indicated:

Onward Christian Soldiers unto heathen lands,
Prayer books in your pockets rifles in your hands;
Take the happy tidings where trade can be done,
Spread the peaceful gospel with the gatling gun.

As the partition advanced, educated Africans faced a dilemma. They discovered they were absolutely helpless to stop it. Furthermore, as Britain held back and the French appeared to be taking over, English-educated Africans felt that if Africa was to fall, it must fall to Europeans they understood and whose language they spoke. Lagos began to fear French encirclement. The *Lagos Weekly Times* moaned, 'we now find ourselves on the threshold of the fate which has befallen Sierra Leone and the Gambia – a colonial failure and a political ruin'. Against the French and German foreigners they began to feel their cultural affinity with the British. 'We "black Englishmen", who have been so large benefited by English benevolence and justice cannot sit still and see her (England) robbed of the well-earned fruits of her sagacity, enterprise and goodwill.'

At the same time, nationalist imperialism emphasizing European racial superiority was deeply offensive. Blyden pointed out that the European brought to Africa 'his prejudices, his faith in a natural inequality and his profound disbelief in any race but his own'. In the final analysis it was the hypocrisy of Europeans in claiming that it was in the best interest of Africans that they be subjugated that aroused the greatest resentment. Herbert Macaulay, with bitter humour pointed out in 1905 that, 'The dimensions of "the true interests of the natives at heart" are algebraically equal to the length, breadth and depth of the whiteman's pocket.'

It was a natural reaction of Africans to European nationalism and hypocrisy and an expression of the sorrow they felt for the passing of African independence that inevitably they made the comparison between the slave trade and the scramble. A Lagos editor in 1891, more in a mood of despair than anger summed up the scramble, partition and subjugation of Africa as:

a forcible possession of our land has taken
the place of a forcible possession of our persons.

16 Collapse of independence

'the Maxim-gun inspires the most profound respect'

The most striking aspect of the conquest of Africa was the ease with which it was carried out. Frequently African armies of 20,000 were defeated by European-led armies of 2,000 or less. Few Europeans were involved, often no more than one hundred, occasionally only a dozen or so. Africa was conquered by Africans trained and officered by Europeans and fighting with European arms. The normal pattern was that a European-led army of African soldiers administered a crushing defeat, following which African resistance collapsed. The European invaders interpreted the feeble resistance as being due to the oppression of African rulers and this led them to over-estimate their welcome and acceptance. It prompted them to forget resistance which had been bitter and prolonged. It confirmed their conviction of their own innate superiority.

With notable exceptions, West African resistance was weak. Some Africans passively accepted alien rule; others tolerated it only as long as they had to, until they had the strength to throw it off. The quality of African resistance can best be understood in relation to the military and political weakness of African states and to European diplomacy.

However, even when African resistance was strong, led by military commanders of superb intelligence and backed by a unified and determined people, where no particular political weakness appeared in the state, it was overcome by the vast military superiority of European weapons. The symbol of this superiority was a late-nineteenth-century invention, the Maxim-gun, which, a Lagos journalist in the 1890's pointed out, overawed the Yoruba rulers by inspiring 'the most profound respect'. A European writer suggested the confidence which the new gun gave the Europeans when he wrote, 'whatever happens we have got the Maxim-gun and they have not.'

Military weakness

The most obvious and decisive factor during the subjugation was African military weakness. By 1885 Europeans, through their control of the import-export trade of the West Coast, had banned the importation of guns and ammunition. The firearms which African states possessed were not modern,

The futility of resistance. A relief from Abomey showing the superior armaments of white soldiers

for it had been commercial practice for European merchants to purchase the obsolete weapons being discarded by European armies and sell them for profit in Africa. Few Africans possessed fast-action repeater rifles; Samori probably had the greatest number; Nana had enough to equip his personal bodyguard. Even fewer had cannon, though the Delta city-states were exceptions. Few, if any, possessed the destructive repeater-action, Gatling or Maxim-type gun with which almost every European-led army in Africa was equipped.

It is not therefore a surprise that the new and powerful Maxim and Gatling-guns dominate African tradition about the partition. They were novel to Europeans as well, for a number of new weapons were experimented with in the subjugation of Africa which only came to popular European attention during the first World war. Goldie's army against Nupe employed such experimental devices as flares, searchlights, special incendiary shells to set thatch roofs alight and Maxim-guns which could be dismantled for easy porterage.

Against these military products of the industrial revolution, the impressive walls of West African cities and traditional massing of troops were not merely useless but indeed provided ideal targets. French destruction of the walls of Sikasso, and the slaughter of Nupe cavalry in their charges against Goldie's gun emplacements, indicated the hopelessness of traditional methods.

227

Even with inferior weapons, however, when Africans abandoned traditional military tactics they could mobilize impressive resistance. Samori avoided walled cities and massed cavalry. The Baoule of the Ivory Coast adopted the strike and retire method of guerrilla warfare, which was especially suitable for foot soldiers in a forest region. Intelligent resistance required that the defenders never face the invader's machines. Such methods appeared cowardly and unmanly and only generals of the stature of Samori could impose them on their troops.

Defensive techniques were hampered by the lack of natural barriers such as the rugged mountains which the Ethiopians used to advantage in saving their homeland in East Africa. The Sahara provided a limited defensive barrier in which the Tuareg and Sanusiyya evaded total submission until as late as the 1920's. However, the vast majority of West Africa with its gently rolling, open savannah was ideally suited for European military methods.

Seldom have agricultural nations been able to compete militarily with the industrialized, a fact which, in addition to others, has driven more and more nations to industrialize. To finance total war African states would have been compelled to organize their citizens into servility in order to extract exportable products from the soil. African leaders had neither the dictatorial powers nor the bureaucracy to do this, and, although Samori attempted such a regimentation, the limitations of his agricultural economy were clear. With a potential of 100,000 soldiers, he had finances to keep 4,000 under arms and 1,000 equipped with modern weapons; to remove more from the land would have created famine. A major exportable commodity was slaves, but the more slaves Samori sold, the more he alienated those whose loyalty he needed. The Mandinka and Asante had gold for export and the resistance of both was at least partially due to the economic power this gave them over states compelled to rely entirely upon agricultural exports.

The coastal states had small populations, often typical of agricultural nations, small even in comparison with European nations such as Belgium. The 'powerful' state of Dahomey had less than half a million people on whose resources it might draw. The Aro were probably no more than 10,000 strong. When Brass was fully mobilized it produced an army of 1,000 men.

Political weakness

The military weakness of African states was partly a reflection of their political situation. Professional military classes were small and standing armies rare. Dynastic rivalry, restless, only partially assimilated subject peoples, a poorly developed sense of nationalism and an almost total absence of racial solidarity combined to make the military effort ineffective.

One of the weaknesses of many African political systems was the absence of clearly defined rules of succession to the throne. Prominent members of the royal lineage or lineages were often potential or actual leaders of opposition factions. Power struggles were intense. The disgrace attendant upon 'stepping down' from high office made, and still makes, the act a rare one. Since holders of such offices usually hold them for life, unless unseated through civil strife, the competition to secure office took on the nature of a life and death struggle. Consequent upon the lack of national feeling neither the contestants nor their followers would submerge their personal or material interests in the national cause. Principles and policies were submerged to personal ambition, since a candidate expected the support of his lineage regardless of the ideological position he might adopt. Thus candidates might accept foreign assistance to gain their ends. The advancing Europeans, without even understanding the political situation, often found collaborators. In the Tokolor empire Ahmad was fighting a number of pretenders while trying to control French advances. In Dahomey, the French found a brother of the displaced king to occupy the throne. In Nupe, Lugard dethroned the Fulani Etsu and replaced him with a candidate from a rival Fulani faction.

The large empires of the western Sudan – Sokoto, Rabeh, Tokolor and Mandinka – were relatively recent creations. Their subject people were either not totally subdued, as was the case with the Bambara under the Tokolors, or were resentful, as the Kanuri under Rabeh, or their loyalty was in doubt, as the Gwari people under Sokoto.

Some Muslims felt that the original reform movements initiated by dan Fodio had either not gone far enough or had abandoned their original aims. There was a succession of more militant, radical and austere reformers, such as Jibrilla in Hausaland and Mamadu Cheiku in the Futas who were challenging the authority of the ruling groups. As the Europeans advanced the ruling artistocracy was plagued on the one hand by groups ready to throw off alien or Muslim rule and on the other by radical leaders, usually of the same ethnic group, calling for a more rigid application of Muslim principles. Rabeh, an admirer of Mahdist radicalism, sought to rally these rebel forces against the invading Europeans but by so doing alienated the conservative leadership of the Sokoto caliphate and Sanusiyya empire.

No African kingdom had developed the powerful nationalism common to European states in the nineteenth century. Asante and Dahomey may have come closest to it. In Asante the concept of the national soul, symbolized in the Golden Stool, was akin to the idea of nationalism. The national spirit of Dahomey was likened to water in a calabash punctured with holes which were plugged by the fingers of the citizens. Each individual thus had a personal responsibility for the national spirit. There was also a procedure by which aliens might become citizens. By recognizing individual responsibility and the fact that citizenship was a condition of the heart and head rather than birth and blood relationships, Dahomey was close to the concept of nationalism.

In the western Sudan, Islam played the unifying role of nationalism in European states. Once the European invaders convinced the Sudanese people that they did not aim to subvert their religion the will to resist and unity of the state were undermined. But nowhere did people hold an absolute loyalty to the state. Generally African peoples of the nineteenth century exhibited an individualism of political behaviour which the nationalist states of Europe would not have tolerated among their subjects.

Considering the general military weakness, it may seem strange that there were few cases of effective inter-African alliances against the European invaders. Jealousy and concern for religious prestige prevented an alliance of the Futa Jalon, Tokolor and Mandinka empires against the French. It was often easy for the European power to secure the alliance of one group of people against another. The British had the assistance of Ibadan against Ijebu, of the Itsekiri and Urhobo against Benin, of the Fante against Asante, while the French found allies everywhere in their march from Senegal to Lake Chad. In addition, like the mercenary troops in pre-nationalist Europe who fought for the side which paid the highest, the European-led armies were made up of African soldiers. Lugard, for example, conquered the Sokoto caliphate with troops who had been born in Hausaland.

In the late nineteenth century the ties of race and colour were as strong to Europeans as the ties of family to Africans. Race meant little, if anything, to Africans. The doctrine of racial solidarity remained a mystifying European belief. There was little feeling that two African states should ally merely because they were African. During the partition, European powers became just another factor in the power struggle between hostile peoples, to be used by one African state against another. One state looked upon a European alliance as an instrument of gaining ascendancy or at least equality with a neighbouring rival. This was in dramatic contrast with the European nations who worked to prevent their rivalries and jealousies from disrupting a unified assault upon the African continent.

British tactics

While British diplomacy was at its best in Yorubaland and close to its best in the Sokoto caliphate, it was at its crudest in the conquest of Benin and Asante. This divergence in approach was partly due to the amount of force at the conquering officer's command. Where he held only limited military means, as with Carter in Yorubaland and Lugard in Hausaland, greater diplomacy was essential. It was also partly due to the attitude of the officers towards their mission. Carter and Lugard thought in terms of a protectorate in which they would change little in the indigenous system, but would merely establish British paramountcy. But the conquerers of Benin and Asante behaved as if they were creating a colony where indigenous institutions were to be destroyed and where the British would rule either directly or through African agents who held little traditional power or prestige.

In 1892 Governor Carter of Lagos created an incident with the Ijebu which led to a crushing and spectacular military victory designed to overcome resistance, as well as to emphasize its futility to other Yoruba kingdoms. Since the Awujale (oba of the Ijebu) claimed that he had advocated peace but had been overruled by his chiefs in council, it suited Carter's purposes to confirm him in his position, as a direct hint to other obas that co-operation would not go unrewarded. Immediately Carter opened treaty discussions with the Egba and Ibadan in which he showed a willingness to treat these powers with considerable respect, to negotiate and not impose his terms. The Egba secured internal autonomy, while the Ibadans rejected the first treaty draft and a new one was drawn up to meet their objections. Others followed and not one Yoruba oba was deposed. Little force was employed but it was always present since Carter dragged his Maxim-gun around the country so that it might duly impress and inspire respect. Had the British adhered to the letter of these treaties their position would have been little more than that of an 'influence', and not one of colonial subjugation. It was not for some years though, after the people were disarmed, that the chiefs discovered that they were powerless to prevent the British from ignoring the terms of the treaty and behaving as outright conquerors.

In the Sokoto caliphate Lugard's tactics were similar, if not as successful as Governor Carter's. Lugard demonstrated his military strength by conquering Nupe and Kontagora. He deposed the Etsu Nupe and replaced him with a rival Fulani candidate. He then wrote to the Amir al-Muminin at Sokoto informing him that he had taken this action because of the oppressive rule of these two emirs, and requested that he nominate someone for the vacant throne of Kontagora.

Through these tactics Lugard sought to indicate the futility of resistance and also that he was not hostile to Islam or the Fulani if they co-operated. On the other hand Lugard posed as the 'liberator' of the subject people from Fulani 'oppression'. Thus the Fulani were warned that if they resisted they might well be replaced by the pre-jihad Hausa dynasties.

Lugard's mixture of force and persuasion brought confusion into Fulani councils. Without a strong lead from Sokoto, Zaria decided to accept, and Kano to reject British overtures. The Amir al-Mumimin had just died and Attahiru, the new caliph, hesitated too long before he decided to resist. In

1903 the British occupied Sokoto and installed a new Amir al-Muminin. Attahiru fled and later the same year was defeated and killed at the battle of Burmi.

There is little doubt that had the caliph called upon his people to resist at the right moment, Lugard's supply lines could have been cut and he and his forces utterly destroyed. However, the Fulani estimate of the overall situation was correct. They could not in the end defeat the military might of the British empire which would be sent against them if Lugard was destroyed. Furthermore, French forces were driving all around the northern frontier of the caliphate and by reports from the Tokolor empire it was obvious that if Lugard could be relied upon he was offering less severe terms of surrender than the French were likely to impose.

The approach of the British to Benin and Asante was entirely different. In Benin the British mixture of force and persuasion caused a serious rift in the oba's council. Oba Ovonramwen preferred to negotiate but a majority of his chiefs desired to resist, a dispute which brought Benin to the verge of civil war. To gain enough time to achieve national unity, the oba attempted by various excuses to delay the arrival of British negotiators. The Royal Niger Company to the east was hoping that Benin might fall to its jurisdiction and attempted to persuade the Bini to resist the overtures of British government agents. It is possible that some militant chiefs hoped to encourage this inter-British rivalry and so save the independence of the kingdom.

To provoke a crisis the British advised Urhobo traders to refuse to pay Benin customs dues and sent a negotiating party to Benin City which ignored repeated Bini warnings to halt. As the party advanced the oba's messengers, while continuing to insist that the British halt, became more and more conciliatory in their attitude. The British interpreted this as growing weakness and expected to be ultimately welcomed in the capital. Had the oba had his way it might well have been so; however, the militant chiefs precipitated war by ambushing and destroying the advancing party.

In 1897 a British army advanced into Benin, burnt the capital and looted it of nearly 2,500 of its famous bronze treasures. Ovonramwen was deported and the British offered positions of importance to chiefs who came out of hiding and indicated their willingness to co-operate. Few major chiefs responded. The British left the throne vacant and made little effort to recreate the Bini political system but ruled directly through African agents after the manner of the French.

Had the Bini chiefs not precipitated actual war it appears likely that Ovonramwen could have negotiated to hold his throne. There was no definite British policy to destroy Benin as a nation. But once they had made the mistake of deporting Ovonramwen they found that Bini principles forbade the crowning of a new oba while the old one still lived. Furthermore,

Oba Ovonramwen (Overami) of Benin

once they had committed themselves to the chiefs who offered their co-operation, it was not so easy to set them aside for the chiefs who had influence in Bini society.

In Asante the result was much the same as in Benin. But while in Benin the British got themselves into a position of direct rule by a series of mistakes and accidents, in Asante the destruction of the nation and direct colonial rule was their avowed aim (see chapter 9). For fifty years the British had ruled the Fante people of southern Ghana directly and they thought in these terms as they planned the subjugation of Asante. They aimed to break up the Asante union, de-stool the Asantehene and destroy the Asante as a nation.

Wars of independence in the Ivory Coast

We have seen how the French allied with African rulers to neutralize them until they could be eliminated at convenience. Such was the fate of the damel of Cayor, Ahmad the Tokolor and Tieba of Sikasso. Occasionally they experimented with the idea of replacing legitimate monarchs with puppets – the Bambara king of Segu, and the king of Dahomey – but this was only a temporary measure until their hold over the state was secure. There were places – the Futa Jalon, the Mossi kingdom and Lake Chad area – where the French permitted the existence of African kings under their rule. In the Ivory Coast there were no large centrally organized states and the French pursued the policy of using the chiefs to sign treaties and then eliminating them so that they could set up direct administration.

Particular attention must be drawn to the unprecedented resistance of the coastal-forest people of the Ivory Coast, who fought for twenty-seven years (1891-1918) to preserve their independence. This was the most prolonged

233

and coherent resistance and, along with Samori, the fiercest struggle against subjugation anywhere in West Africa. Although there were no centralized kingdoms like Dahomey, Asante and Benin, the small chieftancies achieved exceptional co-operation. While the French were preoccupied in suppressing one, two or three others arose to harass them. Because of the smallness of the chieftaincies there were no large armies against which the French could use their artillery and the forests proved ideal for guerrilla 'strike and retire' tactics. Africans insisted that the French honour the protectorate treaties, and did not meddle in African internal affairs and specifically did not interfere with the election of chiefs. The French could never establish their rule if they were bound by the treaties, and indeed to them the treaties were merely to secure allies who could be gradually transformed into subjects. But each time they began this transformation, widespread resistance broke out. The major result of these prolonged wars was that the African leadership class (chiefs and priests) was annihilated more thoroughly than anywhere else in West Africa.

In 1871 when French garrisons were withdrawn from the Ivory Coast, French interests were left in the hands of the merchant firm of Arthur Verdier. Afro-French relations were governed by treaties in which French merchants were given trading rights in return for an annual tribute to the coastal chiefs. Verdier honoured the treaties and sold his goods from Grand Bassam and Assinie. The major markets were inland, to which the coastal people carried French goods and where the products of the savannah and of the forest, as well as the gold of Asante, were exchanged. Between 1887 and 1889 the French negotiated similar tributary treaties with the forest chieftaincies and as far north as Kong in the savannah. By the treaties the French bound themselves not to interfere with African customs, land tenure or government.

Almost immediately the French violated the treaties by demanding slave porters, by meddling in the election of chiefs, and by dispatching two military expeditions to strike at Samori in the north, which failed partly as a result of the opposition of Baoule chiefs. In retaliation Samori sacked Kong, France's ally; the French were proved vulnerable and more groups joined the Baoule in harassing them.

In 1900 the French sought to levy a head tax on the entire population and three years later began the construction of a railway which required the seizing of African lands, and increased demands for slave labour. The tax was a total reversal of Afro-French relations as governed by the treaties. Prior to 1900 the French were tribute-paying aliens; by the new tax law they became conquerors exacting a tribute from their former masters. The tax, slave labour and land seizure brought home to each individual the real intention of the French. The result was a supreme effort to throw the French out of the Ivory Coast which changed what had been a basically Baoule resistance into a general war of independence which forced the French to abandon the interior. By 1908 they were clinging to a small coastal strip, daily fearing the invasion of their seaside settlements.

Africans who had not been militarily defeated but had rather negotiated treaties with the Europeans continued for many years after partition to think of their status *vis-à-vis* the Europeans as being in the nature of a partnership, albeit something of an unequal one. They did not look upon themselves as defeated and subjected people. This was especially true where the French and British worked in co-operation with the chiefs or where the people concerned achieved a rise in status or a trade advantage over neighbouring rivals as a result of European paramountcy. As colonial rule tightened it often became more careless of the people's feelings and Europeans were less careful to disguise their role as conquerors. Treaty obligations were ignored and sooner or later Europeans felt secure enough to demand tribute. For the people this was often 'the moment of truth' when the Afro-European partnership established by treaty was converted into a humiliating African subjection. Europeans blamed the ensuring riots and wars on African unwillingness to pay tax, but really it was African refusal to accept the status which payment of tribute symbolized. Thus it was where European paramountcy had been established through treaties – as among the Yoruba, Ibo and Urhobo of Nigeria, the Mende and Temne of Sierra Leone and the Baoule of the Ivory Coast – rather than through military defeat, as in Benin, Ijebu and Asante, that European demands for tribute (tax) occasioned the greatest resistance.

In 1908 the French sent Governor Angoulvant to the Ivory Coast. He was a man who was prepared to be tough and who attributed French humiliation to the softness of his predecessors. Angoulvant began a methodical military occupation with the purpose of disarming the population. Since Africans avoided open battles and took to strike-and-retire and ambush tactics, Angoulvant was forced into a brutal war in which hundreds of villages were destroyed and their people herded into larger settlements which the French army could guard and thus prevent the people giving support to their fighting forces. One group formerly living in 247 villages were forced into seventeen; another originally in 147 were herded into ten.

By 1915 the country was under the iron discipline of military rule. The French had seized 100,000 guns, imposed £30,000 in fines and deported 220 African leaders. The administration was poor and its finances exhausted by the military effort of holding down a resentful people. To maintain itself slave labour was recruited on a scale larger than ever. In addition, the French, facing collapse before the Germans in the World war, began to recruit

African soldiers for the battlefields of Europe. While the people of the savannah in the north responded to the recruitment campaign, to the coastal-forest people it was just another intolerable burden of subjection. In 1916 the Baoule led another uprising which came almost as close as that of 1908 to expelling the French. In 1917 in hopeless despair of victory a section of the Agni (a people related to the Asante) migrated as a body to the less harsh colonialism of the British in neighbouring Ghana.

The Harris movement, 1914-16

By 1918 Africans of the forest zone of the Ivory Coast were an exhausted, humbled and leaderless people. Killings and deportations over the past twenty-seven years had almost wiped out the chiefly class. When the chiefs were destroyed the priests of the traditional religion attempted to lead the resistance. They, like the chiefs, failed. The people lost faith in the religion and gods they represented. Military failure led to the collapse of political institutions and a weakening of faith in African religious beliefs and principles. For the Ivory Coast people things had fallen apart. It was in this political, religious and social chaos that a remarkable mass conversion to Christianity took place under a Liberian Christian preacher by the name of Harris.

The right to self-determination is probably one of the strongest instincts in any community. When a people make a supreme effort to uphold this right and fail hopelessly they may lose their self-respect and their faith in their institutions and beliefs. A society is one whole and cannot easily be separated into its political, social, religious and economic parts. To interfere with one aspect of a society is to interfere with all; to destroy one, is to damage the society so badly that an entire reconstruction may be necessary. In the chaos which accompanies reconstruction the society gropes for survival. Large elements of the conqueror's culture and techniques may be adopted, for it is only with the instruments of the conqueror that groups are likely to overcome their difficulties and reassert their self-determination. In non-Muslim Africa where religion ran through and bound together the social, political and economic aspects of society, the European's religion was often looked upon as the key to his power and success.

It was not, therefore, unusual in non-Muslim Africa for European conquest to result in a general turning to Christianity. The speed of this movement varied; sometimes it was gradual, gaining momentum as the colonial situation bore more heavily upon the people, elsewhere it was so rapid that mission societies could not cope with it. Occasionally, as in Katanga, Ijebu and the Ivory Coast, it took the form of a spontaneous mass movement of the population.

Prophet William Wade Harris

In the Ivory Coast the Roman Catholic missionaries arrived with the imperial forces in the 1890's and were too closely allied to the conquerors to be trusted by the people.

In 1914 Harris, preaching in English through an interpreter, began to attract attention near Grand Lahou. Harris denounced the old religion, challenged the traditional priests and even converted some of them to the new faith. Thousands followed his advice. Villages cut down their sacred groves, destroyed symbols of the old religion, built churches and elected their own leaders to conduct Christian worship. About 120,000 people were converted in one year, giving Harris the distinction of having inspired the greatest Christian mass movement in West African history.

The wars of independence were not over. A few young men educated in Catholic schools and employed as clerks in the administration and commercial firms became Harris converts and, because of their literacy, rose to positions of importance in the new churches. These men were anxious to influence the movement to support the cause of African independence and to achieve the expulsion of the French from the Ivory Coast.

Originally the French favoured Harris because he was striking at the power of the traditional priests who were encouraging resistance to French rule. In 1916 when they saw that the new Christian leaders were seeking to take over the political as well as religious role of the traditional priests the French deported Harris to Liberia. Although these educated youths failed to turn the movement into political channels, it survived and without foreign aid produced the largest Protestant population of any French West African colony.

In the end – the Maxim

The wars of independence in the Ivory Coast were in some ways unique, and contradict earlier assumptions regarding African resistance. Economically and politically the small chieftaincies were weak in contrast to the centralized states of West Africa. However, this weakness proved to be a kind of strength. Small political organizations could not raise large armies to be crushed by French firepower, nor depend upon walled cities which could be destroyed by French artillery. The wars therefore consisted of multiple risings, small groups striking and retiring, ambushing, and cutting communication lines so that the French found it difficult to profit by their military superiority. Furthermore Africans were able to secure guns; it is not clear whether these were of local manufacture, or were smuggled from Liberia, or both, but the French capture of 100,000 firearms indicated a fairly reliable supply.

Colonialism in the Ivory Coast was not in principle more harsh than French or British rule elsewhere in West Africa but the Ivory Coast administration was particularly clumsy. Instead of securing disarmament and subjugation before imposing the full burden of colonial rule, the French continued through recruitment of slave labour, seizure of African lands and demands for tribute to unite the people in a desperate struggle for survival. The more cautious British in some areas delayed their demands for tribute until as late as the 1920's. In southern Nigeria, for example, they imposed it in a few areas at a time, so that they were able to deal firmly with Africans who resisted it.

Although the Ivory Coast resistance to French rule was unique in its length and intensity, in the end it failed. European military superiority was, as elsewhere, the decisive and triumphant factor. In the final analysis it was the the Maxim-gun which compelled respect, obedience, humiliation and subjection.

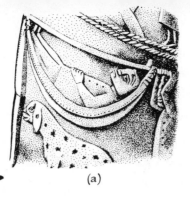

Part **four**

Response and resistance to foreign rule

(a)

(b)

(c)

(d)

(e)

(f)

(g)

West African artists portray their colonial rulers (see over)

(a) *A merchant calculates his profit and loss while carried in a hammock (Nigeria)*

(b) *A European merchant checks his account book (Portuguese Guinea)*

(c) *Queen Victoria, symbol of Britain's might*

(d) *A calculating merchant holding a 'Manila', currency widely used in nineteenth-century West Africa*

(e) *A self-assured French soldier (Dahomey)*

(f) *A German district officer (Togo)*

(g) *An unsympathetic foreign judge (Portuguese Guinea)*

The architects of indirect rule in West Africa

17 West Africans
and indirect rule

British and African aims and assumptions

Nineteenth-century British policy towards West Africa had sought the creation of a westernized class (the missionaries making an important contribution to this process) who would be British partners in religion, trade and administration. As a result Africans rose in the British colonies around Freetown, Bathurst, southern Ghana and Lagos to important positions in the Church, in commercial firms and in colonial government. The partition added large areas to the British West African empire and the problem of administration, personnel and finance became urgent. Most of the newly-conquered territories were controlled through the chiefs who were confirmed in their positions, except in Asante and Benin where the kings had been deported. Due to the changing attitude to the role of educated Africans noted in chapters 10 and 15 and the turning away from the earlier nineteenth-century belief of development, the British brought in European administrators as fast as the growth in finances would allow instead of accelerating the training of Africans for administrative positions. Western educated Africans already in service were gradually replaced and new recruiting for the senior civil service almost stopped, either by custom or by enactment. In 1910 the Colonial Office expressed the opinion that Englishmen naturally expected to enjoy the fruits of their conquests and that it was logical that they should be preferred over Africans in senior positions. This gave official Colonial Office approval to a policy which was already being followed in West Africa.

Like other British conquerers, Lugard in Northern Nigeria adopted the policy of ruling through the aristocracy of the conquered people. This had been a popular policy of imperialists throughout history and was extensively used in African empires of the nineteenth century. From the British view Lugard's system worked economically and satisfactorily and in 1914 he was appointed to join together the various colonies which later made up Nigeria. In his years as Governor General of Nigeria, 1914-19, he began to extend his theories to the peoples of southern Nigeria. After he left Nigeria he laid out his theory of indirect rule in a book, *The Dual Mandate in Tropical Africa* (1922). *The Dual Mandate* became the handbook of British officers everywhere in the empire. Admirers adopted Lugard's methods all over the world. Noted examples were Cameron in Tanganyika, Guggisberg in Ghana and Palmer in the Gambia.

Indirect rule formed the basis of local government. It did not apply to the central government of the colony which was run according to traditional British ideas and practices. The African chief was the instrument of local government. He appointed all officials who were responsible to him. He or his officials presided over the law courts which as far as possible applied African law. His agents levied taxes for the local treasury. Part of the revenue was sent to the central government and the remainder kept for local improvements such as roads, sanitation, markets and schools, and to pay the salaries of local officials.

The chief was responsible to a British official, a resident or district officer, who in turn, was responsible to the central government. The resident also oversaw the operation of taxation, the treasury and courts, but always operating through the chief. British officials were expected to remain in the background making changes appear as if they came from the chief. The major point to notice is that to work ideally, from the British point of view, a chief whose authority was accepted by the people was a necessity for successful operation of the indirect rule system. As has already been indicated in earlier chapters in reference to African political systems in the nineteenth century, and will also be clearly seen later in this chapter, by no means all African leaders had such authority. Where they did, indirect rule worked well from the British point of view; where they did not, it failed from everyone's view, African and British. In the caliphate in Northern Nigeria indirect rule was 'successful' mainly because of the authority of the emirs but partly because it was designed by Lugard specifically for the caliphate where he had intimate knowledge of the society. When he and others began to apply it elsewhere its unsuitability became more apparent.

While Lugard's emirate system in Northern Nigeria was becoming the show piece of indirect rule and was being acclaimed in the English-speaking world, the western educated Africans began to look upon Lugard as the symbol of the worst aspects of British imperialism. Except for its heavy paternalism Africans had little quarrel with the theory which put forward a double duty (dual mandate) of the imperial power to govern in the interests of Britain and the colonial people. This required that each colony must finance its own administration, not become a burden on British taxpayers and provide ideal conditions for the expansion of British trade. In addition, Africans must also benefit and Lugard felt that this was best achieved by government through African institutions, shaping these where necessary to meet modern changes.

Where educated Africans and the British disagreed was on the assumptions which underlay the dual mandate. Were British and African interests identical? Could the colonial governments serve two masters? The British assumed that the majority of Africans not only tolerated but actually welcomed their overlordship and that colonialism would last so long that the ultimate goal of colonial policy need not yet be precisely defined. Experience of the older white colonies led to the assumption that this goal would be self-government. There was, however, little effort to link this vague aim with present policies, which often appeared to be leading in an entirely opposite direction. Africans tended to emphasize the ultimate goal and criticize policy in the light of it. They tolerated British rule because there appeared no alternative. When the world position of the British visibly declined after 1918 Africans began to urge a faster pace towards self-government.

The British assumed that African society had been static for centuries, that their political institutions were therefore fixed and that the population was very conservative. On the contrary many African societies had been passing through important social upheavals in the nineteenth century and African peoples were only conservative when pushed in directions they did not want to go. The British assumed that most chiefs, emirs and kings so controlled power that they could be used to bring change from the top rather than from the normal process of change starting from the bottom. The king of Dahomey, emirs of the caliphate and oba of Benin had centralized a good deal of power in their hands, but in Yorubaland, Asante and Bornu, although the monarch appeared powerful, this power was actually divided in a complicated way in the society. Among other peoples, the Mende, Temne, Fante, Kru, Ibo and Tiv, the chiefs were either under popular control or there were no chiefs at all. Among the Ibo, Tiv and Kru, chiefs or elders were spokesmen, powerless to act without popular consent. More West Africans lived under this system than under ones which placed power in the hands of a single king or chief.

During and after the partition, when the nineteenth-century theory of African evolution towards European society was being attacked as unsound, some Europeans doubted African ability to evolve at all. More liberal views held by people like Lugard felt that Europeans could transform African society but that this would not lead towards a European, but towards a distinctly African, pattern. From this arose Lugard's emphasis on the British role as shapers of African society. Educated Africans emphasized less their inability to develop European forms but rather their lack of desire to do so. Although they wanted certain aspects of European life they wanted also to be free to chose these aspects and not to have this vital decision taken for them by Lugard or anyone else. While the British were proud of their own democratic traditions, they sought to emphasize the autocratic in African tradition. More and more the educated class began to feel that Lugard was opposed to their having those aspects of European life which they wanted, while he was intending to force on them those aspects of African life they wished to discard.

Modern defenders of colonialism point out that empires are not created because of a general love of mankind. From the beginning of the colonial period Africans accepted that the British expected material benefits, but they became more and more impatient with British efforts to hide this under slogans such as 'paramountcy of African interests' and 'white man's burden'. Colonialism presented Africans with their own burden which they were ready to carry as long as they felt there were worthwhile benefits; these included expanding educational opportunities, a voice in policy making, a sharing of senior civil service positions, economic development to bring Africa into the industrial age and a wider nationality in which tribalism could be submerged.

Indirect rule in Northern Nigeria

Following the conquest Lugard confirmed the co-operative emirs in their positions, enthroned a new Amir al-Muminin at Sokoto and permitted the alkali courts and bureaucracy to function as before. British residents were to advise and if, necessary, ultimately to force the emirs to follow policy approved by the conquerors. The caliphate had always been run by local governments and the British took over Sokoto's former position of supervising these local rulers; they also confined the authority of Amir al-Muminin to strictly religious matters. The residents tended to build up the independent power of the emirs, and thus also their own importance as 'the power behind the throne', until they appeared to be working towards separate independent states and thus undoing the unification brought about as a result of the jihad.

If a colonial policy was cheap and produced peace, order and tranquillity, it was judged to be a 'success'. Trouble, arguments and disputes were thought of as failure. But while trouble could indicate rapid social change, tranquillity might mean nothing more than stagnation.

A number of factors combined to isolate the caliphate from the great twentieth-century world movements. By the middle of the nineteenth century the trans-Saharan routes began to decline as a result of the trade contacts opened up on the Niger river by British merchants (see chapter 5). Thus when the Muslim world was beginning its modern transformation the caliphate began to lose contact with it. Colonial boundaries completed this isolation.

In the surrender terms the British promised not to interfere with the Muslim religion and this was interpreted by both parties to mean that

Christian missionaries would not be encouraged. This increased the isolation of Northern Nigeria for it thus missed an influence which was having such a pronounced effect in southern Nigeria. While it was therefore not expected that the British should favour Christianity over Islam, it was not foreseen that shielding the people from the stimulating influence of Christianity would slow down the process of change. The British did allow mission activities in non-Muslim areas, many of which had not been brought within the caliphate in the nineteenth century. These relatively backward areas of the nineteenth century, through their acceptance of the education brought by the missionaries, became some of the most progressive areas by twentieth-century standards. The British did set up a few good non-religious schools for the aristocracy, but they were never popular because they were in competition with the already existing Islamic system. One result of this was that, since the Hausa-Fulani western educated class was very small, and since there was no place in the British administrative system for the products of the Islamic schools, when the British began to build up a civil service, when the railway system came, and when postal services and commercial firms began to employ a clerical staff, these were recruited from southern Nigeria, where even before the first World war a surplus of school leavers was developing. The British never saw the problem this was creating for the day of eventual self-government, for their main concern was that northern Muslim society should be protected from the ideas of these southerners. It was a cheap way of staffing but, as African opinion repeatedly pointed out, it did not lead to the ultimate goal of self-government. Thus, cut off from the Maghreb and Middle East, and protected from southern Nigerian ideas and movements, Northern Nigeria presented a picture of tranquillity strangely out of place in the general upheavals of the twentieth century.

Indirect rule among the Yoruba

It was Lugard's belief that his system could be adapted and modified so that it would work anywhere. When in 1914 he was sent to achieve Nigerian amalgamation he began to introduce to the Yoruba his own particular interpretation of the system of ruling through traditional institutions. The Yoruba states possessed a centralized government headed by obas who held a certain respect for the Alafin of Oyo or Oni of Ife. It was thus all too easy to see the Yoruba family of states as a looser arrangement of the caliphate. Since after the conquest Yoruba obas had been maintained in their positions, Lugard saw his task as the establishment of British rule through them.

In Yorubaland the British wanted to return to the conditions of the eighteenth century and to make Oyo the chief power. The refusal of many

Yoruba to accept this had been a major cause of the nineteenth-century Yoruba wars. In the 1890's the British had recognized Ibadan as one of the most powerful of the Yoruba states but now they sought to make it subordinate to Oyo. The Bale of Ibadan, surrendering to British orders, made his submission to the Alafin and then took his own life knowing that he had acted against the wishes of his people. When the chiefs are carelessly called agents of British rule, their problem should be clearly understood; in Ibadan the issue was clear; refuse the British and lose the throne or obey and lose popular respect. At one time prominent Yoruba chiefs were forced to supervise grass cutting along the roads to punish them for their independent views.

Among the Yoruba the western educated, though small as a group, were becoming influential: in Abeokuta they had in fact taken over control; in Ibadan they were advisors to the chiefs; in Ilesha one had become oba. Lugard ignored this vital development and tried to introduce the system which existed before the rise of the western educated men. In Abeokuta he overthrew their government and reverted to chiefly government; he then decided to elevate Oyo, which was the least influenced by this class and by its standards, and was one of the more conservative of the Yoruba states. It was thus not surprising that the Yoruba western educated class were suspicious of Lugard and ready to lead opposition to British rule.

The British believed that the Yoruba oba possessed a considerable degree of autocratic power, and that by controlling him they could control the whole system. In fact, power was shared among a number of chiefs, representing lineages over which the oba had limited power.

When the British tried to control the oba's selection of chiefs they discovered that his power was much less than they had believed. Titles were often the property of lineages who selected the title holders to represent them. The British, unable to control this selection, resorted to doubtful methods such as threatening to take land from unco-operative lineages and giving it to those who more readily accepted British aims. The Yoruba were in the middle of revolutionary changes in the nineteenth century, which the British either did not understand or took no notice of, and their efforts to return to the system of pre-Afonja days were destined to fail. In addition there were few Yoruba, either western educated or not, who, for internal political reasons, were willing to see their obas' powers increased.

Indirect rule among the Ibo

Regardless of the attempts to adjust a system of indirect rule based on the caliphate, such a system could never work with the Ibo. There were few chiefs whom the British could control; and even if they could control the

Ama-ala, the elders could not control the village meeting, which was the basic institution of Ibo government and of which they were little more than spokesmen. But because Lugard's theories, developed in *The Dual Mandate*, became so widely accepted among colonial civil servants, these men thus lost what has been described as the Englishman's most valuable characteristic in dealing with colonial societies, a refusal to put a practical approach before theory.

Had the British approached the Ibo free from the theories of the *The Dual Mandate* they might have attempted to introduce their own forms of local government, which would have been much closer to nineteenth-century Ibo political theory. British and Ibo democracy were far from being alike but they possessed the common quality that authority came directly from the people, indeed far more directly in Ibo than in British forms. The units of Ibo society were possibly too small for meeting the increased demands of modern government but it would have been better to introduce elected representatives who came from the village meeting and were responsible to it, rather than to give a lineage elder an authority which made him a chief and gave him powers unknown in Ibo society. A jury system would also have been a better replacement for the Ama-ala in court cases than were the judicial powers given to these artificially-created chiefs.

However, the idea of election, or any other transfer of British political philosophy, was distasteful to Lugard and his disciples. A constant question was, how was it to be controlled? With an open mind and imagination the British might have created a system which harnessed Ibo ambitions and developed a system of rule which could have become as much admired as that of Northern Nigeria. The Ibo might well have been considered the most progressive and co-operative rather than the most troublesome of West African peoples.

In Iboland the British had to deal with a society which was undergoing rapid change in the twentieth century. Once incorporated into an amalgamated Nigeria and influenced by the Yoruba western educated class, the Ibo used the co-operative strength of their clans to build schools, educate their promising sons and play one mission off against the other to get the greatest benefits. The Roman Catholics under Bishop Shanrahan in the 1920's caught the spirit of this Ibo movement. Within thirty years the Ibo were emerging into Nigerian public life in a way which was quite unexpected by other national groups. This advance was largely brought about within nineteenth-century social and political institutions, and not within the system which the British were trying to impose.

British administration in Iboland was a series of failures followed by attempted reorganizations. When the British conquered eastern Nigeria they set up a system of indirect rule, and although in the Delta the autocratic House heads served this purpose well, the lineage elders of the interior did not respond happily so that the political officers turned to more direct administration. When Lugard took over in 1914 he was disturbed by this development of policy. He therefore sent a northern officer, Palmer, to 'find' the Ibo chiefly system, over the protests of officers who had been working for years among the Ibo. Palmer 'found' the chiefs, who were given warrants to increase their authority. These warrant chiefs, with their unrestrained authority and control of the courts, were seen by the people as miniature tyrants. When in 1929 the British tried to impose direct taxation, and the famous Women's riots followed, the main targets of attack were the warrant chiefs.

Following the riots a number of anthropologists were sent to 'discover' Ibo traditional government. But Lugard's prestige was still too strong, and although adjustments were made there was no one of sufficient influence among the British to challenge the whole system. So the search for chiefs continued. It was not until the 1940's – just forty years late – that the British began to introduce their own local government system.

Donald Cameron, governor of Nigeria from 1931 to 1935 has been considered a reformer of indirect rule. He checked the growing independence of the emirs in the north as well as the efforts to elevate the Alafin in Yorubaland. He was hailed because he put emphasis on developing the institutions rather than preserving them. Thus he introduced selected western educated men into certain chiefly councils in southern Nigeria. But his 'reforms' were merely adjustments, and were not nearly sweeping enough to meet the needs of a rapidly changing society.

Indirect rule in Ghana

By the early twentieth century the Fante-Ga coastal area of Ghana possessed the largest western educated class in West Africa. Ghanaian contacts with Europe dated back for centuries and as early as 1844 the Fante chiefs had voluntarily given over certain powers to the British. Many of the chiefs were also western educated men and the division between chiefs and western educated was less distinct than in Nigeria. When it appeared in the 1860's as if the British might withdraw from the Ghanaian coast, the Fante Confederation, a body including chiefs but in fact the creation of the western educated elite, prepared a constitution to take over and rule an independent Fante state. This was a definite pointer to the way in which Fante society was moving.

In Asante we have seen how the British tried to destroy the nation and set up direct administration. In fact by making the Asantehene a martyr in exile they forced Asante nationalism and opposition to centre around him. Governor Guggisberg, who introduced the Lugardian theories to Ghana, brought Prempe back to the Asante stool in 1924. This was a popular measure and encouraged the Asante to continue to work towards the reconstruction of their nation. Guggisberg merely recognized Prempe as Kumasihene (chief of Kumasi) but to the Asante people he was Asantehene (king of all the Asante) and the British finally accepted this fact in 1935. In 1943 the British gave back all stool lands which they had confiscated when Asante was conquered. A major concern of the Asante throughout the colonial period was to reconstruct what the British had destroyed at the conquest.

Guggisberg was governor of Ghana from 1919 to 1929. In the coastal regions the western educated were far too strong to be ignored and to secure their support for his scheme of indirect rule he combined it with a number of projects very close to the heart of the western educated class. He began a rapid acceleration of Ghana's economic development, founded Achimota College for higher education in 1927, introduced three elected members into the Legislative council and drew up plans which would increase the twenty-five Ghanaian civil servants in 1925 to 151 ten years later.

As noted above, Ghanaian leadership, both chiefs and western educated, had long co-operated. In 1897 the two groups had come firmly together against British efforts to confiscate land in Ghana and organized the Aborigines Rights Protection Society which upheld Ghanaian rights against any imperial attempt to reduce them. Guggisberg's introduction of indirect rule caused serious divisions in Ghanaian leadership. The chiefs led by Nana Ofori Atta, a capable and western educated chief, were enthusiastic. The western educated feared the revival of chiefly power and also that the chiefs would become agents of British rule. Certain individuals were, however, ready to try the system and Ghanaian leadership was broken into conflicting factions over the issue.

After Guggisberg left in 1929 Nana Ofori Atta and Casely Hayford, prominent leader of the western educated, settled their differences. Then in 1934 the seditious ordinance introduced by the colonial government united Ghanaians once again. Nana Ofori Atta continued to uphold the interests of the western educated by pressing for Africanization of the civil service, which had fallen far behind Guggisberg's suggestions.

As elsewhere, but more prominently in Ghana because of its large western educated class, the greatest complaint against the British version of indirect rule was that it emphasized the conservative and illiterate in society. In 1945, for example, out of 2,471 members of local government, only 614 were educated. This was a sad fact in West Africa's most literate colony. In 1948 a Commission of Enquiry condemned this state of affairs but the colonial government, backed by the Colonial office, said that the Commission had listened too much to city politicians and not enough to the 'solid good sense of the countrymen' who were much attached to tradition. Another commission followed and on the whole confirmed the opinion of the first Commission. Few Ghanaians wanted chieftaincy abolished but few also approved of the emphasis in the system against western educated men.

Indirect rule in Sierra Leone and Gambia

Expediency was again the mother of indirect rule under Governor Cardew of Sierra Leone. In the interior it was a 'success' because Creoles were excluded, there was little commercial activity or development of natural resources and consequently there was little social change. Peace, order and stagnation went well together. Even the little education which was introduced was carefully controlled so as not to create a leadership class.

Even in little Gambia the interior which was ruled indirectly was kept carefully separate from the colony area around Bathurst. Palmer, one of Lugard's most devoted disciples, attempted during his governorship in the 1930's to bring the system into line with Lugard's principles. British conquest had halted a long series of religious wars in the Gambia which had produced various different and opposed systems of government. Finding tradition therefore became a matter of choice. But the system worked, as in Sierra Leone, more because social change was slowed down under British rule than because of any real suitability and value.

The British could only see two alternatives in West Africa: either of maintaining what they believed to be traditional, or introducing their own system. Throughout most of their colonial dominance they pursued the first, and Africans who suggested changes along the lines of British government were dismissed as imitators. Very few Africans wanted to take over the British system completely; most were aware of the necessity for holding on to some aspects of African political thought. They wanted a colonial power ready to experiment, to listen, to accept suggestions, and to proceed by trial and error. It was in this spirit that rural Ghanaians explained that they wanted both their chiefs and their educated men. In the end Africans came to feel that the British were hopelessly without ideas and that little could be done until they had been removed; only then could the experiment begin to create a twentieth-century African form of government.

18 African reaction to the French policy of Assimilation

The French conquest and annexation of African and other overseas territories in the nineteenth century was the work of Frenchmen on the spot in those territories rather than of the French public in France. Indeed, for a long time, French public opinion was either not interested in or hostile to any idea of French colonial expansion. Because the French were largely a stay-at-home people, more interested in protecting their country in Europe than in investing their capital and manpower in foreign parts, the effort of French leaders, such as Jules Ferry, to acquire colonies for France met with strenuous national opposition.

Jules Ferry was, perhaps, the first French political leader to put forward a coherent colonial policy. He believed that the greatness of a country rested on its economic strength. Convinced of the economic value of colonies, he urged that France should embark on a vigorous policy of colonial expansion. Colonies were to supply raw materials and consume French manufactured products. By having colonies, France would thus be able to buy in the cheapest markets and sell her manufactures there at high prices. But the arguments of Ferry failed to rally the French who, having just emerged from a ruinous war with Prussia (1870-71), were determined to avoid further international conflicts. It was with enthusiasm, therefore, that the French Parliament voted him out of power in 1885, after the failure of his colonial expansion policy in Indo-China.

However, during the last ten years of the nineteenth century, mainly due to rapid industrial expansion in Europe and the increase in competition among European powers for colonies, Ferry's colonial policy gained wider support in France, and the French public began to support the idea of colonial expansion. As a result most of the French colonies, especially those in Africa, were acquired during this period, and by 1904 France had acquired a large colonial empire second in size only to that of Britain.

The history of the establishment of the French West African empire illustrates the role played by French merchants and administrators on the spot. The empire began in Senegal which was France's oldest colony in West Africa.

Contacts between the French and the Senegalese, which became regular from the middle of the seventeenth century, were at first primarily for trade. However, from the middle of the nineteenth century, largely because of the pressure put on the Paris government by the French merchants in Senegal and because of the expansionist ambitions of Governor Faidherbe, the French began to acquire large territories in Senegal which soon formed the stepping-stone to further territorial expansion in West Africa. By 1904, the French West African empire, which by 1895 had been constituted into an administrative federation, had spread from Mauritania above Senegal to the northern and western boundaries of Nigeria, and consisted of the territories covered by modern Mauritania, Senegal, Mali, Guinea, Ivory Coast, Upper Volta, Dahomey and Niger.

The policy of Assimilation

French colonialism is distinguished by its theory and policy known as Assimilation. The word Assimilation is the noun derived from the French verb *assimiler*, which means 'to cause to resemble'. The French assumed that their civilization and culture had attained the highest possible standard and set out to impose this standard on other nations whose civilizations they considered to be inferior to their own. They set out on this 'civilizing mission' in the strong belief that the other peoples – be they white, black, brown or yellow – were capable of being assimilated into French culture, and assumed that what was good for the French as a nation was also good for other nations. Thus, the black peoples of Africa and the yellow peoples of Asia were to be transformed into Frenchmen, speaking, living, behaving and thinking like Frenchmen. The territories in which they lived were to be identical to the provinces in France, administratively, economically and politically. Assimilation was thus a comprehensive colonial theory which sought to influence every aspect of the lives of the colonized peoples, and also to mould the colony and its society in the image of France.

The tendency on the part of France to assimilate other nations can be traced back to the seventeenth century; but it was not until the nineteenth century that France deliberately set out to put the theory into practice. In West Africa, the first territory where the doctrine of Assimilation was seriously applied was Senegal. French merchants and government officials were settled in comparatively large numbers in the Senegalese towns of St. Louis, Gorée, Rufisque and Dakar, which came to be known as the *Quatre Communes* (four communes). Here, the French educational and administrative systems were applied; local government institutions similar to those in France, such as municipal councils and a General Council, were set up in 1872 and 1879 respectively; elections were, as in France, based on universal male suffrage, with Europeans and Africans having theoretically the same right to vote and to be voted for. Trade and finance were dominated by the French firms established in Bordeaux in the south-west of France and were consequently

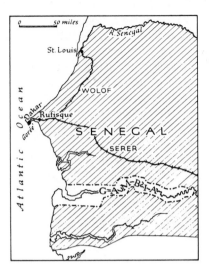

*42 Senegal, showing the Four Communes—
St. Louis, Gorée, Rufisque, Dakar*

greatly influenced by the economic situation in France. Moreover, the black and white inhabitants of the *Quatre Communes* were equally entitled to the protection of their rights under the French judicial system. The colony was represented by a locally elected deputy in the Chamber of Deputies in Paris.

To what extent, we may ask, did the French policy of Assimilation succeed in Senegal? It was both a success and a failure. Senegal was administered in almost the same way as a French province in France, and the Senegalese political situation was often influenced by the political situation in France. Furthermore, the Senegalese economy, which consisted largely of the ground-nut crop, was related very closely to the French economy. However, the final assessment of the success or failure of Assimilation can only be made by an examination of the extent to which the colonized peoples were culturally assimilated. For a culturally assimilated people are a people who have abandoned their original cultural identity for the French one, and have become French in all but colour. In this most important respect the French attempt to assimilate the Senegalese was a failure. Thus, while it was possible to impose French administrative and political institutions, it proved extremely difficult to bring about effective cultural assimilation.

This failure of France to assimilate the Senegalese culturally can be explained in several ways. In the first place, the theory of Assimilation was based on false assumptions. It is true that all men are equal; but it is also true that men differ from one another. African culture is basically different from that of France just as the Frenchman is different from the Chinese. Hence, what was good for the Frenchman was not necessarily good for the

Chinese or the African, for they have different habits, customs, religions and social organization. Secondly, a people's culture is the basis of its very existence; and it is impossible, except over a very long period, to erase one culture and substitute a foreign one. Thirdly, only by a regular system of education, based on indoctrination of the minds of the colonized peoples, can cultural Assimilation achieve some measure of success. Fourthly, the French themselves, realizing that Assimilation pushed to its logical conclusion would mean the end of colonialism, changed their minds and began to reverse some of their moves towards Assimilation. Finally, the failure of cultural Assimilation can be explained by the strong attachment of Africans to their own cultural values and their opposition to cultural imperialism. The case of Senegal, which was reputed to be the most culturally assimilated of all French West African colonies, will illustrate the effect of these factors on the course of cultural Assimilation in French West Africa.

Assimilation in Senegal

The Senegalese way of life was basically different from that of the French. A good example of this is in the concept of family and property. In Europe, the family unit consisted basically of the husband, the wife, and their own children; but in Africa, where the extended family system held sway, a man's nieces, nephews, cousins and distant relatives competed with his own children for attention. In Europe, landed property was individually owned; but land in Africa usually belonged to the family, or group of families, or even to a clan or whole ethnic group. In Africa, individual ownership was the exception rather than the rule. It is not surprising, therefore, that the French attempt to introduce their own system of land ownership in West Africa between 1904 and 1945 met with strong African opposition. Indeed, in Senegal it alienated the people of the towns such as the Lebu of Dakar, who would accept neither the French claim to lands which had come down to them from their ancestors, nor the French opposition to collective African land ownership.

Furthermore, most of the Senegalese were Muslims and their lives were, to a large extent, governed by Islam and the Koran. As Muslims they tended to be polygamous, while the French were by legal definition monogamous. To be fully assimilated one had to be a Frenchman in the fullest sense of the word, and therefore to be a monogamist governed, not by the Koran, but by the French codes. However, the Senegalese were very attached to their religion, and this meant that while they were liable to the French courts for criminal offences they were at the same time liable to the Muslim courts, especially in such civil matters as marriage, divorce, inheritance, birth and death. French Governor General Angoulvant rightly commented in 1916 that the Senegalese Muslims were opposed to cultural Assimilation, not because they hated France, but because of their attachment to their own civilization. The entire pattern of social life in Senegal was so bound up with their basic civilization that acceptance of this French way would have undermined all the normally accepted rules of behaviour.

The nineteenth-century system of education established by France in Senegal was not of a type to promote the cultural Assimilation of the Senegalese. Though the French realized that only a vigorous system of education could accelerate the process of Assimilation, throughout the century this was controlled by the Catholic Missions who were more interested in winning souls for God than in conquering minds for France.

Thus, although Senegal was a largely Muslim country, education was dominated by a Christian community. It is not surprising, therefore, that only a tiny section of the population, the French and Mulatto Catholics and some Senegalese, was able to take advantage of the education dispensed in Senegal. The rest of the population rejected the education offered to them. Because of religious antagonism and because they feared being converted from Muslims to Catholics, the majority of Senegalese did not attend school. It was not until after 1903, when secular education replaced that of the missions, that a larger number of Senegalese began to go to school. Even so, the reforms introduced from 1903 onwards had a different result from that expected by the reformers, for rather than accelerating cultural Assimilation, they accelerated the growth of African political consciousness.

One other obstacle to Assimilation was the reactionary attitude of the French themselves, especially during the period before the first World war. The years between 1890 and 1914 were years of rapid economic development in French West Africa. Commerce expanded, and with this the wealth of the West Africans seems to have improved also. This improvement also helps to explain why the Senegalese became more politically conscious during this period than they had been in the past. They began to claim real equality with the French. The French in Senegal began to fear that they would lose their property if African demands for true equality were gratified. They feared that equality would put an end to the French domination in Senegal and West Africa.

It was a paradox of Assimilation that the architects of its philosophy were unable to accept the consequences of their own ideals; for the very equality of the assimilated would tend to destroy the French colonial empire throughout the world. To prevent this, and to safeguard their economic and political domination in Senegal, at the turn of the century the French began to agitate not only for the rejection of Senegalese demands but also for the abolition of the political and civil rights enjoyed by the Senegalese.

African reactions

The African peoples of French West Africa reacted to the French policy of Assimilation in two apparently contradictory ways. This has been described by President Léopold Sédar Senghor of Senegal as: 'assimilate, but do not be assimilated'. Thus, while they were willing to absorb everything that was good in the French way of life, they were very careful not to become Frenchmen in dark skins in the process. If we take the case of Senegal again, we shall see how this apparent contradiction was expressed.

Between 1790 and 1880 the inhabitants of the towns of St. Louis, Gorée, Rufisque and Dakar, the majority of whom were Africans, were granted French citizenship. The importance of this concession was that those who won it were treated differently from the rest of the African population who were known as subjects. The French African citizens were, in theory, treated like French citizens in France; they could vote and be voted for at elections, and they had the right of protection under French justice. In short, they had the same rights and privileges as Frenchmen, and had to be treated as such. The non-French citizens had no rights whatsoever; they could be treated without respect, and were subject to punishment at any time by the French administrators. This also explains why when, between 1900 and 1916, the French, in reaction against their own policy of Assimilation, demanded that the civil and political rights of citizenship so far enjoyed by the Senegalese of St. Louis, Gorée, Rufisque and Dakar should be abolished, the latter protested very vigorously.

The Senegalese were the first African people to react against the French Assimilation policy. In a period of agitation, which lasted from 1900 to 1916, they opposed French colonial rule by demanding that they should control Senegalese politics. They condemned the concept of racial and cultural inferiority preached by the policy of Assimilation; they demanded equality before the law, equality of opportunity and other equal rights, and they advocated the right to be treated as respectable human beings while retaining their status as Muslims governed by the Koran. In 1916 they won their case through the intervention of the French Parliament. A large part of this was due to the parliamentary intervention in Paris of Blaise Diagne who was elected Deputy in the 1914 elections to the French Parliament. Diagne thus became the first black African to sit in the French Chamber of Deputies and to have an important influence in Senegalese politics. As a result of this intervention, Senegalese rights as French citizens were not only confirmed but also extended to their descendants. Thus, by being naturalized collectively rather than individually as demanded by law, and in retaining their Muslim status, they radically modified the theory of Assimilation.

Exact figures are not available for the number of Africans granted French

Blaise Diagne of Senegal

citizenship up to 1946, the year in which constitutional reforms were carried out in French West Africa. Until then, the normal procedure for obtaining French citizenship was by naturalization but very few Africans opted for this. The total number of Senegalese made French citizens by the French Parliament in 1916 was perhaps 50,000. If we add this figure to the number of their descendants who inherited their predecessor's status, as well as others who were subsequently naturalized, it can be estimated that there were about 80,000 French-African citizens in French West Africa up to 1946 – a tiny figure when compared with a total population of more than 10 million.

Up to 1946, the attention of Africans in French West Africa was concentrated on obtaining French citizenship, while that of the French was focused on preventing them from having it. However, with the reforms in 1946, a law was issued which made French citizenship available to any African in French West Africa who wanted it, regardless of his personal or religious status. This ended the long struggle over 'citizenship'. Historically the significant factor in the Africans' agitation for French citizenship is that they demanded it, not because they were ashamed of their colour, nor out of love for French culture, but simply because they wished to be treated as persons with rights under the law. As respectable human beings proud of their cultural heritage, they wished to be treated as the equals of the French, and to enjoy the same rights and privileges as the French themselves. Equality before the law, and equality of opportunity in education and employment were therefore the main motives rather than any special love of the French way of life.

Negritude

The term 'Negritude' has been used to describe the cultural and political movement of the French-speaking Africans in Africa and the French-speaking Negroes of the West Indies against the French policy of Assimilation. No full definition of this term has yet been given. Mr. Léopold Sédar Senghor,

President of the Republic of Senegal, who is the leading African exponent of the term, has described Negritude as the total cultural, social, and political values of African civilization, and of black Africa as a whole. Cultural Assimilation was justified in the past by the French on the wrong grounds that Africans had no history or culture of their own. Negritude set out to demonstrate that, on the contrary, Africans had contributed and were still contributing to world civilization as a whole. Thus, Negritude was originally an African cultural nationalist movement against the political, and especially cultural, domination of France.

In the first place the Negritude movement was not confined merely to the African continent. It embraced Africans in Africa, and descendants of Africans in the West Indies and in the Americas. Indeed, it may be said to have begun with the successful revolution in 1802 of the African slaves in Haiti under the African slave leader Toussaint Louverture. This important rebellion overthrew French rule and brought about the birth of the first Negro republic in the world. But such violent and successful outbreaks were few and far between, and for the most part the sense of cultural identity among Negroes in the new world was maintained by common expressions of religion such as the 'Negro spirituals', one of the origins of the jazz which has had such a strong influence on popular music throughout the world.

The anti-Assimilation movement soon spread, and between 1920 and 1940 was taken up by the French-speaking West Indian Negroes and black Africans living in Paris. Three leading intellectuals became especially identified with the movement – Aime Cesaire, the famous French-speaking Negro poet from the West Indies, who is said to have coined the word Negritude in about 1939, another West Indian, Léon Damas, and the Senegalese, Léopold Sedar Senghor. As a movement Negritude has not been confined to Negroes and Africans, but has influenced a number of white people. The well-known French writer Jean-Paul Sartre was among the first of them and has contributed a great deal to the movement.

Among exponents of Negritude are many creative writers. In addition to Aimé Césaire and Léopold Senghor, Birago Diop (from Senegal) and Camara Laye (from Guinea) should be mentioned. All these writers express Negritude in both poetry and the novel. In 1956 the First Congress of Negro Writers and Artists was held in Paris, with the aim of defining a new African and Afro-American cultural value. A second Congress was held in Rome in 1959. This time it was the political aspect of Assimilation that was attacked; delegates criticizing the colonial rule of the European powers. Since 1960, however, Negritude has gradually ceased to be associated with organized political protest, and has become identified with President Senghor of Senegal who has emphasized the philosophical aspects of the movement. The First World Festival of Negro Arts which took place in 1966 in Dakar, Senegal, was the work of President Senghor, and was aimed at defending and demonstrating Negritude.

Negritude has been criticized by many people who regard it either as sheer nonsense or as a waste of time. The criticism of the English-speaking Africans has been particularly sharp. For instance, Mr. Wole Soyinka, the well-known Nigerian playwright, has ridiculed it by saying that 'a tiger does not proclaim its tigritude'. In other words it is undignified to draw attention to what is already obvious. But this is a wrong assumption when it is considered that even now many people, especially those of European descent, still deny the African contribution to civilization. What is wrong with Negritude is not that it proclaimed the values of African civilization – it was necessary to proclaim them to a world which denied their existence and used this denial to justify political and economic domination – but rather that Negritude is now out of date.

Since the 1950's Africa has made a great impact on the political world, and researches in African studies, especially in history, archaeology and anthropology, have revealed so much about Africa and her past that it is no longer necessary to continue to protest the cause of African civilization.

That the English-speaking Africans should become the most merciless critics of Negritude is understandable. Under British colonial rule, which did not attempt cultural Assimilation, Africans were able to retain their cultural values almost intact. They are naturally surprised, therefore, to find their fellow Africans proclaiming their African values, since these values, as far as the English-speaking Africans are concerned, have always existed, no matter what Europeans say about them. In criticizing Negritude, however, we must excuse the French-speaking Africans and Negroes for spending so much time in cultural protest for we have seen that this arose from the need to find a positive point around which they could rally in their resistance to the pressure to become black Frenchmen.

Effects of Assimilation

What then has been the effect on modern French-speaking West Africa of the French policy of Assimilation? The reaction in France, between 1890 and 1914, against the consequences of Assimilation, led the French to question the fundamentals of the policy. As a result, by 1920, they had devised a slightly different colonial policy known as Association, which was to some extent, similar to the English colonial policy known as indirect rule. However, Assimilation had gone deeply into the minds of the French, and as a result they never seriously practised indirect rule in the British sense. They always returned to Assimilation.

While Assimilation was a failure because it could not produce Frenchmen in black skins, its strength and partial success is to be seen in the deep mark it has left and its continuing influence in French-speaking West Africa and amongst its inhabitants. Though French-speaking West African countries became politically independent in 1960, they have yet to win economic independence, and the relationship between France and her former colonies is still very close. With the exception of the Republics of Guinea and Mali, all French-speaking West African states belong to the completely French financial association known as the Franc zone. France is almost the only market for their products. They are economically dependent on France and their internal economies are controlled by the French. Their system of education is closely modelled on that of France, and they often seem to have more in common with France than with their fellow African states. In other words, the French-speaking West Africans have only won part of their struggle against Assimilation. The second phase of the struggle, against economic dependence and what is commonly known as the 'colonial mentality', only began with political independence in 1960. Thus while French-speaking West Africa, like the rest of Africa, will eventually win through, progress is slow, and complete decolonization will only be achieved when the French-speaking West Africans have swept away those unwholesome aspects of Assimilation which are hampering their progress towards complete independence.

19 The colonial economy

Colonial economic theory

The economic theory applied to colonies – referred to in France as the Colonial pact – was that colonies must be self-supporting, that they must provide agricultural export crops for the imperial country, and that they must buy its manufactured goods in return. The French enforced this theory more firmly than the British. The countries of French West Africa were forced to sell and buy in French markets even when they could do so more profitably elsewhere. On the other hand the Colonial pact did not oblige France to buy from her colonies. If, for example, Ghanaian cocoa was cheaper, the French could buy it to the loss of their own colony, the Ivory Coast. Thus the Colonial pact was binding on the colonies but not on the imperial country. When France agreed to purchase Senegalese groundnuts at above the world price in 1931, it was the first break in the Colonial pact, the first acceptance by France of economic responsibility for her colonies.

Britain was more liberal, usually allowing the colonies to buy and sell in the best markets, though after the First World War the British placed special taxes on palm-oil going to Germany, and in the 1930's excluded Japanese cotton cloth from colonies where it was underselling her own. The Nigerian Press was quick to point out that while Africans were now forced to buy high-priced English cloth, Britain continued to buy cheaper Norwegian whale-oil, in preference to Nigerian palm-oil. When there was a burden to bear it was the colonies which bore it. The Colonial pact would have been less harsh if the imperial power had been willing to assist with the expensive development projects such as harbours, railways and roads, but these had to be built entirely out of local funds.

Development however, did not mean industrialization, for this would compete with the industries of the imperial country. For example, when groundnut oil mills in Senegal began exports to France in 1927 they were restricted because French oil millers complained of the competition.

Harbours, railways, roads

Freetown possessed the only good natural harbour in West Africa and elsewhere enormous sums had to be spent to create artificial harbours. The French colonies' taxes went into turning Dakar into the best harbour in West Africa. The Ivory Coast did not get an ocean port until the development

Kru men rowing passengers to waiting ships before artificial harbours were built

of Abidjan in the 1930's. Guinea, Gambia and Liberia had no ports until after the first World war; Togo and Dahomey had none when the French left in 1960. Nigerian tax money was swallowed up in creating deep water ports at Lagos, which was opened in 1913, and at Apapa, opened in 1926. Part of Guggisberg's work was in creating Ghana's first port at Takoradi.

Most colonies struggled to finance a cheap one-track railway from the coast into the interior. Railways were begun from Dakar in 1880, Lagos and Freetown in 1896, Sekondi in 1898 and from Conakry, Abidjan and Cotonou in 1900. Many of these railways were not completed until the Second World War and all are quite inadequate. Only Nigeria had enough money, due to the discovery of coal at Enugu and tin at Jos, to create a railway system of two major and three branch lines. None of the railways of one colony linked up with those of any other so that there was no West African railway system similar to the one in Europe. In Ghana the railway still does not connect the north with the south, and by far the largest part of French West Africa has no railway services. The burden of financing even these inadequate railways was especially heavy during the depression, when prices and revenues fell.

With the coming of motor cars and lorries, colonial governments began to build roads to link up with and feed the railway, but not trunk roads to the seaports. New areas could now cultivate export crops which were sent on lorries to the railway. Colonial governments tried to prevent lorries, which were popular because they were faster and cheaper, from competing with the railways by refusing to build trunk roads and by charging high licence fees. Since lorries were usually African-owned this was discrimination against African businessmen.

Railways and roads produced a transport revolution that may be considered among the important results of colonialism. A head load from the coast to Kumasi, which had cost 26s. 6d., cost four shillings by rail. However, it should be noted that the railway also allowed European cotton goods and iron tools to be sold in the interior much more cheaply than those of African manufacture. Only in Mossi country in French West Africa were local iron industries able to compete in price with European imports and African craftsmen, especially weavers and blacksmiths, were hard hit and only survived at all because of the high quality of their products.

An important result of harbour, railway and road building was the growth in population of port cities such as Dakar, Takoradi and Lagos. People from all national groups travelled to the big cities looking for jobs and education. The colonial governments were financially unable to undertake low cost housing and as a result vast sprawling slums developed. Discontent fanned by the press became widespread, and new associations were formed, including churches, trade unions, ethnic and progress unions, and parties agitating for political change.

Export crops and food crops

The major export crops of West Africa were palm-oil, groundnuts, coffee, cocoa and rubber. Iboland and Dahomey remained, as in the nineteenth

43 *West African trade patterns, 1900-39*

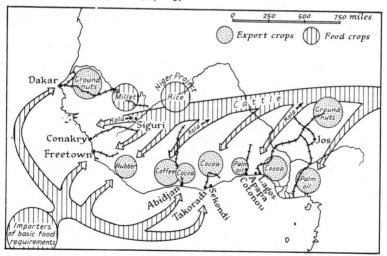

A rubber plantation

century, the leading exporters of palm-oil, although the French failed to keep up the volume of oil exported by the kings of Dahomey before the conquest. Groundnuts, first planted in Senegal in about 1820 as a domestic food crop later became the main export of that country, the area of production expanding with the extension of the railway. Groundnuts also became the major export crop of Hausaland, centred on Kano, once the railway reached that city from Lagos in 1911. Coffee was originally cultivated by Europeans in the Ivory Coast, but it requires more labour than most crops, and ultimately African farmers took over from the Europeans because they were more successful in securing and holding labourers. Ivory Coast became the world's third largest coffee exporter.

Cocoa was West Africa's most important export crop. Ghana became the world's largest producer followed by Yorubaland and the Ivory Coast. Cocoa was first introduced to the mainland from Fernando Po in 1879 by two Ghanaians, the Tetteh Quashie brothers. Its production grew and Ghana's thirteen tons of cocoa exports in 1895 reached 40,000 tons in 1911 and brought an economic revolution to the whole country. From Ghana, cocoa was introduced into Yorubaland in the 1880's, first at Agege, later spreading inland to Ibadan with the railway, and to Ondo along the feeder roads. Aware of the 'cocoa miracle' in Ghana, Governor Angoulvant in 1912 introduced it into the Indenie area of Ivory Coast from where it spread rapidly.

In 1925 Liberia began to pull out of its economic slump when a million acres of land were leased to the Firestone company for rubber plantations. Americo-Liberians also developed plantations of their own and soon rubber made up ninety per cent of Liberia's exports. Foreign-owned plantations however, did not have as revolutionary an effect as where export crops were totally under African control as in Ghana.

Cocoa pods

A groundnut pyramid

In colonies which developed export crops – Nigeria, Ghana, Ivory Coast, and Senegal – there was a rise in both living standards and in government revenue for the development of ports, railways, roads and education. In Senegal groundnut prosperity contributed to small scale industrialization, which included oil and lumber mills, soap, beverage and brick factories, lime works, salt works and fisheries. In Nigeria and Ghana profits went into education, better housing and transport lorries.

Everywhere in West Africa, except Nigeria, the rise in the value of export crops was partly counterbalanced by the decline of food crops and the rise of food prices. This was due to the scarcity of land, the neglect of food crops because of the greater value of export crops, and to the lack of a labour force. Sierra Leone, Liberia and most of French West Africa imported rice even though they could grow their own. Food crops were also neglected by the colonial governments because they did not directly contribute to the welfare of the imperial country. Mali – called the granary of French West Africa – produced a surplus of millet which it sold in the groundnut-producing areas of Senegal, but because of the lack of railways and roads, Mali was unable to transport any of this surplus to other surrounding areas. In 1932 the

French began the Niger Project in Mali to irrigate an area of the Niger Bend for the growing of cotton as an export crop, but African farmers found that rice was more profitable. This emphasis on cash crops was typical of colonial policy, and if food crops were encouraged this was often accidental.

Only in Nigeria was the development of cash crops not balanced by a decline in food crops. In Iboland food crops were grown along with the palm trees. In Yorubaland, around the edges of the cocoa belt, in Oyo and Ekiti, food crop production was increased to feed the cocoa areas. There was also a lively trade in kola nuts going north and in cattle moving south. Ghana, however, was more typical of West Africa generally. With its cocoa revenue it was the wealthiest West African state but more of its money than Nigeria's was spent abroad on rice and other foods brought in by sea, and on cattle coming mainly from Hausaland in the north-east.

Many colonies developed no important export crop and had therefore no money for railways, roads or education. Economic conditions in some were worse than in the nineteenth century and their people fell far behind those in export crop areas. Poverty drove the young men of Mali to the groundnut areas of Senegal in search of work, and thousands of young Mossi left home to work on the coffee and cocoa plantations of Ivory Coast and Ghana. While Mali and Mossi exported 'manpower', Dahomey exported 'brainpower'. Poor as it was, Dahomey struggled to educate its sons who found employment with French firms and with the civil service in other parts of West Africa. Money sent home by all these migrant workers helped to lessen the poverty of their homelands.

The *grands comptoirs* and African merchants

Three great monopoly enterprises controlling wholesale and retail trading, the buying of export crops, banking, and transportation systems on land and sea dominated the economic life of British and French West Africa. These *grands comptoirs*, or combines, were the Compagnie Française de l'Afrique Occidentale (C.F.A.O.) founded in 1887, the Société Commerciale de l'Ouest Africain (S.C.O.A.) founded in 1906, and Unilever, a world-wide organization whose African branch was the United Africa Company (U.A.C.).

The *comptoirs* were usually formed as a result of a long process of amalgamation. For example, in 1880, the African association was formed out of the union of a number of small companies, and after the First World War it joined with Swanzy's and with Miller Brothers, two other West Coast firms, to form the African and Eastern Trading Corporation. In 1920 Unilever purchased the Niger Company and in 1929 joined it with the African and Eastern Trading Corporation to form the U.A.C.

The *grands comptoirs* were involved in almost every aspect of West African commerce. In 1927 C.F.A.O. had 33 branches and 154 trading centres and was making a profit of ninety per cent in good years and twenty-five per cent in poor. S.C.O.A. at the same time had 21 branches and 122 trading centres while the U.A.C. was the dominant company in all British West Africa besides having subsidiary companies in Senegal, Mali, Guinea and Ivory Coast. C.F.A.O. controlled most of French West African river transport, was involved in a number of banks, and dominated the steamship lines serving French West Africa, just as U.A.C. was heavily involved with shipping to British West Africa. S.C.O.A. had palm-oil and banana plantations in Ivory Coast, while U.A.C. held the mineral rights to practically all of Northern Nigeria. So widespread was the *grands comptoirs*' influence that a Ghanaian remarked 'The earth is Lord Leverhulme's [head of U.A.C.] and the fullness thereof'.

The *grands comptoirs* agreed to fix prices so as not to compete with each other and were therefore under no compulsion to give good service, to cater for African tastes or to modernize their businesses. They sent most of their profits to the home country, and colonial governments were too subservient to imperial interests to force them to invest in West Africa by taxation of profits sent abroad.

In Ghana and Nigeria the *grands comptoirs* repeatedly sought to fix cocoa prices paid to farmers. To protect themselves against the 'combine clique' as Ghanaians called it, farmers' unions grew up, the earliest ones being at Larteh and Dodowah in Ghana, and Agege and Abeokuta in Nigeria. In 1914, 1916 and 1921 some Ghanaian farmers held back their cocoa crop demanding higher prices. In 1928 the All Ghana Federation of Cocoa

West African cocoa production

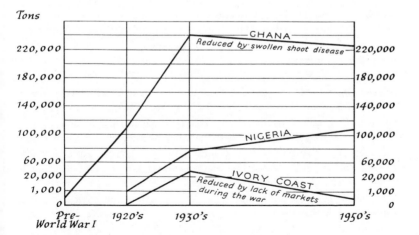

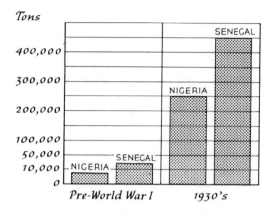

Tons

Groundnut production in
Nigeria and Senegal

Farmers was set up, and in 1930 it organized a widespread 'hold-up' of cocoa. Again in 1937 fourteen firms led by U.A.C. secretly agreed on a fixed price but, led by their chiefs and farmers' unions, Ghanaians not only refused to sell their cocoa, but also boycotted all the retail shops of the firms involved. At the cost of real personal suffering the farmers brought a complete halt to the economic life of Ghana until the price fixing agreement was broken.

Another merchant group, the Syrians and Lebanese, began to move into West Africa in the 1890's. Their numbers grew until in 1935 there were 6,000 of them in French West Africa and even more in British colonies. Organized in close-knit family groups, the wealthy members brought in poor relations and helped them set up in business. They pushed into the small retail trade – beads, cloth, kola nuts, and road transport – until then dominated by Africans. Syrians and Lebanese received much of the blame for the colonial economic system, for African anger against exploitation was often directed against them while Europeans – who wanted to direct attention away from themselves – encouraged the idea that the Syrians and Lebanese were the major obstacle to African commerce.

One of the most lucrative nineteenth-century trades was the exchange of kola nuts from the forest for cattle from the savannah and where the railway, as in Guinea, Ivory Coast and Nigeria, went from the coastal forests to the savannah this trade expanded. Since kola required less labour and brought more revenue than cocoa, many early cocoa areas in Nigeria, such as Agege and Abeokuta changed to kola planting. Asante, however, probably the greatest kola exporter of the nineteenth century, lost some of its markets because there was no railway running north to the savannah.

In the nineteenth century, before the development of the *grands comptoirs*, a number of African merchant princes – Creoles, Brazilians, Ghanaians and Senegalese – made large commercial fortunes. Although they had less capital than European firms, they were more trusted, had greater influence and more access to African kingdoms. As a result a number of Afro-European business partnerships developed which combined European money and African influence to the benefit of both.

After the partition there was a steady decline in the prosperity of these merchants. The political advantages they had enjoyed under African kings became disadvantages under colonial rule, and the old partnerships were no longer necessary to Europeans. Often the merchant princes were crushed between the developing *comptoirs* and the incoming Syrians and Lebanese. Furthermore, while European firms were building up capital reserves, an African merchant's estate was usually broken up at his death among children and relatives, so that while Europeans built one generation upon the other, Africans began afresh in each generation. European firms established branches inland, following first the railway, and later the roads, which cut out African middlemen, especially produce buyers.

Colonial governments seldom stepped in to protect Africans against European competition though they did occasionally do the reverse. Nothing was done in 1895, for example, when the shipping companies gave lower freight rates to larger than to smaller firms, and so made it impossible for African firms to sell as cheaply as the larger European ones; and in the Ivory Coast government action between 1912 and 1925 intentionally cut out Ghanaians from the mahogany industry, in which they had been engaged since 1887, to make way for European firms.

A contrast is provided by the development of the goldfields of Asante with those of Siguri in Guinea. A gold boom followed the conquest of Asante when 400 European companies wanted to mine, and ultimately employed 10,000 Africans. The Asante goldfields, for centuries in Africans hands, passed to Europeans, and except for the wages paid to labourers Africans got little benefit from them; for there was not even an income tax, or a tax on company profits, through which the colonial government might secure revenue for development purposes. In Guinea the French also tried to come in with big companies, but since the deposits were not as rich as in Asante, they failed and gave up the venture. At Siguri every dry season about 100,000 Africans mine for gold which is sold as in the nineteenth century through Diula traders. Thus it appears likely that the poorer Guinea goldfields have contributed more to African living standards than the richer fields of Asante.

Land and labour

The French assumed that they owned the land in their colonies by right of conquest, and in 1904 they declared all vacant land state property. It was difficult to define vacant land because in a system of shifting cultivation land which may appear vacant is in fact merely resting in preparation for a crop in three to seven years' time. The French desired to attract French planters and to encourage Africans to take out individual titles to their land. Considerable land was given to settlers, especially in Ivory Coast and Guinea, but frequently European farmers were unable, as noted previously, to compete with African farmers and much land was later abandoned.

In British West Africa, with its much heavier population, the giving of land to settlers would have created hardship. The educated elite – Creole, Fante and Yoruba – conscious of what settlers were doing in British colonies in South and Central Africa, were determined to prevent the same thing happening in West Africa. In Ghana, the British tried in 1894 to follow French policy by a lands bill which proclaimed unoccupied lands, forest lands and minerals the property of the state. Protest meetings, petitions, demonstrations and a newspaper outcry brought the chiefs and educated elite together in opposition. The *Methodist Times* called the bill 'civilized robbery and British brigandism'. The chiefs demanded that the bill be 'abandoned, dropped and thrown overboard'.

Three years later a similar bill was introduced. To mobilize opposition the elite and chiefs organized the Aborigines Rights Protection Society (A.R.P.S.), and again a storm of protest arose. Since the Church forced the *Methodist Times* to keep out of politics, the Society established its own paper, the *Gold Coast Aborigines*, as its mouth-piece. The chiefs paid for a deputation from the society to go to England where the government was persuaded to drop the bill.

The victory of the A.R.P.S. was a landmark in West African history. The Society brought both groups of Ghanaian leaders together to watch the Colonial government. All along the West Coast it made educated Africans suspect British intentions regarding land. In 1912 a land law in Nigeria caused the formation of an African society of opposition there. This, like its earlier Ghanaian counterpart, also sent a delegation to London. In 1924 Lord Leverhulme, chairman of the U.A.C., began an agitation for plantations in Nigeria. His request was turned down largely because the British were fearful of the gigantic agitation it was likely to cause. Nigerians were frightened that a Kenya, Congo or even Ivory Coast type of settler-dominated colony would result. Although, for centuries the malarial mosquito had protected African lands now that Europeans had discovered artificial immunity to malaria there was little but African anger to stop the incoming of white settlers.

Since colonies had to be self-sufficient, and yet large sums were required for harbours, railways and roads to get export crops out, and European goods into the continent, costs were reduced by the use of forced and unpaid labour.

France relied upon forced labour more than Britain because her empire was larger in area and smaller in population; her colonies also had smaller revenues because cash crops developed more slowly and on a smaller scale, and also because French merchants invested less in their colonies than British merchants. By 1936 British merchants had invested 117 million pounds in West Africa, but French merchants had invested only 30 million. With all these disadvantages the French required more ports and more miles of railway and roads than the British because of the greater size of their empire.

Under French colonial laws every male between 18 and 60 years of age was compelled to contribute a certain number of days labour to the state. Between 1927 and 1936, 15,000 men were forced to labour on the Niger project and on railway construction, and probably as many again were employed on road building and other projects. Forced labour was not abolished until 1946 and was one of the most hated aspects of French colonialism. African chiefs were used as recruiting agents and this much lowered their position in people's eyes. Few revolts against French rule were unconnected with the hated forced labour system, and many young men travelled from home to escape it and to earn wages. About a quarter million a year went to the cocoa farms of Ghana for this reason, and another 70,000 went from Mali and Guinea to the groundnut farms of Senegal.

Conditions under which the forced labourers worked were often very bad, the food was inadequate, the housing poor, disease frequent and the death-rate high. Especially cruel were the conditions in the Cameroons under German rule, where men recruited in the high plateau free of the malarial mosquito were forced to work in the mosquito infested plantations of the lowlands. Lacking the natural immunity of people born in malarial areas, only about ten per cent of them ever saw their homes again.

Africans under British rule suffered less, because wages were offered, but occasionally the pay was too low to attract labourers and the government then recruited labour through the chiefs. The result was very similar to the French system. Originally the Enugu coal mines paid certain chiefs so much for every labourer supplied. The chiefs thereupon forced their people to work, and in 1914 some of them were so hated that they were driven out of their towns. The British army arrested those responsible and a court fined the towns concerned by forcing them to supply 2,000 labourers for railway construction. In Ghana the government used the chiefs to assist the gold mines to recruit labour in the Northern Territories. The chiefs were often reluctant to do this, especially after the influenza epidemic of 1918-19 had killed 25,000 people, thus reducing the farming labour force in the north. Investigations after the Asante goldfield's strike in 1924 showed that most of the evils of forced labour, including an unusually high death-rate, were present in the mines.

Forced labour was justified on the basis that Africans would not work

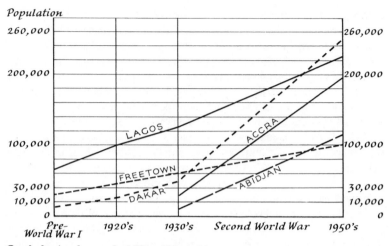

Graph showing the growth of West African cities

without compulsion, and low wages on the grounds that African labour, regardless of its wages, was unproductive. Africans who travelled long distances to find work desired to return home for visits and to marry. Many young workers did not look forward to a life of daily paid labour, and indeed most hoped to settle down and farm. In fact, ample evidence showed that high wages attracted labourers. One of the problems of the Asante mines was that labourers preferred to work on the Asante cocoa farms where the money and living conditions were better. Europeans were slow to see that they had to pay more than a subsistence wage to attract workers since all Africans could get that on farms, and those in export crop areas could earn much more. In any case forced labour is always inefficient labour, and low paid labour only slightly less so.

Until the 1930's neither the British nor French colonial governments recognized the right of Africans to form trade unions or to strike as a legitimate way of forcing employers to improve conditions. Most governments took the attitude of the Governor of Sierra Leone who in 1926 called the railway strike 'a revolt against the government'. The first serious strikes were on the railways and in the mines, notable among which were the Sierra Leone railways strikes of 1919 and 1926, the Senegal railway strike of 1925, the Asante goldfields strike of 1924 and the Enugu coal mines strike of 1925.

The employers' usual method of dealing with strikes was to sack all workers concerned. After the Enugu coalminers' strike of 1925 the men were sacked, and for the next twenty-five years the mines refused to hire labourers from the clans from which the strikers came. To strike, therefore, might hurt not only the men involved, but their relatives, and even their children yet unborn.

Wage levels were tied neither to supply and demand, nor adjusted to prosperity and depression or rising and falling costs. They remained static over long periods of time, and because of the rising cost of living, became worth less and less. In 1896 in Ghana the lowest paid government employee earned £36 per year. In 1919, although the cost of living had risen one hundred per cent (so that £36 would only buy what £18 had bought in 1896) the basic wage remained the same. The wage was then raised to £48 although the cost of living continued to rise in the 1920's so that low wages were actually becoming lower.

Economic slump

While the 1920's had been a period of general economic prosperity the 1930's witnessed the most severe economic depression in modern times. No part of the world escaped. Nor could any colonial government do much about it for even the great powers suffered almost helplessly. Prices of raw materials fell disastrously, and government customs dues were therefore reduced with a consequent reduction in revenues, and in government services. Many civil servants were discharged from their posts and others had their salaries reduced. For the common man money became so scarce as to become almost a curiosity.

The depression, followed by the scarcity and hardship of the Second World War (1939-45), produced widespread disillusionment with colonialism. It intensified the struggle between the *grands comptoirs* and African farmers. The Co-operative movement was born to market export crops and thus by-pass the European firms. Countries with a one-crop economy, which meant almost all West African colonies, were particularly hard hit, and African demands became louder for a wider economic base, for more emphasis upon food crops, and above all for industrialization, especially to produce locally consumed items like soap and buildings materials. Economic disillusionment became political dissatisfaction, and hostility towards colonialism resulted in the birth of modern nationalism.

20 Efforts to reform colonialism

The elite as watchdogs, 1900-18

British colonies in West Africa were divided into two parts, colony and protectorate. In Gambia, Sierra Leone and Nigeria the colony was confined to a small area around Bathurst, Freetown and Lagos; the colony area of Ghana was larger, and included the coastal area of the Fante, Ga and others. Only in the colony areas was modern political agitation possible. Political associations could be formed without permission from the British and newspapers could operate on the whole free of interference. English law was enforced and lawyers were available to check the worst abuses of colonial rule. In the protectorates, however, lawyers were forbidden to practise and associations for political discussion had to conceal themselves as cultural or social organizations.

The colony areas had come under British rule in the early or mid-nineteenth century while the protectorates were the areas added during the partition of Africa at the end of the century. Because of the longer tradition of western education in the colonies there was by 1900 a sizeable number of educated people – called the elite – who through their newspapers and associations acted as watchdogs of colonial rule, protesting against its abuses. Members of the elite were well known to each other all along the coast from Bathurst to Lagos, partly because the core of them were Creoles with ties to Freetown, partly because they were intermarried and had interlocking trading relations and partly because many were old boys of the same schools at Freetown, Cape Coast or Lagos. Many moved freely from one colony to the other in the course of their work. Isaac Wallace-Johnson, for example, had been acting editor of the *Nigerian Daily Telegraph* and general secretary of the African Workers Union which he organized in Lagos in 1931. He moved to Ghana where he worked with the Nigerian, Nnamdi Azikiwe, on the *African Morning Post*. He then returned to Sierra Leone where he organized a political party, the West African Youth League. Thus the elite formed a West African community and thought of themselves as West Africans rather than Ghanaians or Nigerians.

In French West Africa only the four communes – Dakar, St. Louis, Gorée, Rufisque – enjoyed a similar position to English-speaking Africans in the colony areas. Those born in the communes enjoyed the status of French citizens and could form political associations and run newspapers. Since the communes also had a long tradition of education, the elite of French West

Africa were at first entirely Senegalese but later others – especially Dahomeans – began to take advantage of the secondary schools of the communes.

Like their English-speaking counterparts the elite were well known to each other, being old boys of the same schools, especially the famous William Ponty School of Senegal which has been called 'the nerve centre, the most solid link which joined the elite' of French West Africa. The French-speaking elite mostly served in the colonial civil service, had worked in many of the colonies, looked upon themselves as West Africans rather than Senegalese and performed the function of watchdogs of French rule.

The millions of Africans who were not citizens were classed as subjects and they suffered under many more disabilities (such as forced labour and the indigenat) than people in British protectorates. Naturally they could not establish newspapers or form associations without the permission of the French authorities. They could, however, belong to a branch of a French society. Often such branches were set up to conceal discussion of purely African political topics, but, as will be noted later in relation to Dahomey, this could be dangerous.

The West African press was an important element in keeping the elite united. A West African newspaper was seldom profitable. The reading public was small and the habit of many people reading the same copy reduced the number of copies sold. European firms whose advertising was urgently needed were quick to withdraw this if a paper was critical of European rule or wanted to promote ideas of nationalism. The best papers and therefore the poorest were those in which there were few European advertisements.

The life of many papers was short. By 1937 fifty papers at one time or another had been registered in Nigeria. There were, however, a number of good newspapers which lasted between thirty and forty years and left behind a solid impression on African thinking. Some of the most famous were the *Lagos Weekly Record* begun in 1890, the *Sierra Leone Weekly News* begun in 1884 and the *Gold Coast Independent* founded in 1895. In French West Africa newspaper problems were multiplied, because the readership was smaller and the censorship was strict. In Senegal in the nineteenth century newspapers were owned and edited by Frenchmen. Even in the 1950's the most widely read newspaper, *Paris-Dakar*, begun in 1933, was owned and edited by a European. Dahomey's first regular newspaper was *Le Guide du Dahomey* (1920), while *L'Eclaireur de la Côte d'Ivoire* (1935) was the first African-owned paper in Ivory Coast.

In British West Africa the press was the most important single element in the birth and development of nationalism. The press kept a constant eye upon British officials, was quick to point out oppression, kept African claims to advancement and dignity alive, stimulated creative writing and never allowed the British to forget that their ultimate aim was to develop self-governing modern states. The press brought before West Africans the issues of the larger world, especially the black world extending from Africa to America and the West Indies.

The Aborigines Rights Protection Society (1897) was the first important political organization of the elite in West Africa. After its victory over a land issue in 1897 the society, composed of the Fante chiefs and their educated advisors, was a watchdog for Ghanaian interests. The A.R.P.S. did not press for a change in colonialism but tried to make the colonial government aware of Ghanaian public opinion. As the years passed the society failed to organize branches and so lost contact with public opinion. Centred and controlled in Cape Coast, other cities such as Accra denied that the society spoke for the nation. Like so many other political organizations it became conservative and friendly, and British governors saw to it that its leading members mono-polized the nominated seats for Africans on the Legislative Council.

In Lagos the Peoples Union had originally come into being to protect land in the colony and protest against taxation policy and efforts to control the press, but it quickly became a conservative wealthy man's club defending the colonial government. In 1912 the effort of the Governor to get all 'waste' lands under his control brought into being the Anti-Slavery and Aborigines Protection Society, as a branch of the English society of the same name. The advantage of this was that the parent society in London could bring complaints from Lagos before the British House of Commons and the English public; the disadvantage was that the parent society had the right of deciding which issues could be raised and which could not. When a delegation of chiefs and elite set out for London to protest against the proposed land changes, the Society broke into radical and conservative wings in Lagos, and discredited its own delegation. Thus before the first World war no Nigerian political organization was able to function in the same way as the A.R.P.S. in Ghana, as a representative of African opinion.

Blaise Diagne and Senegal, 1914-34

The communes of Senegal from 1848 had the right to elect a member to the French Chamber of Deputies (parliament) in Paris. The communes also elected their own municipal councils like the cities of France. During the nineteenth century those who ran and were elected for office were Europeans, even though the electorate was largely African. French firms usually sup-ported different candidates and by massive bribery and corruption controlled political appointments in their own interest. In the early twentieth century the firms combined to stop both the economic and political competition which had previously existed between them. They became known as the

'Bordeaux clique' because most of them had their headquarters at Bordeaux (pronounced Bordo) in France. The clique began their co-operation by fixing the price of groundnuts, and then followed this up by joint support of a candidate for election.

Just as the Creoles of Sierra Leone by 1900 had begun to suffer from changing European ideals (see chapter 10) so the citizens of the four communes began to discover that colonial governors were seeking to restrict both their privileges of citizenship and their access to higher posts in the colonial civil service.

In order to break the Bordeaux clique and defend their rights the communes in 1914 voted for Blaise Diagne, an educated Senegalese who became the first African to sit in the French Chamber of Deputies. In 1916 he was responsible for the passing in the French Chamber of the Loi Diagne which confirmed French citizenship on the people of the communes while allowing them to retain traditional law in family matters. In 1919 Diagne was re-elected and in addition all municipal seats were won by members of his Republican Socialist Party.

The Bordeaux firms, the French settlers and the administration were alarmed by Diagne's popularity and election victories. A tough governor was sent to Senegal and all Diagne's efforts for progressive reforms were blocked by united European opposition. Diagne sought a compromise and, like the A.R.P.S. and Nigerian Peoples Union, drifted into conservatism and outright support for the colonial system. The compromise was sealed in the Bordeaux agreements of 1923 in which, in return for Bordeaux support, Diagne dropped his radical demands. The Senegalese elite called this a 'sell out' and Diagne only won the 1928 elections with the help of French rigging and falsification of election results.

While Diagne was elected by the four communes and was therefore only responsible to them, all French West Africa expected him to speak for them as Africans. Those outside the communes of Senegal, however, came to feel that he took no notice of their condition and that he was actually ready to sacrifice them for the sake of the citizens. This suspicion made it difficult for any future Senegalese leader to get the support of Africans outside Senegal. This suspicion was based on Diagne's wartime recruitment campaign and his defence of forced labour.

During the First World War Diagne agreed to tour West Africa recruiting men to fight in the French army in Europe. The vast number of men who volunteered, fought and died for France were subjects, not citizens. Those who returned were annoyed to discover that they had achieved little and were still subject to the humiliations of French colonialism, trials without jury or lawyers, arbitrary taxation and worst of all, forced labour. Then in the 1930's Diagne was called upon by the French government to represent it at international labour conferences. Here he found himself, an African, defending forced labour in the French empire in Africa. Little wonder many of the subjects saw Diagne as a 'stooge'.

However, in the rigid world of colonialism before the Second World War Diagne had little choice. The alternatives involved following the path he chose or being thrown out. He felt that there were advantages to be gained from working within the French government; for example in 1931 when the depression began he was able to negotiate a special price for groundnuts which was higher than usual and which helped Senegal over the worst years of the depression. This was the first break in the colonial pact under which Africans got most of the disadvantages and few of the advantages of the colonial economic system. Furthermore, Diagne was hailed and admired by Negroes all over the black world – America, the West Indies and Africa – as someone who, having reached the highest position ever held by an African in the white world, was a symbol of black ability and a rebuke to all those who were writing about the inherent inferiority of the African race.

The black world

Between the two world wars, from 1918 to 1939, the various sections of the world inhabited by black people became more conscious of each other than ever before. Events among Negroes in America and the West Indies were influencing Negroes in Africa and African events were being closely watched by a growing number of new world Negroes. The elite of Africa and the new world began to feel that the elevation of the race must be an international effort, that a victory of Negroes over segregation in America was as important as a victory over colonialism in Africa. Many felt that a black man could not carry himself with dignity, no matter what his degree of freedom, as long as brother members of his race were being humiliated elsewhere in the world.

During and after the First World War the United States and Europe talked of self-determination as the basis of the peace settlement. This was particularly in relation to the ethnic groups of eastern Europe under the Austro-Hungarian empire, who were to be allowed to choose their independence and form of government. The idea was picked up by British colonies such as Canada, Australia, South Africa and India, who had sacrificed much to help win the war and who demanded greater powers of self-government and a seat on the British empire peace delegation. Colonial nationalism in Canada and South Africa after the war continued to press the British, and eventually resulted in their virtual independence in the Statute of Westminister in 1931. The

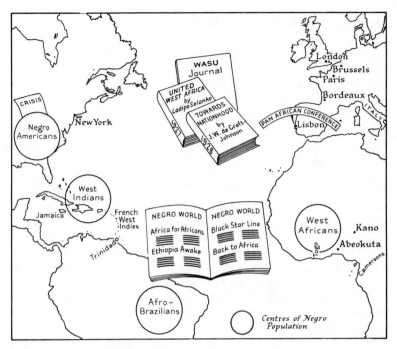

44 *The Pan-African World, 1900-30*

Congress party in India was agitating in the same direction. The Irish, after a bloody war of independence, cut themselves away completely from English domination in 1921 and Egypt secured partial independence in 1922. The latter two events prompted a West African chief to say, 'this is the beginning of the end of the British empire'.

These many triumphs for self-determination had powerful influences in West Africa. The Ghanaian press asked for West African representation on the empire peace delegation and it also raised the question of self-determination for Africa. It came therefore as a considerable shock when the German colonies of Togo and Cameroon were split between Britain and France, in absolute contradiction of the doctrine of self-determination and over considerable opposition, in particular of the Ewe people of Togoland. The results of all these world war influences was the Ewe Union Movement and the National Congress of British West Africa, which will be discussed later.

Washington; Garvey; DuBois

In the meantime events in Negro America were also holding West African attention. The first coloured American to achieve real prominence in the United States was an educator, Booker T. Washington, who advanced his doctrine of race relations at Atlanta, Georgia, in 1895. In what came to be called the 'Atlanta compromise' Washington supported racial segregation and the submission of the Negro to the dominant white group. He claimed that the best way to rise in American society was for the Negro to equip himself with agricultural and manual skills.

In so many ways Washington was like the elite of his day in West Africa, the A.R.P.S., Nigerian Peoples Union, J. K. Aggrey and the conservative Blaise Diagne; he accepted white dominance and because of it could be friendly with American presidents, just as his counterparts in Africa might be friendly with British and French governors. Washington's emphasis upon technical training was also echoed in West Africa. Some West Africans went to train at his technical institute at Tuskegee, and in Nigeria an effort was made to create an institution like it; Achimota College in Ghana was also influenced by similar ideas. Particularly in Liberia, where a number of coloured American missionary societies were working, there was a strong feeling in favour of technical education.

Washington's opponent, and after his death the foremost American coloured leader, was William DuBois, who believed that white Americans must be forced to grant full equality to coloured Americans. He felt that if the coloured people did not resist segregation and agitate for equality they would gradually come to accept the American caste system as normal and inevitable. DuBois was a founder of the National Association for the Advancement of Coloured People and the editor for many years of its magazine *Crisis*. The N.A.A.C.P. stuck to this doctrine and until the present day has been the main organization in the fight for equality and the destruction of the American colour caste system. DuBois in his ideas and leadership was much more like the West African elite which emerged in the National Congress following the first World war.

Before DuBois could establish his leadership among coloured Americans, a man by the name of Marcus Garvey stirred the black world as no one before or since until the rise of Kwame Nkrumah and the modern African nationalists. Garvey was a Jamaican born Negro, one of the most stirring orators of his race, who organized the biggest mass protest movement in American history around his Universal Negro Improvement Association (U.N.I.A.), which by 1923 claimed six million members. Garvey preached racial purity, glorified the colour black, upheld a black Christ and black Madonna and called upon his followers to 'forget the white gods'. His slogans were 'Africa for the

W. E. B. DuBois

Marcus Garvey

Booker T. Washington

Africans', 'the renaissance of the black race' and 'Ethiopia awake'. He demanded the freedom of Africa and prophesied that 'her redemption is coming like a storm, it will be here'.

Garvey began the recruitment of a black army for the liberation of Africa and set up the Black Star Shipping Line which, however small in comparison, was an attempt to invade the white monopoly of world commerce. In 1920 he sent a mission to Liberia to negotiate for the settlement of from 20,000 to 30,000 American coloured families who would be helped to emigrate to Liberia, presumably to be the spearhead for the liberation of Africa. In 1925, with the help of 'moderate' American coloured leaders, the United States government jailed Garvey; it later deported him and, while the influence of Garvey's thought remained strong, the movement itself soon collapsed. The Liberian scheme also failed. But Garvey's ideas have pervaded coloured American and West African thinking ever since.

Regardless of how impractical and impossible Garvey's schemes may have been his words echoed the feelings of millions of blacks; black redemption not as humble beggars but as proud soldiers demanding and forcing concessions; equality in America, freedom in Africa, dignity everywhere; a share in the world economy and a black Christ overseeing all. Mainly in intellectual circles Garvey's journal *Negro World* was eagerly read throughout West Africa. In the colony areas such as Lagos, branches of the U.N.I.A. met openly, while in the protectorate they met secretly.

In Ibadan a group of about a dozen men met quietly to read the *Negro World*. One member wrote 'I must confess I am greatly infused with the spirit of Garveyism and were I to express my mind to the general public am afraid I would be charged for disloyalty. The aliens who rule us would indict me but the men of my own kind would regard it as a spirit of true patriotism. It is admitted that Negroes all over the world are being downtrodden, ill-treated and boycotted; this fact speaks for itself when one looks back to the undignified discrimination of the Lugardian régime which is still being diplomatically practised today.' After reading the *Negro World* this same man wrote in his diary, 'the most inspiring message of Marcus Garvey to the Negro people of the world nearly maddens me. I feel as if I am in America as one of the hearers of his golden speech.' Although the same writer was quite aware of Garvey's impractical plans he believed that his prophecy about Africa's freedom would be fulfilled. On 3 March 1921 he wrote in his diary, 'Garvey though a great champion of the race does not know the aims and aspirations of Africans' but 'my conviction is that Africa *will be free* from European bondage'.

The colonial powers were certainly worried about Garveyism. In Lagos the mission churches unitedly refused their meeting halls for U.N.I.A. rallies. *Negro World* was banned in French West Africa and seized in the mails in

The

Lagos Weekly Record

he OLDEST ESTABLISHED NEWSPAPER, and BEST ADVERTISING MEDIUM in the COLONY of NIGERIA
representing ADVANCED NATIVE OPINION.

| Vol. XXXI No 35 [New series]. | LAGOS, WEST AFRICA. APRIL 23—30, 1921. | Price Ninepence. |

ELDER DEMPSTER LINES.

*Accelerated Service to the United Kingdom, connecting with the Nigerian
Boat Train, calling at Accra, Seccondee and Sierra Leone,
for Mails and Passengers.*

ALSO

**NTERCOLONIAL SERVICE to GOLD COAST PORTS as far as SECCONDEE from LAGOS (inside
the Bar) carrying Passengers and Mails.**

For further Particulars of Sailings, Passage and Freight Rates, please apply to

ELDER DEMPSTER AND COMPANY, LIMITED, LAGOS.

Have You Bought Your Shares

IN

THE BLACK STAR LINE STEAMSHIP CORPORATION?

(INCORPORATED IN U.S.A.)

If not, Please do so TO-DAY.

The authorised Capital has been raised to

10,000,000 dollars

DIVIDED INTO

2,000,000 shares of 5 dollars or 30s. each.

*To give every member of the Negro Race the opportunity of participating in this great enterprise,
Directors have decided to offer for sale in Nigeria 100,000 shares at 5 dollars or 30s. each.*

This is a golden opportunity: seize it and become a JOINT OWNER of the Corporation.

For full particulars please apply to the

GENERAL AGENT,

**BLACK STAR LINE, Inc.,
26, Breadfruit Street, Lagos, Nigeria.**

*An advertisement for shares in Garvey's Black Star Shipping Line, Lagos Weekly
Record, 1921*

Nigeria. To be caught with a copy of it in Dahomey could bring life imprisonment.

Garvey's rise indicated the growing unity of feeling in the black world. Garvey's fall made it all the plainer that the world belonged to the whites. With the fall of Garvey, DuBois attempted to assert his leadership among the American coloured elite and he sought as Garvey had done to approach the problem from the point of view of the black world. He believed that the Negro who was suffering under the caste system in America and the West Indies and the Negro who was suffering under colonialism in Africa must get to know each other better, and realize that the struggles of the blacks for equality were all part of one movement, that American coloured and Africans could inspire and encourage each other, and that a gain for one was likely to bring a gain for the other. In pursuit of this ideal he was the leading spirit of five pan-African congresses between 1919 and 1945.

The first pan-African congress had been held in London in 1900 under the inspiration of a Trinidad lawyer, to protest against the inhumanities practised during the partition of Africa. It was not repeated until DuBois, activated by the ideas following the First World War and assisted by Blaise Diagne, organized the second congress in Paris in 1919 to draw up a Charter of Human Rights for Peoples of African Descent. The conference was mainly attended by Africans living in Paris because the United States, although the main supporter of self-determination for Europeans, was not anxious to see this applied to its own black population, and therefore refused travel permits for coloured people wishing to attend the Paris Conference.

The Third pan-African Conference was held in three sessions in 1921, at London, Brussels and Paris where Diagne presided. The fourth in 1922 was held in London and Lisbon; and the fifth in New York. These Congresses helped to keep the demands of the black world before the public of the world and brought together leaders of the black world. In the 1921 London session there were 41 Africans, 35 American coloured, 7 West Indians and 24 Africans living in Europe. DuBois, a university professor and prodigious writer (his first book appeared in 1896, his fifteenth in 1952), helped to keep the pan-African unity of the black world alive.

Negritude

Black men brought up under British colonialism in Africa and the West Indies or in the caste system of America talked, wrote and agitated for their rights as men spurred on by the discrimination and prejudice which everywhere faced them. The 1923 pan-African congress manifesto summed up this preoccupation: 'We ask in all the world that black folk be treated as men.'

In the French world this was much less the case. While the illiterate blacks were treated with more crudity in French colonies than in English, the black French-speaking elite in Paris, even if less so in Africa, were nevertheless basically accepted as men in French society in a way which Englishmen and Americans found impossible to understand. Although in France Africans were accepted as men, African culture was branded as inferior; Frenchmen believed that their own culture and way of life was superior to all others, and that it was their mission to export it to their African empire.

Most of the African elite accepted this view, but a few Africans and West Indians turned their attention to seeking out the values in African culture to disprove it. This movement was known as Negritude, a philosophy which sought a combination of French and African culture and values, as against the French policy of Assimilation, which required the complete abandonment of the African heritage and adoption of the French. Originally Negritude developed in Paris among West Indians, a West Indian, Aimé Césaire, being considered its father. Negritude was similar to pan-Africanism in that it saw a oneness and basic similarity amongst Africans everywhere in the world. But while the English-speaking pan-Africanists spoke in political terms, Negritude was expressed in poems, novels, drama and even dance. The greatest African contributor to Negritude has been Léopold Senghor of Senegal. Others included the novelist Bernard Dadié, the dramatist Cofi Gadeau, of Ivory Coast, and the Guinean ballet producer, Keita Fodeba.

After the Second World War, while political development in British West Africa began to affect French-speaking Africans, it was the influence of Negritude which influenced English-speaking Africans in a cultural outpouring of novels, plays and dance which showed distinct ideas of combining African and European culture.

W.A.S.U. and Solanke

The hub of the black world, the centre through which American, West Indian and African ideas passed back and forth, was the student organizations in London. The first such organization began in 1917 and had 25 members in 1921 and 120 in 1924. In 1925 the Nigerian, Ladipo Solanke, organized the West African Student Union (W.A.S.U.) which superseded the earlier association and became the centre of social and political activities in which modern militant nationalism was born. In 1928 Marcus Garvey gave W.A.S.U. its first hostel and it published a journal which gave an outlet for nationalist writings.

Many of West Africa's leading modern statesmen at one time or another held executive positions in W.A.S.U. Two of its leading members produced books setting forth West Africa's claims: Solanke's *United West Africa at the Bar of the Family of Nations* (1927) and J. W. de Graft-Johnson (a Ghanaian) *Towards Nationhood in West Africa* (1928). Between 1929 and 1932 Solanke visited the major cities of British West Africa to collect funds for the W.A.S.U. hostel, to organize branches of the society and to get support from the chiefs. Nana Afori Atta, the Alake of Abeokuta, and the Emir of Kano became patrons of the Union.

African students were much slower to go to America for education, but after the return of Azikiwe and Nkrumah from the United States many began to follow their example, and in 1941 an African Students Association with its own magazine, and closely linked with W.A.S.U., was established. Few things stimulated nationalism more than student life in Britain or America. There were contacts with white liberals, socialists, communists (all anti-imperialist), West Indians and American coloureds. There was the powerful nationalism of Englishmen and Americans which made people nationalist in defence. There was open prejudice and discrimination, polite and informal in Britain, crude and institutionalized in America.

Ethiopia

Then in 1935 came the Italian attack upon Ethiopia 'the sole remaining pride of Africans and Negroes in all parts of the world'. Ever since Ethiopia's survival at the time of the partition, when Menelik defeated Italian arms at Adowa in 1896, Africans and Negroes had looked upon that country as a proud symbol of African independence and black achievements, a noble and ancient history and international equality.

When the world was shocked at Italy's action, Mussolini hit back with the language of racism and white supremacy, which all Europeans had used during the partition but which by 1935 had become somewhat embarrassing. Italy felt she was bent on bringing 'civilization' and 'Christianity' to a 'barbarous, primitive and backward' people who were accused of slave raiding and slave holding. Italy was a great and expanding nation. She had come late to the partition of Africa and got very little. According to the doctrine of the survival of the fittest she must expand at the expense of the weaker races. When the League of Nations sought to restrain him, Mussolini scoffed, 'Has the League of Nations become the tribunal before which all the Negroes and uncivilized peoples, all the world's savages, can bring the great nations which have revolutionized and transformed humanity?'

286

The protest of the black world was more prolonged and widespread than ever before in history. There was hardly a Negro organization or Negro city that did not organize a protest. In New York, 20,000 coloured Americans demonstrated in support of Ethiopia. Demonstrations followed in South and West Africa, London and the West Indies, in which young men offered themselves to fight for Ethiopia. W.A.S.U. organized an Ethiopian Defence Committee, and an African Friends of Abyssinia Committee in London was probably the most pan-African Committee ever organized. Those connected with it were three Ghanaians, including J. B. Danquah, five West Indians, a Somali and Jomo Kenyatta of Kenya. The Committee organized a reception for Haile Selassie, emperor of Ethiopia, when he arrived in London to begin his exile after Italian forces had defeated and occupied Ethiopia.

In Nigeria mass meetings in Lagos continued to draw over 2,000 people to demand 'hands off Abyssinia'. Committees were formed in Nigerian cities which had never before engaged in modern political protest. Money poured in for an Ethiopian Defence Fund, young Nigerians offered to fight, and Italian firms were victimized and boycotted. The invasion of Ethiopia brought forward the most national response Nigeria had ever witnessed. So deep was the emotion that even the elite were surprised. The ultimate deal by which England and France 'sold' Ethiopia to Italy convinced many that the white world would stick together regardless of moral or other issues. Ethiopia, as did Garvey's fall a decade before, demonstrated that power lay with the white and not the black world. But the Italian defeat of Ethiopia nevertheless marked another vital step in the growing unity and determination of Africans to change world realities. Political movements in West Africa from 1918 to 1939 must always be seen against this larger black world background.

West African reforms and self-determination

During the partition of Africa the Ewe people had been divided between British Gold Coast and German Togoland. During World War I British and French forces overran Togo and, since the British occupied Lome and the south, the Ewe were reunited. In 1919, without reference to the people, Togo was divided between Britain and France in such a way that the Ewe were more seriously split apart than ever before. The Ewe under the leadership of O. Olympio repeatedly appealed to the British and Americans on the basis of the doctrine of self-determination. So illogical was the division that Ewe on one side of the border had their cocoa farms on the other, and this could result in double taxation for some and none for others. The *Gold Coast Independent* gave wide publicity to Ewe grievances until it was banned by the

French in Togo. One of the first points raised by the National Congress of British West Africa was the bartering around of African peoples by the European nations.

The National Congress of British West Africa, established in 1919 and holding its first conference in Accra the following year, was in its West African outlook the natural expression of the unity of the elite of English-speaking West Africa. The moving spirit behind the Congress was Casely Hayford of Ghana, who consulted with Nana Ofori Atta and R. A. Savage of Nigeria; the congress had the almost unanimous support of the English-language West Coast press. At the Accra Conference attended by 6 Nigerians, 3 Sierra Leonians, 1 Gambian and 40 Ghanaians resolutions were passed requesting the introduction of the franchise, equal opportunities for white and black in the civil service, opportunities for higher education, and a clearer separation of the judiciary from the colonial administration. The conference decided to send a deputation to press its claims in London, since no one colonial governor was in position to act in West Africa as a whole.

The West African governors were annoyed that the Congress went over their heads. They warned the Colonial Office that the deputation represented no one in West Africa. Governor Clifford of Nigeria was particularly scornful that West Africans could ever consider themselves one nationality, and even laughed at the idea that Nigeria could ever be a nation. All the governors insisted that only the chiefs could speak for the people. Due to the attitude of the governors the deputation achieved nothing in London; but the Congress continued to exist, holding a Conference in Freetown (1923), in Bathurst (1925) and in Lagos (1930).

Changes took place in West Africa in the direction the Congress desired even though the British (anxious to discourage political agitation) claimed that these reforms were presented to the West Africans by the British and not forced upon them by Congress pressure. By 1925 a limited franchise had been extended to Calabar, Lagos, Accra, Cape Coast and Freetown. Achimota College was set up in Ghana in 1927 for higher education and the West African Court of Appeal made the judiciary less subject to the control of the governors. However, the elected Africans had no power in the Legislative Council and past pupils of Achimota were discriminated against in the civil service so that the gains were minor.

Meanwhile the Congress, like political organizations in West Africa before it, became conservative and in 1930, when Hayford died, the Congress passed away with him. The common people were never stirred and little effort was made to bring them into the Congress, so that the governors' contention that the elite of the Congress represented no one was at least partly true. People from the interior were dismissed as 'bush'. A party of Ibadan leaders approached the Congress to take up certain local grievances. They were

London deputation of the National Congress, 1920. From left to right seated: Dr. H. C. Bankole-Bright (Sierra Leone), T. Hutton Mills (President of the Congress), Chief Oluwa (Nigeria), J. E. Casely Hayford (Ghana), H. Van Hein (Ghana). Standing: J. Egerton Shyngle (Nigeria), H. M. Jones (Gambia), Herbert Macaulay (Chief Oluwa's Secretary), T. M. Oluwa (son of the chief), F. W. Dove (Sierra Leone), E. F. Small (Gambia)

treated to such educated snobbery that the Ibadan branch of the Congress died and could never be revived. The apathy and even fear of elite leadership was indicated by the few who turned out to vote; seldom more than forty per cent of the eligible voters did so, and the figure was often as low as twenty per cent.

In Ghana the Congress members were soon entertaining the governor, a sure sign that their political enthusiasm was ebbing. In Nigeria big wealthy men, on the whole quite satisfied with colonialism, fought over Congress positions to gather a large following for prestige purposes. Some were interested in removing a few colour bar restrictions but at heart they would have feared major reform. Common men were interested in real reforms but money was a problem and without a wealthy patron no one, whether British or Yoruba, was likely to pay attention to a society of commoners. Many branches which were led by commoners were much more lively than the Lagos headquarters, where the big names fought over position.

In all the colonies the elite leadership won seats in the elections to the

Legislative Council. Those who didn't were nominated to sit by the British governors. In a way the British bought them over by a position and a salary. In Ibadan the British nominated the president of the local Congress branch to the Legislative Council. Thereafter, fearing that he was the eyes and ears of the British administration, the local branch elevated him from president to patron where he did not attend executive meetings and so was excluded from hearing political discussions.

Hayford had stressed that the Congress was a movement of the elite and thereby broke with the old A.R.P.S. tradition of representing both the elite and the chiefs. Some chiefs were ready to accept this, but others rallied under the leadership of Nana Ofori Atta in Ghana and attacked the Congress for jumping over the heads of the chiefs. These divisions, deliberately encouraged by the British, gave them every political chance to kill the Congress. Just before he died in 1930 Hayford expressed his disillusionment with elite leadership:

The African God is weary of your wranglings, weary of your vain disputations, weary of your ever-lasting quarrels which are a drag upon progress and which keep from you, as a people, the good that is intended for you.

Casely Hayford

Dahomey and Hunkanrin

In French West Africa, outside of the four communes of Senegal, politics was a dangerous occupation, as the fate of the Dahomean elite indicates. It was King Tofa of Porto Novo, of the De Lokpon lineage, who invited French protection for his city. At first the French ruled indirectly but gradually, as was their normal colonial custom, they cut down the monarch's powers so much that after Tofa's death in 1908 his son was reduced to the position of a head chief. Traditionally the monarchy had alternated between two royal lineages but the French confined it to De Lokpon because they were 'loyal'. This policy threw the rival lineage led by Sognigbe into opposition to the French régime.

In addition the Muslims of Porto Novo were disunited. Jose Paraiso, a Brazilian Muslim and chief adviser to the De Lokpon lineage, controlled Muslim affairs and in this had full French support. A number of Yoruba Muslims returned from the hajj (pilgrimage) determined to purify Islam in the city. They were particularly disturbed because Muslim affairs were being run by a non-Muslim dynasty and Christian overlord. Thus the Yoruba Muslims' opposition to the colonial government came to be expressed in support for Sognigbe's claim to the throne.

Charles Noufflard's governorship (1912-17) was particularly burdensome; the humiliation of the indigenat, heavy taxation and arrogant officials were combined with flagrant corruption. In 1917 the efforts of a wealthy Dahomean merchant, of a Senegalese lawyer and of Louis Hunkanrin (son of Tofa's chief blacksmith), aided by the support of Blaise Diagne and contacts in Paris, led to the recall and investigation of Governor Noufflard. This was a notable victory and from it Hunkanrin emerged as the leader of the opposition to the colonial administration.

Governor Gaston Fourn replaced Noufflard; and though he was little better than his predecessor he was a more crafty politician. Hunkanrin, who had lived in Paris and made contact with anti-imperialist groups there, returned to Dahomey and organized a branch of the *Ligue des Droits de l'Homme* (League for the Rights of Man). While it was illegal to form political associations, this could be evaded by forming a branch of a French society. The *Ligue* gave publicity in France to maladministration in Dahomey and to demands for reform. In addition Hunkanrin received anti-colonial literature from Paris, including Garvey's *Negro World*.

In 1923 the occasion arose for a showdown when Fourn raised taxes by five hundred per cent just as Dahomey's main export of palm-oil fell in price. Mass meetings were organized by the *Ligue*, and the opposition royal lineage led by Sognigbe and the Yoruba Muslim faction all co-operated in protesting against the new tax. The *Ligue* led a campaign of passive resistance which led to a refusal to pay taxes, boycott of markets and a general strike which included the port workers of Cotonou. As passive resistance spread into the countryside around Porto Novo, Fourn called for troops from Togo and Ivory Coast, and declared a three-month state of emergency during which the army collected the taxes, seized firearms, burnt some villages and compelled others to move.

Fourn treated the affair as a revolt against French rule rather than an effort to bring reform to a colonial administration. There was not even an inquiry into the causes of discontent and as a result Fourn was able to get all the leaders of the rival royal lineage, of the Yoruba Muslim faction, and also

Sognigbe and Hunkanrin, exiled and imprisoned in Mauritania for ten years. There all of them except Hunkanrin died under detention. In one blow the colonial administration managed to rid itself of all its opposition.

The Dahomean efforts for reform indicated the impossible difficulties under which African leaders had to work in the French colonies and partly explains why the colonial empire appeared so peaceful. Restrictions on protest were as strict in the protectorate areas of British colonies but British officials could seldom behave as Fourn did because in the nearby colony area educated Africans controlled newspapers and had access to lawyers, who could have demanded and secured at least a commission of inquiry into such an affair. The communes of Senegal had similar weapons but they were thousands of miles away and could be kept as ignorant of conditions in Dahomey as the Paris government itself.

The Democratic Party and Macaulay

Herbert Macaulay, grandson of Bishop Crowther and son of the founder of the first secondary school in Nigeria, first came to public attention by his exposure of European corruption in the handling of railway finances in 1908. Thereafter he engaged in defending the royal lineage of Lagos, which the British normally treated with little respect unless they had some unpopular policy to enforce, when the Eleko (king) was requested to use his influence on the government's behalf. In 1919 the government took over land in Lagos, and Macaulay, acting on behalf of the chiefs, carried the case to the Privy council in London. He won and forced the government to pay £22,500 compensation for the land. In 1920, in a mood of nasty retaliation, the colonial government deposed and deported the Eleko and appointed another. Macaulay kept up a ten-year fight against the government during which time he was jailed twice, until, again by a Privy council decision, the Eleko was restored to his throne in 1931.

It was partly because of this preoccupation with internal affairs that the formation of the National Congress and its later activities received less attention in Nigeria than might otherwise have been the case. Macaulay was a bitter critic of other educated leaders, and he lashed out in the press against his rivals and one-time friends, setting loose anger, bitterness, jealousy and divisions among Lagos politicians. This prevented the emergence of a coherently-led reform movement in Nigeria on the Ghanaian pattern; indeed it may well have been the Lagos leaders whom Hayford had in mind when he spoke of 'your wranglings', 'your vain disputations' and 'your everlasting quarrels'. In addition, although Macaulay paid lip service to the ideals of the National Congress he did nothing concrete to assist its work in Nigeria.

However, regardless of the division which he created among the elite and despite the fact that he was very much the-Victorian gentleman, Macaulay, like no other politician of his age, could keep in touch with the common people. This was all the more unusual when many potential leaders felt it was below their dignity and status to appear too common. But Macaulay was different. Market women sang his praises, Muslims admired him, and he was always ready to address socially unimportant groups. This, together with his repeated victories in the Privy council over the colonial governors, earned him the reputation as the leader of Nigerian politics and father of Nigerian nationalism.

When the Nigerian constitution was altered in 1922 to permit three elected representatives (one from Calabar and two from Lagos) to sit on the Legislative council, and when at the same time a municipal government was set up in Lagos, Macaulay's Nigerian National Democratic Party swept all seats in the elections of 1923, 1928 and 1933. However, after the restoration of the Eleko in 1931, relations between Macaulay and the British governor gradually improved. As they did so he and his party drifted into conservatism and support for the colonial government. So bitter was the British governor in 1920 that he refused to attend any social function to which any member of the Macaulay family had been invited; but after 1931 the governor actually held conferences with the Democratic Party, and regularly invited Macaulay to government house parties.

The rebels of the 1920's had become the conservatives of the 1930's. Desire for reform had so far disappeared that Macaulay and his chief supporters were almost the only members of the Lagos elite who did not support the 'Hands off Abyssinia' campaign in 1935. The Democratic Party had fallen into the self-satisfied conservatism which had crept over the A.R.P.S. by 1918 and the National Congress by the late twenties. Once the reformers achieved elected positions, once the Governor asked their advice, and they mixed with Europeans and received invitations to government house balls, the tendency was to ignore the continuing abuses of colonialism. It was the way clever colonial governors 'bought off' their critics. It was little surprise that the people lost interest in such parties. In Lagos in 1933, of the 3,000 people eligible to vote, only 700 bothered to do so.

The youth movements

In the 1930's in Nigeria, Ghana and Sierra Leone there was a reaction against the older politicians which developed through the organization of youth leagues. Partly the leagues opposed the conservatism of the old parties and partly they sought to interest many more people than before in politics. They tried to get away from the idea that political protest should be the monopoly of a top elite and confined to the cities of Lagos, Cape Coast and Freetown. There had always been a feeling that the older politicians wanted improvements in their own personal position or at best in the interests of a small elite at the top; the youth leagues attempted to study the problems of their countries from a broader view.

In Calabar in 1932, Eyo Ita organized the Nigerian Youth League mainly to support reform in education. Eyo Ita managed an industrial school, the West African Peoples Institute, which aimed at preparing youths to be self-supporting rather than to spend their time looking for civil service jobs.

In 1934 in Lagos the Nigerian Youth Movement (N.Y.M.) was formed and put forward a charter which sought to encourage national feeling in Nigeria, and demanded self-determination and Africanization. The N.Y.M. also opposed the setting up of Yaba College (Lagos) because it was proposing a standard of education below that which was common in Britain. Later it took up the cause of lorry owners, against whom the colonial government was discriminating, because it feared their competition with the railway. In addition the party established branches throughout the country in order to be truly Nigerian rather than just a Lagos party. In 1937 Azikiwe returned to Nigeria and established his *West African Pilot*. He supported the N.Y.M., which overthrew the Democratic Party in the elections to the Legislative Council in 1938. Some writers would date the birth of modern nationalism in Nigeria from the organization of the N.Y.M. in 1934, because the movement was the first to possess a Nigerian image, and because of its concern for a wide range of national interests, including Africanization, education and transportation.

In the new constitution of 1925 in Ghana, nine Africans had been elected to the Legislative council, but of these only three were elected by the people, and the other six were chiefs selected by chiefs. Many of the elite opposed this emphasis on chiefs, since they were considered to be supporters of the colonial government. Ever since the National Congress had ignored the chiefs, and attempted to assert the claim of the elite as leaders of the people, there had been bitterness between the two groups symbolized by the personal quarrel between Hayford and Nana Ofori Atta.

The National Congress originally boycotted the elections, but Hayford then decided that a boycott could achieve nothing and he ran for election; he won a seat in the Legislative Council. As a result Ghanaian leadership was split and no unified pressure for reform was possible. The chiefs were divided, those led by Nana Ofori Atta remaining in close co-operation with the government, and those following the elite also boycotting the elections. The elite was also split between those centred in Cape Coast, who continued to boycott, and those led by Hayford who were proposing limited co-operation.

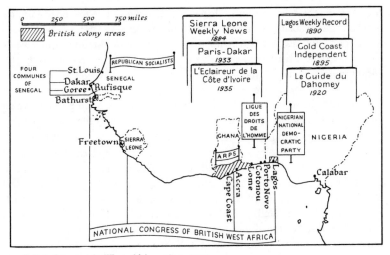

45 *Political protest in West Africa, 1897–1930*

During the 1930's these divisions were gradually healed and greater unity restored among the African leaders. Hayford was personally reconciled with Nana Ofori Atta who, to win the support of the elite, pressed the government for more rapid Africanization of the civil service. In 1934 the government introduced a sedition ordinance which gave it wide powers to control the press and, departing from the major principle of British law, made it the responsibility of an accused person to prove his innocence. Then the cocoa hold-up of 1937 brought the admiration of the elite and proved that the chiefs still had a claim to popular leadership.

In 1938 J. B. Danquah organized the Gold Coast Youth conference. Like its Nigerian counterpart its emphasis upon youth indicated a turning away from the older politicians and its interests centred on the economic and social needs of the country. Again like the N.Y.M. it attempted to involve more people in general national interests. However, unlike the N.Y.M. it was not organized as a political party. Its aims were rather to bring Ghanaian youth together for the discussion of national problems.

The most lively and purposeful of all the youth movements was organized in 1938 by Isaac Wallace-Johnson. In Sierra Leone politics and political protest had been confined to the Creole elite in Freetown, although the city now had thousands of citizens drawn from the protectorate in the interior. The Creole elite was removed from the common people of the interior to a much greater extent than in Ghana or Nigeria. In Lagos, for example, the elite was Yoruba, and bound to the Yoruba of the interior by ties of culture, language and tradition, so that it never lost complete touch with the people.

Members of the Nigerian and Ghanaian elite belonged to extended families of whom the majority belonged to the common class. In contrast the Creoles in Sierra Leone had few such ties with the people of the interior. It was a common Creole attitude to look down upon those from the interior as 'bush', and unimportant in political issues.

Wallace-Johnson strove to change this state of affairs and to combine the Creoles with the Temne and Mende of the protectorate, hoping to involve all groups in his West African Youth League. The league was the first indication in Sierra Leone of thinking in national terms rather than in terms of Freetown and its surrounding colony. As a result it could be said of the League, as of the N.Y.M. in Nigeria, that it signalled the birth of modern nationalism in Sierra Leone. Through its newspaper the *African Standard* the League was the first in West Africa to preach outright socialism and show concern for the 'toiling masses'. But Wallace-Johnson was ahead of his time; he was deported from Freetown for the duration of the war, which at least indicated the impact he was having upon thinking in Sierra Leone.

Conclusion

It was only in the colonies and communes, which contained a tiny fraction of West Africa's population, that Africans had enough freedom to organize political parties, to own and operate a press, and to be defended in court by lawyers, all of which gave them a limited protection against colonial absolutism. This protection happened because those in the colonies were British subjects and those in the communes French citizens; they thus had rights which colonial governments found difficult to ignore. However, over the vast area of West Africa where people were either subjects or protected persons, no such rights were permitted and often political agitation was silenced as was the case with Hunkanrin's supporters in Dahomey.

Between 1897 and 1939 there was a growing militancy in protest movements. The A.R.P.S. sought to protect Ghanaian rights and to protest against colonial excesses. After the first World war the National Congress went further, and demanded much more African participation in colonial government. In the late thirties the Youth movements were asking for greater speed, but it was not until after the Second World War that parties were demanding 'self-government now'. Modern nationalism was by then already born, and it is difficult to say exactly when it began. Certainly individuals were calling for self-government far back in the nineteenth century and the A.R.P.S., the National Congress, and the Youth movemement all echoed this demand.

Nationalism, however, requires a national response and the question is therefore how much support did demands for self-government receive from the people. There appears to have been a greater popular following at each stage. The National Congress had a wider support than the A.R.P.S. or Peoples Union of Nigeria; the youth movements appealed still more widely, and involved people in the protectorates for almost the first time. Possibly this expanding popular support was due to the larger numbers of literates being produced by the schools, and consequently the larger readership of the press. Possibly it also had something to do with the worsening economic conditions in the thirties and during the war.

Another noticeable trend of political organizations was the drift to conservatism. Each movement in turn tended to become a select committee of the elite, out of touch with the people. By 1918 the A.R.P.S. had become nothing more than a few intellectuals in a committee in Cape Coast. In the same way Herbert Macaulay, a popular leader in the 1920's, allowed his party to become a select club which met to pick candidates to run for elections. The Youth movements, which began with wide support, were condemned by the nationalist parties which arose after the Second World War as being parochial and conservative societies.

These developments occurred to some extent because the elite saw itself as the leader of the people and not as their servant; it believed that it knew what the people needed, regardless of what they said they wanted. Colonial governors and colonial policy encouraged this behaviour by a degree of co-operation and by absorbing leaders into the system. The governor nominated A.R.P.S. members to the Legislative Council and consulted them on many issues. Leaders of the National Congress in Nigeria, Ghana and Sierra Leone were elected or nominated members on either the legislative or municipal councils. They discovered that it was difficult to be in the government and to criticize it at the same time.

The best example was Blaise Diagne who first aroused so much popular support, but then agreed to sign the Bordeaux Compromise and went on to hold high office in the Paris government; this lost him his popular support, so much so that the French had to rig the 1928 election to keep him in power. Rather than rig an election the British would have allowed a new radical opponent to win, and would then have turned him into a conservative with a few favours.

Another important theme of this period was the growth in pan-Africanism and the growing awareness of all the parts of the black world of its similar disabilities. In these years pan-Africanism was supported and initiated mostly by American and West Indian blacks but West Africans were drawn more and more into it, and through it to an understanding of black problems in the new world. Garvey in particular, Dubois and to a lesser extent, Washington, had extensive West African contacts, either directly through correspondence or through journals like *The Negro World*. Other contacts were through student organizations in Paris, London and America.

Crucial to the whole growth of nationalism was the fact that the elite often but not always tended to be tribalist and pan-Africanist rather than nationalist. A Yoruba's loyalty was often to Yorubaland and West Africa rather than to Nigeria. Although social friends might be of the same ethnic group intellectual and political friends were often West Africans of all kinds. Thus Solanke organized a *West African* Students Union, Hayford a *West African* Congress and Wallace-Johnson a *West African* Youth League. Hunkanrin in Dahomey relied upon a Senegalese lawyer and a Senegalese Deputy. Because of this West African emphasis these men have been called pan-Africanists rather than nationalists, in the sense that pan-Africanists are nationalists who think of self-government in larger units than those created by Europeans at the time of partition.

In its entirety the period 1897 to 1939 is an important one because it was the time when many of those things which have come to play such a vital role in present-day West Africa were born and first flourished; these included the leadership of the elite and the eclipse of the chiefs, the growing political protest which, as it became more widespread, gave birth to nationalism, and the growing awareness of the black race through Negritude and pan-Africanism.

Part **five**

Return to independence

Women gaily dressed for Ghana's independence, 6 March 1957

a

b

c

d

e

f

g

h

Some of those who led their countries to independence:

(a) *Modibo Keita, Mali*

(b) *Sir Dauda Jawara, Gambia*

(c) *Félix Houphouet-Boigny, Ivory Coast*

(d) *The late Sir Abubakar Tafawa Balewa, Nigeria, killed in the military coup, January 1966*

(e) *Léopold Senghor, Senegal*

(f) *The late Sir Milton Margai, Sierra Leone*

(g) *Sékou Touré, Guinea*

(h) *Dr. Nnamdi Azikiwe, first President of Nigeria*

21 Modern nationalism and return to independence

Second World War, 1939-45

Many parts of the world including West Africa did not entirely pull out of the European and American centred economic crisis of the 1930's until the Second World War. This war produced feverish economic activity which in turn brought about social and political changes so important that they resulted in the African Revolution – which led to the overthrow of European domination and the return to independence. The subjugation and partition had been rapid, 1885-1900. The liberation was just as rapid, 1945-60.

The loss of tropical Asia during the war to the Japanese made Europe more dependent upon the products of tropical Africa. Everything West Africa could produce, palm-oil, groundnuts, coffee, cocoa, rubber and cotton were in steady demand at good prices. More people had more money than ever before but because of their war effort Europeans could not supply their normal manufactured goods to West Africa. Prices rose and people blamed the *grands comptoirs* for price fixing. Local manufacturers began to try to supply the goods no longer coming from Europe, and this, combined with the arrival of European and later American troops and the building of defence installations and airfields, meant that there were more jobs available than ever before.

People flocked in from the country to take up the new jobs. Many cities doubled in size and the already overcrowded slums grew bigger and more congested. While before the war the primary schools had been producing many school leavers, with more money now available during the war an even greater number of parents could afford a few years' education for their children. On the other hand thousands more desired education but could not get it. Thus there were many more people looking for jobs than there were jobs available, and West Africa for the first time began to develop an unemployment problem in the cities. With larger city populations and a far greater number of people able to read, African newspapers, and their demands for social and political reform, were influencing more people than ever before.

The city newcomers, who were often lonely, poor, and in physical need, joined together in numerous associations, including ethnic or progress unions and church clubs, which provided entertainment, help for the sick, for education, for the home village and for lawyer's fees in aid of those in trouble with the law. More and more of these associations turned to political discussion, led by educated members who argued for a return to African self-government and respect for African rights and dignity.

The Germans under Adolf Hitler were outspoken in their belief in white racial superiority, especially of the German branch of the race, and their proclaimed aim was to replace the French and British as the dominant European power. To combat this propaganda and rally the world to their side the allies (Britain and France, and later America) emphasized their belief in equality and the fundamental right of all peoples to self-determination. To win West African loyalty the British made specific promises such as to give an African majority on the Legislative councils and to make money available from British sources – for the first time in British imperial history – for colonial development.

West Africans were recruited in large numbers for military service. The pre-war British West African army of about 7,000 was increased to 176,000 men. The largest colonial army to serve overseas in the history of the British empire was sent from West Africa to fight the Japanese in Asia. West African soldiers fought for a new world and when demobilized after the war were impatient of anything less. Having fought for a free world they wanted a free Africa and were among the most militant followers of the nationalist leaders when the final struggle against colonialism began.

The Second World War exposed the myth of white superiority built up by the segregation of Europeans on their reservations where their frailties were concealed from African view. The great imperial powers were in trouble; France was defeated and Britain with her back to the wall. African soldiers overseas saw the dirty, the illiterate, the drunken, the stupid and the poor of Europe. They also found that Asian nationalists were thinking much as they were. Many European and American troops served in West Africa and after the war there was a further arrival of Europeans to fulfil the promised economic development. Some white service men indulged in habits which revolted Africa's sense of morality. The behaviour of Australian seamen in Freetown became a part of Creole oral tradition. Furthermore the soldiers introduced some of the crudest forms of race discrimination ever seen in West Africa.

On the other hand some allied soldiers were shocked at colonial conditions in West Africa. They made African friends and some took part in secret political discussions which condemned British and French rule. The outcome was that Africans developed a more realistic picture of European life, of both its frailty and even debauchery and of its higher instincts. The basis was being laid for a much healthier African-European relationship after the war.

If British West Africa was economically and socially shaken by the war, French West Africa had an even greater awakening. With the fall of France two French governments emerged, the Vichy régime, a puppet of Germany, and the Free French under General de Gaulle, operating in exile from London. French African sympathies lay with de Gaulle but while French Equatorial Africa declared for the Free French, the colonial régime of French West Africa declared for Vichy. In protest against this action one Ivory Coast chief in 1941 led 10,000 of his subjects into Ghana and placed them at the service of the Free French. French West Africa under Vichy domination extended the system of forced labour, introduced forced cultivation, and kept wages and the prices of export crops low while the cost of living doubled. In addition for the first time racial segregation was practised in line with the race theories of Vichy's German masters. Hotels, clubs and cafés marked 'white only' appeared and African customers were served separately in shops. In contrast to the British colonies, French West Africa suffered severely during the war.

A German-dominated world was not likely to be a happy place for Africans and therefore there was never any hesitation over which side Africans were committed to, neither was there any attempt to take advantage of the weakened position of the imperial power to force a wartime change in the colonial system. English writers stressed the loyalty of their colonies and were therefore all the more startled at the demands which arose immediately after the war. Once the war was won the drive for change began and for the first time it was for revolutionary change, 'self-government now'. All the economic and social frustrations created by the war led to impatience. Everyone hoped to persuade the imperial country into concessions but the mood was militant and some at least were ready to use terror and force.

Impatience increased when after the war Europe concentrated upon her own reconstruction to the neglect of her empires. Once the promised development began it was obvious that in the emphasis on export crops Europeans did not plan a fundamental change in policy but merely a speeding-up of the old policy. Politically, although Britain and France were aware that changes must come, both underestimated the strength and urgency of African feelings, so that the first constitutional proposals were fiercely resented as totally inadequate. It is against the background of the economic and social changes held in check during the war, but bursting forth afterwards, that the establishment of new militant political parties must be seen; these parties included the United Gold Coast Convention and the Convention

Peoples Party in Ghana, the National Council of Nigeria and the Cameroons, and the *Rassemblement Démocratique Africain* in French West Africa.

The Convention Peoples Party, 1949

In 1946 Governor Burns introduced a new constitution in Ghana which provided for an African elected majority in the Legistative council. This was the first colony in Africa to be granted such a majority and it was hailed in European circles as a great political advance. Ghanaians were disappointed because the Legislative Council had only advisory powers and of the 18 elected members, 13 were chiefs who were elected by chiefs and were suspect as being government supporters, and only 5 were elected by the people. In 1947 J. B. Danquah and others organized the United Gold Coast Convention (U.G.C.C.) to protest again the Burns constitution. The then relatively unknown Kwame Nkrumah became U.G.C.C. Secretary.

At the same time swollen shoot disease had been spreading among Ghana's cocoa trees. The only known way of stamping it out was by total destruction of the trees. Between 1946 and 1956 the British destroyed 54 million cocoa

Kwame Nkrumah and other Ghanaian leaders a few minutes after Ghana's Independence, 6 March 1957

trees. Ghanaian farmers naturally resisted the destruction of their wealth and this, combined with all the other hardships of the war and the disappointment with the Burns constitution, led to widespread discontent. Then in 1948, the *grands comptoirs* once again agreed not only to fix prices but also introduce 'conditional sales' which meant that if a customer wished to buy one product he would be allowed to do so 'on condition' that he bought another product chosen by the firm along with it. For example, if a customer wished to buy six yards of cotton cloth he had to buy six enamel plates in addition whether he wanted them or not. This was designed to unload the firms' unsaleable goods. Agitation was led by the ex-servicemen and the traders. Riots developed in which 29 were killed, 237 injured and property (mostly European, Syrian and Lebanese) worth two million pounds was damaged. The colonial government blamed the U.G.C.C., and Danquah, Nkrumah and four others – later called the 'big six'– were placed under preventive detention.

After the riots a committee of Africans – the Coussey Committee – was appointed to advise the colonial government on further political changes. Most nationalist leaders, except Nkrumah, served on it. The result was a new constitution with many more elected members in the Legislative Council and providing for eight of eleven cabinet positions to be held by Africans. After Nkrumah came out of detention he became impatient of the more conservative U.G.C.C., broke with it and set up the Convention Peoples Party which was devoted to positive action. Relying more on the youth than on the older elite leadership he condemned the Coussey committee and the constitution which resulted. To force the pace of political change the C.P.P. declared a nationwide strike and boycott. Nkrumah and others were jailed and the C.P.P. newspaper, the *Accra Evening News*, was banned.

The 1951 election was held while Nkrumah was in jail and under the slogans 'Seek ye first the political kingdom and all things will be added unto it' and 'Self-government now', the C.P.P. swept to victory with 33 seats against 3 for the U.G.C.C. Nkrumah, although unable to take part, was elected to represent Accra. The British governor called upon him as leader of the winning party, to come from jail to government house and asked him to name his cabinet. As leader of the government Nkrumah brought a welcome urgency to a traditionally cautious and slow moving colonial administration. He speeded up Africanization, pushed education and development projects, reorganized local governments which subordinated the chiefs to elected councillors, and in 1953 proposed a new self-government constitution with an all African cabinet.

As long as it was freedom against colonialism most Ghanaians could do nothing but support Nkrumah and and the C.P.P. Now that it was obvious that the British were leaving, attention turned to what kind of government an independent Ghana should have and on this a number of the elite disagreed with C.P.P. policy, and feared Nkrumah's tendencies towards absolute power. The north complained of neglect and both the north and Asante resented the way their chiefs were being pushed aside. They said, 'We are proud of our chiefs and these C.P.P. boys show them no respect'.

Opposition parties sprang up in the north and in 1954 the most important of them all, the National Liberation Movember (N.L.M.) was established in Asante. Violent clashes between C.P.P. and N.L.M. flared up in Kumasi, accompanied by house burning and political murders. In Togo – a United Nations mandate administered by the British as a part of Ghana – a referendum was held in 1956 to decide on its future course. The majority of the people voted for union with Ghana, but the majority of the Ewe people, as they had from as far back as 1919, continued to desire reunion with their brethren in French Togo and rejected union with Ghana. The British and United Nations accepted the overall majority and union with Ghana was carried out. As a result a good number of Ewes joined the opposition again the C.P.P.

With mounting opposition the British government decided that an election was necessary before they pulled out entirely. The 1956 election gave 72 seats to the C.P.P. and 32 to opposition parties. The British accepted the majority verdict, handed over the last remnants of their power and early in 1957 Ghana became the first West African state to emerge from colonialism into sovereign freedom. With Ghana independent, Nigeria, French West Africa, Sierra Leone and even Gambia, small as it was, could not be denied.

The National Council of Nigeria and the Cameroons, 1944

In Nigeria, Nnamdi Azikiwe broke from the earlier more conservative elite leadership and formed the National Council of Nigeria and the Cameroons (N.C.N.C.) just as Nkrumah was to do five years later in Ghana. Ethnic and progressive unions and other voluntary associations all over Nigeria affiliated and became branches of the party. In 1945 in reaction to wartime hardships a general strike swept the country and the N.C.N.C. alone of the political parties supported it. This made the N.C.N.C. popular, especially among the workers.

In 1946 Governor Richards introduced a new constitution which like the Burns constitution in Ghana fell far short of Nigerian hopes. Azikiwe and Herbert Macaulay went on a tour of the country to raise funds for a delegation to go to Britain to demand self-government. Macaulay, a very old man, died on the tour but not before he had given his blessing to Azikiwe's nationalist

Nigeria's New (Richards) Constitution

H.E. Sir Arthur Richards, Governor of Nigeria, proclaims a new Nigerian constitutional reform. The native intelligentsia in welcoming this however sincerely criticised some of the ordinances, which they feared would not work to the best interest of the people.

The Richards Constitution as seen by the cartoonist Akinola Lashekan

leadership. The deputation, drawn from all over Nigeria and solidly national-ist, went to England but achieved little. Enthusiasm slowed down and a struggle began in the N.C.N.C. between Yoruba and Ibo elements. It was this failure of the N.C.N.C. to remain united which partly was responsible for Nigeria's slower march to independence than Ghana, even though the N.C.N.C. had been formed five years before the C.P.P.

The major criticism of the Richards constitution was that it had been designed without consultation with Nigerians. To remedy this the British organized a series of conferences at village, divisional, provincial and national level. The national conference was held at Ibadan in 1950 where ethnic feelings ran high. The Hausa north showed its fear of southern political domination and many Yoruba were uneasy about the recent rise to prominence of Ibo in the nationalist movement. As a result the Ibadan Conference demanded a federal form of government with strong regional governments.

In 1951 a Yoruba party, the Action Group, and a Hausa-Fulani party, the Northern Peoples Congress, were organized. The N.C.N.C. remained the most national party but, since many Yoruba and Northerners had pulled out of it, it became more Ibo-dominated than before. In the next five years ethnic feelings in many leaders triumphed over national feelings. In the Kano riots northerners and southerners were locked in pitched battle. The Action Group threatened to set up a separate Yoruba nation outside the federation and northerners boasted that when the British left they could easily march to the sea.

As a result every constitutional change gave more power to the regional governments and less to the central government which eventually appeared too weak to provide adequate national leadership. While in Ghana many feared that the central government was so strong that it was likely to lead to dictatorship, in Nigeria the feeling was that the country was likely to break up. Hopes were raised when the western and eastern regions gained internal self-government in 1957, and Alhaji Abubakar Tafawa Balewa, as Federal Prime Minister, formed a coalition government of N.P.C., N.C.N.C. and Action Group ministers.

Further fears of disintegration arose when minority groups (which often numbered millions of people) began to demand their separate regions. The Bini in the western region complained of Yoruba domination; the Efiks and others in the East complained of Ibo domination; middle belt groups disliked Hausa-Fulani domination. Nationalists began to fear that, considering the large number of Nigerian ethnic groups, there was no limit to the process of of splitting apart which had begun. Others argued that everyone who wanted a state should be given it but that state powers should be drastically reduced so that a strong central government could develop.

As in Ghana the British required an election before they left. Both the N.C.N.C. and Action Group attempted to organize a countrywide campaign to get support from various groups and thus to expand the basis of their support. They had limited success and generally the N.P.C. won the north, the Action Group the west and the N.C.N.C. the east. The N.P.C. had the most seats and in 1959 it went into coalition with the N.C.N.C. in the federal government under Tafawa Balewa, with the Action Group remaining in opposition. The new nation celebrated its freedom in 1960.

Rassemblement Démocratique Africain, 1946

The end of the war came as a great relief to French West.Africa and in France there was much gratitude for the loyalty of the colonies in the gloomy days when France had been prostrate under German domination. France was in a mood to make generous political concessions to her colonies. However, the *grands comptoirs* and French settlers organized a 'save the empire' campaign which modified the early proposals.

At the end of the war French West Africans did not think of independence but rather of getting out from under the status of subject and achieving citizenship, which the four Senegalese communes had long enjoyed. In the constitution of 1946 (the year of the Burns and Richards constitutions of

Ghana and Nigeria) all power remained in European hands, as it also continued to do in British West Africa. However, the status of citizen was extended to all Africans, which meant the end of the indigenat and forced labour and gave the right to elect representatives to the territorial assembly, the federal assembly in Dakar and the French Chamber of Deputies (parliament) in Paris.

In the same year at a conference in Bamako which drew 800 delegates from French Equatorial and West Africa, Félix Houphouet-Boigny formed a federation of parties called the *Rassemblement Démocratique Africain* (R.D.A.). The R.D.A. allied with the French Communist Party because it took a strong anti-colonial line and copied its excellent organizational methods but not its doctrines, which it felt were inapplicable to African society. By 1950 it had 700,000 members and was the largest political organization anywhere in Africa. It was the dominant party of Ivory Coast, Mali, Guinea, Cameroons, and Chad, and the leading party of Volta, Niger and Congo (Brazzaville).

In almost every colony the colonial administration opened a reign of terror on the R.D.A. because of its wide popularity, its refusal to compromise with imperialism and its communist affiliations. Its leaders were arrested, supporters persecuted, demonstrators shot, newspapers closed and chiefs with R.D.A. sympathies deposed. At the same time the administration encouraged and even financed rival political parties and occasionally falsified election returns so that their favourites would win. The R.D.A. hit back with hunger and workers' strikes and boycotts of French firms; but by the end of 1951 the party was silenced. Since English-speaking Africans often underestimate the nationalist movement in French West Africa, it should be noted that nowhere in British West Africa were the nationalists dealt with so sternly. Furthermore, this repression clearly showed that the achievement of French citizenship was something of a hollow victory.

In these circumstances Houphouet-Boigny broke his alliance with the French Communist Party and looked for a compromise with the colonial administration. In the compromise the administration promised co-operation with the R.D.A. in return for a lessening of its demands and a check upon its militancy. The result was that, with the administration neutral in some colonies and actively in support in others, the R.D.A. emerged victorious in the elections of 1956 in every colony except Senegal and Mauritania. The year 1956 marked the height of R.D.A. influence and power; henceforth opposition to its policy, and weakness within the party organization, contributed to its decline.

Houphouet was a citizen of Ivory Coast which was the headquarters and main stronghold of the R.D.A. Before its rise the Senegalese had been accustomed to thinking of themselves as the natural leaders of French West Africa. This was partly due to the long tradition of education, the large elite, and the economic dominance of Senegal from which, throughout the colonial period, over half of French West Africa's revenues had come. After the war Ivory Coast's development was very rapid and by the 1950's she was challenging Senegal's dominance both economically and politically. Opposition to the R.D.A. came mainly from Senegal where Léopold Senghor organized all the opposition parties of French West Africa against the R.D.A. into a coalition, which aimed to vote together on all African issues in Paris. When the administration was terrorizing the R.D.A. Senghor's coalition had administration support and appeared as conservative and reactionary. However, after Houphouet's acceptance of a cabinet position in Paris the roles of the two political groups appeared to be reversed.

Real differences in the fundamental ideas of the two parties arose after the *Loi cadre* (outline law) came into effect in 1956 under Houphouet's sponsorship. The *Loi cadre* gave much greater powers to the territorial assembly of each colony while the Dakar central government was weakened. French West Africa appeared to be following the Nigerian path and fears began to be expressed that the federation might soon begin to break up.

French West Africa consisted of eight colonies in addition to the associated mandated territory of Togoland. With a total population of 30 million, the individual colonies averaged about $3\frac{1}{2}$ million people. At the time of the *Loi cadre* the French appeared to have decided that the nationalist movement could be slowed down, and their own influence could be maintained if a gradual break up of the federation was begun. France began to feel that she could more easily deal with eight small units of $3\frac{1}{2}$ million people each rather than one more powerful unit of 30 million.

In this the French had the co-operation of Houphouet; economic development was rapidly making Ivory Coast the wealthiest of the colonies and he was consequently reluctant to see its revenues being spent on poorer colonies by a federal government sitting in Dakar, the capital of Ivory Coast's rival. An unusual situation developed in that Houphouet, leading a truly national party with support from all over West Africa, came to take up the cause of development in separate regions. On the other hand Senghor, leading a coalition of regional parties, was putting forward plans to maintain the unity of the federation.

Once the *Loi cadre* came into effect the branch parties of the R.D.A. in each territory tended to grow and develop independently of the headquarters. The R.D.A. was falling apart. But Senghor's coalition also fell apart, and soon there was no real national party covering all of the federation. Only France could now hold French West Africa together and she did not want to do so.

In 1957 the R.D.A. held a conference and the split within its leadership became obvious. Sékou Touré of Guinea and Modibo Keita of Mali desired a strong independent federation which would maintain certain links with

France. Houphouet wanted each colony to govern itself while maintaining individual links with France and of course remaining within the French community. Houphouet was also being attacked for being far too co-operative with France; as far back as his compromise in 1951, the R.D.A. branches in Senegal, Niger and Cameroons had refused to follow him, and had therefore been expelled from the party; the trade unions were also critical of Houphouet's position in the French cabinet, as well as of his support for the use of West African troops on the French side in the Algerian war of liberation, and because of the large number of European settlers who were nominated to stand for election as R.D.A. candidates. More militant groups were attracted to Sekou Toure, a labour organizer who was less soft with French settlers and French firms.

In 1958 General de Gaulle came to power in France. He ordered a referendum in the French African colonies. The choice put before Africans was either association with France as overseas departments, self-governing statehood within the French community (Houphouet's policy) or complete independence for which no prominent leaders or political party had yet asked. There was no chance to vote either for federation or for an independent federation having close links with France (Sékou Touré's policy). In the

The French West African referendum, 1958. Only Guinea voted 'non'. All the others voted 'oui'.

referendum all the colonies except Guinea voted for self-government within the French Community. Sekou Toure had come to believe that the French were the main obstacle to federation and that de Gaulle's proposed self-government within the French community was disguised colonialism. Guinea, acting on the recommendation of Sékou Touré, voted for complete independence, hoping that if all French colonies became independent they might be able to reconstruct the federation once French influence was completely removed. As with the independence of Ghana, this freedom had a wide effect; Guinea was independent and other colonies could not be denied. By 1960 the federation had been dismantled and all the former French colonies became independent states.

Conclusion

This chapter has sought to trace how economic and social changes, brought about in West Africa as a result of the Second World War, built up pressures which exploded in demands for rapid development and greater African participation in government. Constitutions were short lived because the imperial power always underestimated the urgency of demands and because the most militant political party, that is the one which pushed the hardest and fastest for imperial withdrawal, usually won most votes while the conservative and cautious were pushed aside. Within fifteen years of the war's end almost all West Africa had become independent.

In Ghana the centralizers won the day and the country became independent with a unitary form of government. In French West Africa the federation was gradually weakened and then torn down and the various territories emerged as separate states. In Nigeria regional feelings were strong but in the end nationalist feelings were powerful enough to preserve the federal structure.

Of all West African states Ghana was the best prepared for independence because of the value of her exports, her financial reserves, her standard of living, the number of educated people, the longer tradition of political agitation, and the relative homogeneity of its peoples. Ivory Coast and Nigeria were next. Although Ivory Coast had a small population and was short of trained personnel, she had a rapidly growing and flourishing economy. Nigeria with a heavy population, a diversified economy strengthened by the discovery of large oil reserves, and adequate numbers of educated men and women being produced by her five universities, had possibly the brightest economic future of all. Before she could enjoy these benefits Nigeria had serious political problems to solve. Senegal and Guinea would soon be able to stand on their own feet and the diamond and iron mining in Sierra Leone

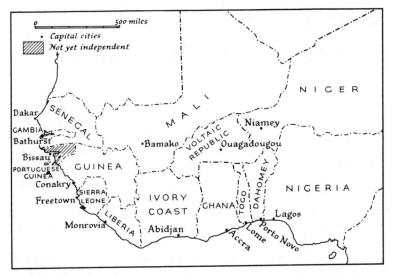

46 *Independent West African states, 1965*

gave promise that she too would soon prosper. However, for Dahomey, with an over-supply of trained men and an under-supply of resources; for Gambia, with a tiny area and population; for Mali, Upper Volta and Niger, which were denied even independent access to the sea, the economic future was not bright. Small populations in countries with no prominent export crop and no discovered mineral wealth meant that France, or someone else, would have to meet as much as fifty per cent of the normal budget to keep the civil servants paid and the schools and other amenities operating.

Epilogue:
problems of modern West Africa

Against this background the new states of West Africa have gone forward to meet the challenge of political independence. While this is not the place to go deeply into the current problems of West Africa, it may be useful to lay down a framework for discussion and further reading.

The new states have faced, within the short period since independence, not merely the difficulties inherited from the colonial period, but also many new problems resulting from independent nationhood and the demands of the people for the better life the new leaders promised would follow independence.

Of all these problems, social, economic, educational and political, probably the most urgent are political.

Problems of unity

Events in West Africa since independence have underlined the need to develop the idea of 'one nation', for the removal of the colonial governments has clearly exposed the differences between groups living within national boundaries fixed to suit European convenience. Whether these differences are religious, ethnic, or merely the result of some areas being favoured with better resources and communications than others, they have led to political instability and even, as in the case of Nigeria, to the brink of civil war. There is great need to find a solution to these problems, which are at present hindering co-operation between countries as well as within them.

Constitutional problems

Within the wider problem of national unity lies the question of the proper form of government for West African states. It is clear that the system of parliamentary democracy introduced by the colonial powers is, in the forms so far adopted, unsuitable for modern African society. Where political parties have frequently been extensions of ethnic rather than political interest, the constitutional provisions of the colonial governments have proved inadequate. Coalitions and one-party states have thus far failed to provide answers, and where 'free' elections have taken place there have frequently been intimidation of voters and 'rigging'. This has led to widespread dissatisfaction and in some instances to army and police intervention.

The economic foundations

Underlying these political issues lie the long-term economic problems of the 'developing' nations. West African states rely heavily upon what are called 'primary products'. These are the products of agriculture (such as cotton, groundnuts and cocoa) and the mineral raw materials for industry (oil, tin, iron, bauxite, etc.). At present, most of the goods needed to improve the conditions of people in West Africa have to be bought by selling these products abroad, mainly in markets dominated by the rich manufacturing countries. To change this pattern means setting up industries, and industrializing agriculture in West Africa; and industry requires huge sums of money for investment in 'capital' equipment – the machines that make the things people need. If a country is not rich, it must seek this 'capital' from overseas, not merely for the machines themselves, but also for equipment to generate the electricity to run them, and the roads and railways to transport them and distribute their products.

In their efforts to industrialize, West African states have followed different economic patterns. The 'socialist' experiment in Nkrumah's Ghana meant more state control of industry and heavy loans from overseas governments, private firms and international organizations. This heavy borrowing and sometimes wasteful use of the capital involved led to debt and difficulty for Ghana. Nigeria's 'mixed' economy in which the state and private industry have gone side by side has led to regional differences over the siting of industry and to the export by expatriate companies of large profits which should have been kept in the country. This coupled with the variable world cocoa price would have led Nigeria into serious difficulty had not oil, which is internationally very much in demand, been found. The 'free' economy of Ivory Coast has led to rapid development of some of the country's resources, but also to very high prices and consequent suffering of the working people.

The correct solution to these problems has not yet been found and it may be that in order to raise capital at home a sacrifice of some of the good things in life, even among politicians and the higher educated, will have to be tried. This system of raising capital is slow and painful and carries with it political consequences which may be unacceptable to nations looking for immediate improvements.

For in order to attract votes and indeed, to retain political power, politicians have frequently found it necessary to make promises of economic improvements which the country's finances could not in fact bear.

West Africa and the world

Above the political and economic problems of each nation is the question of her relationships with the outside world. Rich countries giving aid to African states tend to expect support in such international bodies as the United Nations. West Africa has thus been drawn into international politics and some African countries have been forced to give political support to policies of which they do not really approve. Further, they have found themselves powerless to intervene in such pressing matters as the ending of white minority domination in Southern Africa. The Organization of African Unity has been less effective than most Africans hoped because it has been itself divided over its proper aims and because the nations within it could, at times, be seen to be working against each other away from the conference table. African economic union, which could in itself greatly assist overall development, has been hampered by economic treaties with countries outside Africa, by distrust among African nations themselves and by the desire of individual nations for economic independence rather than African interdependence.

The details of these problems remain the province of current affairs. Perhaps the post-independence period to date has been most marked by the growth of a body of informed public opinion among the people of West Africa: for a state whose government has public opinion solidly behind it has little to fear from other nations seeking outside control and can concentrate on building an economy capable of giving a service to its people comparable with that of the rich countries of the world.

Glossary

Alafin: Title of the ruler of Oyo. He was considered to have descended from the nation's semidivine ancestor.

Almami: Muslim title of a spiritual and temporal leader.

Amir al-Muminin: Arabic term meaning "commander of the faithful"; title assumed by rulers in Macina after the Muslim conquest.

Animism: The belief that there is a soul in every object.

Ardo: Title of pre-Muslim ruler of Macina.

Aremo: Title of the eldest son of the Alafin of Oyo; crown prince.

Arma: Title of pre-Muslim ruler of Jenne.

Aro: An Ibo clan. The oracle of Chukwu, the Ibo supreme deity, was in Aro territory in Eastern Nigeria.

Arochuku: The seat of the oracle of Chukwu, the supreme deity of the Ibo peoples.

Asante: Variant of Ashanti.

Asantehene: Title of the paramount ruler of the Asante Confederacy.

Atlanta Compromise: Booker T. Washington's doctrine that the best way for Negroes to rise in American society was for them to learn manual and agricultural skills. It was presented in a speech he delivered in Atlanta, Georgia, in 1895.

Awowa: Asante word meaning pawns; the term was used for indentured servants.

Awujale: Title of the ruler of Ijebu.

Bashorun: Also *Basorun.* In Oyo, leader of the Council of Notables, Prime Minister.

Bey: Governor of a Turkish province; a title of courtesy.

Black Star Line Shipping Corporation: Marcus Garvey's project for a shipping line that would operate between the West Indies, New York, and Africa. The plan never materialized, but modern Ghana's shipping line is called Black Star.

Bordeaux Agreements: The compromise reached in 1923 between Blaise Diagne, a Senegalese member of the French Chamber of Deputies, and the Bordeaux firms with interests in Senegal. The firms dropped their opposition to Diagne in return for his support of the colonial system.

Bordeaux Clique: A group of French firms, with interests in Senegal, that cooperated to eliminate economic competition among themselves and support a joint candidate for election to the French Chamber of Deputies.

Brotherhoods: See Tariqa.

Cadi: See Qadi.

Caliph: See Khalifa.

Chukwu: Supreme deity of the Ibo.

Colonial Pact: The concept that colonies must be self-supporting, export crops to the imperial country, and buy its manufactured goods in return.

Damel: Title of the ruler or king of Cayor.

Diula: Also Dyula. A Muslim trading class.

Dual Mandate: The theory that Great Britain had the double duty to govern in its own interests and in the interests of the colonial people. This required that each colony finance its own administration, and that it provide ideal conditions for the expansion of British trade. Africans were also to benefit, and it was assumed that this could best be achieved through indirect rule.

Dyalo: A Fulani clan.

Dyula: See *Diula.*

Ekpe: A secret society that played an important political role among the Ibibio.

Eleko: Title of the hereditary ruler of Lagos.

Emir: Also Amir. Independent Muslim chieftain or prince.

Eso: In Oyo, a nonhereditary class of war chiefs.

Fulani: A race of nomads who became important converts to the Muslim religion in the western Sudan.

Golden stool: Throne serving as a national emblem of Asante. It was said to contain the power of all the people of Asante and to bring victory in war. During the wars with the British, who had demanded to sit on it, it disappeared; it was found in 1921.

Grands comptoirs: French term for the great combines that dominated the economic life of British and French West Africa.

Hajj: Pilgrimage to Mecca; one who has made the pilgrimage.

Hijra: Arabic for flight, emigration.

Ifa: Among the Yoruba, a superhuman being, sent from heaven to give personal guidance; the name of an oracle.

Igbo: Variant of Ibo.

Ilari: In Oyo, priest of a local Shango shrine.

Imam: A Muslim spiritual and temporal leader.

Iwofa: Yoruba term for indentured servants or debt slaves.

Jihad: Holy war.

Kachela: In Bornu, men of servile origin.

Kakanfo: Field Marshal of the Oyo Empire; leader of the Eso.

Kambe: In Bornu, freeborn commoners.

Khalifa: Head of an order or brotherhood.

Kokenawa: Bornu administrators.

Kolak: Ruler of Wadi, a Lake Chad kingdom.

Loi cadre: Law that gave semi-autonomy to French African territories.

Loi Diagne: Law that granted French citizenship to Africans in the *quatre communes* of Senegal.

Mahdi: A Muslim messianic leader.

Mahdiyya: A brotherhood, or *tariqa,* popular in the Republic of Sudan.

Mai: Ruler of a Bornu state.

Mallamai: Local magistrates in Bornu.

Mallams: Hausa term for Muslim scholars.

Mandinka: Variant of Mandinga, Mandingo.

Manin Kanendi: Title of the chief justice of Bornu.

Mbang: Title of the ruler of the Lake Chad kingdom of Bagirmi.

Oba: Title of the ruler of Benin; ruler of a provincial kingdom in Oyo.

Ogboni: A secret society of political and religious leaders in Oyo; a secret society among the Yoruba.

Oluwa: In Oyo, the chief Ifa priest.

Omanahene: Asante provincial ruler.

Ona Efa: Title of the chief judge in Oyo.

Oni: Title of the king of Ife.

Order of Blood Men: An organization of runaway slaves formed as protection against the Ekpe of Calabar.

Osi Efa: Title of the controller of palace finances in Oyo.

Otun Efa: Head of the Shango cult in Oyo.

Oyo Mesi: Council of Notables in Oyo.

Poro: Secret societies found in Sierra Leone and Guinea. Boys are instructed in traditional rituals, social duties, and endurance.

Qadi: Muslim judge.

Quatre communes: The four Senegalese towns—Saint Louis, Gorée, Rufisque, and Dakar—in which both Africans and Europeans were allowed to vote and become candidates for election to the French Chamber of Deputies.

Ribat: Fortified monastery where men were trained in religion and in preparation for holy war; walled fortress.

Sanusiyya: A *tariqa,* or religious brotherhood.

Sarkuna: Rulers of non-Muslim Hausa states. Singular, *Sarki.*

Shango: Also *Sango.* Yoruba storm god—according to legend, the fourth King of Oyo. He is credited with having established Oyo's supremacy over other Yoruba kingdoms.

Shuwa: Nomads who rose to power in Bornu.

Sidi: A Muslim title of courtesy.

Tariqa: In Islam, a mystical path; a system of spiritual doctrine and practice; a religious brotherhood.

Vai: A people of Liberia; its language; a script invented about 1834 for use with the language.

Waziri: Bornu Prime Minister.

Wird: Also *werd.* A litany recited at the end of rituals of initiation into a brotherhood.

Zawiya: A Muslim lodge or monastery; in many areas, *zawiyas* became important trading centers.

Further Reading

(An asterisk beside an entry means that a paperback edition is available.)

PART ONE

ABUN-NASR, JAMIL M. *The Tijaniyya, a Sufi Order in the Modern World.* New York: Oxford University Press, 1965.

*AJAYI, J. F. ADE. "The Fulani Jihad." In *Milestones in Nigerian History.* New York: International Publications Service, 1962.

ANENE, JOSEPH C. "Slavery and the Slave Trade," in *Africa in the Nineteenth and Twentieth Centuries,* edited by Joseph C. Anene and Godfrey N. Brown. New York: Humanities Press, 1968.

BOAHEN, A. A. *Britain, the Sahara and the Western Sudan.* New York: Oxford University Press, 1964.

————. "The Caravan Trade in the Nineteenth Century." *Journal of African History* (1962).

*————. *Topics in West African History.* New York: Humanities Press, 1966.

BOVILL, EDWARD W. *The Golden Trade of the Moors.* New York: Oxford University Press, 1958.

COUPLAND, REGINALD. *The British Anti-Slavery Movement.* New York: Barnes & Noble, 1964.

CROWDER, MICHAEL. *A Short History of Nigeria.* Rev. ed. New York: Praeger, 1966.

————. *West Africa under Colonial Rule.* Evanston: Northwestern University Press, 1968.

*CURTIN, PHILIP D., ed. *Africa Remembered: Narratives by West Africans from the Era of the Slave Trade.* Madison, Wis.: University of Wisconsin Press, 1967.

————. *The Atlantic Slave Trade: A Census.* Madison, Wis.: University of Wisconsin Press, 1969.

*DAVIDSON, BASIL. *Black Mother.* Boston: Little, Brown & Co., Atlantic Monthly Press, 1961.

DIKE, K. ONWUKA. "The Rise of Sokoto." In *Encyclopaedia Britannica,* Vol. XX (1966).

————. *Trade and Politics in the Niger Delta.* New York: Oxford University Press, 1956.

EDWARDS, PAUL, ed. *Equiano's Travels.* New York: Praeger, 1967.

*FAGE, J. D. *Ghana: A Historical Interpretation.* Madison, Wis.: University of Wisconsin Press, 1959.

GRIFFETH, ROBERT R. "Samori Toure." *Tarikh* I, No. 4 (1967).

HALLAM, W. "Rabeh: Tyrant of Bornu." *Nigeria Magazine,* No. 86 (1965).

HODGKIN, THOMAS. "Uthman dan Fodio." *Nigeria Magazine* (1960).

————. *Nigerian Perspectives.* New York: Oxford University Press, 1960.

HUNWICK, J. O. "The Nineteenth Century Jihads." In *A Thousand Years of West African History,* edited by J. F. Ade Ajayi and Ian Espie. New York: Humanities Press, 1965.

IFEMESIA, C. C. "Bornu Under the Shehus." In *A Thousand Years of West African History,* edited by J. F. Ade Ajayi and Ian Espie. New York: Humanities Press, 1965.

————. "A Note on Samori Touré." In *A Thousand Years of West African History,* edited by J. F. Ade Ajayi and Ian Espie. New York: Humanities Press, 1965.

KANYA-FORSTNER, A. S. *Conquest of the Western Sudan.* New York: Cambridge University Press, 1969.

KRITZECK, JAMES, and WILLIAM H. LEWIS, eds. *Islam in Africa.* New York: Van Nostrand Reinhold, 1969.

*KUP, PETER A. *A History of Sierra Leone.* New York: Cambridge University Press, 1964.

LAST, MURRAY. *Sokoto Caliphate.* New York: Humanities Press, 1969.

LEGASSICK, MARTIN. "Firearms, Horses and Samorian Army Organization 1870–98." *Journal of African History* VIII, No. 1 (1966).

LLOYD, P. C., et al, eds. *The City of Ibadan.* New York: Cambridge University Press, 1968.

*OFOSU-APPIAH, L. H. *Slave Trade.* Minneapolis, Minn.: Lerner, 1969.

SMITH, H. E. C. "Islamic Revolutions of the Nineteenth Century." *Journal of the Historical Society of Nigeria* II, No. 2 (1961).

TRIMINGHAM, J. SPENCER. *History of Islam in West Africa.* New York: Oxford University Press, 1962.

*WILLIAMS, ERIC. *Capitalism and Slavery.* New York: Putnam, 1966.

YVER, G. "Bornu." In *Encyclopedia of Islam,* edited by H. A. R. Gibb, et al. Vol. 1, New York: Humanities Press, 1960.

PART TWO

AJAYI, J. F. ADE. "Yoruba Warriors in Politics." *Tarikh* I, No. 1 (1965).

————, and ROBERT SMITH. *Yoruba Warfare in the Nineteenth Century.* New York: Cambridge University Press, 1969.

AKINJOGBIN, I. A. "Dahomey and Yoruba in the 19th Century." In *Africa in the Nineteenth and Twentieth Centuries,* edited by Joseph C. Anene and Godfrey N. Brown. New York: Humanities Press, 1967.

ANDERSON, R. EARL. *Liberia, America's Friend.* Chapel Hill, N.C.: University of North Carolina Press, 1965.

ANENE, JOSEPH C. "Benin, Niger Delta, Ibo and Ibibio Peoples in the Nineteenth Century." In *A Thousand Years of West African History,* edited by J. F. Ade Ajayi and Ian Espie. Humanities Press, 1965.

————. "The Southern Nigeria Protectorate and the Aros, 1900–1902." *Journal of the Historical Society of Nigeria* I, No. 2 (1956).

AWE, B. "The Ajele System: Ibadan Imperialism." *Journal of the Historical Society of Nigeria* III, No. 1 (1964).

BIOBAKU, SABURI O. *The Egba and Their Neighbors.* New York: Oxford University Press, 1957.

BOAHEN, A. A. "Asante, Fante and the British, 1800–1880." In *A Thousand Years of West African History,* edited by J. F. Ade Ajayi and Ian Espie. New York: Humanities Press, 1965.

*————. *Topics in West African History.* New York: Humanities Press, 1966.

BOWEN, M. "Nri Traditions." *Nigeria Magazine,* No. 54 (1957).

————. "Obi Oputa of Aboh." *Nigeria Magazine,* No. 22 (1944).

COX-GEORGE, N. A. *Finance and Development in West Africa: The Sierra Leone Experience.* New York: Humanities Press, 1961.

CROWDER, MICHAEL. *A Short History of Nigeria.* Rev. ed. New York: Praeger, 1966.

FRAENKEL, MERRAN. *Tribe and Class in Monrovia.* New York: Oxford University Press, 1964.

*FYFE, CHRISTOPHER. *A Short History Of Sierra Leone.* New York: Humanities Press, 1962.

GREEN, M. M. *Ibo Village Affairs.* New York: Praeger, 1964.

HARGREAVES, J. D. *Prelude to the Partition of West Africa.* New York: St. Martin's Press, 1963.

JONES, ABEODU. "Joseph Jenkins Roberts." *Tarikh* I, No. 1 (1967).

JONES-QUARTEY, K. A. "Sierra Leone's Role in the Development of Ghana, 1830–1930." *Sierra Leone Studies.* No. 10 (1958).

JULY, ROBERT W. *The Origins of Modern African Thought: Its Development in West Africa During the Nineteenth and Twentieth Centuries.* New York: Praeger, 1968.

LLOYD, P. C., et al, eds. *The City of Ibadan.* New York: Cambridge University Press, 1968.

LYNCH, HOLLIS R. *Edward Wilmot Blyden: Pan-Negro Patriot 1832–1912.* New York: Oxford University Press, 1967.

————. "Sierra Leone and Liberia in the Nineteenth Century." In *A Thousand Years of West African History,* edited by J. F. Ade Ajayi and Ian Espie. New York: Humanities Press, 1965.

*MERCIER, P. "The Fon of Dahomey." In *African Worlds,* edited by Daryll Forde. New York: Oxford University Press, 1964.

NEWBURY, COLIN W. *The Western Slave Coast and Its Rulers.* New York: Oxford University Press, 1961.

NZEKWU, J. "Asaba." *Nigeria Magazine,* No. 54 (1957).

———. "Onitsha." *Nigeria Magazine,* No. 50 (1956).

NZEKWU, ONUORA. "Gloria Ibo." *Nigeria Magazine,* No. 64 (1960).

PORTER, ARTHUR T. *Creoledom: A Study of the Development of the Freetown Society.* New York: Oxford University Press, 1963.

SMITH, ROBERT. "Ijaye: The Western Palatinate of the Yoruba." *Journal of the Historical Society of Nigeria* II, No. 2 (1962).

———. *Kingdoms of the Yoruba.* New York: Barnes & Noble, 1969.

TORDOFF, WILLIAM. *Ashanti Under the Prempehs, 1888–1935.* New York: Oxford University Press, 1965.

YANCY, E. J. *The Republic of Liberia.* London: Allen & Unwin, 1959.

PART THREE

AGBODEKA, F. "The Fante Confederacy." *Transactions of the Historical Society of Ghana,* No. 3 (1964).

AJAYI, J. F. ADE. *Christian Missions in Nigeria, 1841–1891.* Evanston, Ill.: Northwestern University Press, 1965.

ALAGOA, EBIEGBERI, J. "Koko: Amanyanabo of Nembe." *Tarikh* I, No. 4 (1967).

———. *Small Brave City-State: A History of Nembe-Brass in the Niger Delta.* Madison, Wis.: University of Wisconsin Press, 1964.

AYANDELE, E. A. "External Influence on African Society." In *Africa in the Nineteenth and Twentieth Centuries,* edited by Joseph C. Anene and Godfrey N. Brown. New York: Humanities Press, 1966.

*BOAHEN, A. A. *Topics in West African History.* New York: Humanities Press, 1966.

BRADBURY, R. E. and P. C. LLOYD. *Benin Kingdom and the Edo-Speaking Peoples of South-Western Nigeria.* New York: International Publications Service, 1964.

CLINTON, J. "King Eyo Honesty II of Creek Town, Calabar." *Nigeria Magazine,* No. 69 (1961).

COOMBS, DOUGLAS. *The Gold Coast, Britain and the Netherlands, 1850–74.* New York: Oxford University Press, 1963.

CROWDER, MICHAEL. *A Short History of Nigeria.* Rev. ed. New York: Praeger, 1966.

*DAVIDSON, BASIL. *Black Mother: The Years of the African Slave Trade.* Boston: Little, Brown & Co., Atlantic Monthly Press, 1961.

DIKE, K. ONWUKA. *Trade and Politics in the Niger Delta.* New York: Oxford University Press, 1956.

*FAGE, J. D. *Ghana: A Historical Interpretation.* Madison, Wis.: University of Wisconsin Press, 1959.

————. "The Administration of George Maclean on the Gold Coast." *Transactions of the Historical Society of Ghana* I, Part IV (1955).

FLINT, J. E. "Chartered Companies and the Scramble for Africa." In *Africa in the Nineteenth and Twentieth Centuries,* edited by Joseph C. Anene and Godfrey N. Brown. New York: Humanities Press, 1965.

————. "The Growth of European Influence in West Africa in the 19th Century." In *A Thousand Years of West African History,* edited by J. F. Ade Ajayi and Ian Espie. New York: Humanities Press, 1965.

HARGREAVES, J. D. *Prelude to the Partition of West Africa.* New York: St. Martin's Press, 1963.

IKIME, O. "King Jaja of Opobo." *Nigeria Magazine,* No. 62 (1959).

————. "Nana Olomu: Governor of the Benin River." *Tarikh* I, No. 2 (1966).

KIMBLE, DAVID. *Political History of Ghana: The Rise of Gold Coast Nationalism, 1850–1928.* New York: Oxford University Press, 1963.

LYNCH, HOLLIS R. *Edward Wilmot Blyden: Pan-Negro Patriot, 1832–1912.* New York: Oxford University Press, 1967.

METCALFE, GEORGE E. "After Maclean: Some Aspects of British Gold Coast Policy in the Mid-Nineteenth Century." *Transactions of the Historical Society of Ghana* I, Part IV (1955).

————. *Maclean of the Gold Coast.* New York: Oxford University Press, 1962.

TAMUNO, T. "Some Aspects of Nigerian Reaction to the Imposition of British Rule." *Journal of the Historical Society of Nigeria* III, No. 2 (1965).

*WARD, WILLIAM E. *Short History of Ghana.* New York: Humanities Press, 1966.

PART FOUR

*ADLOFF, RICHARD. *French West Africa.* New York: Holt, Rinehart & Winston, 1964.

*AJAYI, J. F. ADE. *Milestones in Nigerian History.* New York: International Publications Service, 1962.

*BOAHEN, A. A. *Topics in West African History.* New York: Humanities Press, 1966.

BOURRET, F. M. *Ghana: The Road to Independence, 1919–1957.* Rev. ed. Stanford, Calif.: Stanford University Press, 1960.

*BROWN, GODFREY N. *An Active History of Ghana.* 2 bks., Bk. 2: *Since 1844.* New York: International Publications Service, 1946.

BURNS, SIR ALAN. "Sir Ofori Atta." In *Pageant of Ghana,* edited by F. Wolfson. New York: Oxford University Press, 1958.

COLEMAN, JAMES S. *Nigeria: Background to Nationalism.* Berkeley: University of California Press, 1958.

CROWDER, MICHAEL. "Indirect Rule—French and British Style." *Africa* XXXIV, pp. 197-205 (1964).
*———. *Senegal: A Study in French Assimilation Policy*. Rev. ed. New York: Barnes & Noble, 1967.
———. *A Short History of Nigeria*. Rev. ed. New York: Praeger, 1966.
FOLTZ, WILLIAM J. *From French West Africa to the Mali Federation*. New Haven, Conn.: Yale University Press, 1965.
GAILEY, HARRY A. *History of the Gambia*. New York: Praeger, 1965.
GEISS, IMANUEL. "The Development of Pan Africanism." *Journal of the Historical Society of Nigeria*, No. 3 (1967).
HATCH, JOHN. *The History of Britain in Africa: From the Fifteenth Century to the Present*. New York: Praeger, 1969.
*HODGKIN, THOMAS. *Nationalism in Colonial Africa*. New York: New York University Press, 1957.
*HOOKER, JAMES R. *Black Revolutionary: George Padmore's Path from Communism to Pan-Africanism*. New York: Praeger, 1967.
INGHAM, E. G. *Sierra Leone, After a Hundred Years*. New York: Barnes & Noble, 1968.
JOHNSON, W. "Blaise Diagne: Master Politician of Senegal." *Tarikh* I, No. 1 (1966).
JULY, ROBERT W. *The Origins of Modern African Thought: Its Development in West Africa During the Nineteenth and Twentieth Centuries*. New York: Praeger, 1968.
KIMBLE, DAVID. *Political History of Ghana: The Rise of Gold Coast Nationalism, 1850–1923*. New York: Oxford University Press, 1963.
LEWIS, M. D. "One Hundred Million Frenchmen: The Assimilation Theory in French Colonial Policy." *Comparative Studies in Society and History* IV, pp. 129-253 (1962).
LUGARD, FREDERICK J. C., LORD. *The Dual Mandate in British Tropical Africa*. 5th ed. Hamden, Conn.: Shoe String Press, Archon Books, 1965.
MARKOWITZ, IRVING LEONARD. *Léopold Sédar Senghor and the Politics of Négritude*. New York: Atheneum, 1969.
MEEK, CHARLES K. *Law and Authority in a Nigerian Tribe: A Study in Indirect Rule*. New York: Barnes & Noble, 1968.
MELADY, THOMAS. *Profiles of African Leaders*. New York: Macmillan, 1961.
MORTIMER, EDWARD. *France and the Africans (1944–1960)*. New York: Walker, 1969.
NIVEN, REX. *Nine Great Africans*. New York: Roy, 1965.
PADMORE, GEORGE. *Pan-Africanism or Communism*. New York: Roy, 1956.
PANKHURST, REGINALD. "Menelik II, Emperor of Ethiopia." *Tarikh* I, No. 1 (1956).
PERHAM, MARGERY. *Lugard: The Years of Adventure, 1858–1898: A*

Maker of Modern Africa. Hamden, Conn.: Shoe String Press, Archon Books, 1968.

———. *Lugard: The Years of Authority, 1898–1945.* Hamden, Conn: Shoe String Press, Archon Books, 1968.

PORTER, ARTHUR T. *Creoledom: A Study of the Development of the Free-town Society.* New York: Oxford University Press, 1963.

RUBENSON, SVEN. "Modern Ethiopia." In *Africa in the Nineteenth and Twentieth Centuries,* edited by Joseph C. Anene and Godfrey N. Brown. New York: Humanities Press, 1966.

*SENGHOR, LÉOPOLD SÉDAR. *On African Socialism.* Translated by Mercer Cook. New York: Praeger, 1964.

THOMPSON, VINCENT. *Evolution of Pan Africanism.* New York: Humanities Press, in preparation.

TORDOFF, WILLIAM. *Ashanti Under the Prempehs, 1888–1935.* New York: Oxford University Press, 1965.

PART FIVE

*BOAHEN, A. A. *Topics in West African History.* New York: Humanities Press, 1966.

COLEMAN, JAMES S. *Nigeria: Background to Nationalism.* Berkeley: University of California Press, 1958.

GAILEY, HARRY A. *History of the Gambia.* New York: Praeger, 1965.

*HODGKIN, THOMAS. *Nationalism in Colonial Africa.* New York: New York University Press, 1957.

MELADY, THOMAS. *Profiles of African Leaders.* New York: Macmillan, 1961.

PADMORE, GEORGE. *The Gold Coast Revolution.* London: Dobson, 1953.

POST, KEN. "Nationalist Movements in West Africa." In *Africa in the Nineteenth and Twentieth Centuries,* edited by Joseph C. Anene and Godfrey N. Brown. New York: Humanities Press, 1966.

———. *The New States of West Africa.* New York: Penguin, 1964.

SITHOLE, NDABANINGI. *African Nationalism.* 2d ed. New York: Oxford University Press, 1968.

EPILOGUE

BELING, WILLARD A., ed. *The Role of Labor in African Nation-Building.* New York: Praeger, 1968.

BURKE, FRED G. *Sub-Saharan Africa.* New York: Harcourt Brace & World, 1968.

ČERVENKA, ZDENEK. *The Organization of African Unity and Its Charter.* New York: Praeger, 1969.

COHEN, ABNER. *Custom and Politics in Urban Africa: A Study of Hausa Migrants in Yoruba Towns.* Berkeley: University of California Press, 1969.

*COWAN, L. GRAY. *The Dilemmas of African Independence.* Rev. ed. New York: Walker, 1968.

DE LUSIGNAN, GUY. *French-Speaking Africa Since Independence.* New York: Praeger, 1969.

DODGE, DOROTHY. *African Politics in Perspective.* New York: Van Nostrand, 1966.

*DUMONT, RENÉ. *False Start in Africa.* Translated by Phyllis Nauts Ott. 2d ed., rev. New York: Praeger, 1969.

HATCH, JOHN. *A History of Postwar Africa.* New York: Praeger, 1965.

KILBY, PETER. *Industrialization in an Open Economy: Nigeria, 1945–1966.* New York: Cambridge University Press, 1969.

LEE, J. M. *African Armies and Civil Order.* New York: Praeger, 1969.

LLOYD, P. C. *Africa in Social Change.* Rev. ed. New York: Praeger, 1969.

NIELSEN, WALDEMAR A. *The Great Powers and Africa.* New York: Praeger, 1969.

*NKRUMAH, KWAME. *Dark Days in Ghana.* New York: International Publishers, 1969.

———. *Africa Must Unite.* New York: Praeger, 1963.

O'CONNELL, JAMES. "Trades in the Independent States of West Africa." In *A Thousand Years of West African History,* edited by J. F. Ade Ajayi and Ian Espie. New York: Humanities Press, 1965.

PASSIN, HERBERT, and K. A. JONES-QUARTEY. *Africa: Dynamics of Change.* New York: International Publications Service, 1963.

*POST, KEN. *The New States of West Africa.* New York: Penguin, 1964.

THOMPSON, W. SCOTT. *Ghana's Foreign Policy, 1957–1966.* Princeton, N.J.: Princeton University Press, 1969.

WARD, WILLIAM E. "Emergent Africa." In *Twentieth Century Histories,* Vol. 3. New York: International Publications Service, 1968.

*ZOLBERG, ARISTIDE R. *One-Party Government in the Ivory Coast.* Rev. ed. Princeton N.J.: Princeton University Press, 1969.

Index